There Must
Be A Reason

There Must Be A Reason

◆

My Daughter's Battle With Wegener's Granulomatosis

Myrna Swart

iUniverse, Inc.

New York Bloomington Shanghai

There Must Be A Reason
My Daughter's Battle With Wegener's Granulomatosis

Copyright © 2008 by Myrna Swart

iUniverse books may be ordered through booksellers or by contacting:

iUniverse
1663 Liberty Drive
Bloomington, IN 47403
www.iuniverse.com
1-800-Authors (1-800-288-4677)

ISBN: 978-0-595-47001-3 (pbk)
ISBN: 978-0-595-48806-3 (cloth)
ISBN: 978-0-595-91285-8 (ebk)

Printed in the United States of America

Although Carol's treatment options and the medicines she was given are discussed, often in detail, this is not meant to be a substitute for medical care for any other person who reads this story.

Regardless of similar symptoms, only your doctor can determine the correct treatment for you. I urge you to consult your own physician and not attempt to use this story in any way as medical advice.

Those names marked with an asterisk (*) the first time they appear are not the person's real name. All the other names are true and correct. In other instances only first names are used to protect the individuals' privacy.

To my beloved daughter, Carol
I wish there'd been no story to tell

"If I can ease one life the aching,
… I shall not live in vain."

Emily Dickenson

Contents

List of Illustrations

List of Illustrations

Acknowledgments

There are many people who both helped with or encouraged the writing of this book, and those who helped make life more livable for Carol. I am sincerely grateful and wish to acknowledge them here.

Thanks go first to my son, Kenneth, who believed I had a worthwhile story to tell and told me to "go for it."

Thanks to the late Helen Eisworth, a journalist and dear friend, who encouraged my efforts and did the early editing.

Thanks to Linda Urquizu, a family friend and reference librarian, for securing information regarding the disease; and her brother, Gilbert, for taking Carol to the hospital and for the numerous times he followed her down the mountain from Big Bear to see her home safely.

Thanks to family members, Doris, Bea, Alan, Peggy, Bonnie, and Derek, who supported the writing of this story and never laughed at me for taking on this project.

Thanks to our dear friends Sandy Stover, who lived the story with me; and Tracey Termath, who lived the story with Carol, and for reviewing the manuscript.

Thanks to John T. Plander, MD for advice, concern, and friendship.

Thanks to special friends Adele Jacobs, June Rapoport, and Rheta Steele, who took their time to read the manuscript, and for their support and encouragement.

Thank you to my special friends at the Vasculitis Foundation: the late Marilyn Sampson, who founded the present day organization; the late President and Executive Director, Iva Roe, who encouraged my participation in helping with the growth of the organization; the current Executive Director, Joyce Kullman and her mother, Arlene, for their consistent hard work, support and encouragement; and Patient Support Coordinator, Shannon Morgan, for never failing to supply me with information and materials to further my work of supporting patients in record time. Thanks to all of you for your friendship, also.

Thanks to Philip A. Naecker and his employees for helping Carol create and for hosting the organization's website in its early days. Thanks also for his help and understanding through many of Carol's trials while they worked together.

Thanks to Carol Csomay and Victoria Preuss for their outstanding editing, encouraging comments, and patience with my long-windedness. Carol consistently made me feel good about what I wrote, even when it needed to be changed, shortened, or deleted. Vicki made my characters come alive, my descriptions more vivid, my emotions more heartfelt, and my words more powerful.

Thanks to Cassandra Tondro and Angela LoPresti St. Amant for their encouragement and assistance in finding an artist for this book's covers.

Thanks to the world-renowned artist Sigi Oberlaender for his paintings which grace the covers of this book. In the short time Sigi's known Carol, he was able to capture her perfectly in the "Three Faces of Carol."

My undying gratitude goes to the two physicians, Roger D. Haring, MD and Andrew Saxon, MD, who saved Carol's life and my sanity; who wrote the Foreword and Afterword contained herein, respectively; and who reviewed and encouraged the completion of this book. Dr. Haring is the genius who diagnosed the disease in record time; Dr. Saxon is the genius who found the treatment that put Carol in long-term remission. They are the true heroes of this story.

Thanks to my beloved sons, the fabulous Swart boys, Kenneth, Ronald, and Donald for their help and support through their little sister's trials, and their encouragement in this endeavor. Their love and compassion were always there when Carol and I needed it—and still are.

A very special thank you goes to the love of my life, my late husband, Dick, who lost his battle with cancer in March, 2006. He was always there for us in every way humanly possible, and wholeheartedly encouraged the writing of this book. He believed in me even when I didn't believe in myself. We will miss him forever.

Lastly, I wish to thank my beloved daughter, Carol, for allowing me to tell her story. She personifies courage. I want the world to know I'm so very proud of her accomplishments and the kind, compassionate, loving person she has become in the face of adversity. She fulfilled her mission in life when she found the **Reason**.

Foreword:
By
Roger D. Haring, MD

"Permanence, perseverance, and persistence in spite of all obstacles, discouragements, and impossibilities: It is this, that in all things, distinguishes the strong soul from the weak."—Thomas Carlyle

I first met Carol Swart in 1978, when she was sixteen years old. I was an ear, nose and throat doctor not too many years out of training, practicing in a small community in southern California. Carol came in complaining of a stuffy nose. A stuffy nose in my specialty is a common complaint, but on initial examination, I knew she did not have a common problem. My working diagnosis was either an unusual infection, an ominous sounding condition called Lethal Midline Granuloma, or Wegener's granulomatosis.

While initial biopsies suggested Wegener's granulomatosis, a second opinion from a nearby university medical center disagreed. Now began the first of what was to be a cascade of challenges and dilemmas that Carol would have to face in her lifetime.

Without a definitive diagnosis, it was not possible to recommend a specific treatment. But in the absence of treatment, close monitoring by me and other consultants was imperative.

For the next four years Carol was seen on a regular and frequent basis. The inflammation remained limited to her nasal cavity, and did not show up in her lungs or kidneys as Wegener's usually does. Scarring in the anterior nose, however, made examination and cleaning of the posterior nasal cavity difficult; so in 1983, I arranged for Carol to get another opinion at The Mayo Clinic in Rochester, MN. There, Thomas McDonald, MD was able to make a definitive diagnosis of Wegener's granulomatosis and give recommendations for treatment.

The initial treatment with a sulfa drug was somewhat controversial, but given Carol's age and the reproductive implications—sterility—of a much more potent chemotherapeutic medication, we chose to start with it. When that caused an allergic reaction, she was switched to the other medication. After a severe complication on *that* medication, she faced another challenge and another dilemma.

Here Andrew Saxon, MD, an immunologist at UCLA, entered her life. He was able to chart a course for Carol that, although difficult for her to endure, has resulted in the arresting of her Wegener's.

Still she had other challenges to face.

However, this is not just a story about a person with a serious illness. It is also the story of a mother and her daughter and their remarkable accomplishments in the face of obstacles, discouragements, and impossibilities that came, unwanted, into their lives.

Throughout all these years of medical problems, Carol graduated third in her high school class. She went on to graduate from college and landed a very good job.

While her treatment took its toll on her body and forced her to change her goals and expectations, she did not let it destroy her spirit. She and her mother became active in the national Wegener's Granulomatosis Support Group—now a part of the Vasculitis Foundation. Carol developed its website while her mother served on the Board of Directors and has written this book.

I have a small placard which hung over my mother's kitchen sink that says, "Bloom Where You Are Planted." It was her credo for over ninety-five years, and I can see it easily applied to Carol and Myrna. I have no doubt that they both will continue to bloom, and that their story will encourage the reader to do the same.

I think this book should be required reading for all physicians, nurses, and hospital administrators. It is not often that we are able to follow a patient with a serious medical condition for twenty-nine years.

Carol's and Myrna's experiences have so much to teach us. We need to know that there is more to *healing* than making a diagnosis and prescribing a treatment. There is that intangible sense of caring and trust that all of us need to nurture and provide to our patients and their families.

You are about to share in the journey of two strong souls. The journey began twenty-nine years ago, and continues on today.

Prologue

"The inside of her nose," Dr. Steven Carlson* said as he pushed the top of his glasses against the bridge of his nose, "is not like anything I've ever seen before. I have no idea what's going on in there."

What a strange thing for him to say, I thought. A plastic surgeon takes noses apart and puts them back together often enough to know what the inside of one looks like. It didn't seem logical for him to be puzzled about what was happening inside Carol's nose. I figured it must be another allergy problem; at sixteen, she'd already had more than her share. If I was right, how could he not have seen similar ailments? Doctors may not always be able to cure us, but they almost always know what the ailment is. Did he see a growth? A hole? What could be so unusual? He had to have some inkling of what was troubling our only daughter.

The doctor was at the hospital that day to remove two cysts from Carol's face while she was anesthetized for a nasal biopsy. When he was finished, Dr. Roger Haring, the ear, nose and throat specialist, was going to perform the biopsy.

Dick and I had preferred to avoid the busy family waiting area and remain in the solitude of our daughter's small private room, readying ourselves for the test results. We were close enough to the operating rooms to keep a lookout for someone to give us news of the surgery.

Six weeks earlier Carol had caught a cold—or so we thought. It wasn't getting better; none of the treatments were helping. Dr. Haring was taking living tissue from her nose today in an attempt to find some answers.

I was trying to pass the time, and occupy my mind, with paperwork I'd brought from my office, but the straight-backed chair was uncomfortable. I'm short, only four feet nine inches, and my feet hardly touched the polished floor. Every few minutes I got up, left my papers on the seat and peeked down the corridor, hoping to catch a glimpse of one of Carol's doctors.

"Do you see either of them?" Dick asked.

It was a quiet afternoon at the hospital, and the halls were empty.

"Not a soul," I answered, "Not a living soul."

"Very funny," he said at my attempt at humor.

Dick closed the book he was reading, rose from his armchair, and took his husky five-foot-nine frame over to the wall of windows. The noonday sun poured through open drapes. Pulling his shoulders back to stretch tense muscles, he stood staring out at the parking lot.

"I hate hospitals," he said.

"I know. They're full of sick people."

He gave me a scornful look. An automobile accident, well before we met, had left Dick with a broken back and a long recuperation. He'd had his fill of hospitals.

"How's your book?" I noticed very few pages being turned.

"I can't seem to concentrate."

That was unusual for him. For years he had devoured anything in print with phenomenal speed. I was thinking of telling him he should have brought a more exciting book, but my humor was getting stale.

"What do you think the problem is?" he asked.

"I'm convinced it has to be an allergy to something," I answered. "I've been pretty accurate about diagnosing our kids in the past, including Kenny's appendicitis and Don's pneumonia."

I had always followed up my suspicions, though, with competent medical advice.

"What makes you think it's an allergy?"

"Because if it was an infection, antibiotics would have helped. And if it was a growth, Dr. Haring would have seen it when he examined her, or her X-rays, and said so."

"Then you don't think it's something serious?"

"Not a chance. The doctor used the word unusual, not serious. Allergies are tough to treat and the body develops immunity to various drugs. We saw that happen with the boys."

Carol's three older brothers, Kenneth, Ronald, and Donald—whom she loved to tease by calling them Huey, Dewey, and Louie—had all had many upper respiratory problems. They'd always turned out to be caused by an allergic reaction to something.

I looked down the hall again and recognized the plastic surgeon's short, stocky frame as he came though the operating room's swinging doors, briefcase in hand. He took a few steps forward to where the corridors joined and glanced from side to side. He pushed up his glasses, lowered his head, turned left, and strode off. I hurried back into Carol's room.

"Dr. Carlson just came out of surgery. Maybe he has some answers."

I grabbed my purse and set off down the hall in the direction the doctor had taken, with Dick following close behind me.

We found him in a reception area, seated on a long, tan, plastic bench seat. His right hand searched in his briefcase for something. He had been finished with Carol long enough to have changed out of his surgical greens and was now clad in a sport coat and slacks. I wondered why he hadn't come looking for us with his news, whatever that news might be.

"Hello, Doctor Carlson," I called out as I approached him. "You've met Carol's father." Dick had been with us at one of Carol's appointments with him.

Withdrawing his hand from his briefcase, the doctor made no comment as to his recognition of Dick and the men shook hands. The doctor seemed preoccupied.

"How did it go, Doctor?" Dick asked as we seated ourselves in chairs facing him.

"What? Oh, the facial cysts were excised," he reported, "and the tissue has been sent to Pathology. I don't anticipate any problems."

He made the statement unemotionally and factually, ignoring any mention of the nasal biopsy. Then he got up to leave.

Although Dr. Carlson's presence at the hospital that day was only to remove the cysts, he had previously been scheduled to operate on Carol's nose. I thought he would have been interested in what the inside looked like, and expected him to make some comment about it. Because the cysts were on her face, Dick and I had agreed that a plastic surgeon was the sensible choice to remove them to avoid any possibility of scarring.

Because we knew Dr. Carlson, we'd asked him to do the surgery after Dr. Haring had set the biopsy date.

"How about her nose?" Dick persisted.

If the doctor wasn't going to bring it up, one of us had to.

"It's a mess!" he exclaimed. "I'm so glad I didn't touch it."

Dick looked at me with a puzzled expression, just as I turned toward him. I knew what he was thinking. That seemed like a very unprofessional remark to be coming from a doctor.

During the years we had spent raising four children, there had been previous hospitalizations along with questions for the attending physicians. I had never had an answer as strange and disconcerting as this one. It made no sense.

Dick pressed on, "What do you mean by that? What do you think the problem is?"

He reached for my hand and gripped it tightly.

The doctor told us he had no idea what was wrong with Carol, "except that it isn't cancer." He sank backward into his seat.

I wondered if he added that because it's what most people fear.

"When do you think you'll be able to do the rhinoplasty?"[1] I asked.

Carol had been hoping to have her nose fixed and I knew she would want to know when it could be done.

"I have," he replied emphatically, "no intention of operating on that nose!"

"Why not?" I queried. "What could make that much of a difference?"

He seemed reluctant to continue the discussion.

"You'll have to speak to Dr. Haring," he said. "I don't have the answers."

That was fairly obvious. He got up and left.

Dick and I returned to Carol's room to wait for Dr. Haring, and for her.

"What could be so bad that Dr. Carlson won't ever operate?" I asked, with uneasiness creeping over me, knowing that my husband didn't have any answers, either. "It doesn't make any sense. How could he have no idea what she has? Hasn't he seen enough noses to tell us something?"

"Apparently not," Dick said, shrugging his shoulders. "You heard what I heard."

"Didn't you get the feeling that he couldn't wait to get away from us? He acted so different when I took Carol for consultations about fixing her nose."

"In what way?"

"Oh—friendly, patient, confident. He answered all our questions in detail. Just now he seemed distant and confused, anxious to get away from us. I don't recall ever hearing such a noncommittal answer."

"I suppose he did seem to be in a hurry to leave. Maybe he had another appointment," Dick said.

We continued waiting in silence, together in the same room but alone with our thoughts.

After a while he said, "I wonder where Dr. Haring is."

"Me, too. We certainly have some questions for him."

"Let's hope he has answers."

---

1.   Rhinoplasty is a procedure in plastic surgery in which the structure of the nose is changed.

Carol before diagnosis, with her brothers Don, Ron, and Ken, 1978

1

A new nose?

Carol's story began a few months earlier. It was spring of 1978. She had just turned sixteen and was nearing the end of her sophomore year in high school.

In her room were sixteen sugar cubes, tied up in pink bows and ribbons, trailing from the canopy bedpost. I'd had the sweet bouquet hanging from the dining room archway during her surprise birthday party to be used like mistletoe. It was a custom from my teenage days that I wanted to share with my daughter and her friends.

On her teeth were the braces that Kenny jokingly referred to as the "teen-age status symbol."

"The day they come off won't be one day too soon," Carol frequently said; but just as often she sported a T-shirt reading "Tin Grins Are In." From the day the braces were put on, and throughout the day-to-day wearing of them for the previous year and a half, she hadn't registered any complaints with me, facing the whole process of tooth straightening in good spirits.

Determined to follow the orthodontist's orders, she would exclaim after dinner, "I'll be down to help with the clean-up after I brush!" and race upstairs, her long, honey-brown hair flying behind her. Discomfort didn't seem to be an issue; having something done to make her look better was.

One evening as we made dinner together, she looked up from the potatoes she was scrubbing and asked, "How would you feel about my having my nose fixed?"

I stopped cutting the lettuce, knife poised in mid-air, and asked, "Plastic surgery?"

"Yeah. I really think my nose is ugly and I'd look better with a different nose."

I didn't think anything about her was ugly.

"Well, it's not the cute little nose that you were born with, but I don't think that any part of you needs changing. Besides, you know how superstitious I am." I returned to my cutting. "I don't like tampering with nature. If what you were born with works properly and is socially acceptable, leave it alone. If it works, don't fix it."

"Please think about it, Mom," she persisted.

"OK. I'll mention it to your father and get his opinion," I said.

Actually, I was thinking about ignoring the issue, hoping she'd forget all about it. The braces were necessary and had been recommended by the family dentist; plastic surgery on her nose was not, in my view, a necessity.

While we were getting ready for bed, though, I decided to tell Dick.

"Carol wants to have her nose fixed," I blurted out.

"OK," he said nonchalantly as he came from our adjoining dressing room and headed for his side of the bed.

Dick's always been a pushover for his children's desires. But discussion of medical details is not his favorite topic and he dislikes going to hospitals. I was sure he'd be opposed.

"What do you mean, OK," I said. "I think it's a lousy idea."

"Why?" he asked as he sat down on the edge of the bed and fluffed up his pillow.

I climbed into my side and turned off my lamp.

"I don't like the idea of unnecessary surgery," I said, "and I would have thought you'd say the same thing."

"Why?" he repeated.

"It's bad enough when someone has to have an operation. Remember what the pediatrician said when Kenny had his tonsils out?"

"About what?"

"About the anesthesia. He said when a person is 'put out,' it's the same for a tonsillectomy as it is for brain surgery, and that's the most likely time for trouble to occur. She has no idea what she'd be putting herself through."

"Why don't you wait and see if she brings it up again. Maybe she's not that serious," Dick said, picking up a book.

"That's the best idea I've heard all day," I said, and kissed him goodnight. If Carol didn't mention plastic surgery again, I certainly wasn't going to, and that would be the end of that.

But it wasn't.

It was a busy time for us. Ken, our firstborn, was twenty-one, and graduating from college with a degree in journalism. My mother and stepfather were coming from Florida for the ceremonies and would be staying for a couple of weeks until Don, our third son who was eighteen, graduated from high school.

Ron, twenty, was studying photography at an art college in Pasadena, making the daily one-hour commute with Dick. I had begun working in real estate sales a year and a half before. After years of cleaning toilet bowls, baking cookies, and volunteering for school and civic projects, I had decided to seek something that would supplement our income. If I helped with college expenses, the children could give all their attention to their studies and not have to worry about paying for tuition, books, cars, etc.

With all that was going on, I conveniently forgot to make an appointment with a plastic surgeon to pursue Carol's desire to have her nose fixed. To me, she was just fine the way she was. If something went wrong during the surgery, I would never have forgiven myself for consenting. If an operation was needed, that was different. But we had a choice about this one, and mine was to forget it.

About a week later, Carol cornered me in the kitchen. I could almost feel the question coming.

"Did you talk to Dad about getting my nose fixed?"

"Yes."

"What did he say?"

"Nothing."

"What's that supposed to mean?"

"Well, we were going to wait and see if you'd mention it again. We weren't sure how serious you were about this."

I was cutting up a chicken, avoiding her eyes.

"You don't want me to have it done, do you, Mom," she said, not bothering to make it a question. I was hedging, and she knew it.

She stopped setting the table. She'd already outgrown me by two inches, and could glare down at me as I stood next to her in my low-heeled shoes.

"I never said I didn't want you to have your nose fixed," I said, as I stopped cutting and looked up at her.

"You didn't have to. You usually don't stall like this when I ask you for something."

She'd never asked for anything I was so opposed to, except to go snow skiing when she was thirteen. I gave in that time. Apparently this meant more to Carol than I thought.

"I guess I was hoping that you would change your mind."

"Why?"

"I don't think it's a good idea to operate on something that doesn't need it."

"Mom, you're not being fair. If we can't afford it, say so. If you're afraid of something, tell me. But don't tell me what's not necessary. You don't see what I see in the mirror."

"Maybe you're right," I said. "Why don't you talk to your father yourself?"

"OK. I will."

"Make sure it's after dinner," I said. "He's more receptive on a full stomach."

If she was going to give this a shot, it might as well be an equitable one.

That evening, with Dick and the boys still seated and chattering away as we cleared the dinner dishes, Carol didn't ask her father, she told him.

"Dad," she said, "I'd really like to see about having my nose fixed."

Dick looked at me. I shrugged my shoulders. I hadn't changed my mind, but decided for the moment not to fight Carol on this.

Her father seldom refused her anything. Maybe that was because she always asked for things that were reasonable.

Because Carol is the youngest of four children, and the only girl, I used to say that she was spoiled. But that's not really true. Dick and I doted on her and pampered her, as did all her brothers, because we enjoyed it. In my mind, spoiled means someone who insists on getting her own way and throws tantrums if she doesn't. But that's not Carol. She has always been easy to get along with, never a crybaby, never demanding. As a young toddler, she put up with starched dresses and lace ruffles because I enjoyed "dressing my doll." Her baby and childhood photographs show her full of smiles.

People who meet her like her instantly. A private person who doesn't particularly like talking about herself, Carol will steer the conversation toward whomever she's with; by the time they part, he or she thinks Carol is wonderful. She's usually upbeat, smiling, and fun to be with. One of my uncles remarked, seeing her as a teenager, that, "When Carol walks into a room, it lights up."

Carol's always loved sports. Having three brothers probably contributed to that. At thirteen she had an opportunity to go on a school ski trip. I said "no" and her father said "yes." I think it was the first time we disagreed on something having to do with the children. I was afraid she would fall off the side of a mountain. But she went and all was fine. It was the beginning of her love affair with cold-weather sports.

I never wanted her to have unnecessary pain and believed plastic surgery would create that for her. But maybe it wasn't unnecessary for Carol.

"I think we ought to find out what's involved," Dick said to her.

To me he said, "Why don't you call Dr. Mysko and ask him for a recommendation of a good plastic surgeon. Once we know what it entails, Carol can decide if she still wants it done."

Dr. David Mysko was our family doctor, and it didn't seem that it could do any harm to check out the situation with him.

"OK," I said. "I'll call him."

When she was born and I saw her for the first time, it was apparent she resembled her father. She inherited his beautiful blue eyes, his tendency to become freckled when exposed to the sun, and his beak-like nose.

The freckles, which her pediatrician called, "angel kisses," didn't seem to bother her; but we had known for a long time that she was less than thrilled with her larger-than-average nose. Even so, surgery seemed to me a radical response.

I was still hoping Carol would change her mind, but she was determined.

"Make sure you don't forget to call Dr. Mysko tomorrow, Mom. I put a note on the refrigerator to remind you."

The next day I made the phone call. Dr. Mysko recommended a Dr. Steven Carlson, who had an office in a neighboring town.

Before I called for an appointment, there was one more source to check. I wanted to hear my mother's thoughts on the subject. Although she lived far away, and only saw the children once or twice a year, I felt her opinion was valuable. She's a logical, objective thinker while, in contrast, I'm an emotional thinker. If there's no trouble afoot, I'll borrow some.

I was certain that Mom would say something like, "If nature gave her that nose, it was meant to be hers. As long as she can breathe through it, leave well enough alone."

Instead she surprised me with, "If it's that important to Carol, at least look into the possibility."

"You're not serious, Mom. I thought you'd be against this idea. It's tampering with nature. That's not like you at all."

"It looks like she wants this badly, and you owe it to her to get the information necessary to make an informed decision. She handled the braces well, and she's obviously concerned about her appearance. I think you need to try, for her sake."

"If I had wanted plastic surgery, you never would have let me have it," I said. "Besides, how do you know she wants this so badly?"

"What I would have let you do has nothing to do with Carol," she said, "and if she didn't want this done badly, we wouldn't be having this conversation."

"I'm supposed to be wiser than she is, and I'm just not comfortable with some doctor cutting into her face. What if a knife slips?"

"You're not being reasonable," Mom said. "Once you both hear what the doctor has to say, you'll be better equipped to make a decision. What does Dick say about all this?"

"You know how he is with the kids. He'd say 'yes' to anything they wanted."

"He would never agree to anything he thought might hurt them," she said.

She had me there. That made two against one. Since both Dick's and Mom's opinions coincided, I had to assume there was a possibility I might be wrong. Maybe one could tamper with nature, on occasion.

When Carol came home from school the next day I was ready for her questions.

"Did you call Dr. Mysko?"

"Yes, I did."

"Did he give you any names?"

"He suggested Dr. Steven Carlson, and I called for an appointment. Boy! Did they give me the third degree!"

"What do you mean?"

"The woman I spoke to not only wanted to know all about the details of what you wanted done, but also how I felt about it."

"I hope you didn't tell her."

"No, I didn't say I was not 100 percent in favor of this. She also wanted to know how we intended to pay, since insurance doesn't usually cover plastic surgery if it's elective. She really made me feel very uncomfortable."

"How?"

"It was almost as if she was trying to discourage an appointment. Half of the feeling came from what she said, the other half from the way she said it. I expected her to say, 'We can see you next Wednesday if there's an earthquake and a rainstorm during a total eclipse of the moon.'"

"I think you're probably exaggerating just a little, Mom. Besides, I'm sure they get a lot of calls from people who think they want to go through with one type of surgery or another, and then change their minds," Carol said.

"I suppose you're right. Well, anyway, I was finally granted an appointment. We go next Tuesday."

"Thanks, Mom. I knew I could count on you."

Carol kissed me and scampered up the stairs, most likely to consult the mirrors that Dick had installed across one wall of her lavender-flowered bedroom, to reshape her nose in her mind.

Nothing else about her needed reshaping. At sixteen she had developed a lovely figure. Everything she tried on looked great on her petite four-foot-eleven frame. I often told my friends that taking her shopping was a joy; I was back to dressing my doll again.

When Carol and I arrived for her appointment, Lily,* the woman I had spoken to on the phone, introduced herself and was friendly and pleasant as she handed Carol an information form to fill out.

"You'll have a short wait to see the doctor. You can use the waiting room or the television viewing room."

There was also a reception area; it was one of the largest doctors' suites I had ever seen, and there were no other names on the door besides Dr. Carlson's.

"There's a five-minute explanatory film that you can watch by pushing a button on the front of the TV," she continued. "It explains all about what a rhinoplasty is and how it's done."

I wasn't going to miss this one. Steering Carol into the TV room, I pushed the button and sat down to watch.

"It's only diagrams," I said, visibly disappointed at the end.

"What did you expect, Mom? Blood and guts?"

"Why not? I like details."

"Most people would pass out in front of the TV if they were shown a real operation," she said.

"I guess you're right, but it would still be more interesting to me."

We went into the waiting room. It was crowded, considering there was only one doctor. One patient came in walking with a cane, another had a bandaged hand, but no one with a nose wrapped in gauze was there.

Carol had several additional appointments with the doctor, during which he took numerous photographs of her face, both front views and profiles.

"Are these the before pictures?" she wanted to know.

"They certainly are," he answered.

"Why do you want to change your nose?" he asked her during one of the appointments.

"I don't think it's pretty," she answered.

"What do you want done to it?"

"I want it to be smaller and straighter," she said.

While Carol spoke, Dr. Carlson made copious notes, and nodded.

My curiosity got the better of me, and I asked him, "Why would you ask Carol what changes she wants instead of telling her what you think ought to be done?"

He said, "What I think is not as important as what Carol thinks. If it's her nose that's going to be changed, it should be the way she wants it. My opinion is important, but it isn't the most important."

He added, "It's unnecessary to change something the patient doesn't want changed."

His answer surprised me. I guess I had always thought of a plastic surgeon in the same category as a sculptor, assuming he would change her nose to fit his own specifications and ideas. I was favorably impressed with him.

"You'll be awake during the surgery," he told Carol.

I just got unimpressed.

"We use an office set up specifically for this on the bottom floor of this building," he continued. "You will want someone to come with you that day, because you'll need to be driven home."

Was he kidding? I'd been with her at every visit. Did he think I wouldn't be with her that day?

"Do you mean, Doctor, that you won't be using a hospital?" I asked.

"No. This is an out-patient procedure."

"Why?"

"A hospital would be a lot more costly and would require the use of a general anesthetic instead of a local one, which I prefer," he explained. "A general is much more dangerous and I don't think it's necessary."

It never occurred to me that the operation wouldn't be in a hospital, and I must have had a startled look on my face.

He added, "You'll have plenty of time to think about it."

And, I thought, to check once again with Dr. Mysko for his opinion.

We'd been warned about the dangers of general anesthesia before. But not using a hospital for the surgery gave me visions of a B-movie with sleazy clinics hidden in dark alleys. It was a Catch-22. Now what were we supposed to do?

Surgery couldn't be scheduled yet anyway.

"I can't operate until the braces come off," Dr. Carlson added. "Make an appointment for then."

I heaved a big sigh; I'd gotten a reprieve.

As we were leaving, Lily stopped us.

"When you make the arrangements for the rhinoplasty, we'll require payment in advance, a cashier's check only, and we must have it at least ten days prior to the surgery."

"Can't I pay you with a personal check in sufficient time for it to clear before the surgery?"

"I'm sorry," she said. "We only accept cashier's checks. If we don't have the cashier's check in time, someone else will be scheduled on that day, and you'll have to make a new appointment."

We made up our minds to comply with their request.

That evening I discussed not using a hospital with Dick. He felt just as uncomfortable as I did.

"Ask Dr. Mysko," he suggested. "He hasn't steered us wrong so far."

Graduation days and my parents came and went, and we settled back into our normal routine.

While Mom was in town she made a point of telling me, "I've taken a closer look at Carol's nose and I agree with her. I think you're doing the right thing by letting her go ahead with the operation. It's very important to her."

But I don't give up that easily. Within the next few weeks I went through all my own fearful questions with Carol again and again.

"Do you understand that you'll probably be full of bruises? Are you aware that you will be sore and in a lot of pain? Do you know that you'll be taped and bandaged and not able to breathe through your nose?"

Her answers were always the same. "Yes, I understand. Yes, I'm aware. Yes, I'm willing to go through all that. Yes, I want it that badly."

In spite of my misgivings she was determined to have this operation.

Carol's persistence was not something new to me. Her strong will first surfaced when she was just a few months old. She weaned herself from my breast and refused a bottle with a rubber nipple. She drank her milk from a shot glass as I held it.

As soon as she was old enough to climb down from my lap and speak, she often made it clear that she would do things her own way.

After patiently listening to me voice my fears she went to work begging and pleading with the orthodontist, determined to have him remove her braces early, promising if necessary to wear her retainer for eternity.

The braces came off in August. The date was immediately set for the rhinoplasty.

I had consulted with Dr. Mysko regarding Dr. Carlson's operating room and he concurred with the surgeon. "General anesthesia is much more dangerous.

"I'm familiar with Dr. Carlson's set-up there," he added. "It's not something you need to be concerned about."

When you pay a doctor for his advice you should probably take it.

Dr. Carlson's fee was paid in advance, as demanded, by cashier's check. Dick went with us to that appointment.

"Would it be possible for us to see where the surgery will be done?" he asked.

"Absolutely," Dr. Carlson replied, and took us downstairs to see the operating room himself.

"It seems that you're a little uncomfortable with these arrangements. Perhaps I can put your mind at ease, or answer any questions," he offered.

He opened the door so that we could see in.

"I can't take you inside the room," he added, "or we'd destroy the sterility."

"It's not necessary for us to go in. We can see what we need to," Dick said.

There was an operating table in the middle of the room, enormous lights overhead and on stands, and lots of equipment on the floor and attached to the walls.

"It looks just like all the operating rooms I've seen in hospitals," I said.

My fears regarding the quality of the room had been put to rest.

Before we left his office, Carol was given a prescription for Seconal™[2] with instructions to take two the night before the surgery and another two the next morning prior to leaving home.

"After seeing the room they'll be using, I feel more comfortable about this whole thing," I said. Then I read the prescription. "I wonder why he wrote this for a dozen pills if Carol will only need four."

"You're borrowing trouble again," Dick chided.

I had the prescription filled; Carol never used it.

---

2.   Seconal™ is a brand of sleeping pill.

Carol, 2½, and Myrna, "dressing her doll," 1964

2

Meeting Dr. Haring

After the payment was made to Dr. Carlson, and a week before the scheduled surgery, Carol developed symptoms of a cold. There was always the possibility that she'd had an allergic reaction; allergy problems had bothered her all her life. When she began sniffling as a week-old infant, I'd thought she had a cold, unusual for breast-fed babies. Looking back now, I realize it must have been the beginning of allergic reactions to surroundings. Now it was often impossible to distinguish a cold from an allergy when she had congestion or a runny nose.

I had a feeling the doctor wouldn't want to operate if he thought she had an infection.

"The cold's really not that bad," Carol said. "I don't see any reason why I can't have the operation. Besides, you already paid for it."

"It's too risky when you have any kind of infection. The doctors don't want respiratory problems during surgery. But, it's his decision, OK? Let him say which way to go."

"OK."

When I phoned the office to let him know of the cold symptoms, Dr. Carlson chose to postpone the rhinoplasty.

Even though I had agreed to the surgery, made the necessary arrangements, paid in advance, and certainly wasn't happy to see Carol suffering from a cold or allergy, I was glad the surgery had been postponed. I felt a strange sense of relief. Since Carol was well aware that I wasn't overjoyed about the impending surgery, and I couldn't explain my feeling of apprehension, I didn't say anything about it to her or anyone else.

She got the usual cold and allergy medicines for a week with no visible results. Nothing had changed; Carol showed no improvement. It was time to see Dr. Mysko, a tall, authoritative man with rimless eyeglasses, dark wavy hair, and a big, bushy mustache. Every time I had a medical question for him, he had an answer I could live with. He'd always been able to help whatever we had that hurt. I trusted his judgment.

After examining Carol, suspecting a secondary infection, he prescribed an antibiotic and told me to bring Carol back in a week.

At the end of the week there was still no change. This time Dr. Mysko took a culture from her nose to send to a laboratory for possible growth and examination. Then he prescribed a different antibiotic.

Three weeks after the cold symptoms first appeared, there was still no change. When we returned, Dr. Mysko told us the culture had not grown anything at the laboratory, prescribed a stronger antibiotic, and ordered a set of sinus X-rays.

Specifically, Carol's symptoms were a stuffy nose, headaches near or around the frontal sinuses, and intermittent pain through the maxillary sinus areas, which seemed typical of the common cold or nasal allergies. What was not typical, or common, was the total lack of response to the usual remedies.

"The X-rays show some abnormalities," the doctor said. "My advice is for Carol to see a specialist as soon as possible."

"What do you mean by abnormalities? Are there any growths?" I asked.

"No, but there are areas that should be black if there's no infection and white if there is. They're cloudy. The radiologist doesn't understand what he's seeing either."

"Could I see the X-rays?" I asked, having never seen them except on TV and having no idea what to look for. Dr. Mysko put the films on a light box and pointed out the areas he'd discussed.

This was the first time a doctor didn't have an answer for us and it was a little frightening. But, that's why one sees a specialist.

"Do you have someone in mind?" I asked.

"I recommend Roger Haring. He's an ENT," he answered. "I'll have one of the girls call for an appointment for Carol if you'd like, so there'll be no delay. I'll let him know what's been going on and see that he gets the X-rays."

I've always had a lot of confidence in doctors and believed that practically anything could be cured with a pill, an injection, or an operation. Doctors had saved Don's life when he was nine months old and Ken's when he was nine years old. They had found ways to treat or cure our illnesses at other times. They had to help Carol now. Most of the respiratory problems in the family had been allergy-related and treatable, even if not curable. This one might be more troublesome, but we had dealt with troublesome problems before successfully.

We were able to get an appointment with Dr. Haring in less than a week.

The atmosphere, when we entered Dr. Haring's office for Carol's appointment, was a friendly one. The receptionist handled incoming calls with concern and compassion. The rest of his staff had a similar attitude.

A young lady called Carol's name, and we both got up to go to the examining room.

"My name is Carla," she said. "Dr. Mysko sent your X-rays over, and Dr. Haring is just checking them now. He'll be with you shortly."

As we followed her into one of the largest examining rooms I'd ever been in, I asked, "Is it all right if I stay and watch?"

"You might as well say 'yes,'" Carol said, "because she's going to anyway."

Carla laughed, and said, "As you can see, there's plenty of room. You certainly won't be in the way."

She showed Carol to the examining chair. I seated myself in one of several straight-backed chairs along the wall, and Carla left the room.

"This looks like an old converted house," I said to Carol. We knew we were in a residential neighborhood. "Did you notice the fireplace in the waiting room? It's been covered over so it can't be used for fires anymore."

"You know, that's funny," she said. "I thought I saw a chimney outside."

"I guess these rooms were probably bedrooms in the house's past life."

Both of us have always found old houses fascinating. We discovered that the bathroom had a bathtub, not a typical fixture in a medical office building.

Dr. Haring entered and introduced himself to both of us. He was fair-skinned, medium height, slender, and had a slightly receding hairline. Looking at my daughter seated in his examining chair he said, "You must be Carol."

"Yes, and this is my mom."

"How do you do, Mrs. Swart. You're welcome to stay during the examination. As you can see," the doctor gestured toward the open expanse of the examining room, "You won't be in the way."

"I'm glad you said that," said Carla, who had rejoined us. "Carol said she's going to stay anyway."

We all chuckled and relaxed. I liked this doctor.

"I've spoken to Dr. Mysko," Dr. Haring said, "and he explained what has occurred so far."

Turning to Carol he said, "Your X-rays are somewhat unusual. What problems are you having?"

"My nose is constantly stuffed, and I've been having a lot of headaches and pain here." Carol pointed to the areas on her cheeks.

"Where are the headaches?" he asked.

"Here," she pointed to her forehead, just above her eyes.

"Does it ever hurt behind your eyes?"

"Yes," she answered. "Sometimes it feels like there's something behind them, pushing them out."

"I'd like to take a look in your nose, now," he said.

I watched as he examined Carol using his headband with the little round mirror, a flashlight, and an instrument to widen her nostrils that looked just like long eyebrow tweezers. Then he turned off his flashlight, took off his headband, and described the interior of Carol's nose as "unusual."

He went on: "It looks as if someone has taken sandpaper and rubbed the inside of her nose raw."

When he let me have a look, I understood what he meant and felt his description was apt. There were angry red spots, some infected with pus, and scabs, which the doctor referred to as crusting, where the infected spots were healing.

"What's the inside of a nose supposed to look like?" I asked.

"Just like the inside of a mouth," he answered.

It was easy to see why he had used the term unusual.

"Just before all this started, Carol was going to have a rhinoplasty," I said. "Right now, I'm glad we didn't go ahead with it."

"I don't think a plastic surgeon would have touched her after seeing what's going on in there," he said.

"I'm going to give her Keflex™, a broad-spectrum antibiotic," he said. "Dr Mysko told me what Carol's been taking and this is much stronger. It's going to be expensive too."

Who cares, I thought. Let's get this thing over with so she can get on with her life.

Turning to Carol he said, "I'd like to see you in a week. If there's still no improvement, I would like to biopsy the tissue from inside your nose and see if we can find out what's going on."

"Nothing she has taken has given her any relief from the stuffy nose and it seems that the pain in the sinus area and resulting headaches are becoming more severe," I told him. "Carol's not a complainer, so when she says it hurts, it must be pretty bad."

"Do you need some pain medication, Carol?" he asked.

"That would help," she answered.

Besides giving Carol a prescription for the Keflex™, he wrote one for emperin with codeine.

Another week passed with no change in the symptoms.

Dr. Haring made arrangements for a biopsy to be performed at Henry Mayo Newhall Memorial Hospital, our local hospital.

"During the biopsy," he told us, "Carol will be put under using a general anesthetic."

"Dr. Mysko suggested that these two cysts," I said, pointing to one on Carol's right cheek, and another on her left jaw, "should be surgically removed. As long as she's going to be under, would it cause you any problems if they were taken out then? I thought I'd call Dr. Carlson who was going to do the rhinoplasty, and see if he's available."

"It's all right with me," Dr. Haring said.

I called Dr. Carlson's office and had no trouble setting up his part of the surgery. No one gave me a hard time; they still had my money.

In preparation for the biopsy, Carol had blood and urine tests. The doctor had also ordered several X-rays of her head and chest, including her first CAT scan, which Carol described to me afterwards.

"It was like an all-around X-ray. The machine circled my head a few times, moving down a little each time. A small X-ray beam was directed horizontally and vertically. Then it was fed into a computer and assembled in an image displayed on a video screen. I could see slices of my skull."

Using this type of X-ray, doctors should be able to identify any destruction a disease has caused as well as search for tumors. The scan was filed for future comparisons.

Carol prepared for her hospitalization as if she were going to a party. She was concerned about what to wear, whom to invite to visit with her, and what she would get to eat. After all, a biopsy was a way to find out how to get rid of her troubles—certainly not a serious operation—definitely not anything to worry about. She was anticipating very little after-pain or discomfort. She was decidedly not prepared for any major problems.

Neither were we.

Besides the clothes and toiletries necessary for her stay, her suitcase was packed with high hopes for an easy solution.

Carol checked into the hospital that October day with Dick and me hanging on each arm. Along with the usual questions, like name, rank, and insurance number, the woman in admitting asked, as she was filling out the various forms, "What is the reason for admission?"

"Severe sinus/nasal infection," I answered.

"Do you smoke?" she asked Carol.

"No," Carol answered.

She then paired Carol with a roommate who chain-smoked.

Before long, clouds of smoke began to envelop the room. Not wanting to be troublemakers, we said nothing for the moment.

A nurse came in and took Carol's vital signs.

"The smoke's pretty bad, isn't it?" she whispered to us.

"And she's here for respiratory problems," I said.

"Something ought to be done about that," the nurse remarked.

"I'm just trying to decide how loud to yell," Dick said. "She can only take so much of this."

The nurse continued with her duties, and asked Carol for a brief medical history. Just as she was finishing up, another nurse passing by the room recognized Carol and came in to visit.

"This is Lacey's* mother, Mrs. Doyle*," Carol said, introducing the nurse to us. "Lacey is the one I've been tutoring in math."

Carol's science teacher, George Peterson,* occasionally used her as a baby-sitter. She got to know his wife, Sally,* an elementary school teacher who offered Carol the opportunity to tutor one of her students who was having trouble with math. She saw Lacey several times a week and had gotten to know Lacey's mother, a nurse.

"Carol's doing a terrific job with Lacey," Mrs. Doyle told us. "She's learning a lot and looks up to Carol as a big sister. That's quite a young lady you've raised. You should be proud of her. Not many teens would take the time to help someone else."

Dick and I glowed with pride as we thanked her.

She turned to Carol. "Why are you in here?" she asked.

"I have some weird sinus infection that I can't get rid of. I'm going to have a biopsy tomorrow morning to see what they can find out."

Then she came closer and lowered her voice.

"Didn't you tell them downstairs that you wanted a non-smoking room? That must be murder on your sinuses."

"We didn't know we had a choice," I said.

By this time, Carol's roommate had three visitors. All four of them were smoking.

"And Admitting knew you were here for a respiratory problem?" She motioned for Dick and me to follow her into the hall. "You'd think they'd have enough sense not to put her in a room with a smoker. Would you like to have her transferred to another room?"

With our eager assent, she disappeared down the hall. In a matter of minutes, she was back.

"There's no other semi-private room available; Carol's getting a private room at no extra charge."

Two orderlies were at the nurse's heels ready to move Carol. The bed, with Carol in it, was wheeled down the hall to a private room and the orderlies left.

"This one even has a shower in the bathroom," Carol noted after she got up to survey her new quarters. "Of course the other room had a better view; all we can see from this one is the parking lot."

"Shut up and enjoy your privacy," I said.

"This is a perfect example of the saying: it's not what you know, but who you know that counts," Dick said. "You seem to have friends in the right places, sweetie."

Several of Carol's classmates knew of her problems with the cold that wouldn't go away and came to visit that evening, bringing her silly gifts suitable for a four-year-old. Teresa brought play dough; Linda brought Colorforms™; Valerie brought a coloring book and crayons; Brad brought her a stuffed animal. They all laughed gaily as she unwrapped her presents. It seemed even funnier to me when I reminded Dick that every one of her friends was part of the school's gifted program.

Mr. Peterson even turned up to see her, bringing a box of candy.

Her brothers all came to visit, also. When they were little children I used to tell them it was their job to take care of and protect their little sister. They did, and still do.

None of us had any idea what tomorrow, and the biopsy, would bring. At that point, it didn't matter to Carol. This was a good excuse for a mini-party. Dick got soft drinks from the vending machine for Carol's visitors.

Her brothers and friends brought Carol a lot of joy that evening. If she was supposed to be apprehensive and full of gloom and doom, someone forgot to tell her. She was enjoying the attention.

When a nurse checking on Carol walked in and observed the atmosphere, she remarked, "I can see you're really upset about tomorrow."

The nurse didn't chase anyone out until after 10:00 PM when they were getting ready to leave anyway.

We had been told that Carol would be taken into surgery at 10:00 AM, and planned to be there to kiss her and wish her good luck. For superstitious people like me, it's important to my peace of mind.

When the surgical nurses came to take her to the operating room, they covered her head with a white paper cap. We watched as she was transferred to a gurney, covered up to her neck with a sheet and strapped in. We kissed her, wished her good luck, and watched them wheel her off to surgery down the hall, around the corner, and through the double doors. I watched this scenario with a lump in my throat.

Then we returned to Carol's room to wait an eternity. A nurse's aide saw us going back and said, "Did you know there's a waiting area with coffee and tea at the end of the hall?"

We took a look, but Carol's room seemed to be a better choice for us.

"This is much more peaceful," I said to Dick. "We won't be disturbing anyone and vice versa. I'd like to be alone with my thoughts."

It was frightening to realize that my baby was sick and no one seemed to be able to help, at least so far. But this couldn't possibly be anything serious. I was convinced Dr. Haring would find something that was easy to fix and fix it. Horrible things happen to someone else's children—not to mine.

Dick chose the armchair by the window, settled into it and opened a book he'd brought. I picked a straight-backed chair close to the door and appointed myself "chief lookout and doctor watcher."

A box of real estate flyers I'd brought with me needed the selling price changed, so I took out my red pen and got to work. It was a perfect way to keep my hands busy, but my mind wandered.

This was not the first time we'd had a child in the hospital. There was Ken's tonsillectomy and emergency appendectomy and later Don's stomach problems.

Everything had happened so quickly the day Kenny's side hurt. The pediatrician and I were certain by 10:00 AM that the problem was appendicitis. It was confirmed about 2:00 PM by the surgeon. By 5:00, Kenny was in surgery.

I had brought my knitting to pass the time then. I was in the habit of bringing some kind of needlecraft to doctors' offices, on trips, or any place I thought I might have to wait. That way I never felt I was wasting time. As I knitted, while awaiting news of Kenny, Dick said I reminded him of Madame Defarge.[3] When Kenny had his tonsillectomy, Dick waited at the hospital while I stayed home with the other three. Carol was just an infant then.

The worst scare we'd previously had was before Carol was born when Don was a baby. The whole family had come down with the flu. Within three days the rest of us were over it, but Don was deathly ill and needed hospitalization. He was diagnosed with severe dehydration and gastroenteritis. It took another three days with Dick keeping a constant crib-side vigil, along with twenty-four-hour nursing care, before Don was pronounced out of the woods. He spent a total of nine days in the hospital with private nurses for seven of them. We were worried, of course, but we were comforted by the fact that the health professionals knew what they were treating.

This time was different because no one seemed to know what to do to relieve Carol's pain and symptoms, let alone what was causing them—and she wasn't getting any better. We both had good reason to be frightened, but if I told Dick I was afraid for Carol, that would be admitting that this thing that was troubling her might be serious. I wasn't ready to do that.

Dick interrupted my brooding. "Don't you think it's been long enough? This wasn't supposed to take all day."

"I'll check again."

It was then that our strange and disconcerting encounter with Dr. Carlson took place. He was the first one to come out of the operating room and, while he reported that his portion of the surgery had gone well, he left us with more questions than he answered.

"Here she comes," Dick said, as two nurses in surgical greens wheeled Carol into the room. There was an IV attached to her arm.

In spite of her many freckles, she looked so pale. The white paper cap was still covering her hair; and her blue eyes, framed by brows and lashes so fair that it looked like she hardly had any, were wide open, searching for a familiar face.

A weak, "Hi," emanated from her parched lips as they broke into a smile.

"Hi, angel face," I said, using a childhood endearment. "Nice of you to drop in."

A tall, thin nurse transferred the IV bag to a pole on the bed, and then the two of them moved all one hundred five pounds of Carol off the gurney and onto the bed.

"She's doing just fine," said the other nurse as she wheeled the gurney away.

The taller nurse stayed to adjust the flow of the IV and to take Carol's vital signs. She recorded her findings on a clipboard, put up the bed's side rails, and left.

Carol's nostrils were packed with gauze; there was another large wad of gauze taped just underneath her nose to keep the packing in place. We learned that the nurses referred to that particular dressing as a mustache bandage. If it had been black instead of white, and if she had been wearing horn-rimmed glasses and smoking a cigar, Carol could have entered a Groucho Marx look-alike contest. The thought made me smile, and relieved some of my tension.

She could only breathe through her mouth. Her lips were beginning to crack. When I saw that, I made a mental note to bring some A&D™ ointment when I returned later.

Dick and I walked over to opposite sides of the bed.

"Hi, sweetie, how do you feel?" Dick asked, as he bent over the bedrail and kissed her forehead.

"OK," she murmured.

It reminded me of a time when she was a toddler, running a high fever. The pediatrician came into the examining room and asked Carol how she was. She told him, "fine," and the doctor and I chuckled about our culture's pat answers, knowing that if she were fine she wouldn't be there.

Being as short as I am, I couldn't reach over the bedrail to kiss my daughter.

"This is not fair. I can't kiss you without a stepstool," I commented as I blew her a kiss. "Is there anything you want?"

"Please close the drapes." The anesthetic had not worn off and she was drifting in and out of consciousness. "The sun is too bright."

Dick walked over to the window and drew the drapes.

"Does your nose hurt?" I inquired.

"No, but my throat does," she said.

"Maybe the doctor will have a suggestion for that."

"I wonder where he is," Dick muttered from across the bed, "and why we haven't seen him yet."

After an unsatisfactory conversation Dick had with a nurse about Dr. Haring's whereabouts, the surgeon strolled into the room.

"Hi, Mr. and Mrs. Swart," he said with a pleasant smile. "I thought I'd find you here. I was told you were in the waiting room. When I didn't see you there, I went down to the cafeteria to look for you. I thought you might be having lunch."

"Hi, Dr. Haring. I'm afraid food was the last thing on our minds," Dick said.

"We were told you had left the hospital," I said.

"Not yet," he said. "I had someone to check on." He nodded his head in Carol's direction.

Taking his hands out of his pants pockets, he walked toward the bed. He was clad in a sweater and slacks.

"How are you feeling, Carol?" he asked, as he placed his hand on top of hers.

"Sleepy," she said, "and my throat hurts."

"That's from the tracheal tube inserted in your throat to assist with breathing during surgery," the doctor said. "Try to drink as much as you can. That should help."

"How bad am I?" Carol wanted to know.

"Nothing we can't handle," he said.

Dick and I simultaneously let out a big sigh.

You can tell yourself over and over again that there's nothing to worry about, but hearing it just once from the doctor makes it so much more meaningful. He didn't look worried, either.

But then he turned to us and said very directly, "I think I have a diagnosis."

---

3.   Madame Defarge is a character from Charles Dickens' novel *A Tale of Two Cities*. She knitted during the beheadings.

3

The Disease Has a Name

"I suspect Wegener's granulomatosis," Dr. Haring said. "I have only seen one other case of Wegener's before. At least that's what they thought it was, and that was during my residency at Stanford."

That had to be ten or more years ago, I thought. If he hadn't seen this disease since then, it couldn't be anything to worry about. If it were deadly, it would have a national organization, lots of publicity, and probably a TV movie of the week, I decided.

"The pathologist will let us know in a few days whether or not my suspicions are correct," he continued.

"What is it?" Carol asked.

Dick and I were full of questions, too, such as: "How serious is it? What's the prognosis? How is it treated? What will make her better? What can we do? What should we do? When can she go back to school? Will she have any restrictions until she's well again?" And of course the most important question of all: "There's a cure, isn't there?"

Dr. Haring was very candid with us.

"I'll have to check my medical books to find the answers for you," he said. "This is not the kind of disease I see every day. Give me some time to do my homework and the pathologist time to examine the tissue. If it is Wegener's, we can all sit down and discuss what to do for Carol, and what to expect from the disease."

I was not worried because I had no idea what he was talking about. All my mind was willing to grasp was that if this disease was uncommon, then no one could be really sure if that was Carol's problem.

Dr. Carlson had been very definite about what he saw not being cancer. It didn't seem to me that anything else she might have could be that bad.

Without facts, there was no reason to panic anyway. Maybe the pathologist would be able to clear things up.

If I had been thinking clearly, I might have realized that Dr. Haring more than suspected Wegener's. With malpractice insurance being what it is, no doctor will say he suspects something unless he's pretty darn sure.

I was so positive we had nothing to worry about; it's surprising that I didn't grow ostrich feathers because my head was stuck so far into the sand.

"I'll be in to check on you this evening," the doctor told Carol, and to us he said, "I don't anticipate any problems. She can go home tomorrow. I'd like to see her in my office the day after."

Carol had dozed off, so we left for home.

Dick and I had driven to the hospital in separate cars. Neither of us spoke as we rode the elevator down to the lobby and made our way out. I felt numb as I stepped outside the hospital into the chilly October air.

"I'll see you at home," Dick said as he kissed me and we headed for our cars. What a pleasant-looking day it was. The sun was still shining brightly and there wasn't a cloud in the sky. As I steered my car out of the parking lot, I moved as if I had been hypnotized. Be a good little girl, Myrna, and don't make a fuss. The Chinese and Japanese believe evil spirits can only follow a straight path. You have a crooked path to your front door and that means trouble can't find its way into your home. Tomorrow everything will be all right, I told myself.

Halfway home it hit me like a bomb! There was no usual prelude of throat lumps, but all of a sudden it was: Oh my god! My baby's got something nobody knows anything about! The tears began rolling down my cheeks as the "whys" and "what ifs" began running through my brain.

What if it's not something simple? Why would Dr. Carlson have drawn a blank? Why would Dr. Haring have to do research before he could tell us about it? What if it's something deadly? What if she's going to be disfigured or incapacitated? What if she's—I could hardly get my mind around the word—dying?

You're being ridiculous, I told myself. Dr. Haring didn't give us the impression that it was serious or deadly. You're getting carried away and making a big deal over nothing.

Nothing devastating had ever happened to me, so it couldn't happen to one of my children. We can handle unusual as long as modern medicine can deal with it, and the doctor had said it wasn't anything he couldn't handle. She's not going to die from this—whatever it is. I dried my eyes, blew my nose, and composed myself before walking into the house. Carol's brothers would be waiting for news. With little to tell them, I still had to make it cheerful. I decided not to share my fears with them, and I certainly didn't want them to know I had been crying.

When I walked in the front door, they were sitting on the red velvet couch like three bumps on a log. Questions were hurled at me from all three of them.

"How did it go?"

"Is she OK?"

"It's nothing serious, is it?"

"Is she up to company?"

I don't remember who asked me what, but I gave them my best smile and filled them in on the little information I had.

"And wait till you see the silly bandage she's wearing. She looks like Groucho Marx without the glasses.

"Look what we got her."

They had all been working weekends at Magic Mountain, a nearby amusement park, and had bought her a giant stuffed troll, the park's mascot. It was three feet tall. She would love it.

"I think she'll be ready for you and that thing in a couple of hours."

Feeling that their questions were answered for the moment, they helped themselves to the necessary reinforcements from the refrigerator and disappeared upstairs.

Dick got home about an hour after I did, although we were about ten minutes from the hospital.

"I stopped off at the library," he said. Then he pulled a slip of paper out of his pocket. "This disease is more serious than I thought."

My heart skipped a beat as I followed him into our bedroom and he half-read, half-told me what he had jotted down.

"Wegener's granulomatosis is believed to be an autoimmune disease. Though its cause is unknown, it is clear that it is exceedingly rare. It attacks and destroys …"

I gasped and covered my mouth with my hand. Destroys is such a strong word.

"… the mucus membranes of the nose, sinuses, larynx, lungs, and kidneys, although not necessarily in that order," Dick continued, "and can be confined to only one place in the body without spreading to others.

"It shares so many clinical features with other upper respiratory syndromes that physicians can only diagnose it with certainty if a biopsy is performed. Even then, it takes a sharp, unhurried pathologist to go beyond what his eyes tell him, to seek answers through books."

Dick stopped reading and commented, "I wonder how sharp the pathologist from Henry Mayo is."

I wondered, too, but was choked up and finding it difficult to speak.

"Until the mid-1960s," he went on, "a diagnosis of Wegener's was tantamount to a death sentence."

He paused again and looked at me. Was my face as white as his?

"Since then," he continued, "it's been found to respond to treatment if begun early enough. The researchers have not been able to pinpoint the disease to any particular age, ethnic group, race, religion, or part of the world. It doesn't appear to stem from another illness, or use of or abuse of drugs. No relation has been found between the patients' vocations, avocations, or travels. It is not contagious or inherited."

He may have continued on; I don't remember.

This is serious, I thought. No, it can't be, my mind denied.

As we stood in our bedroom, panic washed over me. The torrent of tears once again came pouring out like an avalanche. My legs felt rubbery and started to fold under me as I backed up toward the bed and sank into it sobbing.

"That won't do either of us any good," Dick said, "and if you let her see you like this, she may get the idea that her situation is much worse than she's been told."

Dick had been raised with the idea that grief is a private matter, and that one must not show it—to anyone.

His comment set a tone. It was the last time he, or anyone else, for that matter, saw me cry because of Carol's illness for a long, long time. But it wasn't the last time I wept.

In order for Dick to comfort me, he would have had to convince me that everything was going to be all right. But he was probably too frightened himself to do that.

At times when tears would burn my eyes and I would get a lump in my throat, I wished for someone's shoulder so that I could pour out all the heartache. A few people were too close; they had their own tears. The others were not close enough, and I could never let go in front of them. Over time I learned to release my emotions when it was convenient: I was able to cry in the car, in the bathroom, in the closet, in the kitchen, and in any other place where I could be alone. I often wished it could have been in Dick's arms, but he had his own grief to contend with and I believed he expected me to be strong.

Outwardly, I guess I was. I've often wondered why I let the people in my world believe that I am so brave, when in my heart I know that I am scared to death.

Dick's always kept his emotions locked within him. I imagined the sorrow must have weighed heavily upon him and he wished he could tell me what he was feeling, but that's not his style.

He and Carol always had such a loving relationship. I loved seeing the adoring way he looked at her when he thought no one was watching, and would remember how it was with them when she was a little girl. No matter what she was doing or whom she was with, everything would come to a screeching halt when he walked in the door in the evening after work. He would scoop her up in his arms and give her a giant bear hug as he asked her about her day. Often before bedtime, she would climb into his lap as he sat in the recliner, and snuggle against his chest, neither one speaking, but just enjoying the closeness.

I had grown up without my father—a child of divorce—and missed those special father-daughter times. My heart would almost burst with love watching them—for Dick being the loving father to our children that I never had, for Carol returning that love to him as only a daughter can. The looks of affection they shared could light the world.

Now real fears loomed on our horizon. How could Carol, at the tender age of sixteen, handle the knowledge we had just acquired? I made myself a silent promise that day in my bedroom: I would find a way to make her well if it took me to the ends of the Earth and my entire lifetime. We would weather this storm and emerge all the better because of it. I also promised myself never to let her know how afraid I was for her life. I planned to hide my fears and not discuss them.

Oh, how I wished for someone to talk to who knew something about this disease firsthand. But we seemed all alone in the world. Not only did we have no contact with anyone else who had Wegener's, but also most people—including doctors and nurses—hadn't even heard of the disease.

I phoned Carol the next morning to find out how she was feeling and if she was ready to come home from the hospital.

"I'm ready," she offered. "Dr. Haring took the packing out of my nose a while ago."

She added, "Teresa called me last night and I told her what Dr. Haring thinks I have. She looked it up in one of her mother's medical books."

"And what did the book say?" I asked, wondering if Teresa had told Carol anything drastic.

"That they don't know where it comes from and that it could be fatal."

She sounded detached.

My heart skipped a beat. Thank goodness this was over the telephone and she couldn't see the blood drain from my face. Carol had heard the worst.

Who could know what she was thinking or feeling at that moment? Did she experience a feeling of helplessness? Was she afraid of not being able to function normally? Did she believe she would get well? She wasn't letting on, yet.

"Yes, I knew that," I told her, trying to keep my cool. "Dad stopped at the library on his way home. I think it would be a good idea to see what the pathology report turns up. Dr. Haring didn't seem to be particularly worried. At this point we're not really sure what you have anyway.

"I'm surprised you remembered the name of the disease. I didn't think you were awake enough to know what was going on when Dr. Haring was talking to us."

"It's my life, Mom."

I guess she was not as nonchalant as she appeared to be.

Two days later, the pathologist confirmed Dr. Haring's diagnosis.

4

Coping

A few nights after we were told of the pathological results, with my superstitious mind at work as we were getting ready for bed, I asked Dick, "Have things been going too well for us? Are we being punished for not having had hard times? Has our luck run out?"

In his logical, clear-thinking manner he said, "If we were being punished, the disease would be terminal. This isn't. I think we're pretty lucky that this is treatable."

His answer made me feel better, even if I didn't feel lucky. Fortunately, besides being superstitious, I've always been optimistic, too, and so I had to believe that tomorrow would bring better news. He kissed me goodnight, turned off his bedside lamp, and was soon off in the land of Nod. The ease with which he fell asleep was one of our family jokes. His reason was always the same: "I have a clear conscience."

As I lay there beside him, breathing the cedar-tinged aroma of the wall by the bed, I would listen to him snore for hours. The royal blue velvet drapes fluttered at the windows; the moonlight made a silhouette of the macramé canopy I'd spent hours on a ladder to create. Someone remarked once that I always had such romantic bedrooms. But it was difficult to think of romance that night when there was so much pain in my heart.

I lay there in the dark wondering how our lives would change. Although we were told that Carol was not in danger of dying, the uncertainty still was terrifying. Why was this happening to our family? Would anything ever be the same again? How would Carol's brothers react to her illness? They were not only good friends with her, but were unusually devoted to their little sister. When someone in the family is seriously ill, there's no question that the whole family is affected. While the patient suffers from physical problems, the rest of us fight the emotional kind.

I found myself buying her things she neither needed nor wanted just because I felt guilty that I was healthy and she wasn't. I wanted her to have material things because she was being cheated out of something we couldn't buy—good health. So many times I wished I were able to give her some of mine.

Her brothers began, individually, to take her more places to have fun. Just in case there were going to be fewer tomorrows, they didn't want her to miss anything.

We didn't show each other how scared or worried we were about Carol's recovery or the effects of the illness. The doctor had said she would be fine. We had to believe that or go crazy. One word from him could turn our world upside down.

I had convinced myself that Carol would pull through this. I don't know if I could have gotten out of bed in the morning if I had allowed myself to think that she was going to die.

By not expressing our fears to one another, I guess we were coping and trying to maintain some semblance of normalcy.

Frequently unable to sleep, I would wonder, why in heaven's name my baby, a sweet-tempered, loving child, was being made to suffer.

I'd heard people say: "What comes around goes around," and until this believed there was truly justice in the world. But what could Carol possibly have done to deserve something like this? I don't know how many times I asked myself, Why are there rotten people walking around healthy when Carol is sick? Who decides these things?

I remembered feeling that way, on a much smaller scale, when Carol had asthma as a baby. Once after she had experienced a particularly bad night, I was dragging my bones around the house, looking like a zombie, totally exhausted from both lack of sleep and worry. Dick's mother, Julie, had stopped in, as she did frequently, to visit. She, herself, suffered with asthma for many years and knew what the attacks were like.

"What's wrong with you? You look like death warmed over," she said, using one of her favorite expressions.

"I was up most of the night with Carol. She had another attack and we had to take her to the hospital for a shot of adrenaline.

"Why, oh why," I continued my lament, "if there's a God in heaven would he let a child suffer?"

I'll never forget her answer as long as I live.

"The sins of the parents," she said, quoting from the Bible, "are visited upon the child."

Hearing that brought to mind every insignificant thing I'd done in my past that I considered bad or wrong, and I feared Carol was being punished for them. If religion worked that way, I wanted no part of it. If there was a particular point in my life when I stopped believing in God, I think that was it.

I often wondered how other families handle things like this and keep from going out of their minds. What do I say when someone asks how Carol is? Do I really want the world to know? I can't imagine answering, "Most of us are fine, but one of us is seriously ill with a rare disease that might kill her."

How could I tell someone what I know, don't know, or am afraid of knowing without the tears? Does Carol want the world to know? What kind of future is in store for her? Would she ever be able to live a normal life for a normal life span?

If Carol was afraid of what the disease might do to her, she never said so. I never heard her cry, even behind a closed door.

In fact, throughout all her life she had almost never cried.

When she was born, I was awake during the delivery. She was taken to the other side of the room. I could see her tiny arms and legs moving, but she never made a sound.

"Is she all right?" I asked the obstetrician, who knew that I already had three sons and was thrilled to know that I had just given birth to the daughter I had so desperately wanted.

"She's just fine," he exclaimed.

"Why isn't she crying?" I asked.

"She has nothing to cry about," he answered.

Each time she was brought to me for a feeding, she was fast asleep. I never heard her voice until I brought her home.

Friends and neighbors, even Dick's mother, who never saw Carol without a smile on her face, would ask me, "Doesn't she ever cry?"

I hung noisy toys on the crib. Jingling or clacking meant the baby was awake. Upon entering her room, I was greeted with a smile.

Two of her brothers shared a room with bunk beds when Carol was about two. I would put the ladder up on the top bunk during the day, so I wouldn't have to worry about her climbing up and falling off. At least that's what I thought. When my little monkey couldn't find the ladder, though, she climbed up the end of the bed at the footboards and, of course, fell off.

Hearing the thud from the other end of the house, and using mother's intuition, I knew what had happened and rushed her to the doctor to make sure nothing was broken. By the time we entered the office, bruises started to form and she looked as if she had been beaten. Of course, she still hadn't shed a tear.

As the doctor entered the examining room I turned to him and said, "I swear to God I did not beat this child."

The doctor chuckled and said, "I wasn't worried about that. People who beat their kids seldom go to the same doctor more than twice."

After examining her, the doctor reported, "Nothing is broken, the bruises will disappear in about a week, and she'll be fine."

"Can you believe, Doctor, she never cried?"

Carol guarded her privacy. If she cried about the unknown in those early days after her diagnosis, no one knew.

"It's much too soon to concern yourself with all the what-ifs," Dr. Haring told us at Carol's next visit. "I'd like Carol to see a rheumatologist[4] for another opinion on how to treat her."

He recommended we make an appointment with a Dr. Bernard Andrews.*

We didn't get along with Dr. Andrews right from the start. His speech was difficult for us to understand and he mumbled a lot. Dr. Haring had warned us about that.

It didn't appear that he would be doing anything different or new for Carol. He examined things like her fingernails, and asked her questions about pains in her joints, which seemed to us strange and not pertinent. She responded negatively to the question of joint pains. After all, the trouble was in her nose and sinuses. He never bothered to explain what he was searching for or why. We were not yet experienced enough to push him for explanations. We had been used to doctors explaining things without our having to ask. It seemed like a serious lack of communication on his part.

I was angry because he didn't have an instant cure, and wondered what good he was and what we needed him for.

Dr. Andrews' intentions, after his initial examination, were to order blood tests, chest X-rays, and urinalyses regularly to see if the disease was spreading. He didn't tell us what he hoped to find, or not find, with the tests or what he would do with the test results. In short, his communication skills were sadly lacking, and we weren't willing to accommodate his shortcomings.

"Is there a treatment for Wegener's?" I asked.

He seemed reluctant to answer when pressed. Then he told us that the recognized treatment was chemotherapy and it was much too soon to consider that. But again he didn't tell us why.

We decided to take those questions to Dr. Haring. He made it a point to find the answers for us.

We knew little of the side effects of chemotherapy. We were desperate for someone to explain what to do and it was obvious to me that Dr. Andrews wasn't going to be the one.

He did, however, give us the best simplified explanation of Wegener's.

"The disease," he said, "is an overreaction of the immune system. The body usually gathers its forces to fight a disease and kill a germ. Carol's body is overreacting and trying to kill a germ that isn't there. So her body's fighting forces, the internal army, so to speak, is going after healthy tissue and destroying it."

When Carol's examination was finished, and it was time to settle the current charges with Dr. Andrews' receptionist, she asked, "How is she?" I assumed she was trying to be pleasant.

"I don't really know," I said.

To this, the woman replied, "Well, she's not dying, is she?"

A chill went through me as I answered, "I don't know that either."

After I was out of Carol's listening range I asked Dick, "How could that woman have been so insensitive when she's working for a doctor?"

"She just didn't know how to handle the question," he said. "Try to put this in perspective. You're afraid and concerned about someone you love, but the whole world isn't willing to share that."

Dick was right. I was desperately afraid for someone I loved dearly and wasn't willing to concede that the whole world didn't share my feelings or my fears. And it brought back another such memory.

"Remember when Don was so sick with gastroenteritis? I was carrying him into the hospital before you got there and a nurse's aide passing by took a look at him. He looked so awful, he was gray instead of pink and his eyes were sunken deep in their sockets. 'I hope he makes it through the night,' she said.

"Don't those people think that families have feelings? Aren't they given any sensitivity training or instruction of any kind when they go to work for doctors or hospitals?"

He had no answer so he just shrugged.

It was apparent that communication was certainly not Dr. Andrews' staff's strong suit, either.

"If it's too soon for chemotherapy," I told Dick, "I'd like to know what we can do for her. I'm unhappy with all these loose ends and I don't like the words, 'wait and see.' I heard them too much as a child from my mother."

"Next time you go to Dr. Haring, ask him about going to the Mayo Clinic," Dick suggested.

"Where is it?" I asked.

"It's in Minnesota."

"Why would we want to go there?"

"It's supposed to be the best diagnostic clinic in the country, maybe even in the world," he said. "Since this disease is rare, it would be nice to know what their opinion is. After all, Valencia[5] is not the center of the universe. How do we know the pathologist who saw Carol's slides knows what he's doing?"

"That's a good point. I'll mention it."

I discussed Dick's idea at Carol's next appointment with Dr. Haring.

"I would always welcome another opinion," he said. "However, I don't think that anyone anywhere would do anything different for Carol at the present time. All indications are that we shouldn't treat the disease itself, only the symptoms, unless it becomes absolutely necessary."

"What do you mean by absolutely necessary?"

"I mean if it's a question of saving Carol's life. Then we would discuss chemotherapy. The consensus among the doctors I've consulted at UCLA is to treat the symptoms and observe the reactions, since symptoms of Wegener's have been known to abate with no treatment at all. Advice is usually sought at the Mayo Clinic if the type of disease is unknown; but we know what disease we're dealing with, and we know it can improve with no therapy at all."

"But what if it gets worse?"

"Then we'll take steps necessary to deal with whatever arises," he answered.

I sighed and slumped in my chair, but made no comment.

"If Carol were my daughter," he added, "I assure you I wouldn't do anything different than what we're doing."

That was good enough for me. We had come to trust Dr. Haring a lot.

After I told Dick what the doctor said, the idea of going to the Mayo Clinic was put on hold.

"If all Dr. Andrews is going to do is take tests regularly," I asked Dr. Haring, "couldn't Dr. Mysko do that, since we all have confidence in him, and like and trust him? Besides, he's so patient about answering our questions."

"There's no reason why he can't," Dr. Haring said. "If that's what you want, that's what we'll do.

"The purpose of the tests and X-rays," Dr. Haring continued, "is to monitor the progress of the disease and any responses to treatments, or lack of them.

"In the meantime, I'll see Carol monthly to check her nose and throat, and what I can see of her sinuses. That way I can keep track of whether the disease is spreading to other places, and observe how it's progressing in her nose."

At every visit he cleaned the crusts out of her nose, looked at what was going on underneath and into her larynx. He reported to me whether there was more or less crusting than the previous visit, and that there was no apparent spread. The disease continued to be confined to her nose and sinuses.

Before this menacing blow, we had been so happy in our little world. The children were doing well in school and they had a lot of friends. After many years of negotiating government contracts while working in the aerospace industry, Dick had joined an engineering firm as legal counsel two years before and was secure and happy in his work.

After twenty years as a housewife, I enjoyed selling real estate, which I had begun the year before. If I had a talent for anything, it was getting along with people, and real estate is a people business. The whole family enjoyed the extra paycheck and, although we were a very long way from rich, we were at least able to pay our bills, send the children to college, and still have a little left over.

When we had moved to Valencia three years before, the Santa Clarita Valley was a sleepy bedroom community of about sixty thousand people, with no department stores, one indoor and one outdoor movie, one bowling alley, one motel, a junior college, and the Disney brothers-funded California Institute of the Arts. Of course there was the usual assortment of restaurants, supermarkets, and small specialty stores. But most people went "over the hill" to the San Fernando Valley to do their big shopping.

Living in a suburb of Los Angeles, we were all beginning to question just how much knowledge and ability some small-town doctors had. After all, we were just minutes from UCLA, a huge medical facility with a reputation throughout the country for performing miracles. And we certainly could use one.

I was sure they would have all the answers and the cures. How much did our doctors know? How many patients did our doctors see that might have any disease this rare? Should we be seeking outside advice? Was the pathologist competent?

We frequently discussed getting another opinion to confirm or refute what we'd been told.

After many discussions with each other and both doctors, Dick and I made a joint decision to just let the doctors treat the symptoms and observe Carol's and the disease's progress for the time being.

Dr. Haring had told us more than once that while this disease was very serious and could be fatal, Carol was not in a life-threatening situation. We had nothing to lose by observing her and her symptoms for a while, instead of trying to pursue answers where there weren't any, at least not any that were different. If Carol wasn't getting worse, we weren't losing ground.

No one had really decided how much time "a while" was going to be. We would all just wait and see.

While we were waiting and watching, Dr. Haring prescribed antihistamines to try to keep Carol's nose unstuffed, pills for the sinus and headache pain, and antibiotics to keep the infection under control because bacteria colonize in the mucus.

Carol was to continue with her normal routine of living, including school and other activities. She had no restrictions whatsoever.

We trusted and had confidence in Dr. Haring because he always told it like it was. He also told us what he didn't know and what steps he was taking to find out. He welcomed our questions, and any answers that were not immediately available were offered at the next opportunity. Whenever I mentioned UCLA, he encouraged our pursuing answers there, but made sure that we knew he stayed in touch with the doctors there for up-to-date information. The doctors he conferred with, he told us, agreed with his approach and the treatment Carol was receiving. He spoke to Carol as a friend and told her everything, whether she wanted to hear it or not.

About the time we were beginning to seek answers to her problems, Carol found out that one of her friends was dying of an incurable cancer. I had very ambivalent feelings of sorrow, guilt, and relief at the same time because while Carol's illness was bad, it wasn't as terrible as what was happening to her friend. She wasn't dying.

Under normal circumstances, high school students seldom give much thought to death and dying, thinking that they're all invincible. I've often wondered just how much of her own personal fears were entwined with her friend's situation. But Carol's never been one to discuss her feelings, fears, hopes, wishes, or dreams. In that respect, she's very much like her father; it's all locked within her. Like many science-minded people, she spoke only about the facts.

The school nurse was given a brief description by phone of Carol's health situation.

"You might consider contacting all of Carol's teachers individually," she suggested. "That way you can inform them of Carol's disease and any medications she takes."

That way there'd be no doubt as to what pills she carried with her and why.

There was no sense coddling Carol. She wouldn't have stood for that. When the children were little and any of them were sick, I always believed in chicken soup and Jell-O™ as cures, along with lots of special attention. They also were temporarily released from their chores.

This was definitely not going to be the case with Carol, who was not about to spend time in bed if she could be up and doing something constructive. And while she did not turn down my homemade miracle cures, she wasn't going to count on them healing her, either.

When there were a few bad days in succession and Carol had to stay home from school, either because of the pain, or the effects of the medication, or both, we hoped she would be allowed extra time to make up work or take tests if the situation was known.

I set up conferences with each of her teachers at the high school and, with one exception, all of them expressed concern for her well-being and a willingness to cooperate, if necessary. The exception, a woman who taught history, gave me the impression that she thought this was a play for sympathy, and that if the problem was ignored it would simply disappear. We would all have been overjoyed if that had been true.

Some of the instructors, especially Carol's math teacher, indicated that Carol was usually so far ahead of other students that her absence might give the rest of them a chance to catch up.

In spite of her physical problems, Carol's junior year went well and no problems erupted in school. She continued to be hardworking and ambitious, and the cheerful disposition she usually displayed did not change. She maintained a high grade point average and participated in extra-curricular activities, including singing with the school choir, occasionally accompanying soloists on the piano, and skiing whenever possible. In addition, she served as president of the school's ski club in her junior and senior years.

Don was already in college, commuting daily to and from a local university. Whenever he could get away, he accompanied Carol on ski club trips. She had talked him into going on one when he was still in high school, and then convinced him that he enjoyed it; so when Carol's friends weren't available, she always had her brother to ski with.

Dick and I were delighted with the idea of Don accompanying Carol on ski trips. It meant there was someone looking out for her.

"Actually," Don told us, "I don't take care of Carol; it's usually the other way around."

Just before the ski club's bus took off on one of their trips, I had been requisitioned by Don and Carol to bring to the school their duffel bags, ski equipment, and snacks they had set aside. Driving up at the appointed time, I could see Carol giving orders and directions to the members as they paraded, arms loaded, on and off the travel bus. She looked like a general marshalling her forces.

I was perfectly willing to drop the stuff off wherever Carol wanted and take off for home. She acknowledged my arrival and asked me to wait, adding that she would be with me shortly. After a few minutes had elapsed, Don and Carol came to where I was waiting, unloaded the things, and in front of all their friends, kissed me.

I would never have expected that kind of affectionate behavior from teenagers in public, but Carol reminded me, "We couldn't leave without kissing you good-bye."

During the eight months following the biopsy and diagnosis, Carol had monthly chest X-rays and urinalyses, reports of which went to both Drs. Mysko and Haring. She also had check-ups with Dr. Haring, who looked inside her nose and down her throat with his flashlights and mirrors. Her larynx continued to show no signs of the disease.

The disease seemed to be traveling from the front to the rear of her nose, and burning itself out, a term the doctor used. The chest X-rays and urinalyses were normal, indicating that the disease had not spread to the lungs or kidneys either.

Carol's schedule and routine changed very little during those months. She continued with her normal activities both in and out of school, and made it very plain that she expected to do her usual chores around the house.

When she saw Dr. Haring for her monthly check-ups he would frequently remark, "I don't know how she can be smiling with what I'm seeing inside her nose."

Just before Christmas vacation from school there was a dance, the Winter Formal, to which Carol had been invited. She told me she would need a long dress and wanted me to help her shop for it. I've always loved long dresses, and while my mouth was saying, "OK. Pick a day and time that you'd like to go," my mind was screaming: Whoopee! Hooray! We're going shopping for a gown.

We covered four major shopping malls in our search for a formal that suited us both. I had always pictured my little girl in ruffles and lace, and in one store pulled my idea of the perfect gown for her off the rack. It was white, off the shoulder, with tiny lace ruffles encircling the skirt from the waist to the floor. For a belt, there was a narrow pink velvet ribbon, fastened with a small spray of flowers. I urged her to try it on along with those she had chosen.

When she walked out of the dressing room in that gown, she looked terrific to me, and I said so. In front of the full length mirror, she frowned a little and turned to view herself from different angles. Finally, she offered her opinion: "All I need is a staff and a few lambs. I look like Little Bo Peep!"

Even the saleslady chuckled at that one.

Carol finally chose a slinky, burgundy, one-shouldered dress that we both felt looked classy. I never looked at the price tag until it was time to make the purchase. Whatever she wanted was what she was going to get.

During her winter break from school, Dick and I took Carol to Utah for a week. With her growing enthusiasm for skiing, her present that Christmas was to be new skis, boots, poles, and the trip. We continued trying to make it up to her for being sick, even though she tried so hard to live her life as if she weren't.

Just before we left for Utah, Ron came down with the flu and while we were gone, Don got it also. Just after our arrival in Utah, Carol also came down with the flu. It was the first time since being diagnosed with Wegener's granulomatosis that she was sick with something unrelated to the disease.

Dick had rented a one-bedroom condo for us that had a sofa bed in the living room. We spent the first two days tiptoeing around the living room so we wouldn't disturb her as she slept. Fortunately, it didn't last the whole week and she was able to ski for several days.

She enjoyed the trip and the attention. The boys never mentioned that we had done nothing similar for them. Giving her more began to be a way of life for all of us. Carol never asked for anything extra because she was sick, or tried to use her illness for any advantage. More often than not, she tried to ignore the disease and keep up with demands even healthy people might shy away from. Maybe she was trying to prove to herself that she could live a normal life.

Shortly before our Utah trip, I happened to be alone in the house, doing my usual round of chores. In Carol's room, a lavender-flowered burst of indoor springtime, I spotted the skis and poles standing in the corner. All my fears bubbled up to the surface. I sat down on her bed and wept.

It was OK in my mind to let the dam break; no one was watching. Oh how I wished to be able to take away her pain. When I knew she was hurting, it hurt me too. All the things that seemed to matter to me before—a college education, a good marriage, a houseful of children—seemed unimportant. I wanted, more than anything, for her to be well.

We know the chances are great that we will outlive our parents, and that one spouse will outlive the other, but it's *unthinkable* that we might outlive our children. I cried for the frustration, but not for the hopelessness, and there was no one to tell me I shouldn't cry. I felt relieved when it was over, and I hoped to be better able to carry on.

My real estate career had the typical crazy hours, but it afforded the flexibility to be with the children when it was necessary, and juggle Carol's doctors' appointments and tests. There was also the freedom to be home with her on the days I felt she needed me.

Working with people on an emotional level—it can be very exciting and stressful to buy or sell a house—helped to take my mind off my fears and worries, and probably saved my sanity.

Interactions with so many people occasionally led to the disclosure that my daughter was seriously ill. Many were kind enough to inquire about her and offer their good wishes for her recovery.

One of my business associates, in an unsuccessful attempt to make me feel better, told me that tests are only sent by God to those who are able to handle them. I could handle anything, but why should my baby be so burdened? She didn't need to be tested. It wasn't fair.

Some religious people offered to say prayers for her. When I relayed some of these conversations to Dick, who shared my lack of belief in organized religion, he said, "Don't discourage them. We need all the help we can get."

I would often find myself lying in bed at night trying prayer myself. Just in case there was someone up there listening, it couldn't do any harm. I tried not to remember that some of my religious friends would tell me that all prayers are answered, and that sometimes God says no.

Although we hadn't indulged the boys with cars of their own, new or used, until they began college, we decided to buy one for Carol. We tried to justify this to the boys, although they never asked us to, by telling them how important it was for a young girl not to be stranded somewhere because she was driving an old junk heap. But we all knew the reason. Carol had been through so much for her young years; she had worked so hard in school, and was entitled to some extras. Life hadn't been that easy for her during the preceding year and we were still trying to make up for it.

Unfortunately, some of this attitude backfired as far as the boys were concerned. I had begun to minimize problems they had, withholding the emotional support that was due them from their mother. If they lost a job, a girlfriend, got a lower test grade than they thought they deserved, I reminded them that they wouldn't die from it.

One day Ken sat me down and let me know that he and his brothers were aware that Carol's situation was much more serious than theirs. He told me it wasn't fair to make light of their problems, though; they needed a mommy, too.

They deserved the compassion and the hugs regardless of the fact that their difficulties might be over in a day, a week, or a month.

I was even doing something similar to my mother. She was getting older and experiencing some serious health problems of her own. Although she was hardly what one might call a complainer, I had begun to minimize her problems, also.

I hadn't even realized I was shortchanging the boys and Mom, and I'm so glad Ken had the wherewithal to let me know. He made me realize I had to stop saying, "I know it's terrible, but you can walk away from this; your sister can't walk away from her problems."

I hope I've changed that attitude. I know I've been lucky: The boys have never gotten angry with or alienated from me when they've been verbally turned away. They know what I've gone through because they've experienced similar thoughts and feelings of their own.

Don had driven Carol to school before, but he was now in college and the extra car he had used then was no longer available for her. A car of her own would give her the freedom to stay after school when her extra-curricular activities necessitated it without being stranded. She also needed a car to go to classes at the junior college during high school hours.

June of 1979 was approaching. Dick and I felt it was time to get another opinion to see how Carol was progressing. As far as we could tell, there was no change either in her symptoms or test results. Dr. Haring indicated that, other than the progression of the disease from the front of her nose to the rear, there was no change in what he was observing.

At each visit, Carol greeted the doctor with her usual smile.

"How are things going?" he would ask.

Her answered fluctuated from, "OK," to "Last week I had a couple of bad days," to "It's been really bad since I last saw you."

When this happened, it was always news to me. Unless she was in severe pain, I never heard about it, and knew no one else did either. Dick often asked me how Carol was feeling.

"Who knows?" was my response.

Unless we knew she was bad enough to be in bed or taking pain pills, she simply didn't discuss her illness, and didn't complain.

She was so comfortable in Dr. Haring's presence, even when he had to hurt her while removing crusts that had formed in her nose, that it seemed like she was visiting an old friend.

It was obvious he also liked her from the start. Why not? She was bright, charming, friendly, enthusiastic, delightful, and sophisticated. At every appointment, he spoke to her about what ailed her, but also asked her about her school and social life. And he gave her answers his full attention.

"We have this science project going where four of us are building a computer."

It was an experience that probably began a love affair between Carol and computers. She talked more about what was going on with that project than almost any other I could remember. The science teacher had a computer at home. She often baby-sat for his children, and he jokingly told us that he felt it was his computer she was really baby-sitting with.

Dr. Haring, also a skier, commiserated with her when no snow fell in the local mountains or nearby ski resorts.

"We were going to Squaw Valley[6] with the ski club last weekend, but there wasn't enough snow," she told him.

"I know. Our family was planning a trip to Mammoth[7] and ran into the same problem," he answered.

They talked about the future.

"Have you thought about which college you want to go to yet?" he asked.

"I think Berkeley," she answered, and then "Ouch" as the doctor poked and prodded inside her nose.

"I'm sorry I had to hurt you. Why Berkeley?"

"Oooo. Because they have a great science department. I'm considering pre-med."

"If you do decide to go pre-med," he said, "I'll be happy to write a recommendation for you."

He questioned her about the various classes she was taking in which they had a common interest.

"How's physics going?"

"Great," she said.

"It wasn't great for me. I barely squeaked by."

I don't think he barely squeaked by any class; he probably sailed through with flying colors.

He told us he had three sons and a daughter, who was the youngest, just like Carol. They would discuss family outings and she would tell him about places we had all gone when she was younger that she thought his family might enjoy.

"You ought to take your kids to Calico[8] the next time you're looking for a place to go for a day trip. It was really interesting, seeing the old buildings and the silver mine. But don't go in the middle of July; it's very hot then," she told him.

It seemed as though they could discuss anything and everything with each other. If a "caring doctor/cooperative patient relationship" was a strong factor in the healing process, Carol certainly had that in her favor since the beginning of their association.

I accompanied Carol to almost all her appointments. She didn't need me there, but I always wanted to hear the latest news, whether it was good or bad. Fortunately for me, Carol didn't discourage my going. Not letting the pain incapacitate her, she often drove me to the doctor's office instead of the other way around.

Several times, Dr. Haring told me that if the costs were becoming a burden, he would be happy to work with me in whatever way I found easy to manage. With both Dick's and my paychecks and good insurance, though, it wasn't a problem.

Although we were glad that the symptoms weren't getting worse inside Carol's nose, we were unhappy that they weren't getting better either. About eight months after the initial diagnosis, Dick and I thought it would be a good idea to have Carol examined and re-evaluated at UCLA. We knew its reputation put it in the top five of all the medical centers in the country.

"At this point in time," Dr. Haring said, "I think that's a good idea. Do you have someone you'd like Carol to see there, or do you need a recommendation?"

"We don't know a soul there. Who would you suggest?"

"Dr. Carl Thompson* of the Head and Neck Department. Would you like me to make the arrangements?"

"Yes, that would be great."

Dr. Haring told us that Dr. Thompson had an excellent reputation.

The medical center was less than an hour's drive from home. I was elated and excited because I hoped to have all my questions answered and that there would be an instant cure for Carol, just like on television movies. But there was one thing I had forgotten.

In 1979, Wegener's granulomatosis was still considered so rare it had never even been mentioned, let alone cured, on television.

---

4. A rheumatologist is a specialist in rheumatology which is the study of disorders characterized by inflammation, degeneration, or metabolic derangement of connective tissue and related structures of the body.

5. Valencia is a small community in the northwest corner of Los Angeles County, now referred to as Santa Clarita.

6. Squaw Valley is a ski resort near Lake Tahoe and the California/Nevada border.

7. Mammoth Mountain is a ski resort in the Sierra Nevada Mountain Range in central California.

8. Calico Ghost Town is a restored silver mining town in California's Mojave Desert, now a tourist attraction.

High school ski club trip, 1978

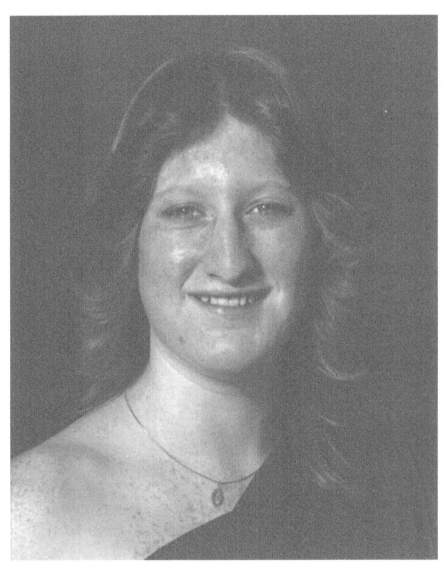

Carol in one-shouldered gown showing natural nose, 1978

First pair of skis, 1978

Adjusting new ski boots, 1978

5

A Second Opinion

We were told to arrive early when checking in at UCLA because there would be a lot of paper work to be completed before the patient saw the doctor—bureaucratic red tape. We had been used to personalized treatment from Dr. Haring, and our experience with the local hospital hadn't been unfriendly.

The atmosphere was very impersonal. It seemed as though the patients had numbers instead of names and the people who worked there didn't seem to have much compassion. I was left with a feeling of anonymity. Since we didn't know any better, we thought all large institutions of that ilk were the same.

The room we were taken to was small and cramped. For the doctor's use there was a small swivel stool with wheels near the examining chair. I had the feeling that our presence was an imposition and Dick and I were in the way.

No introductions were exchanged when a very tall, clean-shaven man wearing a white lab coat entered, apparently Dr. Thompson. Did he know if he was in the right place? I wondered. Did he assume we were Carol's parents?

He looked young considering his great reputation. His manner was so reserved as to seem unfriendly.

After examining Carol's nose, the doctor reported to us some of the same information we had been hearing from Dr. Haring.

"The disease is progressing from the front of her nose to the back, and appears to be burning itself out." Then he asked Carol, "Have you been sniffing anything like drugs or glue?"

"No, I haven't," she answered.

She's always been so straight-laced that we found that question almost amusing, but, of course, the doctor had no way of knowing and he had to ask.

Apparently, the doctor had not been informed of Carol's previous tests either, so he had not reviewed them. The situation wasn't giving me a strong feeling of confidence.

"I think it would be a good time, in this stage of Carol's illness, to do another biopsy of the nasal tissue," he said.

That sounded logical, and would give him evidence from which to form an opinion.

The doctor went to the intercom and ordered a surgical tray and consent forms.

Oh my goodness, I thought. He's going to do it here and now.

The three of us all exchanged glances, but no one said a word. After all, this was a competent doctor with a remarkable reputation. Dr. Haring had told us so. We assumed he knew what he was doing.

The tray and forms were brought in, and we signed what was necessary.

"Can we stay?" I asked.

"It's up to you," he said, as he shrugged his shoulders.

I had no intention of leaving the room.

Sensing our apprehension—could he see me holding my breath?—the doctor said, "This way of doing the biopsy is quicker, easier, and cheaper."

When he said that, it was the first time I actually gave any real thought to the costs that Carol's illness had incurred. We had adequate medical insurance through Dick's employer. I wondered how people with no insurance would cope. If a life-threatening illness rears its ugly head, those who aren't insured might not survive. That thought is very scary. With the staggering number of people in this country who don't have or can't get insurance, with diseases such as Wegener's left untreated, the outlook is bleak and often a death sentence.

He made several attempts to cut some tissue from inside Carol's nose. Each time an instrument touched her, she went from a moan to an emphatic yell. At one point, it seemed like her body raised off the chair. While Carol was not a complainer, neither was she a martyr. What he was attempting to do was obviously extremely painful, and she wasn't about to keep it a secret.

She was so tense and her nose was so sore that after the doctor tried three times she said, "I don't think this is going to work."

"I think you're right," he said to Carol. "We'll have to admit you."

The doctor made the necessary arrangements and she was admitted to the hospital within a few days. The procedure was to be done under a general anesthetic, as before.

Carol checked into the medical center the afternoon before the surgery, accompanied by Dick and me.

"Can I have a private room?" Carol asked.

"If we can get you one," Dick answered.

There was a private room available, and we gladly agreed to pay the extra cost. If that was all it took to make her happy, it was little enough for us to do.

Early in the evening when we were visiting with Carol, a group of people who seemed to be foreigners—most of them were not speaking English—marched into the room. They were not wearing name tags that I could see, and didn't bother with introductions to Carol, or to Dick and me, either. As they approached the head of the bed, a man in front, who appeared to be their leader, began speaking to Carol. We tried to listen to what he was saying but because of his heavy accent he was difficult to understand.

She began to raise her voice, saying, "No. No. No. Where's Dr. Thompson?"

Carol's not generally an excitable person and it's unusual for her to be apprehensive, particularly with both her parents close by.

Dick interrupted the man. "Just a minute. I don't know who you are or why you're here. She's under the care of Dr. Thompson. We will honor instructions from him and no one else. Now please leave."

En masse, the group did an about-face and marched out with no one uttering a word of explanation.

It was our first experience with the curiosity of medical students who wished to observe a patient with Wegener's, an opportunity that wasn't likely to present itself too often to interns or residents.

"Thanks, Dad," Carol said. "They made me really uncomfortable."

"What did that man say?" I asked.

"I couldn't understand him very well, but I think they wanted to take me somewhere and I didn't want to go."

Carol had gotten used to being assertive, but Dick suggested that it might be time to become aggressive.

"Don't let anyone do anything to you that you're not comfortable with, or don't want them to do. If anyone gives you trouble, I'll deal with them," Dick told her.

Up until that time, none of us had ever been concerned about what we were told to do or what was done to us in a hospital.

Later that evening, a young man knocked on Carol's door and waited for an invitation to enter.

"Is this Carol Swart's room?" he asked.

"Yes, it is," Dick told him.

"I'm Dr. Bernard Weinstock," he said, "one of Dr. Thompson's assistants. He asked me to take Carol's case history. Is that all right with you?"

"That's fine," Dick said.

I said, "OK."

Then he turned to Carol for her agreement.

"That's fine," she said, also, and answered all his questions.

Dick and I did him the same courtesy. The message must have gotten through to someone that we were used to being treated like human beings and were not going to settle for anything less. During the course of his interview, Dr. Weinstock said, "By the way, are you aware that you kicked out the chief resident in the Head and Neck Department?"

Dick answered this one. "No, I was not aware he was the chief resident because he never introduced himself to any of us. I hope he learns to communicate better in the future."

The biopsy was scheduled for seven o'clock the following morning. Dick and I planned to be there in time to kiss Carol and wish her good luck as we had done before. Unfortunately, she was taken to surgery at six o'clock.

Disappointed, we settled down to wait in her room and informed the nurses. No doctors came looking for us after the surgery. We weren't surprised.

When Carol was brought back to her room from Recovery, she was as white as the sheets covering her, and took much longer waking up this time than she had at the last biopsy. Once again, she was sporting a mustache bandage.

We spent the day in her room with her, observing how and when her vital signs were taken, and watching her sleep. When she awoke, we approached the head of the bed.

"Hi, angel face," I said. "I'm so sorry we missed you this morning," The bedrails were in the up position and I couldn't reach her again.

"Hi, sweetie. They must have taken you early," Dick said, as he leaned over to give her a kiss on the forehead.

"I wondered where you were," she said. "I didn't know what time it was. Remember, I gave you my watch last night."

I nodded.

"I was really scared," she said with a trembling voice.

"What do you mean?" Dick asked, with a puzzled expression.

"Of the operation?" I asked, also confused.

I couldn't ever remember her voicing a fear in her entire life.

"A nurse came in and gave me some pills that she said were supposed to relax me and make me sleep, but I don't think they worked. Then she told me it would be a few hours before they came to get me for surgery, but it seemed like just a few minutes later this really big man in street clothes ..."

"Not a hospital uniform?" I asked.

"No," she said, "street clothes. He whisked me away so fast I felt like I was going to fall off the bed."

"Weren't you strapped in?" Dick asked.

"Yes," she answered, "but loosely. Anyway, I asked him why I was going so soon and where my parents were. He didn't answer me. Then I asked him where he was taking me, in case he had the wrong person, but he still didn't answer me. Finally, I told him that if he wouldn't answer, would he please take me back to my room until my parents arrived. He never changed direction nor uttered a single word."

"I wonder if he even spoke English," I said.

"I felt like I was being kidnapped. It was frightening."

And we were angry. Dick gave me a knowing glance, but chose not to comment. There was no sense in making Carol any more uncomfortable.

"When did you know you were in the right place?" Dick asked.

"Well, they left me in the hall a really long time. I guess I must have fallen asleep."

"That must have been the surgical holding area," I told her. "They did the same thing to me when I had the hysterectomy. I thought they were taking me to surgery, but they were only taking me someplace else to wait."

"What happened then," Dick asked. "Did you wake up before the operation?"

"I woke up," Carol continued, "when the bed I was on started to move again and I saw a lady behind me pushing it. I think she was a nurse; she was wearing hospital greens and had a mask around her neck. I asked her where I was going and she told me they were ready for me in surgery. Then she asked me my name, my doctor's name, and why I was here."

"That was a hell of a lot more comforting," I said.

"Then she looked at my hospital ID bracelet," Carol continued, "and wheeled me into the operating room.

"Dr. Thompson came in and asked me if I was sleepy yet. I told him I was and he said the whole operation wouldn't take long. Then I knew I was in the right place with the right people."

"I'm so sorry we missed you, baby, and I'm so sorry you were scared."

I was beginning to feel very uncomfortable in that hospital.

"If anyone had kidnapped you, they would have brought you back fast," Dick said.

I noticed a slight grin showing from underneath her bandage.

"We're not leaving you any more today," I said.

And we didn't. When one of us was hungry or thirsty, we brought food or drinks to the other. The rest of the time we sat and watched Carol sleep. Dick read, and I worked on the needlepoint I had brought with me.

We had been told that she could go home in the late afternoon or early evening, depending on how she felt.

If Dr. Thompson saw Carol after surgery, we didn't know about it. At that point our confidence in him was zero.

Dr. Weinstock, however, did come by to check on her.

"She'll be released as soon as we're able to control the bleeding in her nose," he said.

The biopsy had been done at 8:00 AM, and the bleeding was not controlled until 10:00 PM. Then we were told she could leave.

On the way home Dick reminded me, "You know, from the time we entered the medical center until we left, we never laid eyes on—nor had any communication, either before or after the surgery, from—Dr. Thompson."

I had brought Carol's pillow and a blanket so she could lie down and ride in comfort. "I'm really glad to be going home," she said, as she stretched out on the back seat.

The next day she spent lounging on the living room couch, watching TV—both activities unusual for her. Like most teenagers, she enjoyed the privacy of her room and she rarely watched TV.

"Can't stand to be away from your Mommy, can you," I teased.

"I just wanted to be downstairs where the food is," she teased back. "I didn't have much to eat yesterday."

It was obvious to both of us that she was happy to be home in comfortable surroundings with familiar people.

That evening Carol talked Don into taking her to the movies.

"This is ridiculous," I said to Dick. "She has no business going out right after surgery."

He overrode my objections—again. "If she didn't feel well enough, she wouldn't want to go," he offered. "Besides, how much trouble can she get into watching a movie? It's the same as being here and watching TV."

I had lost another argument.

One of her friends phoned to see how she was feeling, knowing that she'd just been through another biopsy. She was surprised that Carol wasn't home in bed moaning.

Although we were very disappointed with our experience at UCLA and the treatment she received, with what we perceived as an apparent lack of compassion during our first encounter there, we liked the diagnosis.

A few days after the biopsy, we went back to UCLA for a post-operative exam.

"There's no trace of the disease," Dr. Thompson informed us. "If it was Wegener's, it would have spread to other parts of her body by now. Whatever has been causing her problem is getting better by itself anyway. Continue doing what you're doing."

We felt that was great news even though it left us very confused. It appeared that she was getting better without treating the disease at all. But what was it that she was getting better from?

"If she doesn't have Wegener's," I asked, "what does she have?"

"I don't know," the doctor answered.

When I pressed him to put a name to what she did have, he said, "Acute rhinitis."

"Isn't that an infection in the nose?" I asked.

"Yes," he answered, "but if she's getting better, what difference does a name make?"

"How many cases of Wegener's granulomatosis have you seen?" I asked.

"Three."

That was astounding. In an institution the size of UCLA, figuring the number of patients who pass through their doors each year, with most WG symptoms presenting in the head and neck, that was a phenomenally small number, in spite of the rarity of the disease.

"Did they all get better by themselves?" I asked.

"I don't know," he answered. "I never saw them again."

On the way home, I said to Dick and Carol, "I can understand why he never saw the other patients again. They probably went to see another doctor. He's far from the friendliest doctor we've had the occasion to consult."

"He doesn't have to be friendly to be competent," Dick reminded me. "But I agree."

In the end, we decided to take Dr. Thompson's advice and continue what we were doing. We couldn't think of any reason not to. Not getting worse is OK with us, but getting better is great.

The possibility of a trip to the Mayo Clinic was raised again, since if Carol didn't have Wegener's, we wondered what she did have. Her apparent improvement, however, made the trip seem unnecessary. As long as she wasn't getting worse, what difference did it make what she did or didn't have? But I couldn't help feeling that it did make a difference, and wanted to know for certain. However, there seemed to be no need to push for additional opinions at that time.

Her friend with cancer, who unfortunately had been getting steadily worse, was being treated at UCLA also. Besides our visits there for Carol, we made a few extra trips to see him. His family had no complaints with his treatment, so we couldn't be sure whether the problem lay with the way Carol's case was being handled, or my interpretation of it. Maybe we were expecting too much.

I would occasionally cross paths with the young man's mother, and she never failed to ask about Carol's progress.

Once I asked her, "How do you handle it?"

She obviously knew I meant the heartache of watching her son suffer, knowing he would not get well.

"He talks about going back to school when he's better, and I just don't tell him that he's never going back. I believe he's aware of that. I think I would have ended my life if I were in his shoes. But I simply take it one day at a time; what other choice do I have?"

6

Choosing a College

A Summer Scientific Seminar is sponsored by the Air Force Academy in Colorado Springs, CO, every year to recognize achievement and further interest in the sciences for high school juniors. I think it's also a subtle advertisement for Air Force recruitment.

Teachers are asked to nominate worthy students; nominees must possess academic superiority in general, and academic excellence specifically in science. Three teachers must submit letters of commendation for a nominee. Only two hundred high school juniors from across the country are selected.

Several may be nominated from the same school, but only one can be chosen. Carol was one of three nominated from her school. All three nominees submitted their applications to the Academy and were then subjected to a personal interview by a visiting representative. Students must make their own travel arrangements to the academy, but no other costs are involved. Meals and lodging are provided.

During her high school years, Carol had been asked to baby-sit with the children of several of her teachers. Besides knowing her academic ability, they had the opportunity to get to know her as a person outside of school. It never occurred to her that these associations would serve an additional purpose. There were more than enough teachers in a position to recommend her for the award. Carol was chosen!

Although I was concerned about her being away from home so soon after surgery, she obviously was thrilled and had no intention of missing this opportunity.

She felt the experience at the academy was fascinating and rewarding, and did not allow her health problems to interfere. A cousin of Carol's science teacher's wife lived in Colorado Springs; he and his family took Carol sightseeing up to Pike's Peak during her last day there, and then saw her safely onto the plane for her trip home.

The high school awards ceremonies took place during the week Carol was in Colorado, so Dick and I were invited to attend and accept the science award for her. We didn't know that she had also been chosen as one of the Top Ten juniors for academic excellence for 1979. That was a nice surprise for us.

The junior class top achievers were honored during the seniors' graduation ceremonies. The top ten were seated up front, across from the speakers' platform. Our whole family was there to see Carol, who placed third in her class, join the other nine being presented a keepsake medallion, strung on a ribbon to wear for the occasion. She clearly had made certain that her illness had not held her back that year.

In the spring, when it looked like things were going well for Carol, Dick booked a Caribbean cruise for the two of us for the coming October. I had misgivings. What if she needed us and we couldn't be reached?

I discussed the trip with Carol and the boys and, in fact with almost everyone I knew. Each person did his or her best to convince me that everything would be all right. There were plenty of friends available should an emergency arise. Carol did everything she could to allay my fears. We left written permission for the doctors to treat her if necessary, and for each of her brothers to seek medical care for her, since she was still a minor.

I kept using the phrase, "If the ship goes down …" with instructions to the boys, until one of my co-workers who had been on a similar cruise heard it and made me realize how ridiculous I must have sounded to the children.

Right after Thanksgiving, Carol's friend died. When we went to pay our respects, her friend's mother was still concerned about how Carol's health was holding up.

Carol had worked hard during her senior year. She was determined to go to a good university and knew that high grades were the only way to get there.

By the end of her junior year, Carol had already completed all the math and science classes offered at her high school. Before high school was over, she had taken biology, chemistry, calculus II and III, physics and, for fun, psychology at the local junior college. She excelled in all.

During graduation award ceremonies in 1980, Carol received more citations than any other student. But the award Carol wanted the most was a scholarship established by the parents of her friend who had died: it was to be given in his memory to someone who excelled both academically and socially as he had. There was a standing ovation, and very few dry eyes, in the audience when Carol's name was announced.

The principal presented a special award to Carol as he told the audience of her academic excellence—her junior college courses, the science seminar—her leadership of the ski club for two years, and her service to the school and community, such as organizing a skate-a-thon to raise money for a memorial to her friend, tutoring an elementary school student and being chosen as a speaker for the graduation exercises.

In addition, she was presented with another medallion for being a top ten senior, and was awarded a life membership to the honor society known as the California Scholarship Federation. This recognition enabled her to wear special gold cords on her graduation robe. There were also scholarships from the Bank of America and the DAR, and another science award, all for academic excellence. She truly stole the show.

While the awards were being presented, baby pictures of the graduates—previously requested from the parents—were being projected on a giant screen for the audience to view. I had submitted my favorite baby picture of four-month-old Carol in which she had a kewpie doll curl on top of her head, and, at the other end, pink ruffled panties I had insisted Dick bring to the hospital when she was born.

With my own parents in attendance, I can't remember ever being so proud of my daughter in all my life as that awards night, or crying so much. After all the tears I had shed because of her illness, it was a nice feeling to be crying for joy.

Another graduate had been asked to sing at the ceremonies. The music from the show "Annie" was popular at that time, so she sang the song, "Tomorrow." Whenever I hear that song, I'm transported in memory back to that night. I get a lump in my throat and tears in my eyes remembering all the honors amid the uncertainty of what her tomorrows would be like.

Because she had done so well in high school, Carol had her pick of colleges and she made up her mind that she wanted to go away to school. The boys had stayed close to home when they sought higher education, and I wasn't sure I was ready to have my baby leave home, particularly after all the health problems that she had experienced. But she had worked so hard for the awards and wanted to go away so badly, I didn't see how I could stand in her way.

Carol narrowed her choices to three within the University of California system: Berkeley, Los Angeles, or Riverside. Dick, Carol, and I took a couple of days off from work and school to tour the campuses.

Berkeley came first. We flew to Oakland, rented a car, and drove to the campus to meet our tour guide. She began by telling us that there was a 60 percent chance that Carol wouldn't be able to secure on-campus housing. The facilities were already overcrowded. The surrounding areas did not appear to be the kinds of neighborhoods in which Carol was used to living.

When I asked about on-campus safety, the guide only commented, "Well, I don't think we hold the record for being the safest of the UC campuses. The girls are encouraged to use escorts."

The campus itself was a very beautiful one, with the typically hilly terrain of the San Francisco area. But dorm rooms meant for two beds had been redone to accommodate three. It looked like there was hardly room to breathe, let alone space to study.

As we came back to our starting point, there were some students demonstrating for and against something political. A few were holding an enormous American flag and singing "God Bless America." The police and reporters, complete with nightsticks and television cameras respectively, were there. It did not look like a situation I'd ever been involved in before, but certainly did look like something you'd see on the six o'clock news.

Our tour guide concluded the tour by apologizing. "I'm really sorry it's so quiet on campus here now," she said. "It's exam week, you know."

We were all very quiet on the way home, each deep in his or her own thoughts. I didn't know what Dick and Carol were thinking, but all that kept running through my mind was: I'll be damned if that's the place I want to send my baby—my only daughter. Quiet indeed!

Soon after our Berkeley encounter, Tammy, the older sister of one of Carol's friends, came by for a visit. Coincidentally—though Carol says there are no coincidences—she wanted to talk about her college experience, not realizing we were at the threshold of making a decision.

Having chosen her father's alma mater in the midwest, about a thousand miles from home, Tammy told us weekend trips were expensive and impractical. She was so homesick that first semester and spent so much time crying that she couldn't wait to get home. She was planning to transfer to a commuter college. Dick and I were surprised because we were listening to a young lady we knew to be self-assured, well-adjusted, and level-headed. It was so out of character for her to talk like this. Not only did we make a mental note of what she said, it seems that Carol did, too.

Carol had not been having a very hard time with her illness just then, but I didn't think it was a great idea for her to be very far away from her doctors.

When we began to talk about UCLA, we had to consider the fact that housing was very scarce on that campus, as at Berkeley. Although it was possible, if not pleasant, to commute there, Carol wanted the living-on-campus experience.

Attending a high school recruitment meeting, we learned of a unique pre-med curriculum, known as the bio-med program, that UC Riverside had to offer. Carol was very interested and we went on a tour of that campus.

Riverside was very different from Berkeley, not as physically beautiful, but much more quiet and peaceful.

Looking around the vast campus, Dick remarked, "Well, what do you know; not a single demonstration going on!"

Our guide looked puzzled, so he explained, "We recently had a tour of Berkeley."

She gave us a knowing smile and nod as we continued on.

"Are there any housing problems?" I asked.

"None," she said. "Anyone who wants to live on campus can; there's plenty of room. While most of the rooms are set up for two students, there are a few private rooms to be had under special circumstances."

My mind was already trying to think up a special circumstance. Carol had never shared a room with anyone and I wasn't sure how she would like that.

"How safe is the campus?" Dick wanted to know.

"UC Riverside has the reputation of being the safest of the nine UC campuses with the lowest crime rate. Coeds are urged, however, to use certified campus escorts after dark just to be cautious."

"What do you mean by an escort?" I asked, having heard the term used at Berkeley, also.

"A male student volunteer, who's been thoroughly checked out, presents special credentials to the coed, and wears an escort armband when he is called upon to see a girl safely to and from campus buildings," she answered. "The armband is issued to an escort on duty and must be turned in at the end of the evening so it can't be passed to someone who is not qualified or certified."

UC Riverside was looking better by the minute. I was hoping Carol felt the same.

Our tour guide went on to tell us that the university was equipped to handle six thousand students and there were only four thousand five hundred registered. She added that classes were smaller than normal, with more individualized attention.

The student gave us a tour of the dorms also, including the recreation rooms complete with pianos and enormous fireplaces, the cafeteria and the utility rooms. We were also shown tiny kitchens where a student could warm up pre-packaged meals, and laundry areas with large sinks for hand washing delicate items. There were even ironing boards, although students had to bring their own irons. It was exactly what I had in mind for my little girl.

"You can join your daughter for dinner here anytime," she said. "That includes any of the five places to eat on campus."

I sincerely hoped Carol would choose Riverside. I already had!

Within a few days Carol made the announcement that she wanted to go there and we were overjoyed. It was close enough so that she would be able to come home on weekends if she desired, but far enough away to assert her independence. She wasn't going to be too far from her doctors, either.

After graduation Carol wanted to visit her grandparents in Florida and Mom was anxious to show off her granddaughter to her friends. Whenever she had seen my mother and stepfather it was always in California and she wanted an opportunity to see them in their natural habitat.

The evening Carol arrived in Florida, I phoned Mom to see how she weathered the trip and how she was feeling. Carol was tired but otherwise OK.

Mom added, "Thank you for sending her to me." The adoration in her voice was very touching.

We thought it would be a great experience for her. She enjoyed her visit and the attention and even felt well enough to do some sight-seeing.

We had all been so worried about her future and were pleased that Carol's health seemed to be improving.

After her return from Florida, she got a job working in a water testing laboratory at what was then known as James M. Montgomery Consulting Engineers, Inc., the same company that employed Dick.

Her interest in science made her a perfect candidate for the intricate workings of the laboratory. The supervisors liked her work performance so much that they wanted her to come in weekends, school holidays, and any other time she could manage it.

At that time no one there knew of her illness. As a very conscientious worker, she gave her employers more than their money's worth. Many of the people she worked with were quite a bit older than she, some as much as ten to fifteen years. They became good and lasting friends with the age disparity making no difference.

During the summer Dick got a new car—the Corvette he had always dreamed of—and there was some question as to what to do with his old car, which was still in great shape. Ken needed another but didn't want anything as big or as loaded as the one Dick had been driving.

"Why don't we see if Kenny would like to have my car, and I'll take Dad's?" Carol suggested. "I think that's what he's looking for."

"That means she'll be driving to and from college and around Riverside with the convenience of electric windows, electric doors locks, and an electric seat," Dick said. "Much safer, in my opinion."

"Dad's car doesn't get the great mileage you're used to," I reminded her.

"I don't drive that far anyway," Carol answered.

It was the logical thing to do, and Kenny was very happy with the choice.

Because Carol and Dick were working at the same place, they drove to and from work together. They loved to speculate about the strange looks they would get from adjacent cars on the freeway.

"They're probably wondering what an old geezer like me is doing with a young chick," Dick would remark and then add, "It's got to be the car."

Then Carol would comment, "Chevrolet pays me to ride with him. It helps sell more Corvettes."

While these wonderful things were happening to Carol, she still suffered the headaches and the pain in her sinuses. I didn't realize it was as often as it actually was because she hardly complained at all.

She made an effort to avoid the stronger pain pills unless they were taken at bedtime. When Carol had a social engagement and her headache would become too severe, she cancelled or postponed her plans. Frequently I wasn't aware of it until weeks later.

Sometime during the summer her sense of smell disappeared. It seemed as though it would return for short periods of time and then leave again. We were at a shopping mall one day, on a descending escalator, and the popcorn aroma was wafting upward.

"Let's get some popcorn," Carol said. "It smells good."

"OK," I said, not giving it a second thought.

Then it struck me. "You smelled the popcorn!" I exclaimed.

She hadn't realized it either from the surprised look on her face.

"Oh my gosh! I really did! I didn't even think about it," she said excitedly.

We couldn't wait till we got home to tell Dick. It had been so long since she had smelled anything at all.

We rushed through the front door and I began yelling, "She smelled the popcorn in Sears," at the same time she was yelling, "I smelled the popcorn, Daddy."

It's a good thing there was only family present. Any strangers would have thought we were out of our minds, but Dick was just as excited as we were.

Unfortunately, the excitement was short-lived. Her sense of smell left again. We kidded her about how lucky she was whenever there was a dead skunk in the neighborhood.

The construction of a memorial to Carol's friend who had died was completed the fall after graduation on the high school campus. Carol was invited to give the dedication speech. Although she didn't make a lot of trips home from college after the first few weeks, she would not have turned down this particular request. Her touching speech was highly complimented by her friend's parents, the principal, and many others. She presented a copy to her friend's parents before she left.

Carol and roommate, Air Force Academy, 1979

Myrna and Dick on cruise, 1979

Carol at high school graduation, 1980

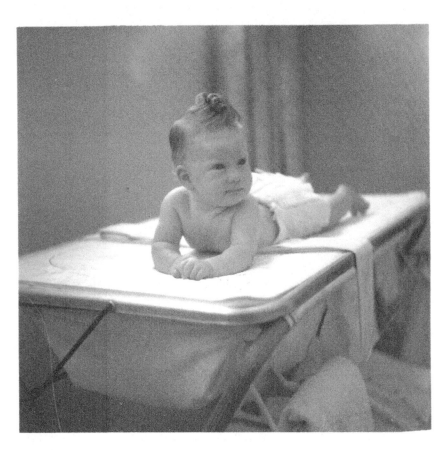

Carol at four months old, 1962

7

The College Years

Because UCR has a great reputation for its bio-med program, and because Carol was so good in science and interested in medicine, she chose that for her major. However, the program was so structured that it left her little or no time at all for what was becoming her first love: computers. After giving bio-med a good try for the first year, she switched her major to computer science, a subdivision of the math department.

While involved in the bio-med program, Carol did volunteer work in the emergency room of a nearby hospital. It must have been interesting for her to be on the other end of a stethoscope for a change. It gave her some knowledge that was to do her in good stead later on, particularly what to look for in the way of vital signs, and how to interpret blood pressure readings.

The first two years of college she spent in the dorms. For most of the first year she had a roommate—a new experience for Carol. It worked out well and she enjoyed the company.

Unfortunately, her roommate was a basket lover. With a wall full of baskets collecting dust, it began to prod Carol's old allergies into action. Before long she was having numerous asthma attacks, which I thought she had outgrown.

The resurgence of the old problems evoked memories of many late night runs to the hospital for injections of adrenaline. At the time, I had not had any personal experience with wheezing, the main symptom of asthma, and it scared me. It sounded a lot worse than the doctors would tell me it was. Listening to her gasp for breath, I was so afraid each one would be her last.

After a trip to the emergency room, and the accompanying shots, which acted as stimulants and made it difficult for her to sleep, Dick and I would often take her into our bed. All the books on child rearing said that was a terrible thing to do, and we could be asking for trouble in the future. But I had to know that her breathing was normal before I could go back to sleep, and it was hard to tell that from down the hall. When her breathing became normal, I would take her back to her own bed and things would be fine until the next attack. She never asked to sleep with us; she liked her privacy even as a toddler.

One night she actually called a halt to sleeping with us all by herself. The two of us were lying sleeplessly in the bed listening to Dick snore. She sat bolt upright in bed and announced, "I can't sleep here. I'm going back to my bed because Daddy makes too much noise!"

Years later, when she and I discussed that incident, we always found it funny; Dick never did.

The asthma attacks abated until Carol went to college. Don had been getting weekly allergy shots so I took her to his doctor. He gave Carol the requisite skin tests, the results of which were the usual ones in our family: sensitivity to trees, grasses, pollen, dust, etc. The doctor determined that Carol would also need desensitization shots.

"Why don't you check with the University Health Center?" Dick asked. "I'm sure they're equipped to handle desensitization shots and probably do it all the time for students."

Carol made the necessary inquiries and followed up with arrangements at the health center. She began getting the shots regularly—at a dollar a pop—and as her sensitivity was built up she was able to taper off the shots. At least that was one health problem we were able to get under control.

For her sophomore year, she was able to secure a single dorm room because of her allergy problems.

When describing the room to us before we saw it, she said, "I don't want you to think it's small, but it's referred to as the 'closet' single."

Since I'd always done the interior decorating in the house, I didn't realize she had talents in that direction, also. My tastes are quite different from hers and, eternally wanting to please me, she let me decorate her room at home. She would have preferred modern décor with chrome and glass instead of the French provincial style with the canopied bed that I had selected. But when asked what she wanted for her bedroom she answered, "You're doing a great job with the rest of the place, Mom. Do it the way you want to."

When I finally got to see her closet single, it looked like a page from a decorating magazine. She'd done a fantastic job.

Wanting to please me had always been Carol's way of life as far back as I can remember. When she was old enough to join the Brownies I got involved also, thinking I was doing it for her. After a while it became obvious that it was the other way around; she was involved because of me.

In January, 1981, Don transferred to UC Riverside from the commuter college he was attending, joining Carol in her home away from home. Before then, whenever he visited her, our gregarious daughter had a room full of girlfriends, a situation which Don referred to as a smorgasbord. I think that may have spurred his decision to change universities.

Being constantly concerned about Carol's health, I hoped with Don there she would have someone to watch over and take care of her. Later, it became apparent that it was the other way around, just like their skiing trips when Carol was in high school.

After Ken graduated college he had gotten a job as a newspaper reporter. Because the newspaper office was sixty miles from home, he had moved out. Ron was working in photography and had gotten an apartment of his own, also. With Don and Carol away in Riverside, Dick and I discovered we had a lot of time alone. It was surprising how clean the house stayed.

That winter during a long weekend we rented a condo in Big Bear Lake, a ski resort in the San Bernardino Mountains, about one hundred miles from Los Angeles. Carol invited two of her new college friends, John and Tracey, who were destined to become life-long friends. We were grateful for the chance to get to know them, and I began to understand how well they had gotten to know Carol.

It was interesting when John told us about a weekend he had decided to go home, only to discover that his parents had gone out of town, and how disappointed he was.

I was puzzled. "What difference did it make, John? You had the house all to yourself."

"I didn't come home to have the house all to myself," he told me. "I came home to see my Mom and Dad."

I turned to Don and Carol and asked, "Don't you two come home for the privacy of your room, to do your laundry, or enjoy a change of scene?"

"What makes you ask that?" Carol wanted to know.

"Because it never occurred to me that you come home to see Daddy and me."

"Why else would we come home?" Don questioned.

"I never guessed it was just to see us."

It was a real eye-opener for me. John seemed to have a way of opening doors in my mind.

At the end of the weekend as we were preparing to leave and everyone was loading their respective cars, Dick asked, "Have the girls left?" We were all going in different directions, and Carol and Tracey were headed to a concert.

Before I had a chance to answer, John said, "Carol would never leave without kissing Mommy and Daddy goodbye."

For a moment I thought he was teasing us until I realized he was just letting us know the score.

Moments later she raced up the stairs calling out, "I'm leaving," and kissed us goodbye.

Since she'd gone away to college and had been living in the dorms for two years, she was usually so glad to be home with the peace and quiet and good food that she was almost disgustingly cheerful, affectionate, thoughtful, and helpful.

For a long time after Carol had gone to college, Dick and I didn't go down there to see her. One day Carol asked why.

"I think that you're the only parents who haven't come to visit," she said.

"We were waiting for an invitation," I answered. I had seen a TV program that depicted a daughter getting annoyed because she had started college and her mother was always underfoot, even signing up for some of the daughter's classes. "I didn't want you to think we were checking up on you."

"Well, I would never think that. I'd be happy to see you and Daddy any time you'd like to come."

After that we made periodic trips to Riverside and often took a few of her friends out to dinner with us.

The first Thanksgiving that Don and Carol were both in Riverside, they brought home with them for the weekend a few friends who lived too far to travel home.

I'm not a turkey lover, so sometimes I would make other things like lasagna or roast beef for Thanksgiving. But because they had invited friends, Carol and Don specifically ordered turkey, with all the trimmings—a traditional Thanksgiving.

It was interesting to hear from some of them that Don and Carol were the only siblings they knew who not only talked to each other, they actually seemed to like each other. Comments like that really warmed our hearts.

Although there were occasional problems with Carol's nose, and she came home for regular check-ups, for the most part I thought the WG was under control. The disease progressed toward the back of her nose and was continuing, according to Dr. Haring, to burn itself out. That was the good news. The bad news was that scar tissue was forming and Carol's nostril openings were becoming smaller, resulting in restricted breathing and obstruction of the doctor's view during examinations of the inside of her nose. The doctor was also concerned about drainage because there were still encrusted and infected areas.

If her headaches and sinuses were bothering her, no one knew because she never complained. Carol's and my phone conversations might as well have been taped and rerun; they all sounded the same.

Mom: "How are you feeling?"

Carol: "OK."

Mom: "No, I mean *really* how are you feeling?"

Carol: Possible answers: "OK," "Crummy," "Don't worry about it Mom. I'll let you know if there's a problem."

It drove me crazy because I never knew. But I had to trust her. If there was a problem, I had to believe I would hear it from her.

"Sometime in the future," Dr. Haring said, "we may have to think of removing the scar tissue. If it's not bothering her too much we won't bother it."

He was, of course, aware of the allergy problems and the treatment that Carol had been receiving for them.

Carol had many new friends, classes were going well, and skiing became her escape. She lived for winter when she could get away to a nearby ski resort and partake. She had become an avid skier and even won a few medals in local NASTAR races. When she couldn't find a friend to go with her, she could always talk Don into going.

During the summer she worked at the laboratory again, giving her a chance to renew old friendships.

Carol still seemed to be doing well, and Dick and I were beginning to breathe easier about her situation. If she was having difficulties, she didn't tell me; she handled them. When we're not in the middle of a crisis, those of us not fighting a disease tend to forget that life is never truly normal for someone who is.

Once she told me, "I am not a disease; I'm a person who happens to have one. It doesn't define me."

In the summer of 1982, she began working with large, sophisticated computers—again at Montgomery Engineers—and the real love affair began. The computers seemed to love her back.

Between the end of work and the beginning of school, John invited Carol to go on an eight-day backpacking trip in the mountains—her first wilderness adventure. All my instincts as a mother told me to forbid her to go. But, as was becoming the custom, Dick's opinion differed. Had I turned stodgy and old-fashioned, I wondered, or just overly cautious because of what she'd been through?

"Why don't you want her to go?" Dick asked.

The answers were easy: "It's too long. It's too tiring. What if she has an asthma attack? What if a snake bites her? What if the gear she has to carry becomes too heavy? What if she wants to come back after three days?"

"You don't like the outdoors, and you can't conceive of eight days without indoor plumbing, can you?" Dick asked.

"What if they get lost?" I asked, ignoring his sarcasm.

"Ask Carol to explain the trip in detail. Then ask Dr. Haring if he thinks it will be detrimental to her," he offered.

I supposed that was fair. Carol explained that there was an experienced guide, a friend of John's, who was also a college teacher, and had escorted classes on wilderness trips. A route had to be filed with the Forestry Service, and strictly followed. That way the authorities would know where to look for the hikers in case a problem arose. They even carried a snakebite kit.

I checked with Dr. Haring and he thought it was a wonderful idea—my misfortune that she had a doctor who also liked the outdoors!

As long as I was giving in, I decided to make sure she was well-equipped, so she and I went shopping for clothing and supplies.

When I took her to meet the group at the assigned time and place, she made me promise not to make any remarks about being without indoor plumbing for eight days.

My instincts were wrong and the trip was a roaring success. Participants took turns being the navigator, and the guide taught the hikers all about nature as if they were in a class. At night they discussed placement of the stars and how to find constellations. For weeks afterward she talked of little else.

Don graduated that June and Carol was the only one of our children still in college. He helped her to convince me that she needed the space and privacy of an off-campus apartment. Dick, Carol, and I spent a day in Riverside looking at apartments. They varied. Some were the size of a postage stamp; some were dingy; some did not appear to be safe enough for a young single girl—especially one with a mother who was a died-in-the-wool worry wart—who might be coming home in the dark. Then we found a two-story building with a swimming pool in the central courtyard. With all the apartment entrances off the courtyard, people could probably see other people lurking outside someone's door.

"I just put that sign out today, and the apartment isn't ready to show," the landlady said.

We were so insistent that she agreed to let us see it. It was on the second floor. I liked it already. When she opened the door and we stepped inside, we knew this was the one.

There was a large entry hall, a spacious living room, and a wood-burning fireplace. Windows on either side of the fireplace let the afternoon sun in and the room was bright and cheery. Beyond the living room were a tiny dining room and a huge kitchen. Directly off the kitchen was another hallway that led to a large bedroom. Even the bathroom was spacious. Compared with Carol's closet-single dorm room, this apartment looked like the governor's mansion. It was definitely not typical student housing.

"How far is this from school?" I asked Carol.

"About two or three miles," she answered.

"There's certainly plenty of room here," Dick said.

"Look at the closets, Mom," Carol yelled from the bedroom. "I may have to buy more clothes to fill them up.

"I love the idea of a fireplace, too," she added.

"This kitchen is fit for a gourmet cook. Too bad we don't know anyone who can make use of it," I teased. Carol was definitely on her way to becoming one.

"I think I'd like to rent some storage space in your kitchen," I told her. Considering that it was a one-bedroom apartment, it had enough cupboards for a family of ten.

As we walked through the courtyard so the landlady could show us the laundry and parking areas, I noticed that there were several little old ladies in the building. Making a mental note of that, I hoped they would be nosy enough to keep an eye on Carol.

We had some genuine worries about Carol's living alone: she wouldn't know if any food had spoiled because of the odor. She could no longer detect smells of any kind.

"Do you have any suggestions to tell if something is spoiled?" she asked.

"Keep track of the dates when you buy things," I answered. "Make a judgment according to color and texture. Then follow a hard and fast rule: when in doubt, throw it out!"

Another worry we had no answer for was a possible gas leak. The stove, heating unit and log lighter on the fireplace were all gas appliances. The gas company purposely puts an odor in the gas so that people living with these appliances can detect a leak if one occurs. With no sense of smell, Carol was out of luck.

In October, I got involved with a couple of women who were interested in starting a Toastmistress Club in the Valencia area. With double-digit interest rates, 1982 was a terrible year for real estate, one of the worst in history. I needed something to occupy my time until things picked up. Because I had been involved with a Toastmistress group in the past, they enlisted my help.

Now that Carol was a seasoned public speaker, she was very encouraging. She expressed a desire to attend meetings during the summer when she was home, and when she happened to be in town at other times. Getting her encouragement, I went ahead with the project.

When Carol was available, she participated in the meetings, and enhanced her speaking abilities. Even though she was a good deal younger than most of the participants, she earned the members' respect and affection. If she was at home on a meeting night and I didn't feel well or had to work, she would fill in at a moment's notice. I always heard from the women later that she had done a marvelous job with all of the speaking assignments.

Carol came home for the Christmas holidays, short-tempered and sarcastic. After so many years of being such a happy young lady, usually bubbling with laughter, I was puzzled. Was she having problems at work? School? A romance that wasn't working out?

I let a few days of this moodiness go by, wondering what was going on and feeling hurt by her sarcasm. This wasn't the way my little girl usually behaved. But because we were no longer seeing her day by day, I sometimes tended to forget she was still fighting a life-threatening disease.

Then I remembered.

Carol and Tracey, 1981

John, 1981

8

Relapse

"Has your nose been bothering you?" I asked.

"Yes. I've been feeling pretty horrible."

"Why haven't you said anything?"

"Why bother. There's nothing you can do about it."

I was upset with her cryptic answer, but she was absolutely right. No one had done anything yet to take away her pain.

"Usual problems?" I asked, hoping it wasn't and at the same time knowing that it was.

"Yes. Pain in the sinuses, the inside of my nose hurts, and the headaches are worse."

"If you didn't want to tell me, why didn't you call Dr. Haring?"

"I was hoping it would go away again," she snapped, "and I'm sick of complaining. In fact, I'm sick of being sick! I thought this stuff was all over, and now it's coming back," she said, dejectedly.

I was angry, too.

It was easy to understand why she was losing her usually sunny and cheerful disposition. I wanted to take her in my arms and kiss away the pain, but she didn't want to be held or touched at all.

We began increasing the visits to Dr. Haring. Since college was two hours from home, the doctor suggested that we use the college health center for X-rays, blood tests, and urinalyses, and have them send copies of the results to him between appointments.

As before, the test results showed nothing unusual, but the nose, if one could look beyond the scar tissue, showed plenty. According to Dr. Haring, all the old problems had definitely come back, in spades. This was apparently typical of this disease.

Carol also went to see Dr. Mysko because she began having joint pains. There was slight swelling in her ankles, knees, fingers, and shoulders, but thankfully not concurrently.

He couldn't find any other reasons and attributed the symptoms to the possibility of rheumatoid arthritis, "Even though," he told Carol, "it doesn't follow the classic pattern."

Apparently the classic pattern of that disease is symmetrical pain and/or swelling. Both the knees or both the shoulders would have the problems together, or on the same side of the body. For example, it would not be the right shoulder and left knee.

It never occurred to any of us that the joint pains might have a connection to Wegener's so we never mentioned it to Dr. Haring. We'd completely forgotten that a few years ago Dr. Andrews had asked questions about joint pains.

Dr. Haring suggested Carol see Dr. Andrews again. That's when I remembered his mentioning the joint pains and began to realize the validity of his previous questions. We realized that maybe we hadn't been fair to him. His reputation seemed to be so good among the other local doctors. This time we got along fine with him. Maybe we were being more reasonable, receptive, or cooperative. Unfortunately, he had nothing new to offer.

"Just continue what you're doing. Treat the symptoms," he told us.

As the months wore on, all the symptoms that had seemed to be fading had returned, full force. Carol looked pale and tired, although she still complained very little.

People outside the family wouldn't have detected a difference, but Dick, her brothers, and I began to sense an underlying moodiness that had never been there before.

As she neared her twenty-first birthday, she had more reason to complain than any of us were aware of.

We wanted to do something special for this birthday with the whole family and began to make plans, feeling we had every reason to celebrate the day I had brought her into the world.

"Daddy and I were thinking about coming down to Riverside next Wednesday and taking you to dinner."

"That's exam week, Mom. Can we celebrate when they're over? Besides, John asked me out to dinner, and we'll be spending the rest of the evening studying."

"OK, we'll postpone our celebration. You let us know when you're ready."

Two days later she phoned me in the morning.

"Mom, my nose hurts worse than it's ever hurt before, and even though I know it isn't, it feels like it's broken."

"When did it start?"

"It's been hurting for a couple of days, but it wasn't that bad at the beginning. I thought it would go away, but it didn't. Anyway, I had to take my exams."

"Have you taken any pain pills?"

"Codeine."

"How many?"

"About four or six, I think. I don't remember. I didn't sleep all night."

She sounded awful.

"Would you like me to come get you? I think you should see Dr. Haring. It's probably an infection."

"I guess I can drive, but I'm a little dopey from the codeine."

"You sound very dopey. Stay where you are and I'll come get you."

"But it's a two-hour drive, Mom."

"I think I can handle it."

I called Dr. Haring's office and requested an appointment for later that day. I also called Dick to let him know what was going on and what I suspected, letting him know he'd get an update later.

During the drive my mind kept replaying, like a never-ending tape, what Carol had said about her nose feeling like it was broken. That brought back other memories. The only time she'd ever broken a bone was her right ring finger. My tomboy daughter, who played with a dump truck and a bug keeper while the other girls were playing with Barbie dolls, had been playing football during baseball season. Carol had always been much more athletic as a young child than I would have thought any little girl of mine would be. I used to sit indoors and do various kinds of needlecrafts and also loved to read. But my only daughter was always outside, involved in some kind of sport. Having three big brothers must have influenced her.

They always said she had the best pitching arm in the family. And many summers during her elementary school years, her softball coaches consistently put her in the outfield, since she was one of the few little girls who could throw the ball as far as home plate.

When I arrived at her apartment, Carol looked terrible. She was pale, her eyes were sunken back into her head, and her face was puffy. Because her nasal passages were so severely blocked, drainage from the sinuses was next to impossible. If nothing was broken, and there was no reason to believe differently, the only thing to cause that much pain had to be an infection.

"One look at you and Dr. Haring is going to put you right in the hospital."

Her nose was so sore that when I came close to her to kiss her, she pulled back and, to my dismay, didn't want me to touch any part of her face.

We drove non-stop to the doctor's office. When we arrived, the doctor was with us in moments.

"Where does it hurt, Carol?"

"Here." She circled the entire sinus area with her hand, "and my nose hurts really bad."

After taking a quick peek, he apologized as she moaned loudly.

He turned to me. "It's almost impossible to see in there," he said, "because the scar tissue has closed off so much of the passageways. She's in so much pain I don't want to poke around. It's not going to do her any good anyway."

He was right, of course. There was no doubt that she was hurting badly. Every time he touched her she seemed to jump a foot off the chair. Through all the examinations I'd observed that he had a very gentle touch. Every other word he uttered was an apology for causing her more pain in his attempt to evaluate the situation.

"She's not smiling today," he observed.

Then to Carol he said, "I believe you have a large pocket of infection in there, and I'd like to put you in the hospital. That's the quickest way to get large doses of antibiotics into you. I think that will be the best way to deal with this."

It was what I expected.

In a matter of minutes we were on our way to the hospital. It seemed like we waited an interminable time for Carol to be admitted. While we were waiting, I phoned Dick to bring him up to date.

Then I sat down with Carol again to wait.

"Mom, I really need to lie down," she said after a while.

There was hardly anyone else in the waiting area. I walked up to the receptionist and began to bark, "I've gone down to Riverside to pick up my daughter at college and she had a two-hour drive here. When the doctor examined her, he wanted her put in the hospital immediately. If you people are too busy to admit her, I wish you'd let me know so I can take her to another hospital. She needs to be in a bed *now* and we can't continue to wait here until someone gets around to admitting her."

As I finished my speech, I realized it was the first time in my life I had ever spoken to anyone like that. It's totally against my nature to be forceful, assertive, or aggressive. I imagine there must be something to the phrase maternal instinct. My baby was hurting badly, and enough was enough.

Moments later we were in the admitting office.

"Can I have a private room?" Carol asked.

There was one available. Carol let the attendant take her up in a wheel chair.

After she was settled in her room and her vital signs were taken, I gave the nurse a brief history. She had never heard of Wegener's granulomatosis, and asked me to spell it.

Carol was hooked up to two intravenous solutions: one for the antibiotic and one for the glucose. I'm sure she must have needed the nourishment. She told me she hadn't felt like eating that day and probably hadn't had much for the past couple of days, either. When you're not feeling well, the last thing you want to do is cook.

She was given periodic pain shots and although food was brought in regularly, most meals were returned uneaten.

I spent many hours sitting in her room during the next few days, even though we hardly spoke at all. I wanted to be available in case she wanted something—anything from a Coke© from the cafeteria to a magazine at the gift store. Although she rested, she didn't seem to sleep much.

If nothing was pressing at work, I could spend the whole day at the hospital, doing my needlecraft, reading, and keeping quiet, but being close to her. I never asked if Carol wanted the company; she didn't protest my being there. There was little else that could be done for her but offer moral support. I needed for her to know she wasn't going through this alone.

During this hospitalization, Carol began to question medications that were brought in or injected.

The questions were:

"What is that?

"What's it for?

"What's the dosage?

"Are there any side effects I should be aware of?

"How often is it taken?

"When will I get the next dose?

"Does it come in different strengths?"

I have to admit I was a little embarrassed at first because in my day good little girls did what they were told, took what they were offered, and didn't ask questions. How times had changed.

The nurses weren't the least bit reluctant to explain the name, contents, dosage, purpose, and side effects. If a particular nurse didn't know, she would find out. Invariably, on a later visit to Carol's room she would have the information.

On the whole, they seemed pleased that she was taking an active interest in her care.

I was glad I hadn't interfered, especially the night when a nurse brought in the wrong pills. When Carol asked what they were, the nurse gave her a drug name and dosage.

Carol surprised both of us when she said, "Those don't look like the pills I had before, and I know they don't come in twenty-five milligrams, only fifty and one hundred."

A few moments later the nurse returned with another little white paper cup.

"You were right," she said to Carol. "These should be the correct ones."

"Yes, these are the right ones," she agreed.

I sat up and took notice, wondering how often the wrong medication is given. It staggers the imagination. That was the beginning of *everyone* in our family questioning any and all medicines they're given.

We've also made it our job to inform our friends and extended family members of this episode. Without question we have all become more vigilant about drugs we're given in hospitals.

Carol also questioned whoever took her vital signs as to what readings they got, and told me whether her blood pressure and pulse readings were normal. They usually were.

Watching someone you love in pain can be an emotionally difficult thing to do. It certainly was for me, but it was better than being somewhere else, wondering what was going on.

Sometimes I was only good for pouring her another drink of water, or getting her another blanket, but it was one more thing she didn't have to ask, and possibly wait, for.

Dick was able to join us in the evening. She seemed to perk up a little by then. Maybe it was her father's presence, or the fact that he tried to show up with some cute little present, like a stuffed animal.

"You realize you didn't have to go through all this just to get a gift," Dick would tease her.

Her brothers would take turns wandering in and out of the hospital, except for Ken, who by this time was living three hours away in Palm Springs. He was able to visit on weekends. We suggested that he not make the trip because most of the time all we were able to do was to watch Carol try to sleep. But he wanted to do what cheering up he could and it seemed to work.

She perked up the most when any of her brothers came to visit—or maybe she just put up a front for them. It's hard to know. None of them missed an opportunity to come and offer their moral support. They did a great job of hiding their concern and always had a joke to tell her, or something to discuss that would help take her mind off the pain. It was a great source of comfort to Dick and me to see that the boys weren't too busy if they thought she needed them.

"There's little doubt as to what her problem is," Dr. Haring told us. "The scar tissue has become so profuse and the nasal openings so minute that not only is breathing very difficult, but drainage is almost impossible. Nasal mucosa becomes trapped and bacteria build up. All the drainage that the rest of us have in our heads is no longer working for Carol. She can't blow her nose, either."

Dr. Mysko also looked in on her, mainly to make sure the rest of her body didn't need attention.

"Although the most important thing right now is to clear up the infection," Dr. Haring said, "it's also becoming important to consider removing the scar tissue, since this problem is bound to recur."

That evening I related to Dick what Dr. Haring had said.

"How would you feel about taking Carol to the Mayo Clinic?" I asked him.

"Well, we're definitely at a crossroads," he said.

"That's why I think we ought to go to Mayo. Find out once and for all what we're fighting, get the experts' opinions, and then make a decision."

"I'm in favor," Dick replied. "Ask Dr. Haring what he thinks about it."

I supposed we should have asked Carol what she thought about it, but we were used to making the decisions about the children's health care, and it never occurred to me to ask her advice. Even though she was now twenty-one, to me she was still my baby and my responsibility.

When Dr. Haring realized we were seriously considering going to the Mayo Clinic this time, he told us he thought it would be a good idea.

"I'd very much like another opinion," the doctor said. "We're fighting a very unusual disease about which little is known, and I, for one, certainly don't have all the answers. Another opinion may only back me up, but I would welcome it under any circumstances. If Carol were my daughter, I think I would take the same direction that you are."

That did it. The decision was made. We felt we would be able to handle the time off from work as well as the expense beyond what our insurance covered.

"If she's definitely going to the Mayo Clinic," Dr. Haring said, "I wouldn't want to touch Carol surgically or remove any scar tissue at this time. I would like the doctors there to see her as she is now. That way they'll be able to make their own decisions and draw their own conclusions."

"I have a strange feeling about the possibility of surgery," I told Dick. "If the disease is no longer active, and this is only the result of having had it, wouldn't surgery to remove the scar tissue be like opening Pandora's Box?[9] Could it possibly trigger a new episode of Wegener's, or whatever it was that Carol had?"

The other side of the coin was that once and for all we might be able to find out whether or not Carol really had Wegener's, and perhaps discover how to treat whatever she did have.

It was our understanding that the doctors at the Mayo Clinic were world renowned experts in diagnosing medical problems.

While Carol was hooked up to an IV, she could have only sponge baths. Most of the time I was able to assist her. But she could hardly wait to get home and wash her hair.

After three days of hospitalization, it appeared that the infection was under control and Carol was feeling considerably better. Her IV was removed and she was released.

Dr. Haring suggested that Carol begin irrigating her nose several times a day with a nasal rinse to try to keep it a little cleaner, and cut down the chance of more infections. Carla explained to Carol how to do the irrigation and what to use during the process. She gave Carol a small pink plastic hand-held irrigator and referred to it as the "pink pig."

It's interesting that the nasal rinse called Alkalol®[10] and the Nasal Wash Cup (which has been nicknamed the pink pig) are the only items that this particular company manufactures. Its sole purpose, since it was formulated in 1896, is to soothe irritated nasal tissue and cut through mucus. After reading the label, I told Carol, "This mixture sounds like something from a witch doctor's bag."

"Don't knock it, Mom," she said, defending it. "It's pretty good stuff."

The doctor told Carol it was OK for her to return to school when he released her from the hospital. She was able to finish what was left of the school year. When unable to reach her for a few days at a time, I would ask John to go to her apartment and report back to me, which he graciously did.

After we made the decision to go to the Mayo Clinic, Carol insisted that the trip be put off till the end of summer. That gave her the opportunity to work until we left. We set up the trip for her to be back in time for the fall quarter.

Work and school continued to be very important to Carol. They were her means of escape, especially when it wasn't ski season. Goodness knows she needed an escape.

Every summer since high school, Carol had been employed. This summer was no different as far as she was concerned. Montgomery Engineers, the company she had worked for the three previous years, wanted her back and that was fine with her. Unfortunately, their budget wouldn't allow for the hiring of another employee when she was ready to start.

Dick and I were as disappointed as she. We felt this was a more important summer for her to work than the last few had been. That way her mind would be occupied.

We got lucky. This time I had a friend in the right place. Tom, a client of mine, worked with computers.

"Would you happen to know of a summer job that my daughter could apply for?"

"Which computer languages does she know?" Tom asked.

"I don't have the foggiest idea."

"I know someone who's looking for a summer hire. She needs to know …" He began throwing names of computer languages at me.

"You're speaking a foreign language," I joked.

"Have her give me a call," he said.

She called my client, told him about her experience, and he referred her to his friend, Lance.

We knew that if she were able to get the interview, she would probably get the job.

She must have said all the right things because Lance hired her on the spot. She was thrilled. After he saw what kind of work she was able to do, he was thrilled.

That job was one of the best things that had happened to Carol in a long time. She not only gained more knowledge and experience working with computers, but also learned how to handle herself in the business world as a working woman. I especially loved her story of how she took care of a male chauvinist who kept trying to treat her as a secretary. One day she decided she had to let him know that writing reports and running errands for him was not what she had been hired for. When he asked for a cup of coffee, she suggested they find someone to do that for both of them. After requesting that she prepare a report for him, she stated that she was working on a software project that Lance was waiting for. He got the message and that was the end of that problem. She had discovered early in life how important it was to speak up for herself.

There were several occasions for me to speak to Tom about business he and I were transacting, but it wouldn't have been in good taste to ask him about his friend's opinion of Carol's job performance. However, Tom told me the next time we spoke, "By the way, your kid is working out great."

She was asked if she would consider working full-time, if she wasn't going back to UCR, or part-time if she was. It was very flattering, but the drive would have been three hours each way—out of the question.

Carol dated a young man several times during the summer who worked for the client company. We knew that he was completely unaware of her illness, and that she preferred to keep it that way. She seemed to be keeping him at arm's length, and I wondered if it was because of the uncertainties she faced. She never discussed it though, and we didn't ask her.

For our trip to the Mayo Clinic, Dr. Haring had inquired and gotten a reference.

"A Dr. Thomas J. McDonald has been recommended," he said. "Someone from Dr. McDonald's office will be in touch with you shortly."

Carol's initial thoughts and feelings about going to the clinic seemed to be mixed. Although she hid her fears well, they existed. That was obvious from the questions she posed:

"What if they don't come up with anything new?

"What if they find something worse?

"What if we don't like their treatment or suggestions?

"What if they concur with everything and also want to operate?

"Will I be able to make the trip home right after surgery?

"Couldn't I just spend the money on another ski trip or two?"

When the call came from the Mayo Clinic, the woman I spoke to, who identified herself as Kathy, was very friendly and accommodating. We set a date for the examination, and she explained the procedures we were to follow.

"Upon entering the clinic, turn left, go to the reception desk, and identify yourselves. One of the people behind the desk will guide you to your next destination," Kathy said. "Carol will be scheduled for several routine tests in the morning, and will see Dr. McDonald in the afternoon, after he has had time to look over the tests."

What a nice surprise. She had called Carol by name. Dr. McDonald planned on seeing the tests *before* he saw Carol. That was certainly logical. I figured it was time for me to be optimistic and give them a chance.

"I'll be sending you written instructions in the mail explaining all this," she added.

"Do you think Carol's slides and X-rays would be of any value to Dr. McDonald?"

"By all means. Bring the X-rays and, if possible, send the slides on ahead."

It was obvious that appointment coordinators from the clinic were used to dealing with out-of-town patients and geared to handling details that would facilitate matters. When the packet came, it included information on lodging and how to find one's way around town, also. We noted that most of the motels and hotels had hourly shuttles to the clinic during the day.

There were many times during the summer when Carol voiced the opinion that the trip was a lousy idea. However, as her parents, we pulled rank. Although she voiced misgivings, she didn't refuse to go. Someone asked me what we would do if she did.

"Frankly," I said, "that thought had never occurred to me."

We would not have accepted Carol's veto. This was not a choice of piano or horseback riding lessons. Our reasons for wanting to go were no secret, and although this particular trip may not have been the one Carol would have chosen for herself except in desperation, nevertheless there was no question in my mind about her going. Our only aim was to help find answers to what was becoming a much more serious health problem.

I don't really feel Carol ever fought the idea of going in her mind. If there were anything that disturbed her about the trip as a whole, I would say it probably would have been fear of the unknown. But while Carol might have been afraid of the answers, she would never have been too scared to ask the questions. Her scientific curiosity would have pushed her toward the quest for knowledge.

As the summer wore on, it became clear that our decision to go to the clinic was the right one because her symptoms were definitely not abating.

In my desperation to find ways to help her, I began reading books about faith healers such as Edgar Cayce. Because Wegener's is so rare, even he hadn't cured anyone of it. I facetiously mentioned these things to Dr. Haring once, and he, too, said there were times he would have liked to believe a witch doctor could wave some feathers and rattle some bones because modern medicine didn't seem to be doing her much good.

Dick usually made jokes about my heading off in those weird directions, but he understood my need to keep busy doing something that I thought might be even a little constructive, as long as it wasn't destructive.

In Carol's usual way she kept busy working.

One day Dr. Haring discovered that Carol had computer knowledge. "I just bought a personal computer for my family," he said, "and they are in need of instruction. Are you interested in a tutoring job?"

She was delighted to be of help to him after all the help he had given her. She spent several evenings a week for a few weeks at his home teaching his wife and children how to use their computer. Mrs. Haring and the children became quite friendly with Carol, which didn't surprise Dick and me at all.

Because it was necessary, on occasion, for Carol to change the hour or day she was to work with the Haring family, she was given their home phone number. It went into our family directory in case we ever had trouble getting through to him.

Dr. Haring's children were enamored with her, and, according to him, looked forward to the time Carol would spend with them and their computer.

Getting along well with children seemed to be second nature to Carol. While in the sixth grade she was offered an opportunity to work with the deaf or hard of hearing preschoolers.

I had the occasion to understand just how much Carol had profited by that association. Another family had come to visit us at our vacation home in the mountains when Carol was twelve. She and the older children were going to take the younger children for a walk in the nearby woods. One little boy named David had a clicker, a noise-making toy from a game, and was downright adamant about relinquishing it. Carol got the little one's jacket, and while she was zipping him into it, explained to him, "We might get lucky enough to see a rabbit or a deer in the woods but the clicker might scare the animals. It might be a good idea to leave it here in the house."

The toddler walked over to where the older children were putting the game away, handed them the clicker and told them, "I don't want to scare the animals."

No amount of coercion could have gotten it away from him before his conversation with Carol.

Later that day I asked her, "Where did you learn to handle situations like getting the clicker away from David?"

"When I was working with the preschool class," she said, "I learned that hard-of-hearing children are more easily frightened. They have to have things explained more thoroughly in order to get them to cooperate. I found out when I was baby-sitting that explanations also worked well with children who don't have handicaps."

She handled the children that she baby-sat with so well that after she went away to college, we used to get tiny gentleman callers, about six or seven years old, wanting to know when Carol would be back so she could baby-sit them.

I obtained Carol's biopsy slides from Dr. Haring, packed them in a shoebox with lots of sterile cotton as padding, and mailed them to Dr. McDonald.

"Come by my office just before you leave," Dr. Haring suggested, "and pick up my bulging file. Dr. McDonald will probably want to look over my notes. You should probably stop by the hospital and pick up a complete set of Carol's X-rays."

"Doesn't the hospital staff need some authorization from you?"

"Absolutely not," he said. "The X-rays belong to you, and they won't refuse."

He was right. They didn't. We took those with us instead of sending them on ahead.

Our plans, appointments, and reservations were all set. The night before we left, Don presented Carol with a travel gift: a small tape recorder with headphones.

He told her, "Listening to Mom and Dad's music coming and going is more punishment than anyone should have to endure."

She was delighted with her present and used it throughout the trip.

The day after Labor Day, 1983, the three of us set off for Rochester, Minnesota and the famed Mayo Clinic.

---

9. According to Greek mythology, Zeus presented Pandora with a box and told her not to open it. But curiosity got the better of her and she opened it, releasing all the misfortunes of mankind such as plague, sorrow, poverty, crime, etc., into the world.

10. Alkalol is a mixture of purified water, menthol, eucalyptol, thymol, camphor, benzoin, oils of wintergreen, spearmint, pine, and cinnamon, potassium alum, potassium chlorate, sodium bicarbonate, sodium chloride, alcohol, and caramel color.

Dr. Haring and family

9

The Mayo Clinic

Carol's appointment was for Monday, September 15th. We had decided to drive to Minnesota, hoping Carol would enjoy seeing a little bit of America on the way.

Our route took us through Yellowstone Park with "Old Faithful" geyser, and Jackson Hole ski resort, both in Wyoming; and Brian Head, Utah, a ski resort that Carol was interested in seeing with the hope of going there someday. We also stopped at Mount Rushmore in South Dakota, which was awe inspiring, and the caverns near the monument.

About halfway to Rochester, Carol said, "I'm really glad we're going."

"Why?" I asked. "Has your nose gotten worse?"

"Yeah, it has," she said. "I hope they can help me."

We pulled into Rochester the day before Carol's appointment. Besides her problems, I developed one of my own: a killer toothache!

A visit to the Mayo Clinic is quite an experience. From the moment we entered the town it was obvious that it exists only for the clinic. As one might expect, it's the tallest building in town. Most of the motels have hourly shuttles to and from it during the day. Almost all directions are given with the clinic as a reference point; for example, "it's three blocks past the clinic," or "it's half a mile east of the clinic." In addition, guided tours are offered of the clinic, the town of Rochester, and the Mayo brothers' home, Mayowood.

Because of Minnesota's severe winters, there are several underground tunnels connecting the clinic to shops, restaurants, nearby hotels, and a parking garage.

Although we had never given it much thought, we were surprised to find that the clinic is not a hospital. The doctors practicing there make use of two hospitals: Methodist, which is connected by an underground tunnel, and St. Mary's, which is two blocks away on surface streets.

Rochester is not a money-hungry town by any means. The hotels, motels, and restaurants are more than reasonable. We couldn't believe how inexpensive the clinic parking garage was—only $2 a day. All of this makes sense; one does not choose to go to the Mayo Clinic for a vacation.

Appointments are arranged so that one may easily go from one part of the clinic to another, wasting as little time as possible, but also allowing for those who may not be ambulatory.

Several tests were scheduled for Carol's first morning there.

I had brought a large stack of X-rays.

We had learned during the past five years that each doctor wants his own fresh tests from which to draw conclusions, and to be absolutely certain that nothing important has been missed. The doctors there were no exception.

The clinic is a rather plain-looking, unimpressive nineteen-story building—but it's only unimpressive on the outside. That all changes when one walks in the door. After seeing the way it operates—no pun intended—Dick concluded that it's an administrative wonder. While the efficiency is remarkable, no one is made to feel like a number instead of a human being.

Everything proceeded just as Kathy had explained it.

The brochure put out by the clinic says the doctors will see anyone without an appointment, but suggests one to shorten the waiting time.

We checked in at the front desk and Carol introduced herself to a very pleasant lady. She said, "Oh, yes. You must be Carol. We've been expecting you." Then she handed Carol an envelope with her name on it.

"These cards are your appointment cards," she said. "They're for the tests you're scheduled to have done and the doctors you're to see. The times are noted on the cards. Here's a map of the clinic. This is where you are now." She pointed to a spot on the map. "This is where you'll go for your first test. If you have any questions or problems finding your way, ask someone in the reception area on any floor to help you."

She was pleasant, courteous, and friendly—nothing at all like the medical center at UCLA.

Part of the basement is the laboratory. We were to start there since the tests were scheduled to be done first thing in the morning, before breakfast. That would give the doctors an opportunity to review them and be prepared for Carol in the afternoon.

With her envelope of computer cards clutched in her hand, each one specifying an appointment or test of some kind just as we'd been told, with times and floor, room, or section numbers, Carol proceeded to the laboratory with Dick and me following close behind.

The waiting area was enormous, circular in design, with a skylight in the center of the ceiling, obviously in a spot where there weren't nineteen floors above. There were plants in the middle of the area under the skylight. The various rooms for testing were around the perimeter. Because of the fame of the clinic, staggering numbers of people come from all parts of the world, seeking help and hope. I wondered how many were able to get both, and whether or not Carol would be one of them.

Most of the tests went smoothly, with no incidence. Immediately after the blood test, however, Carol felt a little dizzy. We'd been told that it's a very normal reaction, and one which Dick had experienced on occasion. The technicians were thoroughly prepared and had her lie down for a while. One was even thoughtful enough to ask her if there was anyone waiting for her, and came out to the waiting area.

"Will the person accompanying Carol Swart please come forward?" she called over the intercom.

Dick and I both went to the front of the room.

The technician explained, "Carol had a minor reaction, known as a vasovagal reaction,[11] to the drawing of her blood. We're having her lie down for a few minutes until the dizzy feeling goes away. She asked that someone let you know."

Our little girl was concerned about *us*.

"That's very considerate of you," Dick said.

This thoughtful attitude was noticeable throughout the entire facility.

We learned that the clinic and affiliated hospitals were teaching centers just like our nearby medical center at UCLA, and that the doctors work in teams. Everyone who came within three feet of Carol was introduced to her and then to Dick and me. Explanations followed the introductions without our having to ask anyone who they were or what they were doing.

When we arrived for Carol's afternoon appointment, I handed over the stack of X-rays and Dr. Haring's file, both of which I had been guarding with my life.

The waiting room was about the size of a movie theater. Because of the large number of doctors available, there didn't seem to be a long wait. We had another occasion to witness the courtesy with which the various patients were treated, including those who had come without an appointment and had a much longer wait than those who had one.

When Carol's name was called, we all walked up to the front desk and she was told what room to go to.

"We're her parents," I said. "May we accompany her?"

"Yes, of course," the receptionist said. "There's plenty of room."

The examining room we were all taken to was quite large, particularly in contrast to those of our medical center back home. Besides the chair that raises, lowers, and tilts that all ENTs use, there was a long bench against one wall. Whoever set up this area did not expect the patient to be alone.

When Dr. McDonald and two colleagues entered, he immediately introduced himself and the doctors with him, first to Carol and then to Dick and me. He looked like everyone's mental image of the ideal doctor: white-haired, ruddy-cheeked, self assured, not quite medium height, slightly stocky, and as cordial as if we were in his front parlor.

He began by saying to all of us, "Thank you for coming to the Mayo Clinic and allowing us to examine Carol. Now tell me what has brought you here and how you happened to choose me. Did my good friend, Carl Thompson, send you? He's a wonderful doctor, you know."

I remember thinking at the time that it's too bad we tend to judge doctors by their bedside manner, since that has no bearing on their competence, only their personality. Dr. Thompson had always been so stern-faced, cold, and formal. I don't ever recall seeing him smile.

Carol told her story, and Dick and I filled in parts here and there.

"We've reviewed this morning's tests," the doctor said, "the X-rays you brought, and several of the doctors here have viewed the slides you sent. Thank you for sending them on ahead. We have all concluded that the slides show overwhelming evidence of Wegener's granulomatosis."

At last, I thought, a confirmation of Dr. Haring's diagnosis. Good for him. They were well-prepared, too, and ready for Carol, a big step in the right direction.

The doctor made no assumptions that we knew what each test was for, or what it was supposed to tell him. He explained each one in great detail using layman's terms. Then he gave us an opportunity to ask questions. It was easy to feel complete confidence in him immediately, and to be convinced we had come to the right place for help. There was absolutely no doubt about his ability to communicate, and he proceeded to give us answers almost before we asked the questions. His bedside manner was impeccable; he had charisma to spare. Marcus Welby[12] would have been jealous.

Our first impression of the clinic, and the kindness, compassion and courtesy with which we were treated, led us to believe that perhaps all was right with the world. We never changed our minds about the clinic and told everyone we knew how great we felt it was.

"I'll be going through Dr. Haring's file later today," Dr. McDonald added. "It was very nice of him to send it along with you, and I thank you for bringing it, also." Turning to Carol he said, "Now I'd like to have a look in your nose, young lady.

"Considering that the scar tissue is so profuse," he said, "it's difficult to see much."

That was certainly a confirmation of Dr. Haring's opinion.

After that, Dick and I were asked by Dr. McDonald, "Would you mind stepping outside for a few minutes so I can talk to Carol privately?"

Of course Dick and I complied, and within a few moments Dr. McDonald joined us in the hall. Both of us later confessed to each other how our hearts were pounding with fear, expecting bad news.

But he quickly told us, setting our minds at ease, "It appears that no disease is present at this time." He added, "It looks like she's cured herself."

It's a good thing I was sitting down. For the very first time in my life, I felt faint. I also had a lump in my throat and tears stung in my eyes. I grabbed Dick's arm to steady myself just as he reached out for me.

The doctor continued, "I wanted to give Carol an opportunity to tell me anything she might have to say in private.

"Even though she came with her parents, she's a grown woman and I have to respect her privacy. But we're also very cognizant of your concerns. If you weren't concerned, you wouldn't be here. We'll try to be sensitive to your feelings."

He couldn't have been more sensitive. How nice it would be, I thought, if that were the rule with doctors and hospitals everywhere, instead of the exception.

Following their examination of Carol, all three doctors said they found no active disease. Hearing those words, I felt like a great weight had been lifted, and erased all doubt about whether or not this was a worthwhile trip.

Dr. McDonald indicated again, and those with him concurred, "It's really difficult to be certain of our diagnosis with all the scar tissue in her nose. Those after-effects of having had Wegener's could very well be the cause of her problems now—not necessarily the disease."

I was curious to know how wide their experience had been with treating Wegener's patients, so I asked Dr. McDonald, "How many Wegener's patients have you seen?"

He answered, "I guess about fifty." But then he added, "Many of them had the disease in such an advanced stage that there was little that could be done for them.

"One of the biggest problems with Wegener's is that it's so difficult to diagnose, and many people are treated for numbers of other things before anyone realizes what they have. By then it may be too late.

"Carol was lucky that she had such an early diagnosis. The doctors treating her must be extremely competent."

Three cheers for Dr. Haring and the pathologist at Henry Mayo Newhall Memorial Hospital! And we mistakenly thought the doctors and pathologists at UCLA would be better equipped to make a diagnosis because of its size, reputation and assumed quality of the physicians. We had also questioned, early on, whether or not the small-town doctors in Valencia knew enough or had enough experience to diagnose Carol correctly. Dr. Haring had seen one other patient and hit the nail on the head with his diagnosis. Dr. Thompson had seen three other patients and he still failed to diagnose Carol correctly.

Dr. McDonald went on to say, "It's unusual for Wegener's to be confined only to the nose, and Carol is lucky in that respect, also."

Something he didn't tell us was that he, along with other doctors, had done extensive research into Wegener's and had written a number of papers about their findings.

"What has been done for Carol," Dr. McDonald continued, "was exactly what should have been done."

Another round of applause for Dr. Haring.

"What kind of treatment is there for Wegener's when treatment is necessary?" I asked.

He answered with one word and no hesitation, "Chemotherapy."

He then added, "The scar tissue that is now blocking Carol's nasal airways should be surgically removed."

"Dr. Haring suggested that last spring," I told him.

"After the removal of the scar tissue," he continued, "a plastic material called Silastic™[13] should be placed inside Carol's nose and held in place with a stitch or two to inhibit the regrowth and additional scarring. The Silastic™ should stay in place for about four to six weeks and then should be removed.

"It would be a good idea to take another biopsy during the removal of the scar tissue to insure that the disease is no longer active.

"The surgery need not be performed here, but if that's what you choose to do, I will be available the day after tomorrow.

"If you decide that Carol should have the surgery here and now, I would like to recommend that she first have a thorough examination to make certain she is physically fit for surgery. The doctor able to make that evaluation is Dr. Richard

DeRemee, whose specialty is thoracic[14] diseases and internal medicine. I've taken the liberty of checking in case you would need to know, and he can see her tomorrow morning.

"Depending on Carol's recovery speed, she could be released from the hospital Friday or Saturday, and you would be able to return home immediately.

"There are several options open to you, and the surgery is completely voluntary."

Now two doctors we trusted said it was necessary.

"It can be done back in California instead of here," he went on. "If Carol chooses to have the surgery done here and if for some unforeseen reason she isn't able to tolerate the drive home, although that doesn't usually present a problem, she could fly home. Cabin pressure in an airplane will not cause her any discomfort, either, if you choose that way to go.

"If she has the surgery done here, she could fly back and have the Silastic™ removed here, go to the medical center and have Dr. Thompson remove it, or have Dr. Haring remove it at his office."

Removing the Silastic™ did not seem to be a big deal. We were not pressured to make a decision, either for Carol to have the surgery, or if she chose to have it, where it should be performed. We were given lots of alternatives. For the surgery, we could use our medical center at home, or Dr. Haring could perform it, or we could just forget about the whole thing and go on the way we had been going, at least for a while.

"For scheduling purposes, could you let me know tomorrow if you want me to operate?" Dr. McDonald asked.

At this point the doctors left the room.

Occasional interruptions occurred during some of Carol's visits with Dr. McDonald, but we never felt neglected. They were trying to take care of as many patients as they could with as little time lost as possible. The pauses also gave us a chance to catch our respective breaths. We had the opportunity to reflect on and evaluate what we had just heard. We were also able to pose any questions we had to each other and subsequently to the doctor.

A few times during an examination and/or consultation another doctor who wished to discuss something with Dr. McDonald came into the room.

When these interruptions would occur, Dr. McDonald would introduce Carol, Dick and me to the interrupting doctor, saying, "This young lady has come to us from California. She has had Wegener's, but appears to have cured herself."

The interrupting doctor usually took a look at Carol's nose after asking permission, asked some questions, or made some pertinent comment.

"What do you think about having the surgery done here?" Dick asked both of us the next time we were alone.

"I don't think we have to be in any hurry to remove the scar tissue. On the other hand, it's the same thing Dr. Haring's been telling us," I answered. "What's your opinion?" I asked Carol.

"I like him," she said, "and they seem to know what they're talking about. I don't know whether we should have him operate or wait."

"Maybe we all need a little more time to think about it." Dick said.

"I think that's a good idea," I said. "I think we just decided not to decide yet."

The doctors returned, and before anyone had an opportunity to make any additional comments, another doctor, introduced to us as Dr. Louis Weiland, a pathologist, came into the room to momentarily speak to Dr. McDonald.

"This is Carol Swart, from California. She's had Wegener's," Dr. McDonald told him.

"Oh?" said Dr. Weiland, "How do you do. May I see your hand?"

Carol answered in the affirmative. Dr. Weiland picked up her right hand to look at it and began feeling the finger joints.

She held out the left one and asked, "Is this what you're looking for?" Two joints were slightly swollen.

Joint pains? Dick and I looked at each other in amazement. Then we remembered that Dr. Andrews had mentioned them long ago. But we never knew until that moment the possible connection between joint pain and Wegener's.

"Have you experienced any joint pains or swelling elsewhere?" Dr. Weiland asked.

"I've had some pain in my shoulder, ankle, and knee," Carol answered as she pointed to the ones that had given her trouble, "but not all at the same time."

"We had discussed Carol's joint pains with Dr. Mysko, our family doctor, some time ago," I said, "and he felt it was a form of arthritis. None of us ever mentioned it to Dr. Haring because it never occurred to us that it had any connection to Wegener's."

"Joint pains are very common to Wegener's," Dr. Weiland said.

A discussion of joint pains ensued. Because of the doctors' apparent knowledge of the disease, my confidence in their ability to help Carol kept increasing minute by minute.

"Do you have any more of these?" Dr. Weiland asked as he continued to examine Carol's hands.

"What are you looking for now?" I questioned.

"These tiny red dots," Carol explained.

Then she pointed out different places on her body where she had noticed these dots.

"This is typical of vasculitic diseases," the doctor offered, "and that's what Wegener's is."

When this episode was over, the doctors left the room again for a few minutes.

"You're right," Dick said to Carol. "They certainly seem to know what they're talking about."

"Maybe we should have him operate," I said, turning to Carol.

"Let's go for it," she said.

When Dr. McDonald returned this time, Dick said, "We've made a decision. We want you to remove the scar tissue."

"Good," he said. "I think you'll find it much easier to breathe when it's out," he said to Carol.

"That's what I'm counting on," she said.

"Let me make an appointment for you with Dr. DeRemee for tomorrow morning. We'd like to make sure you're physically fit for surgery," he said picking up the phone.

After speaking to someone he replaced the receiver and said, "You're all set. You see Dr. DeRemee at 10:00 tomorrow morning and I'll see you again in the afternoon at 2:30."

"I'm happy that something's going to be done," I said.

Dick and Carol agreed.

Now I had another problem to deal with—finding a dentist who could see me immediately. I couldn't last the day with no relief from the pain I had developed the day before.

That morning between Carol's tests, I'd searched the clinic halls for a public telephone and had not seen any.

"Where can I find a public telephone?" I asked a clerk.

"Is it a local call?" she asked.

"Yes, it is," I said, wondering what difference it made with a public telephone.

She directed me to a corridor adjacent to the waiting room, where the reason for her question quickly became apparent: The Mayo Clinic had free telephones on each floor. There was a sign above each phone requesting that it be used for "local calls only or please use your calling card."

I found a dentist within walking distance of the clinic who would see me right away, and saw him several times that week, including one painful night at 11:30.

I mention this only because this dentist and his office staff had the same attitude that everyone at the clinic had: kindness, consideration, compassion, and a willingness to help in any way possible. They never asked for a penny, only my address so that they could send me a bill. That would never have happened in California.

Carol saw Dr. DeRemee the following morning. Dick and I were asked to remain in the waiting room this time.

"I'm fit for surgery," she told us after her examination.

That afternoon we had a brief visit with Dr. McDonald. He told us when to check in at the hospital—he would be using Methodist—and what time the surgery would be performed.

"I'll be in to see you immediately after surgery to explain what I find," he said to Dick and me and then added as he turned to Carol, "Would you mind if I ordered some pictures taken of your nose?"

"No, that's fine," she said.

We had noticed some time ago that a portion of the bridge of her nose had begun to cave in a little in the center. Dr. Haring had used the term, "saddle-nose deformity," and since the depression was across the middle of the bridge, like a saddle on a horse, it's easy to see how that term had come into being.

Once again it occurred to me how strange it was that Carol had planned for and wanted a change in the shape of her nose. This definitely wasn't how she had envisioned it, but there was no denying that it was not the same nose that she had five years ago.

I was torn between superstition and logic. One part of my brain couldn't help wondering if we had tempted the evil spirits by seeking an unnatural change; the other part believed those thoughts to be ridiculous.

While all the doctors referred to Carol's new nasal structure as a deformity, the family thought it didn't look deformed but was an improvement over her natural nose. But we would all have much preferred that the change had come about in the way she had planned, with temporary pain, not with the suffering she had endured so far.

We knew from the various doctors' observations that the disease had destroyed portions of the septum inside Carol's nose. They had made it plain that the destruction shouldn't cause Carol any trouble by itself.

The photo-taking session was reminiscent of the many pictures that Dr. Carlson had taken when he thought he was going to change the shape of Carol's nose. It would have been interesting to compare the photographs.

After telling Dr. McDonald about that he had said, "I would like to see those pictures if you could get them."

When the photographer finished, we were directed to a dimly lit cubicle apart from the examining rooms of the clinic. Dr. McDonald had told us a hospital representative would assist us in filling out the necessary hospital forms and consents. Anticipating the need for them, I had brought several insurance forms. The lady seemed pleasantly surprised that we had come prepared. She explained where to go and what to do when Carol was to be admitted at 7:00 PM, her assigned time. Then she thanked us for coming to see her. She was finished and that was that.

Dick couldn't resist asking her, "Don't you people want any money?"

She smiled at his question and said, "The hospital will bill you for what your insurance doesn't cover, but thank you for asking. Have you given your address to the front desk?"

He answered, "Yes." Then he told her, "Carol has seen several doctors and has had a number of tests done at the clinic and they haven't asked for money either."

"Would you like me to send one of your insurance forms to the clinic office?" she asked.

"We'd appreciate that," I said. "We weren't sure where to take it."

"Consider it done," she said. "Thank you for your cooperation. I hope everything goes well."

What a wonderful feeling that kind of attitude gave us.

Knowing the general reputation of hospital food, Carol wanted to eat before she checked in. At the appointed time we arrived at the hospital. The lobby resembled a hotel with armchairs and small tables. After a short wait, including an apology from the receptionist for not taking her immediately, Carol was taken to a three-bed room.

A nurse came in to take her vital signs, which Carol monitored and questioned.

"Would you like a supper tray?" she asked.

Before there was an opportunity to answer, she turned to Dick and me and offered to order trays for all three of us. In other hospitals it seemed like a battle to get a glass of water.

"Thank you, but we just finished dinner," Dick told her.

Carol began settling in for the night. Unfortunately, she was disturbed by the television that the other two patients were watching. She didn't want to be rude and ask them to turn it off.

We casually mentioned that to a nurse and, in the twinkling of an eye, Carol was moved to a private room.

The floor layout of this hospital seemed to be more efficient than most we'd seen before. It had a semicircular wing with all the patients' rooms opening directly to the nurses' desk, not down the hall and around the corner like so many others. It seemed that the communication between the patients and nursing staff would be quicker and easier with that arrangement.

Dr. McDonald and a young man, who we came to believe was his favorite protégé, visited that evening, and were pleased but not surprised when we commented favorably on the treatment we had been receiving so far.

The doctor explained again, in great detail, what he would be doing with the inside of Carol's nose during surgery, and the length of time it would take.

"By the way," he said, "why don't you wait in her room during the surgery, regardless of what the nursing staff tells you to do. I think you'll be more comfortable here."

Whatever else Dr. McDonald does, I think he reads minds, also.

He reminded us again that he and the young man who we guessed was probably a resident would see us here immediately after the operation to apprise us of their findings.

Although visiting hours at the hospital were comparable to other hospitals, we were left pretty much alone, and not even reminded when it was time to leave. Those nurses who spoke to us were aware that we were a long way from home. Perhaps they thought Carol would be more comfortable with the sight of a familiar face.

At the appointed time on Wednesday morning, Carol was taken to surgery. We were there to kiss her goodbye and wish her good luck. This scene was becoming much too familiar. One of the nurses asked us if we would like to wait in the waiting area. When we said we'd rather wait in Carol's room, she said she would let the doctor know where to find us, and no one bothered us.

After the allotted time had passed, Dr. McDonald and his shadow entered Carol's room with such broad smiles that we didn't have to ask how the surgery had gone.

The doctor explained the procedure to remove the scar tissue one more time.

"Tissue from three places in Carol's nose was removed and sent to Pathology for examination.

"Silastic™ has been placed inside her nose and fastened to the septum, or what was left of it. We placed a stitch on each side and one in the center," the doctor reported.

He drew us a little diagram during his explanation. While his bedside manner left nothing to be desired, he was definitely not an artist, to which he attested. But he made his point and we got the message.

"I was prepared to insert a nose button in what I thought would be a hole in the septum," he continued, "but the area that was destroyed was so big that the insertion of the nose button was impossible. The largest one kept falling out."

He had a bag full of nose buttons and showed us several. I had never seen anything like them before. They were of a soft, rubbery material, peach-colored, and reminded me of two plumbers' washers of different sizes, joined in the center. Apparently one side is pushed through a hole in the septum, and the large end on the other side holds the apparatus in place. The largest one was about the size of a quarter; the hole in Carol's septum was much bigger.

Then he gave us the best news of all.

"While a very large portion of the septum has been destroyed by the Wegener's, *no trace of the disease appears to be present at this time.*

"Carol tolerated the surgery very well, and the loss of most of the septum should not prove to be a problem for her. The surgery accomplished what we had hoped it would; it opened the breathing passages and should make it a lot more comfortable for her to breathe normally."

About the time Dr. McDonald finished explaining what had transpired in surgery and the positive results, Carol was being wheeled into her room. She was mostly awake, had good color in her face, and appeared to be in good spirits, probably because she could see that we were all grinning from ear to ear.

She said she felt good, that is, for someone who had just been through surgery. She was wearing the now too-familiar mustache bandage.

Thursday was a good day for Carol. Her recovery was going well and if nothing changed, she would be released Friday evening. That meant that we could start for home Saturday morning.

Fortunately, it was a good day for her because it looked like her parents were going to the dogs. Not only did I have a terrible time with the abscessed tooth the night before, and was so doped up with pain pills I wasn't sure what day it was, but Dick developed a sore throat overnight. That presented another interesting meeting with a health professional in Rochester.

I had gone down with Dick to the emergency room of the hospital to see about getting help for his throat. The doctor on call took a culture.

"We've come from California to have our daughter treated here," Dick explained. "She's just had surgery on her nose and we'll be driving home with her in two days."

"In that case, the results of the culture will take too long to be of any use to us," the doctor informed Dick. "I don't think it's prudent to wait to treat you under the circumstances. I'm going to prescribe an antibiotic to speed your recovery.

"If you have a virus or an allergy, the medicine won't do you any good. But it won't do you any harm, either. How long do you expect to be on the road?" he asked.

"About a week," Dick answered.

"Well, this should keep you on your feet," he offered.

Like my encounter with the local dentist, this doctor was compassionate and considerate. It was a real novelty to be treated with so much thoughtfulness from hospital personnel.

"Who do I see about paying my bill?" Dick asked, when the doctor was finished with him.

"Don't concern yourself," the doctor answered. "You gave them your address and insurance information for your daughter?"

"Yes, I did," Dick said.

"A bill will be sent to you," the doctor concluded.

In this day and age of outstretched hands seeking immediate payment, it was hard for us to believe that any business would be that trusting of people whose home was halfway across the country.

There is an escort service between Methodist Hospital and the Mayo Clinic, another convenience for the patients. As on college campuses, the escorts are young male volunteers. Their job is to take patients from the hospital to the clinic in wheelchairs via an underground tunnel so that the doctors are able to examine them in their offices instead of having to go back and forth to the hospital. Those who are escorted from the hospital to the clinic are usually patients who are almost ready to go home. The wheelchairs are used to conserve the patient's strength and guard against injuries from falling, for much the same reasons that patients are usually escorted to the outside door of a hospital in this manner when they're being discharged. The service appears to save some time for the doctors while offering comfortable transportation for the patients regardless of the weather. Men are used because of their greater physical strength.

On Friday afternoon, Carol was escorted in a wheelchair by a very friendly young man to Dr. McDonald's office for a final post-operative examination before going home.

After a brief look to make sure the Silastic™ was where he had placed it, and that Carol's body was handling the foreign matter satisfactorily, Dr. McDonald phoned Dr. Haring in California. He reported what had taken place in detail. The pathology reports had come in and the biopsies showed no evidence of active disease at this time.

Those were beautiful words.

Dr. McDonald told Dr. Haring that he would be sending a written report. By the time he was ready to hang up, he called Dr. Haring by his first name and thanked him for sending Carol to the Mayo Clinic.

"It can come back again, can't it?" Carol wanted to know.

"Yes. That's a possibility," the doctor answered. "We're still learning about Wegener's."

After reviewing the options, we all agreed that Dr. Haring would be the one to remove the Silastic™ in four to six weeks, depending on how long Carol was able to tolerate the foreign material in her nose with no ill effects.

The doctor repeated that it looked to him like Carol had cured herself. He thanked us once more for letting him have the opportunity to examine and treat Carol.

He told us again, "Everything that's been done for Carol in connection with this disease has been exactly the right thing. You're very lucky."

Three more cheers for Dr. Haring.

"While luck may have had something to do with it," I told him, "we're also very picky about our doctors."

A nurse came into the examining room and gave Carol instructions on post-operative care, including details on how to irrigate her nose. She was given a small pink plastic hand-held irrigator, which the nurse told us had somehow been nick-named the pink pig—our old friend. We'd thought Dr. Haring and his nurses had a patent on that nickname. It was interesting to learn that they used the same gadget here and called it by the same nickname. The irrigation was to be done four times a day.

"Will I get my sense of smell back?" Carol asked.

"Honey, I can't answer that one," Dr. McDonald said. "Sometimes it comes back and sometimes it doesn't."

"Would anything be accomplished by sending Carol's slides to the Air Force Pathology Lab?" I asked. "Dick and I had heard about the lab and I thought it might be of some benefit."

"It can't do any harm," the doctor answered. "Would you like me to take care of that?"

"That would be great," Dick said. "You never know what good it might do."

"Consider it done," Dr. McDonald said.

"What about the CDC?" I asked.

"Let's send the slides there, also," he said. "One never knows what might turn up."

We all thanked Dr. McDonald several times and left.

On Saturday morning we checked out of our motel and started for home. Even though we were very enamored with the Mayo Clinic in general, and Dr. McDonald in particular, we were glad to be going home.

Dick was stopped for speeding on the way. I guess we were all getting a little anxious.

The police officer looked into the car as Dick was getting his license out of his wallet and asked, "Is everything all right?"

Perhaps he was wondering if we were having an emergency. Dick looked at me with a questioning expression. I thought of telling the patrolman where we'd been and why. Turning around to look at Carol, I watched her remove her earphones and tune in instead to what was going on in the front seat. She was sitting up looking perfectly normal. I couldn't help thinking, it's all right now. It was bad for a while and could have been worse. But it's all over and she's just fine, recuperating from surgery with a nose full of plastic, but it's OK now. You can do anything you want to us. My little girl is over the disease and is going to be hale and hearty from now on.

The patrolman must have sensed some apprehension because he asked again, "Is everything OK?"

Since I hadn't said anything and wasn't going to, Dick silently got my message. Smiling, he faced the man in uniform and said, "Yes, officer. Everything is fine."

The trooper looked to me for confirmation and I verbally agreed. He didn't give Dick a speeding ticket, but warned us to be careful, indicating that the patrolmen in the neighboring state would be on the lookout and might not be as inclined to let us go with just a warning.

Carol complained of little discomfort on the way home, and we were able to make a couple of sightseeing stops. One was at Sandia Peak in New Mexico for a tram ride, and another was at the Grand Canyon in Arizona. She was suitably impressed by the Grand Canyon. It was her first time there and she kept calling it, "incredible."

The day we were at the Grand Canyon was another bad day for me with my sore tooth. Dick and Carol left the car to walk over to a sightseeing spot. I stayed behind to take my pain pills, which can cause nausea and dizziness. I was having trouble on both counts, and when leaving the car to join them, I was carrying a small plastic cup of 7-Up™ and obviously unsteady on my feet. When I caught up with them, Dick and Carol were chuckling and couldn't wait to tell me that they'd overheard two old ladies who were watching me, thinking I was drunk and had something stronger than a soft drink in my cup. They were shaking their heads as one said to the other, "And this early in the morning, too." It was about 10:00.

Dick had been taking slides of our side trips. Some time later when we had occasion to view them carefully, we found it interesting that there was only a little change in the shape of Carol's nose in those pictures. Since the collapse of her bridge seemed to have taken place so soon afterwards, we believed that it probably happened right after the surgery; the Silastic™ must have been holding the bridge up as the scar tissue had been doing before. Chronic infection had caused the softening and eventual breakdown of the cartilaginous skeleton that had determined the shape of her nose.

---

11. A vasovagal reaction is sudden dizziness or fainting.

12. Marcus Welby was a character played by Robert Young in a television series, the epitome of the perfect doctor.

13. Silastic™, a word derived from a combination of silicone and plastic, developed and patented by John Holter, is a flexible inert silicone rubber used in prosthetic medicine.

14. Thoracic diseases are those related to the chest.

10

Short-Lived Elation

Within an hour after we arrived home, I phoned Dr. Haring's office to see if he was available to see Carol. I was anxious to tell him in person all that had happened. He was in that day and when Janet told him I was on the phone, he got on immediately.

"How did everything go?" he asked. "How's Carol?"

"I thought you might want to see for yourself. Can we bring her down to the office?" I asked excitedly.

"Come right on over," he said. "I'd like very much to see for myself. I'm anxious to hear all about the Mayo Clinic, too."

"We're on our way," I said, and hung up the phone.

The car hadn't even had time to cool off.

Janet ushered us into an examining room as soon as we got there, and the doctor was right behind her. Both she and Carla stayed to hear about the trip, with Janet only leaving momentarily when the phone rang, and returning to hear the rest of the story.

"You look great, Carol. Tell me all about your trip," he said.

Carol related her experience with and opinion of the clinic, the hospital, and the doctors.

"Dr. McDonald is speaking at a seminar here in Los Angeles in a couple of weeks, and he said he'd like to meet you," she told him.

"I know which one you mean and have already received the information. I had planned to attend this before, but now I'm especially eager to meet Dr. McDonald and compare notes.

"I don't want to disturb the Silastic™ or cause you any discomfort," he went on, "so I'm just going to peek inside your nose if you don't mind."

"Oh no, that's all right," Carol said. "It feels a little weird, but it doesn't hurt."

He put on his headband, turned on his flashlight and looked. Then he listened to Dick's and my versions of our clinic visit.

"I'm really delighted that things went so well for you," he said matching our enthusiasm. "I'm certainly pleased with the outcome as I know you are." Then specifically to Carol he said, "I want to remind you of the importance of irrigating."

"I know, I know," Carol said. "They even gave me another pink pig."

"It's important that you try to avoid hitting your nose …"

"Or getting punched in the nose," she interrupted, as we all laughed.

"Right," he said smiling. "Also, don't blow your nose. Let me know immediately if there's any bleeding or unusual pain."

"OK," she agreed. "Dr. McDonald told me that, too."

"At least they have their stories straight," Dick joked.

"I'd like to see you in about six weeks to remove the Silastic™," the doctor continued. "I don't see any reason why you can't go back to school. When does it start?"

"Registration is the day after tomorrow," she said.

"Carol misjudged the time classes were supposed to begin, and she has no time to spare getting back to Riverside and ready for the fall quarter," I said.

"Dr. McDonald said there wasn't a trace of Wegener's in his biopsies," Carol announced proudly.

"Yes," Dr. Haring said. "He told me that, too."

"Well," Dick said, "we'd better get home and unpack, and let the doctor take care of sick people."

We parted company with broad smiles on all our faces, happier than we'd been in years. I thought the worst was over and now we could all get on with our lives.

We had pulled into our driveway on Wednesday, and class registration was on Friday. After one day at home, Carol returned to her apartment and registered for her junior year. I wanted to go back with her in case she needed care or someone to clean her apartment. But she insisted she would be able to handle everything herself.

After she left, I worriedly told Dick, "Any kind of surgery is a shock to the body. I think she should rest as much as possible for a few weeks."

"Well," he answered, "the doctors seemed to feel that her going back to school shouldn't pose any problems, even with the Silastic™ stitched in her nose."

"That's true. I guess if two competent doctors say it's OK, who am I to question them?"

But old ideas die hard, and I was concerned. Things were better than they'd been for such a long time. I didn't want anything to ruin it.

My parents had been so worried about Carol that they drove west shortly after we got home, anxious to see for themselves that she was better. Rather than have them drive down to Riverside after their long trip, Carol came home to visit with them on the weekend.

"Are you sure you're all right?" I asked her.

She looked totally worn out.

"Stop worrying, Mom. I'm fine. I've been working very hard at school," she answered.

But she just didn't look fine.

After she left, I asked Dick, "Don't you think she looked pale and tired?"

"Yes, I do," he said. "But you have to remember it's been such a short time since the surgery, and I'm sure her body needs time to rebuild itself."

He was right, of course. A healthy body has the power of regeneration that one fighting a long-term disease hasn't.

"Well, I hope it's temporary and she'll look better when we see her next time."

"Carol is a good deal tougher than you think she is," Mom said.

Maybe it was unnecessary worrying. But that's a mother's right. I couldn't just turn it off.

At exactly four weeks to the day after the surgery, Carol called about 7:00 AM. She has most decidedly never been a morning person, and it was unusual to hear from her that early. The phone woke me up and I was groggy. A quick glance at the clock and a listen to an almost inaudible, "Mom?" on the other end of the phone told me I was hearing trouble.

"What's the matter, sweetheart? You don't sound good."

"Mom, my nose hurts again as if it was broken."

She sounded so pathetic. The disappointment was obvious in her voice.

"Stay put. I'll get some clothes on and come for you. It shouldn't take me too long."

"Thanks, Mom. I don't feel much like driving."

"Isn't this kind of early in the morning for you to be up?"

"I didn't sleep at all last night," she moaned. "It really hurt badly."

"Why didn't you call last night?"

"I thought it might get better or go away," she answered, "and I wouldn't have to bother you."

Why did she have to be so damn considerate?

"When it started getting light," she continued, "I figured it wasn't going to get better and maybe I needed you."

"I can't call Dr. Haring yet. The office isn't open this early."

I was thinking out loud, over the phone, waking up and gathering my wits about me.

"The answering service won't do us any good and there's no sense disturbing him at home. He can't do anything until he sees you. I'll call from your apartment. I should be able to reach someone by then," I continued.

I couldn't even let Dick know. He would still be on his way to work.

On the way down to Riverside, I kept thinking: It doesn't sound good. This shouldn't be happening. She shouldn't be in this much pain. Drainage from the sinuses should no longer be a problem.

For almost a month, the only problem the Silastic™ had given Carol was a feeling that was just a little weird, or so she had said. How could that feeling become fierce pain all of a sudden? Could it be an infection caused by her body rejecting the foreign material? But if that's true, why did it take a month to happen?

When I got to Carol's apartment, she looked about as bad as she had the last time—pale, eyes sunken back in her head, face puffy.

Oh no. Not again.

"Hi baby," I said lightly, putting my arms around her as she let me in the door.

"I'm glad you're here," she sighed.

"Have you eaten anything?"

"I had some toast. My stomach's a little queasy from the codeine. That's all I wanted."

"I'll bet the Silastic™ is causing the problem this time. I think it's been in long enough. Dr. Haring will probably take it out and put you in the hospital again."

Carol said nothing, but looked disgusted and despondent.

I called the doctor's office and Janet said, "Bring her right in; we'll be waiting."

We drove directly there. My suspicions were correct as they had been last May. Once again it seemed obvious we were dealing with a massive infection.

Dr. Haring took a quick look at her nose and felt her cheeks.

"It's slightly swollen. I think it's infected. The Silastic™ will have to come out," he said. "I'll try to hurt you as little as possible."

The doctor approached Carol with the instruments, and her body tensed up as she gripped the arms of the chair. She moaned softly as the tweezer-like instrument touched her, which I had since learned was called a nasal speculum. But Dr. Haring was so fast with Carla assisting that with three scissor snips, the Silastic™

and everything that was growing on it or stuck to it came out easily. The doctor placed what he had taken from Carol's nose in a metal tray for Carla to dispose of. The large amount of matter that he had removed should have given her some relief from the pressure. She seemed to relax slightly.

"I'd like to put you in the hospital for a couple of days. I think the Silastic™ was the cause of the trouble, but I'd like to be sure there's not something else going on in there," he said.

"I figured as much when I saw the shape she was in," I said.

"How long will I have to stay?" Carol asked.

"That depends on you," Dr. Haring answered. "You'll know when it's time to go home before I will."

He then wrote the necessary instructions, and we were on our way to hospital admissions.

Previously at the hospital, Carol had been given an identification card about the size of a credit card to carry with her. I noticed the hospital personnel make an imprint of it when she had outpatient tests. It also made the admission process quicker and easier. We had hoped there'd be no need to use it as an inpatient again.

Carol was placed in a private room and, knowing she would welcome the peace and quiet, I felt the extra cost once again would be worth it.

By letting the receptionist know ahead of time that Carol was in a lot of pain and needed to be in a bed as soon as possible, I probably speeded things up a bit. It didn't take as long as the last time.

When Carol was getting settled into her room, we were reminded that we were back in a facility that wasn't quite as concerned with patients as the Mayo Clinic was.

"We're not in Minnesota anymore," I told Carol.

It took making a fuss just to get her a pitcher of water. She hadn't had anything to eat with the exception of a piece of toast, and it was now the middle of the afternoon.

"You'll have to wait till dinner time," the nurse said, when Carol asked for something to eat and drink.

That's what you think, I thought. There was always the cafeteria, and plenty of restaurants close by had take-out. She would be fed.

After her vital signs were taken, which she again monitored—"What's my temperature? What's my blood pressure? What's my pulse rate?"—and was settled in her room, I caused enough of a disturbance to get her some soup and Jell-O™. We both agreed that would hold her until dinnertime.

Besides being hooked up to an antibiotic and glucose, she was provided with a face mask. From it was supposed to flow a combination of oxygen and warm, moist air to facilitate breathing. There were several times during this hospital stay that the respiratory therapists had to be summoned because the mask wasn't working properly. There weren't many people who could figure out how to make it work—a very frustrating situation.

It's a good thing she was being given the glucose because she didn't seem to eat much of anything during those few days.

I spent many hours at the hospital as I had done the last time, reading, doing paperwork or needlecraft, in order to be close to Carol, for whatever good it might do. Maybe she would just like to look up now and then and know that someone who loved her was near.

Spending long days at the hospital really wore me out, and kept me from taking care of many of my own personal needs. But I wouldn't have chosen to be anywhere else. My mother wasn't always there for me; I had to be there for my daughter. I had to break the cycle.

With all that time to think, some of my own childhood memories came flooding back to me.

I was about four or five years old. How could she have disappeared so quickly? One moment she was by my side; the next she was gone. My mother and I had gone on an excursion from which only one of us would return. I didn't know it then, but we were on our way to a children's home—an orphanage. My father had left us, Mom had to go to work, and Grandma was sick. There was no one to take care of me.

I remember sitting in a large, brightly lit office. A friendly woman dressed in a business suit had told me it was all right to play with the dollhouse. I'd never seen a more magnificent one: three stories high, completely furnished down to the grand piano with raised lid, area rugs, bathroom towels, and draperies on the windows. I looked but didn't touch.

After Mom and she talked for a while, we went outside to a courtyard. Actually it was just a small square of cement enclosed with a very high chain link fence. I looked away for just a moment, and Mom was gone. I remembered screaming hysterically all the while knowing it would do no good.

The weeks that followed were like a nightmare. The other children who lived there were older and didn't want to be my friends. They just wanted to tease me and push me around. Boys and girls got undressed and bathed in the same huge bathroom. I wasn't used to that. It was embarrassing.

When afternoon snack time arrived, bread and jam sandwiches were brought to us on trays with a choice of white or chocolate milk. The others always got there first, pushed me out of the way, and took what they wanted. The white bread sandwiches with the red jam would always be gone; so was the chocolate milk. All that was left for me was the dark bread with the yellow/orange jam and white milk. For a long time after we were married, Dick wondered why I never bought wheat bread or apricot jam.

The fire escape that afforded access to the building from the courtyard was off limits to the children except for emergencies. One afternoon, because I walked slowly and was always the last one into the building after recess, someone locked me outside. I had to climb the fire escape to get back into the building. Although I was reprimanded, not punished, I had been out in the cold damp air too long; nature doled out the punishment: an ear infection.

Once when my children were little and running in and out of the house, Ron locked the door and the rest of them couldn't come in. He probably still wonders why I came completely unglued and began screaming, "Don't ever lock anyone in this family out of the house as long as you live!"

To this day I know none of my children have ever locked each other out of anything since.

Lying in bed, trying to endure the pain in my ear, I wanted only one thing: my mother. The days passed so slowly, almost like years, as I lay in the crib-like bed. I hated having to look through the bars. It was nothing like my bed at home. However, in this children's home only the older or bigger children had beds without sides. It was humiliating.

The days dragged by till Mom came. I was so happy to see her I cried. That seemed to make her feel bad and she wanted to buy me a present. I wanted a coloring book and crayons, but was afraid if she left me to buy them she might not come back and I would never see her again. She promised she would come back and take me home. I had to believe her. She couldn't leave me and break her promise to her sick daughter.

She did come back with the coloring book and crayons. In a few days she took me home.

When I was alone with my favorite doll, I told her a secret and made a promise to myself. If I ever had a little girl and she got sick, I promised I would never leave her alone.

I have kept that promise and made sure to be there with Carol whenever she needed me, and for as long as she wanted me, until she chased me home. I don't know if it helped her, but it helped me to be there—just in case.

Although several of Carol's friends phoned her, she spoke to no one. Even the young man she had dated during the summer called. When he asked what she was in the hospital for, I told him she was being treated for a bad sinus infection. If he wanted more information he would have to get it from her.

Both Tracey and John were very concerned because they knew what she had been through already. They had been just as pleased as the rest of the family when they thought she was cured. Whenever they called, they wanted updates on her condition, which I gratefully supplied.

John was a chemistry major in the pre-med program at UCR and had looked up all the information he could find on Wegener's, what little there was at that time. He kept us informed as to his findings, but there wasn't anything we hadn't already heard about.

"Why isn't she being treated with cyclophosphamide?" he asked. "That's the recognized treatment for Wegener's."

"She doesn't have it anymore."

"Then what's her problem?"

"This is a result of having had the Silastic™ in her nose which, of course, is a foreign object. Her body decided it had harbored this foreigner long enough and began to reject it."

That explanation seemed to have satisfied John, even if only for the moment.

I told Dr. Haring about John and his research. Most doctors would have brushed it off as coming from an inexperienced, nosy kid who didn't know or understand anything about what was going on. But Dr. Haring was always so open-minded and so receptive to new ideas that he told us to tell John if he discovered anything new he would appreciate hearing about it.

It didn't seem as if those of us who visited were able to do much for Carol beyond helping her fill out tomorrow's menu choices. She didn't really seem to care what food was brought to her or, for that matter, if any food was brought at all. But it gave us something to do together.

She probably complied with choosing menu options to humor us, sensing our helplessness, hopelessness, and need to be of some assistance. We thought that this would be the last time she'd have to go through anything of this sort. After all, the disease was supposed to be gone, and the doctors, with the help of antibiotics, should be able to clear up an infection within a reasonable time.

"I'm going to contact Dr. McDonald," Dr. Haring told us, "and let him know what has happened. Perhaps he will be able to suggest something."

At Dr. Haring's next hospital visit he had this to report:

"I called Dr. McDonald and he suggested we try a new drug called Septra™.[15] He's had good luck using this for Wegener's patients."

Carol was given the new drug.

After three days, Dr. Haring felt the infection was under control, and Carol was feeling considerably better. He released her from the hospital.

"It's all right for you to go back to school, Carol," he told her.

I didn't agree. It was difficult for me to get over the feeling that more rest might have helped. But school was important to Carol and, if I'd learned anything by now, it was that she needed to be constructively active. Besides, since he knew what she'd been through, it was difficult for any of us to believe that Dr. Haring would agree to anything that would hurt her.

Ron drove her back to Riverside, since we'd left her car there. We all hoped we had seen the end of hospitals, IVs, etc. and that most of her—our—troubles were history.

During the weeks that followed, when we thought things were going great, Carol was actually only doing OK. Some days she was able to attend classes; some days she didn't even get out of bed. She had this bad habit of not wanting to worry us, so we didn't know how she was feeling. When she knows everything that can be done is being done, she's inclined to give the methods a chance.

In touch with us frequently, she told us things were OK, or maybe better. We were all aware that everything that was wrong was not going to become right overnight, so OK was something we had learned to live with.

Then there was a strange phone call from her.

"Mom, I don't know what happened to my car."

Thinking that something was mechanically wrong with it, I asked her, "What is it doing—or not doing?"

"No, Mom. Something happened to my car. It's not there."

"Not where?"

"Not in the carport."

Her apartment had assigned spaces for the tenants, and that's where she parked her car.

"When did you last see it?" I asked. "Did you loan it to someone?"

None of us had ever done that.

"No. Did any one of you come down here and borrow it?"

Although we have extra keys to all the cars in the family, none of us would borrow each other's car without asking, and certainly not when it meant driving an hour or two away to do it.

Then it sank in. Oh my God. As if she hadn't had enough troubles with her health …

"Your car's been stolen! Have you called the police?"

"Yes," she said, "and they came down here and took a report. They need to see some proof of ownership."

"That's easy. I can bring the papers down."

Thank goodness my files were well-organized.

"How long has it been since you used the car?"

"A few days," she answered.

That told me plenty. You don't go far in the Riverside area unless you're driving. That meant she hadn't been out of the apartment for a while and obviously hadn't been to classes, either. She was probably in bad shape again.

"Do you feel as rotten as you sound?" I asked.

"Well … this week hasn't been that great," she answered after a long pause.

"OK. I'll be on my way down in about half an hour. I want to call Daddy and see if there's anything he thinks should be done as far as the police are concerned."

"I'm really sorry about this, Mom."

"There's no need to apologize; it's not your fault, sweetheart."

We had paid off the loan on the car and had just dropped the collision and comprehensive insurance, keeping only the liability. If in fact it was stolen, we were out of luck.

When Dick heard from me about the latest catastrophe, he said, "Stop at the police station and make sure they have any information they might need about the car," he offered. "Then get a copy of the police report before you pick Carol up. That way she won't have to wait. She must be feeling pretty rotten again if she hasn't been out of the apartment for a few days."

That was a good idea. If they kept me waiting any length of time, Carol wouldn't have to be uncomfortable.

Once more I was on my way down to Riverside. Under the circumstances, Carol certainly couldn't come to us.

I followed Dick's suggestion and stopped at the police station first, giving them the information they wanted and obtaining a copy of the police report. Then I picked Carol up and brought her back home to recuperate from her latest crisis.

We never saw the car again, nor did we ever hear anything about it. To add insult to injury, the casualty loss rules had been changed by the IRS at the beginning of the year. We weren't even able to deduct the loss on our income tax return.

Carol was naturally very upset and perhaps thought we might blame her in some way. We tried to make it plain, putting everything in perspective, that if we could get her health back for her, losing one thousand cars wouldn't bother us. It certainly wasn't her fault that the car had been stolen. She and the boys were so conscientious about locking things up that they often locked the cars in a locked garage.

While Carol was home we went shopping for another car for her. Then we shared the available remaining cars with each other for about a week while she returned to school.

She chose a small, four-wheel-drive car, assuming she would be well enough to go skiing during the coming winter. We weren't about to discourage those thoughts. All along we had been told that she would get well. I believed it then, and I believe it now. It would be impossible to face tomorrow if I didn't.

Living in southern California, it's impossible to survive without a car, which is frequently the only means of transportation. It's often been said that in that part of the country the gas pedal is an extension of the foot. Carol came home to pick up her new car, gave back the one she had been using, and then returned to school. During all these happenings, she was still taking the Septra™.

Five days after that, her phone call described these new symptoms: "I've been hot and cold, perspiring and shivering. I'm completely covered with a rash, and I have one of the worst headaches I've ever had."

I phoned Dr. Haring before leaving for Riverside.

"Carol seems to have a fever and a rash," I reported.

Janet wasted no time in putting the doctor on the phone. I repeated the information.

"If she hasn't already done so, have her discontinue the Septra™ immediately. Instead of coming to the office, take her directly to the hospital emergency room. Have them call me when you arrive. I'll order some tests and they can get started on them right away."

After filling Dick in on the latest, I was back on the road again. During the two-hour drive, there's a lot of time to think, and my mind took full advantage of it. There was no doubt as to where she was headed after I picked her up. But why?

I mentally reviewed her childhood illnesses. When she was very young, just barely able to sit up, Carol had suffered a lot of ear infections. When one of the first ones occurred, she was just a few months old. She kept batting at or pulling on her ear with her hand. When I told the doctor about that, he said she was trying to tell me that her ear hurt, an unusually smart reaction for someone so young. Just about the time the pediatrician decided it would be advisable to remove her tonsils, the earaches stopped.

She had a couple of bouts of pneumonia and numerous asthma attacks.

Nothing had ever kept Carol down for long. The doctors frequently said how brave she was, and we probably took it for granted.

She hadn't had the measles. Could the rash be that? The boys had that disease before she was born. It probably wasn't that. As a baby, she had been given the necessary preventative shots.

The rash, she had said, was flat and didn't itch. That meant it wasn't chicken pox. The boys had that disease before she was born, also.

She'd already had German measles, but it's possible to get them more than once.

It could also be a reaction to the Septra™. I'm allergic to sulfa, one of the components of Septra™, and so is my mother.

Ron drove down with me so he could drive her new car home. I was not about to leave it unattended in the spot where the last one had been stolen.

My poor baby sounded so desperate. How much can one small human being take? Most twenty-one-year-olds were getting ready for graduation, planning for the future, or settling down with a spouse and having children. Carol was just trying to get from one week to the next without another crisis.

"Before we go home," she asked, "can we stop by the campus so I can cancel my reservation for the All-Cal?"

It broke my heart to hear her ask that. Every year UCR joined with seven other UC campuses during winter break for what they called the All-Cal Winter Carnival. Several busloads of students were transported to a popular ski resort, often in Colorado.

"It doesn't look like I'll be able to go, and I don't want to keep someone else from going who might be able to use my reservation."

It was so like her to be considerate of others even when it looked like her own world was falling apart. Canceling the trip was the last thing she wanted to do. She enjoyed those trips so much and always looked forward to them.

"Will they return your money?"

"I hope so," she said. "They'll probably keep a portion as a cancellation fee."

She saw a few people she knew on campus and, in spite of her rash, fever, and pain she stopped to chat with them. She didn't want them to think she was unfriendly or ignoring them. I marveled once again at her thoughtfulness.

The drive home was a difficult one for me. I can't remember seeing her look worse. Her face was flushed, her hair needed washing, and her eyes had gray rings around them. I wanted nothing more than to cuddle her in my arms and kiss away her pain like I did when she was little. But she had long since drawn the line on cuddling. Unless it was hello or goodbye, she shied away from being touched at all.

It was so hard to act only slightly concerned, like most mothers do when their child has a rash or fever. But here we were again, dealing with who knows what.

She was freezing and wanted the heat on; I needed the air conditioning. She was hurting and needed to rest; I wanted to know the details of what had happened—when did the rash first appear, when did the fever start, how high was it, and whether her nose was better or worse.

This had been going on for a day or two before she called me. She was worried and tried hard not to show me; I was worried and tried hard not to show her. We were a sorry pair.

I wanted to scream: Why didn't you call for help? You know I'm there for you always.

"I really feel dumb, Mom, having to keep calling you to come get me. It's embarrassing and it's such a big deal for you to have to drive two hours each way."

"Have I complained? Besides, who else would you call if not your mother?"

It didn't matter how many times I had to drive the two hours to get her. If it would have helped her I would have driven to the moon and back—anything to get her back on her feet and on with her life.

She was trying so hard to be brave and to handle her problems without giving us something new to worry about. Her desire not to add to the family's apprehensions had caused her self-imposed isolation.

All I could think of to ask her, without starting a scene, which she certainly didn't need, was, "Are you hungry?"

We couldn't even take her temperature because none of us thought to buy her a thermometer.

It was after office hours when we arrived at the emergency room. We were informed that Dr. Haring had phoned in instructions. He had ordered blood and urine tests for Carol.

For the first time, Carol had a discussion with a laboratory technician about the way her blood was to be drawn. She was beginning to have trepidations regarding strangers with hypodermic needles and vials.

It's not uncommon in people who've had numerous blood tests for their veins to actually shift or move away from a needle that's being inserted. After the technician failed to find a vein that didn't shift, Carol barked, "I'm tired of being practiced on by someone who can't find veins. Send in a person who knows what they're doing; you can practice on other patients."

Frequently, those attending to a patient's needs in hospitals fail to recognize the patients' fears or how much pain they're experiencing.

My sweet-tempered daughter had never insulted anyone in the past. I was witnessing the plight of a grown woman who had been through hell with no end in sight, and she was not about to be unnecessarily abused. Always having been proud of the way she had handled uncomfortable situations in the past, I had to admit that this was no exception. She said and did what she felt was appropriate. It was her body, and she was determined not to let anyone hurt her any more than was absolutely necessary.

"I just came from a soccer game," Dr. Haring announced as he came through the door. He named two of his children who had been playing and, of course, Carol knew to whom he was referring.

"I left them in the car. When I told them I was going to take care of you, they promised to be good," he said. "When I didn't hear from you earlier, I knew the hospital would page me."

Before telling the doctor about her latest ailment, Carol asked him if their team had won. She had become very fond of his family and it seemed that the feeling was mutual.

"I told my wife about this," he said, referring to the rash, fever, and headache, "and she said, 'Can't you do something for her?'"

We all felt no one was trying harder to do something for her than he was.

After examining Carol, the doctor left the room for a short while. When he returned he told us, "I've taken the liberty of calling Dr. Ellsworth Pryor. He's an infectious disease specialist. At this point, I don't know if these symptoms are related to Wegener's, the Septra™, or something new and different."

"I'm allergic to sulfa and so is my mother. I'll bet that's what Carol's trouble is," I said.

Dr. Haring shrugged and said, "Dr. Pryor should be arriving shortly. He was eating dinner when I called. I'm going to take my children home and I'll be back in a little while. I'm having Carol placed in isolation until we can determine what she has."

That took care of the private room option. Carol was wheeled into a room in an isolated part of the hospital. A hospital gown over my clothes was required every time I was with her, just in case she had anything that was contagious. By this time Dick had joined us, also wearing a gown. We looked like a pair of bookends.

I think she welcomed being in the hospital this time. She seemed scared and angry, and was feeling rotten.

Dr. Pryor arrived shortly. He was a soft-spoken short, slender black man with tight curly hair. He seemed to be very low key.

He examined Carol with me in the room, and then began asking her questions, getting a history of what had gone on for the past five years. But I didn't get the chance to tell him my version of what had happened to Carol during that period of time.

"I can tell him, Mom."

I shut my mouth and listened to her account of the events leading up to her present admittance to the hospital. However, during her retelling of the story, it seemed to me she had left some things out which might be important. It was the first time I realized that our viewpoints about some details and time sequences were slightly different. It occurred to me that it would have been a good idea to have kept a journal or made a list of what had happened to her, with dates, to assist the doctors in the event that this was going to be more drawn out than we'd originally thought. I made a mental note to make that list. That was probably the beginning of this book.

Dr. Pryor ordered some more blood tests in addition to the ones Dr. Haring had, and gave us some inkling of what he thought the present problem might be. Even though he was only guessing, at least he was doing it out loud. I'd begun to appreciate doctors who didn't see the point of keeping us in the dark.

"It's one of three things," he said, "A, a strange virus; B, toxic shock syndrome; or C, an adverse reaction to the Septra™."

We had been hearing about young girls using tampons during their menstrual cycle and experiencing toxic shock.

My vote was for a reaction to the Septra™.

"You've been to the Mayo Clinic," he continued, "and I'm just a little nobody from Valencia, California, but I'd like to know why Carol isn't being seen regularly by a rheumatologist."

He looked at me for an answer.

Neither of us had one for him. It was strictly a personality conflict with the local rheumatologist.

It was time to insert an IV again. She was getting a little smarter about the hook-ups. When a technician approached, Carol began asking for a pediatric needle.

Being small and slim meant she didn't have a lot of fleshy spots on her body to stick needles into. She was also getting so—as she put it—"sick and tired of incompetent people hurting me."

She'd had enough of her own pain without others adding to it. When the technician began to question Carol's suggestion of a pediatric needle, she didn't bother to argue. Instead she ordered, "Please send in the head nurse."

When the head nurse arrived, Carol asked her, "Would you please put the IV in yourself? You'll probably need a pediatric needle. I have very small veins."

The nurse looked at Carol's hands, arms and wrists and agreed that a pediatric needle was a good idea.

Considering Carol had done such a good job of speaking up for herself, Dick and I felt confident about leaving her when we walked out of the hospital that night. She would get what she needed, even if she had to cause a commotion to do so. If feelings had to be hurt, they weren't going to be hers.

Outside the hospital, she was a lamb; inside, lying in a bed, she had turned into a lion.

This hospital stay was one of the most difficult for Carol, and for us, also. She stayed through Thanksgiving, and we missed her dreadfully at the dinner table. Because it didn't seem fair to the boys not to, I cooked the traditional dinner, but in a slip-shod way, and we ate it half-heartedly. Turkey had always been one of her favorite foods.

When Ken walked in to see her, he pointed to the two bags hanging from the IV pole and asked, "Which one is the turkey and dressing, and which one is the pumpkin pie?"

Ken was able to spend more time with her during this incarceration, as he called it, and it was obvious that this helped her morale.

Don and Ron were up to see her every day, and that helped, too.

Because it was a holiday weekend, Dick and I were both there so much that she began to chase us home, saying, "You don't have to stay here with me. Don't you have better things to do, like Christmas shopping?"

One day when we were on our way to the hospital, one of our neighbors called a greeting to us as we were getting into the car.

"I see you're off Christmas shopping again," he said.

"I wish we were," I said.

We brought him up to date on what had been happening with Carol. The last time we had spoken to him, we had just returned from the Mayo Clinic, thinking everything was and would continue to be fine. He, like so many other friends we would see while this was going on, hardly knew what to say. We had not gone out of our way to let people outside the family know about Carol's illness and the course it took because we knew Carol didn't want visitors other than family in the hospital.

Like the previous hospital stay, she was given a breathing mask with oxygen and water vapor to assist her breathing and soothe her nasal passages. Also like the last time, the apparatus worked intermittently, and the technicians had to be called often. They even had trouble getting the elastic that held the mask on adjusted properly.

What upset us the most was that no one seemed to give a damn. One should have been able to feel secure in the treatment they or their loved ones were receiving in a hospital. With breathing apparatus that didn't work, and no one attempting to fix it, how secure can it make you feel?

We had no heart for Christmas shopping, but knew we had to do some for our out-of-town relatives, and to be fair to the boys, too. Besides, when she was feeling better, Carol would appreciate her presents.

When we were with her, we would try to feed her, cut her food when necessary, talk to her when she felt like it, or just be there if she needed a runner because the response wasn't quite as quick as she wished when she pushed the call button. Regardless of what the hospital staff thought of Carol, I was pretty sure they couldn't wait to get rid of me.

When your child tells you she can't stand the pain, and what she's being given doesn't seem to be doing the job, you feel so helpless yourself. I decided that there was no devil because I'd offered to sell my soul to him so many times for some relief for her. If watching your child suffer and standing by helpless doesn't tear your heart out, what will? It seemed as though nothing would alleviate the headaches Carol continued to have.

She was given shots of Demerol™ periodically, but it might as well have been sterile water for all the good it was doing.

In desperation, after several days, Dr. Pryor said, "I'd like to do a lumbar puncture.[16] Do you have any objections?"

I had none.

It was such a hopeless feeling. Would things ever get better? Would Carol ever be pain free again? Deep down inside I knew they had to get better because nothing could be worse than constant pain.

If a spinal tap would help give the doctor answers, none of us were going to object. Carol was certainly willing to try anything.

"May I stay and watch?" I asked.

He shrugged his shoulders.

"If you want to," he said.

While the doctor was getting the tray, a nurse prepared Carol by washing her back, and painting it with an antiseptic solution. Then she told Carol to curl her body up into a fetal position.

"That will separate your vertebrae and make it easier for the doctor to get the needle in," she explained.

The doctor returned with the tray and unwrapped the equipment.

Getting in front of Carol, the nurse helped hold Carol's knees up to her chest, chatting all the while to try to take her mind off what was happening.

I was seated toward Carol's back near a window. It was a bright sunny day outdoors. Besides the natural light, the nurse had turned on all the lights in the room.

I watched as Dr. Pryor inserted a hollow needle into the lumbar portion of the spinal canal. The cerebrospinal fluid began to fill the needle and drip out of the end, like water from a tap, into a vial. That's probably why the procedure is often referred to as a spinal tap.

When Dr. Pryor had collected as much fluid as he needed, he withdrew the needle and held some sterile cotton on the puncture until it was replaced by a bandage. Then he held the vial up to the window. As the sun streamed in through the glass, the fluid was so clear it almost sparkled.

"This looks good," he remarked. "I'll send it to be analyzed, but I don't think our problem is here."

"I could have told you that, Doctor," I said. "I watch all the medical shows, and if the spinal fluid is clear, we're not in trouble, are we?"

He just grinned at me and shook his head.

Whatever was causing Carol's current troubles was still in question. The spinal tap didn't give the doctor any answers.

"These procedures are quite painful," the nurse said to Carol. "You're a very brave lady."

Once again she didn't shed a tear. We never heard her utter so much as a whimper or a gasp. How does she stand it?

I noticed the nurse's name tag; her name was familiar.

"You used to sell real estate, didn't you?" I asked, remembering she had previously worked for the same real estate company that I currently did.

"I sure did," she answered.

"Since they're both people businesses, which do you like better?" I asked.

"Oh, nursing, without a doubt."

"Why?"

"Because when I walk out of here after my shift, I'm finished until the next time," she said. "No one bothers me for the next sixteen hours. It's different with real estate. The buyers and sellers own you. They call you at all hours of the day and night with their petty fears, and God help you if you've gone shopping and are not available. They think you've deserted them.

"I'll take nursing any day. You don't make as much money, but you're not paying for it with the aggravation."

I had never thought about my job in quite that way. When I returned from the Mayo Clinic I knew that I had gone sour on selling real estate, but I hadn't been ready to admit it or rationalize it even to myself.

She had vocalized my experiences—the feeling of being owned by the clients. I had no time or energy left these days to devote to them. I'm an all-or-nothing person, and I gave more to my clients than most of the other realtors I knew.

One evening, as a nurse was adjusting the flow of Carol's IV, bells began ringing indicating a dire emergency, and she took off down the hall. The liquid had been flowing much too quickly and now it was totally out of control. Within minutes, Carol's hand began to swell.

"We better see if we can find someone to fix this," Dick exclaimed, and we both went running madly around the hospital in different directions looking for someone capable of re-adjusting the flow. We finally found a nurse and almost dragged her into Carol's room to make the necessary adjustment just in time to prevent some major emergency of our own. Carol had been squeezing the IV tube with the fingers of her other hand to slow it down.

"What in the hell would have happened if we hadn't been here?" I asked Dick.

"And she had been unconscious," he added.

How dare the staff neglect one patient for another?

The nurse that adjusted it looked at Carol's hand and remarked, "That's not too bad. The swelling should go down shortly."

She had helped us and I didn't want to sound ungrateful. But I wondered how concerned she would have been if it were her own daughter. A vein could easily burst under those circumstances.

Soon thereafter, Carol learned how to work the electronic gadgets on the IV pole, and to adjust the flow herself. As long as she was awake, she was determined never to let that happen to her again.

After a couple of days in bed, Carol asked me, "Do you think you could help me wash my hair? A one-handed sponge bath is hard enough, but I don't think I can handle a one-handed shampoo."

She'd always been so fastidious about her grooming, so this was a good sign.

"You're right," I agreed. "A one-handed shampoo is out of the question. I'll bring your shampoo when I come back this evening, and we'll find a way."

After dinner I went searching for a suitable place to take Carol for her shampoo.

"I found a room that has a large, low sink. There's even a plastic pitcher in there. I'm ready if you are."

Although Carol had been hooked up to IVs, she was allowed off the bed to go to the bathroom.

"Are you walking or should I scrounge up a wheelchair?"

"I can walk," she said. "just take it slow."

All three of us—Carol, her IV pole, and I—went down the hall and around the corner to the special room where the forbidden task was performed—forbidden because the nurses or aides wouldn't allow it without the doctor's permission. We kept forgetting to ask and didn't want anyone to call any of the doctors for something non-medical. They probably wouldn't have bothered the doctors anyway.

We knew how important it was that we not get the arm with the IV wet. Also, we both made sure that the bag hanging from the IV pole was not too close to running out. If the bag was almost empty, the electronic equipment it was hooked up to would start to beep. The first time it happened, I panicked.

"I'd better hurry and get this done so we can get you back. They don't have any idea where we are."

"Don't worry about it, Mom. If the beeping drives them crazy because they don't know where it's coming from, that will be my revenge for all the times they're slow to answer the call button. Some of them act like they're doing me a favor if they get me a drink or another blanket."

Our excursions down the hall became the highlight of her evenings.

After that, each time we snuck out of her room to wash her hair I later reported the incident to whichever doctor appeared first after the dastardly deed had been performed. He always gave us his OK after the fact. Each doctor's comment was usually something to the effect that whatever was going to make her feel better was all right with him.

When the headaches were tolerable, and Carol was able to eat a day's worth of meals, she was released. She had been hospitalized for four days. Although no diagnosis had been determined, the doctors felt there was no reason to keep her. By this time, I'm certain there was no doubt in Dr. Haring's mind that if anything was amiss, he would be at the top of my phone call list.

Dr. Haring made a point several times of telling me that whenever Carol needed him, he would be available.

"Don't hesitate to call at any time. Besides normal office hours," he said, "I can see Carol on weekends, after office hours, in the middle of the night, or whenever you or Carol feel it's necessary. At no time will you be disturbing me."

He had even told us where he would be on Thanksgiving day and gave us a phone number in case we needed him.

After Carol was released from the hospital, she told me, "I'm going to withdraw from school for the rest of the quarter. I've missed so much of the instruction that I really have no choice."

When she told Dr. Haring, he said, "I know how much school means to you and what a difficult decision this is."

In a way, it was admitting defeat, even though we all believed it would be temporary.

This was the first time Carol had to be hospitalized not because of her illness but because of the treatment for it.

Remembering how Carol enjoyed working with computers, one Saturday morning Dr. Haring showed up on our doorstep with two of his children by his side and a computer in his arms.

"When they found out I was bringing this to Carol," he said, "they wanted to come and visit. I hope you don't mind."

I couldn't believe my eyes. He couldn't have looked more like an angel if he had sprouted wings.

"A doctor friend of mine rented this for a few months and discovered that he wasn't using it," he explained. "This place where he rented it wasn't going to give him a refund for turning it in early. When I heard that, I told him I knew someone who would make good use of it for the remainder of the time."

She was absolutely thrilled with it. Although she had told me a lot about what computers could do and what she could do with them, I finally had an opportunity to see for myself and was genuinely impressed, more with what she knew about them than what they could do. It was hard to believe that a doctor would go to that much trouble for a patient. But then both doctor and patient are very special people.

With all the time spent at the hospital, in doctors' offices, or on the road with Carol, I was beginning to find that my job was too much to handle, and I began to think about doing some withdrawing of my own.

One evening, a client who was purchasing a house called to express the fear that the roof on the home she was buying might not last for more than ten years. She made such a fuss about it as I listened and then tried to placate her. All the while I kept thinking, you're worried about a roof which can always be replaced, and I have a child whose irreplaceable life may very well be in danger. My patience with other people's problems was ebbing.

After I hung up and explained to Dick what had been said, I commented, "Someone's making a living shouldn't have to be based on another person's whim. Some people are looking for the impossible and I'm tired of trying to get it for them."

"If that's the way you feel about it, quit," he said, being logical again.

Evening calls from clients were a way of life in my business, but it began to appear to me that their problems were so totally insignificant compared to the one I had at home.

That night I decided to take a leave of absence from work until things settled down at home. I was emotionally wrung out but I couldn't show it to my clients or even to the family. I had to hold myself together because it was obvious that my emotional strength—or that which I'd led everyone to believe I had—was needed at home. Something had to give in order to relieve the pressure I felt, and the job seemed to be first in line.

I turned my work over to my friend and colleague, Sandy, and gave notice. I was confident she could handle both her business and mine along with the clients.

I also resigned or took a leave of absence from other extracurricular activities, including the Toastmistress Club that I had helped to organize and was currently serving as the vice president and program chairman. The previous year, I'd been elected to the local Read Estate Board as a director and resigned from that, too. I wanted to devote my daytime energy to Carol, and felt that whatever was left over should be for the rest of the family, and not the outside world.

I wasn't the only one that stress was taking its toll on. I noticed some serious differences in Dick's well-being, also. He'd always been one of those exceptionally healthy human beings who rarely took time away from work unless he came down with something like the flu and couldn't stand up. Twice within the past month he'd had to call me to come to the office in Pasadena, an hour's drive from home, and pick him up because he wasn't feeling well enough to drive. He looked so tired lately. Worrying about what was happening to Carol wore us both down.

The thought occurred to me that it was time to consider putting the house up for sale and moving closer to Dick's work. If I wasn't going to work, the clientele I had built up through the years wouldn't mean a thing. That had been the prime reason for staying in Valencia.

All the reasons for moving were good ones. It would mean we were an hour closer to UCR for Carol when she was able to return. All her doctors assured us it was a *when* and not an *if* regarding her returning to college. We would be an hour closer to Ken, too. It looked like the time was right for a move.

Don and Ron had plans to move out on their own if we moved to Pasadena, so a commute for them wasn't even a consideration. The whole idea was beginning to look better by the minute and we began to verbally kick it around.

Meanwhile both Drs. Haring and Pryor had decided not to use Septra™ for a while. It was too bad because they could see a marked improvement in Carol's nose. They indicated that it would be putting the Septra™ to a good test to try it again at a later date. If there was a reaction, it would certainly tell them what had caused the most recent problem.

Carol was to remain on heavy doses of antibiotics. She went back to college long enough to withdraw from the quarter—she had missed too much. We were all sorry, but I felt it would take some of the pressure off her. Then she could concentrate on getting well and resume her studies after the first of the year.

Ten days after Carol had discontinued the Septra™, the doctors decided to try that drug again. Dr. Pryor had now become regularly involved in Carol's case and would continue to be until we had resolved the drug reaction or infection problem one way or the other. Carol was to begin taking the Septra™ again on Saturday, December 3rd. 1983 was drawing to a close; we were happy to see it go.

---

15.   Septra™ is a combination of trimethoprim and sulfamethoxazole.

16.   Lumbar puncture, commonly referred to as a spinal tap, is the introduction of a hollow needle and stylet into the subarachnoid space of the lumbar portion of the spinal canal.

11

The Culprit is Found

Shopping together for clothes, shoes, etc. had become one of Carol's and my favorite pastimes through her high school years.

When she learned to drive, and later when she got her own car, and even later when she went off to college, Dick asked, "Why is she still going shopping with you instead of one of her friends?"

"I don't know and I don't care," I answered. "I'm not going to look a gift horse in the mouth. Many girls her age have nothing to do with their mothers and I don't want to put the idea in her head to go with someone else."

Curiosity got the better of me, though, and after she had gone shopping with someone at school I asked her, "Why don't you shop with your friends more often?"

"Because you always tell me the truth about what looks good or lousy on me while I'm trying it on, whether I want to hear it or not. A friend will say that everything I try on looks great because they don't want to hurt my feelings. But if you think an outfit doesn't do anything for me, you say so."

Luckily, she does the same for me. I know I've chosen the wrong thing when she says, "You don't want that, Mom. It makes you look like an old lady."

The day she was to begin the Septra™ again, we started out on a shopping excursion. Dick used to laughingly tell anyone who called looking for either of us that when we went shopping we could be gone for days.

She took one dose only of the Septra™ as we headed for the stores. Usually Dick didn't go with us, but this time he did.

We were about an hour past her ingestion of the medicine when she complained her head was starting to hurt.

Dick and I were in the checkout line with the clothes we had chosen.

"Give me the car keys," Carol said. "I want to lie down."

That was unusual. She had never done that before. It would have been so easy because my car had an electric reclining passenger seat. But she hadn't used it in the down position all those times she had been picked up in Riverside. Even coming home from Rochester, I don't remember her lying down at all.

"Let's forget about these things," I said, referring to the clothes we had intended to purchase. "We can come back and get them another time."

"No. Go ahead and pay for them. I'll be OK," she said, and left for the parking lot.

After a minute or two, I decided to let Dick battle the rest of the check-out line himself, and went out to the car to see how she was. In the few minutes it took me to reach the car, she was beside herself; she looked awful. The pain was evident on her face, her eyes were red-rimmed, and it was as if she couldn't sit still.

"My head hurts really, really bad, Mom," she cried.

It was the first time I'd seen tears rolling down her cheeks since she was a child. She had been through so much pain and frustration in the past five years, and I'd never seen her cry before this. My heart was breaking for her.

Dick couldn't have been more than five minutes behind me. I had some codeine in my purse and said, "Let's get a drink for her at the drive-in across the street. She can take a pill."

She took the codeine and we immediately started for home. By the time we got there, about a half hour later, she was crying hysterically and yelling, "I can't stand it; it hurts so bad."

It was difficult not to be hysterical myself. I wanted to take her in my arms and hold her tight enough to squeeze the pain away. But she hurt so badly, she couldn't stand being touched at all.

She walked into the house and went straight to bed. She took another codeine, even though I knew we should wait four hours between doses—something had to be done to give her relief.

Then I called Dr. Haring's answering service and was put through immediately.

"Give her the pain pills I prescribed, and see if they help," he said.

"She's already taken two," I told him, relating how and when the pills had been administered.

"Give them just a little more time," he said. "I'm on my way to pick up my children, but I'll be wearing my beeper, and will be available all afternoon and evening."

We waited for a short while, hoping the pain pills would take effect, but it was as if she'd taken sugar pills. They offered no relief at all.

"It hurts worse than anything has ever hurt before," she moaned.

"Maybe you need a hug to go along with the medicine," I said and held her and rocked her for a while, hoping it would help her to relax and calm down.

As we rocked back and forth there on her bed in each other's arms, it reminded me of a cartoon book the children had when they were young. It was drawn by Bil Keane who draws the "Family Circus" cartoon and entitled *I Need a Hug.* That title had almost become the family mantra. Oh how I wished the old healing methods of a hug and a kiss still worked like they used to.

After a while, she pulled away and said, "I'm sorry, Mom. It's just not working. I'd rather not be touched at all."

By that time I, too, realized the pills weren't working either, and was not about to give her any more.

I went back to phone Dr. Haring's service again. I had already decided to use the home phone number stashed away in case of an emergency if the answering service wasn't fast enough. But it wasn't necessary. He was on the line in seconds, ready, waiting, anticipating.

"Bring her to the emergency room," he said.

By this time the car must have known the way to the hospital with or without me.

We arrived at almost the same time as the doctor.

While lying on the examining table, Carol lifted her blouse to show me her stomach.

"I'm starting to get a rash again," she said.

"There's absolutely no doubt now as to what the cause is," I said.

Dick and the doctor agreed.

Her rash, fever, and headache from two weeks ago were all back after only *one* dose of Septra™.

Looking back, I don't know how I made it through that afternoon except that I was stronger than I thought. But if I became hysterical she would have been worse off than she already was.

Whatever good the Septra™ did for her nose wasn't going to make any difference. It was obvious that the rest of her body couldn't tolerate it. This was not a symptom of the disease; it was an illness caused once again by the treatment.

She was back in the hospital for another four difficult days. She was not only feeling worse than she had ever felt before, she was angry. All of us had believed that these troubles were over. With everything that had occurred, it was more than likely the disease was full blown again. She was not in remission any more, but having a major relapse.

We knew she couldn't continue the way she was going, but we weren't quite sure of the direction to take. It was like the pieces of a puzzle all beginning to fit together, and none of us liked the picture. If the previous surgery at the Mayo Clinic was going to open Pandora's Box, it had done a great job.

There were phone calls from her friends again, but Carol spoke to no one. The young man she'd met while she was working at the summer job called her again also, and it was difficult to skirt the problem. This was the second hospital stay that he knew of in just a few short weeks. Once again I told him nothing about the disease and said it was a bad reaction to some medicine she'd taken. It wasn't a lie, but it certainly wasn't the whole truth, either. I felt, however, that it was her decision as to who should know what. After all, it was her life. He was probably the only one of her friends who didn't know the whole story. I wondered if she avoided telling him because of a lack of self esteem or a feeling that an illness is a manifestation of inadequacy. She never told me; I never asked.

Her friend, John, questioned me again. "Why hasn't cyclophosphamide been considered? And since Wegener's granulomatosis is an autoimmune disease, why haven't you taken Carol to an immunologist?"[17]

"It was never suggested. We've been getting good care from ENTs."

"My niece was seen by an army of doctors before a treatment decision was made," he continued. "Since Wegener's is so rare, why hasn't Carol been seen by a large number of doctors instead of just a few?"

"John, your niece was a baby," I said. "She couldn't tell the doctors what hurt. Cyclophosphamide isn't being used because we were told the Wegener's was no longer active."

"Then how come she's so sick?" he asked. Then, as an afterthought, concerned that he might be stepping out of line, he added, "Listen, I'm just at the beginning of the study of medicine and a long way from practicing. I'm not questioning your decisions or asking you to justify anything you've done. It's just so frustrating, and I've been so worried about her. There must be something that can be done. You know, I've been doing a lot of research on this disease."

"I know. Carol told me. Dr. Haring would like to know if you discover anything new or different. Believe me, we understand your concern and frustration. Dick and I are feeling the same thing."

His questions made me feel like an ostrich again that just lifted her head from the sand. Those were questions we should be asking the various doctors.

I knew that cyclophosphamide was the recognized treatment for Wegener's. It wasn't being used because we'd all believed that Carol no longer had that disease.

But if she didn't have Wegener's, what did she have? Why was she so sick, with little or nothing helping?

The day after Carol was released she wanted to drive, by herself, to visit the young man from work. He lived in a neighboring town, about forty-five minutes away and she planned to spend the night. I was adamant about not wanting her to go.

"What if you're halfway there and don't feel like driving? What if you need medical attention during the night?" I asked.

A dozen more questions arose, but it didn't do me any good. Carol had made up her mind that she was going.

"Do you want to lock me in my room and chain me to the bedpost?" she asked.

Well, obviously that was not a plausible plan, although I considered it for about 30 seconds. The two of us had locked horns and neither wanted to back down. It was an uncomfortable situation because we usually got along so well.

It was time again to call Mom and ask her opinion. I needed reassurance that my objections were valid because I wasn't getting any support from Dick. He was perfectly willing to let Carol go.

"If she feels well enough," he said, "it's a good indication that she is well enough."

But again, Mom didn't back me up. I wonder now why I kept asking her opinion if it never agreed with mine. She did give me some advice though, two words of which I've had to remind myself on so many occasions since then: "Let go."

"You have taught your daughter well, and she's extremely capable and level-headed. She's been through so much," Mom said, "that she isn't going to do anything to put herself back into the hospital."

In retrospect, I believe Carol wanted to get away from anything and everything that reminded her that she was sick, including us. Bed had become her jail with me as her warden. If she couldn't handle a situation, whether it was driving halfway somewhere, a middle of the night emergency, or something more monumental, she knew where help could be found. My trying to keep her close to home was not going to make her well, any more than tying her to the bedpost and feeding her chicken soup.

While Mom's advice was not what I wanted to hear, I guess I had it coming. Most of the time she didn't give an opinion, but pushed me toward making my own decision. My child-rearing efforts were different; when my children asked for an opinion, they got it.

I had always been able to find a way to make the children well when they were sick, but felt so helpless this time, as if I had failed Carol. Why couldn't I find an answer for her? It never occurred to me that there might not be one.

That same afternoon my sister, Doris, called from Las Vegas. She had come from Michigan to attend a convention with her husband, Gene. When we discussed it months before, Dick and I had planned to join them there before all these problems with Carol had resurfaced. Doris and I had not been together for a very long time, and we were overdue for a visit.

Since Carol had been in such bad shape, we couldn't begin to think about leaving town. When Doris learned what had gone on since we'd returned from the Mayo Clinic, she was shocked. So many of our friends and relatives thought, as we did after that trip, that Carol was cured, or at least on the mend, and that most of her health problems were behind her.

Doris had wanted to let us know that her son would be getting married the following May so we could begin making plans to attend the wedding. We didn't know if we dared make any long-range plans to leave town, and decided we would just have to wait and see what condition Carol would be in later that year.

Dr. Haring was beginning to talk about chemotherapy, but I wasn't ready to listen. In my mind chemotherapy was for people who had cancer, and that was deadly. I did not want to believe that this disease could possibly be that bad.

I was enveloped in a cloud of denial. This was my little girl, my only daughter, the daughter I had so badly wanted twenty-one years ago. How could I admit, even silently in my own mind to myself, that her life was in such grave danger that we had to resort to chemotherapy? This had to be a nightmare, and tomorrow morning we would wake up and all would be OK.

Once I actually dreamed that Carol's illness had never happened. It was so disappointing after waking to discover that nothing had changed.

Dr. Haring was well aware of how vehemently I was opposed to chemotherapy, and made it plain, especially to Carol, that "No one is going to nail your feet to the floor and force a pill into your mouth."

We had to decide together what would be the best thing to do to try to make her well and keep her well. But he kept reminding us that chemotherapy was the only known treatment to arrest Wegener's.

"Why are we talking about treating Wegener's when Dr. McDonald said the disease was no longer active?" I kept asking.

No one had any answers, and Carol was definitely not getting better.

Dr. Haring knew that we liked him the best of all the doctors that Carol had seen and trusted him the most. He also knew that he hadn't convinced us that Carol needed the drastic recommended treatment, but knew he had to.

"Another biopsy would tell us whether the disease is active again," he said. "If this one shows the Wegener's as active, we'll have to talk about treating it more vigorously."

"I hate to have her go through another biopsy; it's been such a short time since the last one," I said.

Everyone agreed. But there was no other way to determine what was going on in her nose at this point.

Carol was at the end of her rope. "I'll try anything," she said. "If it takes another biopsy, then let's get it over with."

Because it was very close to Christmas, the biopsy was scheduled for early January 1984.

The holidays came and went and our family hardly noticed. For the first time in many years, we didn't put up a Christmas tree. Our hearts just weren't up to celebrating. I never thought the situation was hopeless; I was just so afraid of what might lie ahead. Carol couldn't continue the way she was going and I didn't like the alternative that was being offered.

When I phoned Mom to bring her up to date, she told me, "Don't worry. Everything will be all right."

"How can you say that, Mom? You have no way of knowing," I barked into the phone. "No one knows how this will turn out. That's a ridiculous thing to say."

I apologized later after realizing it was not a prediction but a prayer she had offered.

There wasn't much that cheered any of us up during those days. No one really understood the emotional pain that we were going through, even if they had been through something similar.

Instead of our usual two hundred Christmas cards, only about two dozen were sent out, and only to those friends who would want to know something about what was going on with Carol, and to business associates of Dick's.

"We'll be using a general anesthetic," Dr. Haring told us, "but Carol will be designated as an out-patient. She'll be able to go home as soon as she wakes up and her vital signs are stable. I know her care at home will be more than adequate and I think she's had enough of hospitals.

"Before the biopsy," he continued, "we'll do another CT scan. I'd like to see if any more destruction has taken place."

Carol told me afterwards that the scan was done once again without dye being injected into her veins. She was getting used to the strange machinery.

"There is definitely something going on," Dr. Haring said after seeing the scan, "and it confirms the need for the biopsy."

While the surgery was being performed, Dick and I waited silently in a tiny waiting room furnished with half a dozen straight-backed chairs and two small tables with outdated magazines.

We hardly spoke beyond, "Do you want a drink?" or "What time is it?"

Our hearts were too heavy to talk about Carol, and neither of us had enough energy for small talk; we were so emotionally drained.

When Dr. Haring entered the waiting room, we had only to look at his solemn face to learn what he had found. It doesn't take long to realize that how a doctor looks when you're about to get news is every bit as important as what he has to say. He had no bright, cheerful smile for us that day.

He sat down with us and explained what he'd seen in the tissue he removed from Carol's nose.

"We'll be getting a formal report from Pathology," he stated, "but there's no doubt in my mind that the Wegener's is active again. It must be halted."

In my heart I knew that he knew what he was talking about.

"I guess if anyone knows what it looks like, you should, Doctor," Dick said with anguish showing on his face. "No one's seen more of the inside of Carol's nose than you."

"Where do we go from here? What do we do now?" I asked.

He reminded us once again, "Chemotherapy is the only known treatment."

Those words were followed by an unbearable silence. I wanted to scream and pound my fists against the wall. But nice grown-up people don't do that. It was as if I were frozen to my chair and my body was numb.

To soften the blow the doctor said, "Perhaps it would be a good idea to see Dr. Thompson at UCLA again and get his opinion."

Dr. Haring wanted a confirmation. Even a skilled physician such as he doesn't take drastic measures on one's own.

Wonderful, I thought. Maybe we would have a repeat performance. He might say it's not Wegener's, but it didn't matter because it was getting better all by itself. Then we would all live happily ever after.

But we all knew that that was not going to be the case.

Although Dr. Haring looked more worried than I ever remember seeing him before, or since, he never voiced the opinion that Carol wouldn't get well. If he ever thought it, at least he didn't say it.

Carol had not come up from recovery yet, and there was nothing more that Dick could do. I sent him on his way to work and waited for Carol alone. After a while a nurse came into the waiting room to tell me that Carol had been brought upstairs and I could wait in the room with her until her release.

There were several beds in the holding room, and one of the others was occupied. A curtain was drawn around us.

Carol looked like Groucho Marx again with her mustache bandage.

"You're getting to be an old hand at this," I said smiling when she opened her eyes.

When had the sparkle left them?

"Did you see Dr. Haring?" she asked.

"Yup."

"What did he say?"

"Nothing we don't already know."

I so wished there were an answer she would have liked better. She closed her eyes and drifted off to sleep again.

"She should be ready to leave in about an hour," the nurse said. "Her vitals are all stable. When she's awake and feels like leaving, then she can be released."

As we were driving home, I told Carol about Dr. Haring's suggestion of seeing Dr. Thompson again. She made no comment pro or con. At least she didn't have the fear that decisions were being made behind her back. Whatever there was to know, Carol always knew just as soon as we did.

I made an appointment with Dr. Thompson, determined not to give chemotherapy a chance, nor him, if that was his suggestion.

It terrified us all. It's common knowledge that while the chemicals are working to fight the disease, they also harm normal cells. I conjured up pictures of bald heads and constant vomiting. Dick and I, and certainly Carol, all felt that chemotherapy was absolutely the last resort, and we would consider it only when they told us that was all there was to save Carol's life. In effect, Dr. Haring had. We had just chosen not to listen.

A few days before Carol's appointment, the movie, "The Terry Fox Story," was going to be broadcast on HBO. Terry Fox was the young Canadian man who lost a leg to cancer and then ran across Canada on the remaining one to raise money for research and treatment.

"I'd like to watch it," I told Dick.

"Why? Aren't you depressed enough?"

"I might learn something about chemotherapy."

That evening we sat down in front of the television set to watch the movie. Carol was up in her room. I hadn't mentioned it to her. She seldom watched TV and since we weren't sure what to expect, there seemed to be no reason to subject her to any dramatizations that might not be authentic but could be upsetting.

When the film progressed to the hospital scene after a chemotherapy treatment, complete with retching in the background and bald heads, we both decided we didn't want to watch it any more and turned it off.

At Carol's appointment with Dr. Thompson, he examined her and then stated, "I feel it's necessary to treat Carol aggressively at this time. I don't think she is going to get better by herself."

Dr. Haring had told us the slides were sent to the medical center again.

"What are you basing your opinion on, Doctor? Have you seen Carol's slides?" Dick at least had the wherewithal to ask.

"I know they've arrived here, but there was a clerical mix-up and I've not had an opportunity to view them," the doctor answered.

So what else was new?

"My opinion is based strictly on what I see inside Carol's nose and her medical history of the past few months. I would suggest you give some serious thought to chemotherapy."

This led me to wonder if his experience had been expanded in the four years since we'd seen him, but decided not to ask.

"Is it a foregone conclusion that nothing else will help?" I asked instead.

"Nothing in medicine is certain," he answered.

Did he sense our total lack of confidence?

"I think it might be a good idea to have Carol evaluated by Dr. Andrew Saxon. He's had some success along these lines."

"What kind of doctor is he, and where does he practice?" Dick asked.

We were at our wits' end and would talk to anyone.

"He's right here at UCLA," Dr. Thompson offered. "He's an immunologist."

I remembered my conversation with John. He had asked why Carol hadn't seen an immunologist since Wegener's is considered to be an autoimmune disease.

"That sounds like a good idea," I said. "Can you make the arrangements for us to see him?"

"I'll have someone from his office call you to set up an appointment as soon as possible," the doctor said.

On the way home I told Dick and Carol about my conversation with John. We all agreed that what John had said was more than interesting. Carol told us she was aware he had done massive amounts of research on Wegener's. She had another friend in the right place.

At the next visit to Dr. Pryor, who was still seeing Carol, she told him we would be seeing Dr. Saxon. She knew that Dr. Pryor had studied medicine at UCLA, and thought he might be interested in knowing to whom she was being referred.

He was very interested and passed along this information:

"While I was at UCLA as an intern, I think Dr. Saxon was a resident. He was referred to as The Boy Wonder."

We all agreed that if we had to choose a doctor for any reason, one who was referred to as The Boy Wonder would probably be our first choice.

Carol and I were eager to meet Dr. Saxon and anxiously awaited an appointment call from the medical center.

Meanwhile, my sister-in-law, Bea, who lived in New York, had been kept apprised of Carol's condition as we had done with the rest of the family. She happened to tell a friend of hers, not knowing his son was a lung specialist. Her friend told his son about Carol and that she was a Wegener's patient. Coincidentally, the specialist gave his father a research paper written by four doctors from the National Institutes of Health about their experiences in treating more than eighty Wegener's patients.

Carol tells me often that there are no coincidences.

That paper clarified a lot of details for me because it had so much information about both the disease and the treatment. The authors had found that Wegener's responded to anti-cancer drugs, particularly cyclophosphamide, along with corticosteroids.[18] Their treatment had produced extraordinarily favorable results. Over 90 percent of the patients treated with cyclophosphamide recovered and were still living! That's better odds than a person has crossing the street in some large cities.

I began to look upon chemotherapy with much more favor. Odds like that are difficult to sneer at. I'd been walking around looking like doom personified, literally fighting a known and recognized treatment. No one called the results a cure. But a recovery, or remission, for an indefinite period of time was a lot better than we had dared hope for.

Carol's headaches and sinus pain were bad and getting worse.

"Could the surgery at the Mayo Clinic have reactivated the disease? Did it really open Pandora's box as I had feared it might?" I asked Dr. Haring.

"In my opinion, the answer is unequivocally no. The surgery was necessary to open the breathing passages and could not have caused a reactivation," Dr. Haring told us.

"Why then did the biopsy at the Mayo Clinic show Carol to be free of the disease just weeks before? What would have happened if the surgery had never been performed? If the disease was not active in September, why was Carol having trouble during the summer?" I bombarded Dr. Haring with these questions.

"I'm sorry. I don't have the answers for you. But I do believe the surgery was necessary," Dr. Haring said.

I was convinced that the surgery had started some problems again, even though it had solved others.

"Have you given any more thought to chemotherapy?" Dr. Haring asked.

"We've thought and talked of little else," I told him.

"*I'm* convinced the disease is active again," he said.

It seemed like that word *chemotherapy* was coming at us from all directions.

"Even though the disease is still confined to Carol's nose," the doctor said, "the nose is too close to the brain for all of us not to be concerned. There's no way of telling if it can be stopped if it were to reach the brain."

If he was trying to scare us, it was working. The danger alerts were becoming bigger and louder.

None of us wanted to take the chance of doing nothing, or even think about the possibility that the disease might reach the brain. He was beginning to wear us down.

Within a few days we were back at UCLA for Carol's appointment with Dr. Saxon.

---

17. An immunologist is a specialist in immunology, the study of the reaction of tissues of the immune system of the body to antigenic stimulation. An antigen is a substance that causes the formation of an antibody and reacts specifically with it.

18. Corticosteroids refer to any one of the natural or the synthetic hormones associated with the adrenal cortex which influences or controls key processes of the body.

12

Meeting the Boy Wonder

When Carol's name was called, we were all ushered into another small, cramped examining room with a small desk and two chairs on one side of the room and a flat examining table on the other side. The atmosphere was different from the rest of UCLA. These people were friendly.

A man of medium build with fair skin, light-brown hair flecked with gray and a bushy beard to match, entered with three other people. He introduced himself as Dr. Saxon and then his entourage, one by one. The tagalongs were residents in immunology. He had a positive, enthusiastic manner and a twinkle in his blue eyes.

So this is the boy wonder, I thought. Not really knowing why, I liked him immediately. Later Dick and Carol told me they did, too.

"You're welcome to stay during the examination," he said to Dick and me. "In fact, we'd like you to stay. I think you'll find it interesting. We will all be examining Carol with a rhinoscope,[19] an examination called a rhinoscopy.[20]

"I hope you don't mind," he continued, "that all of us will be involved in the examination. I hope it won't upset anyone that we'll be discussing what we see inside Carol's nose as we're looking and offering comments."

My mouth said, "Of course I don't mind." My mind was saying, hooray. It's about time we were in on the action.

The doctor sprayed the inside of Carol's nose to deaden the nerves so that the examination wouldn't be painful for her.

Good! Someone was taking her comfort into consideration.

He took a strange-looking contraption out of a silver metal case, about the size of a fat attaché case, and plugged the dangling cord into an electrical socket.

"This is a rhinoscope," he said.

"With this instrument," he explained, "it's possible to see much further inside the nose than the instruments that are normally used by an ENT."

On the business end of the rhinoscope were fiber optics, which lit up when the contraption was plugged into the wall socket. On the other ends, what you might call the looking ends were two things that looked like small fat telescopes. While one person held one telescope to his eye to look through it, another person could do the same with the other telescope and they could discuss what they were seeing.

The fiber optics were on the end of a flexible black pipe, like the kind that attaches a stethoscope to the earpiece. It was easy for the one operating the rhinoscope to use the fiber optics as pointers. It was even possible for the patient to be the other person viewing what was being observed and discussed.

Every one of us was given the opportunity to look inside Carol's nose, including Carol herself.

When it was my turn, I could see that almost the entire inside, or what was now left of the inside, of her nose was a green blob, shades of that old Steve McQueen horror movie, "The Blob." Only this time the horror was real. The blob pulsated as she inhaled and exhaled.

The septum was gone. The thin bones and membranes that are found inside the average nose were gone. In fact, the entire inside of Carol's nose was a giant, hollow cavity, with just nubs—that's what the doctors called the little stumps—where there once had been bone, cartilage, and tissue.

She no longer had air passageways, or the little hairs attached to them to warm the outside air or catch the dust—just one huge cavity.

After everyone had a turn, the rhinoscope was put aside to be sterilized for future use, and Dr. Saxon spoke to us.

"I've seen her slides," he said, referring to the ones Dr. Haring had obtained from the most recent biopsy and forwarded.

Wow! It was comforting to know that he was prepared.

"I feel that the Wegener's is definitely active at this time," he continued.

We'd already established that Wegener's granulomatosis is an autoimmune disease; Dr. Saxon is an immunologist. In fact, his business card said he was the Chief of the Division of Clinical Immunology at UCLA Medical Center, purported to be one of the largest and most prestigious medical centers in the country. We had to assume he knew what he was talking about.

"It's imperative," he said, "that we begin chemotherapy, and soon. We have to keep the disease from spreading."

He and Dr. Haring were certainly singing the same song.

"Within the next week or two," Dr. Saxon continued, "Dr. Fauci, from NIH, will be here at the Medical Center. He's one of the leading experts in the country on the treatment of Wegener's granulomatosis. I intend to discuss Carol's case with him and I'll let you know his opinion and recommendations."

"Would it be possible for Carol to see Dr. Fauci?" I asked.

"Probably not," Dr. Saxon said. "Her chart and history will be more meaningful to him. As long as you're going to get the expert's opinion, it doesn't matter how, as long as it helps Carol."

Dr. Fauci's name sounded very familiar; but why?

When we got home I found the research paper Bea sent me. Voila! Dr. Anthony S. Fauci was one of the authors.

Things were beginning to fit together in my mind. Maybe we were finally on the right track. These people seemed to know what they were talking about, and there was the evidence to back it up in my hands. Maybe we had better listen to them.

Dr. Saxon called a little over a week later and said, "Tony Fauci would like very much to see and talk to Carol. Would it be possible to bring her down here to the medical center tomorrow?"

You bet it was possible.

"You tell us where and what time and we'll be there," I told him.

If it meant getting an opinion and being evaluated by the leading expert in the country, I would have put Carol on my back and crawled there on my belly if necessary. By this time, Carol had read the research paper herself and knew all about Dr. Fauci and his work.

"Guess who wants to see you tomorrow?" I yelled to Carol while climbing up the stairs to her room. "Dr. Fauci is in town and Dr. Saxon just called. He wants to know if we can bring you in tomorrow morning."

Carol had been lying down and she sat up with an animated look on her face. "That's terrific, Mom. I think I'll make a list of questions to ask him."

That was my analytical girl!

"Do you think Dad can go?"

"Wild horses couldn't keep him away. I'd better call him and let him know what time."

The boy wonder is really wonderful, I thought! And he hadn't even done anything yet.

This time when we arrived at Dr. Saxon's section of the medical center and checked in with the receptionist, we were escorted to a huge conference room instead of a small examining room. Within minutes the room was overflowing with what we presumed to be residents, interns and doctors of all ages, shapes, sizes, and specialties. There must have been at least forty of them, possibly more.

It was too bad John wasn't with us. The group looked like the army of doctors that he had hoped would evaluate Carol.

Dr. Saxon arrived with his team from the previous week, along with Dr. Fauci, who he introduced to us. Dr. Fauci's apparent youth was surprising considering the magnitude of his reputation and experience. He must have been a boy wonder himself. He was slender, and clean shaven. All the others were wearing white lab coats. Dr. Fauci was in a sport jacket and slacks.

The rhinoscopy was repeated, including the use of the numbing spray. Everyone there, without exception, had an opportunity to look inside Carol's nose. All three of us were asked questions by many of the participants about the history and progress of the disease. Then we were all given an opportunity to ask questions of our own.

Because Wegener's was considered so rare, every patient's case history could contribute information that might one day answer many questions asked about the disease.

"If I begin a program of chemotherapy now," Carol wanted to know from Dr. Fauci, "will I have deformed children in the future?"

Dr. Fauci answered, "It's more likely that you would not become pregnant. Chemotherapy will probably destroy your eggs."

Carol asked, "Will I lose my hair?"

"Some people do and some don't." he answered. "There's no way of telling how your body will react."

"How long will I have to be on chemotherapy?"

"Approximately two years is the average," the doctor answered. "It's been my experience that the patients who continue therapy for a year *after* there are no signs of active disease have the best results."

Oh boy. Two years worth of poison—on purpose.

He followed his answers with the statement, "Chemotherapy is an absolute must at this time. If the disease is not arrested it will spread."

All the doctors we'd seen recently weren't saying it in so many words, but it was now coming through loud and clear. Her life was at stake. There was no other choice.

"The therapy must begin soon," Dr. Fauci told us with an urgent tone in his voice.

"How soon is soon?" I wanted to know.

"Within four to six weeks," he replied. "If you wait any longer you will be courting disaster."

---

19.   A rhinoscope is an instrument for examining the nasal passages.

20.   A rhinoscopy is an examination of the nasal passages.

13

Chemotherapy—Another Word for Hope

When you've pulled your last ace out of the hole, there are no more cards left to play. One of the leading experts told us what we had to do. When you pay an expert for his advice, it makes sense to take it.

We began to realize that chemotherapy is another word for hope. If nothing could be done, the situation would be hopeless. At least something *could* be done, and that was hopeful. If it worked, that would be a miracle. We were certainly ready for one. But it's a miracle that's paid for dearly when one looks at the list of possible side effects of anti-cancer drugs.

When there's a possibility that a loved one's life may be shortened because of illness, it becomes so much more precious than you ever realized it was. You'll try anything, go anywhere, or do anything that will help improve the prognosis.

The question now was not whether to begin chemotherapy. Rather, we were asking, "When? Where? How? And with whom?" These questions were dumped in Dr. Saxon's lap a few days later at Carol's next visit with him.

"I would be more than happy to treat you, Carol," he offered. "But you might want to consider having one of your local doctors handle the treatment."

Then to me he said, "If she has any bad reactions, or she feels sick and needs to be seen, she'll be a lot closer to home. The last thing you want to do when you don't feel well is travel an hour to a doctor or hospital."

"That makes sense," I said.

He's very considerate of his patients, I thought.

We assumed Dr. Haring would handle the treatment, but at Carol's next appointment he said that Dr. Pryor was the one who was better qualified to take care of that. Although he'd seen Carol several times, we really didn't know much about him, his experience, or his competence. Dick and I wanted to make sure

155

we were doing the right thing with the right person. There's no question that chemotherapy is the most serious of treatments.

Dr. Haring's opinion of Dr. Pryor carried a lot of weight with us, of course. Once again we also sought Dr. Mysko's opinion. He, too, felt that Dr. Pryor was more than competent and a good choice. So Dr. Pryor was chosen to handle the chemotherapy.

The chemotherapeutic agent to be used was Cytoxan™.[21] That was the same drug that John had spoken of, and the one used in Dr. Fauci's study, also.

At Carol's next visit with Dr. Haring, he tore out the page about Cytoxan™ from his previous year's copy of the *Physicians' Desk Reference* and gave it to her. Never being one to pull punches, he wasn't going to start now. He knew she had to know the bad things that might happen to her, along with the good things that had been part of Dr. Fauci's study.

Possible known side effects of any of the antineoplastic[22] drugs include brain, heart, lung, and liver damage; dysfunction of the reproductive organs; altered immunity; memory and learning problems; secondary cancer; crippling; and death. Additionally, the possible side effects of Cytoxan™ were numerous and dangerous: nausea, vomiting, and loss of appetite; increased frequency of infections because it lowers the white blood count; easy bruising and bleeding if the platelet[23] count decreases; skin rash; blood in the urine, painful urination due to inflammation of the bladder, and possible permanent scarring of the bladder if the patient doesn't drink enough fluids; loss of hair; sterility; scarring of the lung causing shortness of breath; and a slight but definite risk of developing cancer or leukemia. That was just the beginning. The list was staggering. But what choice was there? The alternative was worse.

My own research brought out the fact that remission is achieved and maintained by drugs that are toxic to humans. There were to be periodic check-ups and evaluations by Dr. Saxon. Carol would continue to see Dr. Haring on a regular basis so he could keep track of what was going on inside her nose and sinuses as before.

At her next appointment with Dr. Pryor, Carol was prescribed two fifty-milligram pills to be taken once a day, the dosage determined by her body weight. It had never occurred to me that chemotherapy could be administered orally, just like aspirin, and not only intravenously.

Along with the Cytoxan™, Carol would be taking a corticosteroid called Prednisone™. That drug had its own set of possible side effects: the body might turn off its ability to make corticosteroids on its own; appetite could increase along with weight gain; easy bruising; slow healing of cuts or abrasions; lowered resistance to infections, masking signs and symptoms of infections such as pneumonia; stomach upset and, on rare occasions, peptic ulcer. Also on the list are increased body hair; diabetes, which causes increased thirst and appetite as well as excessive urination; softening of the bones, especially in the spine, which causes the back to become bent forward; weakness of muscles; increased emotional sensitivity such as overreactions to irritations, joyful and sad events, or disappointments; cataracts; acne; and retention of water and salt, sometimes causing high blood pressure and swelling of the ankles. The dosage was high on that drug—forty milligrams—and it was to be steadily decreased.

Prednisone™ was to be taken every other day, and was supposed to help minimize infections. Both drugs were considered immunosuppressants, drugs that weaken the body's immune system.

Although weight gain is a major side effect of Prednisone™, the only hint of Prednisone's™ weight effects for Carol was what was termed a "moon face," round puffy cheeks.

"I'll want to see you once a week for a while," Dr. Pryor said to her.

Then to me he said, "I'd like you to take her temperature several times a day, write it down, and report to me at her weekly visits."

To both of us he said, "At each weekly visit I'll draw blood and send it to the laboratory for tests to be conducted."

"What kind of tests?" Carol asked.

"We have to continually check your white corpuscle count," he answered.

"Why?" I asked.

This time Carol answered.

"The white blood cells fight infection. If the white count goes down too low …"

"She's right," the doctor added. "Too few white cells could make her susceptible to all kinds of infections."

To Carol he said, "Take the pills in the morning, and drink, drink, drink all day long to flush out your kidneys and bladder."

He wrote two prescriptions, handed them to Carol, who handed them to me, and then off we went to the neighborhood drug store.

There were so many thoughts that ran through my mind that day in February, from the time Dr. Pryor handed Carol the prescriptions to the time the pharmacist handed me the little bag with the two bottles of pills. Are we doing the right thing? Will this help her or hurt her? Will there be the side effects I read about? Will she be able to tolerate them if there are?

What if she's one of the 10 percent on which chemotherapy doesn't work? If it does work, how long will it be before we know? Will she lose her hair? If she does, how will that affect her emotionally? Will her skin be affected? And once again, are we doing the right thing?

The only thing she asked Dick and me with reference to the chemotherapy at all was, "If I lose my hair, can I get a wig?"

She surely had more thoughts than that, but she never voiced them. I don't know if she spoke to anyone else about her feelings. She certainly didn't share them with me. But mine weren't shared with her, either.

We all tried to act so nonchalant about the beginning of the treatment so we could hide the fact that our hearts were breaking. Why Carol? She did not deserve this. It wasn't fair.

I wished so many times that I could have had this disease for her. I told her once even though I had said it many times to Dick.

"No you don't, Mom. Believe me, you don't!" she said.

I only know what she went through by my own observations. Unless she told us what she was feeling, we never knew. I would rather have gone through it myself than to have watched her suffer.

We knew we had to move forward. There was certainly no going back, and we couldn't stay where we were. The road we traveled, we hoped, was the road to recovery.

Although the pills were expensive, about $2.30 a pill at the time, we knew if they did the job, and Carol got well again, they would be priceless. Like most parents, we would have paid any price to give her back her health.

One of my grandmother's favorite expressions was, "When you have your health you have your wealth."

As a teenager listening to her say that, thinking I'd probably live forever, it meant nothing. But all that had changed. Nothing could buy for Carol the good health she didn't have.

Somehow I expected a comment from the pharmacist, even if it was only a warning, but none was forthcoming.

Dick even asked me, "Did the pharmacist say anything about the prescription?"

"No. No remarks of any kind were made."

By this time, as one might imagine, the people in the pharmacy knew us well. We had, unfortunately, become very good customers.

The pills were white with blue specks in them.

"This reminds me of the Salvo™ tablets we used to take on vacation to wash the clothes when you were little," I told Carol, "only they were much bigger. If it cleans out the germs just like the big ones cleaned the clothes, we'll be doing fine."

For the first few days after Carol began taking the Cytoxan™, she stayed in bed, probably either because the medicine made her sick, or because she was depressed. She never said why; it was her business. She was entitled to her privacy. She had more than enough reasons to be depressed.

We saw her at mealtimes and when taking her temperature. She ate very little, but always came downstairs to the kitchen to eat. I would have brought a tray up to her if she had wanted it, but she seemed to have welcomed the company, particularly at the end of the day when Dick and the boys were home.

Her temperature was always normal; all during the chemo treatments she never ran a fever.

John and Tracey phoned her several times during those first few weeks. She spoke to them each time they called. In fact she spoke to every friend who called. There were so many from college who we'd only heard of but never met. They didn't forget her, and we'll never forget them, or how they kept in touch and kept up her morale during the time she needed it most.

"You know what Tracey asked me?" Carol disclosed one day.

"What?"

"Have you barfed yet?" Carol replied.

It's good that they were able to make light of this. Anyone knows that laughing is better than crying.

If there is a God and he blesses anyone at all, I hope he starts with friends who hang in there when someone they know is seriously ill.

They didn't treat her any differently. To them she was the same old Carol. The value of those special friends can never be measured.

We all used a light approach and did not treat this episode like Doomsday. Besides, if we didn't believe she was on the road to recovery, we were putting Carol through a lot of bad days for nothing. But in our hearts we knew we weren't dealing with anything light. If there was any doubt as to how toxic the medicine was, all we had to do was remember its name.

The next time John called I reminded him of all his questions and how everything he suggested had come to pass. Carol had been evaluated by an army of doctors; she was being treated by an immunologist and was taking cyclophosphamide. He seemed a little embarrassed, but it was important to tell him just how right he was. I believe he's going to be a fine doctor someday, and I'm not the only one with confidence in him. After he graduated from UCR with a degree in chemistry, he was accepted into a number of highly respected medical schools. He chose Johns Hopkins University to continue his studies.

Dr. Haring called frequently just to ask how things were going. He even wanted to know if her friends were keeping in touch and was so pleased when he learned that they were. It was obvious that he truly cared about her as a person and not just as a patient.

Carol had heard that eating pasta while on chemotherapy helped to keep you from being too nauseous, so she put in her order for macaroni and cheese, and spaghetti, two of my specialties. She never said it worked, but never said it didn't either. It made her happy and kept me busy.

When we went to Dr. Pryor for the weekly visits, he drew the blood himself. Carol would tease him about drawing her blood, or anything else she could think of. He was very reserved and not too talkative, but Carol managed to find things to discuss to which he would respond. They got along great, which was so important during that kind of treatment.

He was never hesitant about saying he didn't know if she questioned him about some phase of the treatment for which he didn't have answers. He always made sure he found out and told her at a subsequent appointment.

Since I was no longer working, my time was my own. Many former clients called just to say hello, as they always had in the past. When it didn't concern business, Sandy suggested they call me at home. Of course she gave them no information about Carol and her health problems.

One client called to ask me to attend the funeral of her infant child who had died a few days after birth.

"Are you going?" Sandy asked me.

"How can I not go?" I asked her in return. "When someone makes a request like that it's difficult to turn them down. Their child is gone; I still have mine. It's only fair that I help them grieve."

As I stood on the hilltop at the cemetery that chilly day with the wind whipping my coat around me, watching the tiny casket being lowered into the grave, the thought that kept running through my mind was: *not my child.* I couldn't fathom the time would ever come when that might happen to me. I would not outlive Carol. *This treatment would work and she would outlive me!*

Another client who was a registered astrologist did a health chart for Carol and a life chart for me, at my request.

According to the stars, she told me, I was expected to live to a ripe old age and Carol would outlive me. Astrology had always seemed interesting but I was never quite sure whether it was true or not. I wanted very much to put my faith in something. It was just one more ray of light for us and did no harm.

When Carol had doctors' appointments that were near lunchtime, and she was up to eating out, we began to try different restaurants. It was a little bit of an outing for her and helped to break up the day. It was at one of those lunchtime outings that she finally, after having been sick for six years, asked out loud, "Why me?"

I felt like screaming: "It's time for the nightmare to be over. It's all been a bad joke. My child is not sick at all. The doctors were wrong. We'll all wake up tomorrow and everything will be fine."

Instead, my answer was calm. "At least this is treatable. It could have been worse. You could have been handed a death sentence like your friend from high school."

As I spoke, my skin crawled with goose bumps. But I couldn't cry in front of Carol and had to postpone my tears until alone.

If I had dwelt on all the "whys" or "if onlys" I would have lost my mind. I had long since passed the "why Carol" stage and was trying to handle the "now what?" Was there a reason that she had been chosen?

Without the words being spoken, we both knew that she had a close brush with death and that the struggle was a long way from over.

We had to believe she was now on the mend, with good health just around the corner, or none of us could face tomorrow.

Dr. Haring reminded her frequently of the importance of regularly irrigating her nose. He gave us some information on an attachment for a Water Pik® especially for that purpose. One was purchased for her, but eventually she went back to irrigating by hand, saying, "The water pressure was too high, even on the lowest setting. It hurt. The attachment was probably made for normal noses."

The last biopsy had been performed on the day Carol would have registered for school. Knowing she would probably be starting chemotherapy with so many uncertainties about the side effects, she decided not to register for the winter quarter, but to wait till spring. The doctors felt this was the wisest course of action. All her strength could then be concentrated on getting well.

Dick and I decided to keep Carol's apartment, even though it would be sitting empty and costing us money, because we felt it would do psychological damage if she thought we didn't expect her to complete her education. Besides, the cost to move and store her furniture was probably as much as the rent.

We talked again about moving Dick closer to his work.

"If we put the house up for sale, prospective buyers will be wandering from room to room. It might disturb some of your privacy," I told Carol.

"It won't matter," she said. "Let's do it."

---

21.   Cytoxan™ is the trade name for cyclophosphamide, an antineoplastic.

22.   Antineoplastic refers to a chemotherapeutic agent that controls or kills cancer cells.

23.   Platelets are the smallest of the cells in the blood and are essential for the coagulation of blood.

14

Introduction to a Pain Clinic

Since the house had been redecorated three years before, it looked great and, as we were fond of saying in the real estate business, it would show well. That, in my opinion, would help move it quickly. Due to my success in real estate work, the family felt I knew what I was doing.

Right after the house was listed for sale, I invited all the salespeople from my office over for a customary buffet lunch. The purpose of feeding them was to encourage agents, who might not otherwise come, to preview the house. If they liked it, perhaps they'd show it to a buyer they were working with who would then fall in love with it. My co-workers all knew I had taken a leave and why.

"You won't have to be up," I told Carol. "It won't hurt a thing if they miss seeing your room."

"Well, you'll need help, won't you?" she asked.

"If you feel up to it."

I loved having her beside me in the kitchen but didn't want to put unnecessary pressure on her.

When my colleagues arrived, Carol was up, dressed, and had even put on make-up for the first time since she'd begun the chemo. She looked great and, as usual, was a lot of help. No one would have guessed the monumental "dragon at the door" she was fighting by looking at her that day.

Those agents who knew me a little better let me know how pleased they were to see Carol up and about, looking so well. It was a joy watching her being friendly and charming. Did she know how proud I was? How much I adored her?

The house sold in six days. That meant Carol and I would be busy house hunting in Pasadena and packing for the next couple of months. As long as she was feeling up to it, she wanted to participate.

Dick and I had both assured Carol if she didn't want to change doctors after we moved, we'd commute. It would mean we would only do it occasionally and it was the same commute Dick had done twice a day for many, many years.

Looking for another home was just one more shopping excursion for Carol and me. It gave her something to do, she was company for me, and she could always be counted on for an honest opinion.

We looked for several days, although never for long periods because Carol tired easily. My schedule was adjusted to hers.

Driving through some of the areas of Pasadena where there are stately homes, some even bordering on mansions, made me realize how little wealth mattered. No amount of money could change what had happened to Carol.

Interestingly enough, when we made a choice in March it was a townhouse Carol and I had seen on our first day looking.

We had both agreed, "Daddy would like this one."

The master suite was upstairs in this townhouse; it had been on the first floor in the house we were leaving. There was a second bedroom for Ron on the same floor. At the last minute he had decided not to move out with Don.

One half flight up from the second floor was a third bedroom that Carol chose. She nicknamed it The Penthouse and afterwards we all called it that.

During the packing I kept finding photographs of Carol from healthier times and before her nose collapsed. If one looked closely they might see that those boxes were stained with tears.

Carol seemed to have adjusted to living with chemotherapy by the time the packing was finished. She took the blue-flecked pills every morning. Although she didn't see Dr. Pryor every week after the first few, she did see him every other one. He didn't want to let too much time go by without checking her blood and urine.

Real estate had picked up again and things had gotten busy at the office. Sandy had kept me well-informed as to what was going on when she would call to inquire about Carol.

I started back to work, temporarily, to give her a hand.

Although many people asked about Carol, others were reticent to ask me, so they questioned Sandy, who gave them updates.

It seemed that when someone heard the word chemotherapy, they automatically associated it with cancer and a death sentence, just like I had. There were many surprised faces when they heard from me that Carol had adjusted nicely and was beginning to feel better.

Occasionally I would run into someone I hadn't seen in a while who would ask about Carol. When chemotherapy was mentioned, they would usually say, "Oh I'm so sorry" and start to back away as if it might be contagious. Each such comment was countered with the explanation that there was nothing to be sorry about. At least we had a treatment; some diseases have none.

They were also assured that this treatment had more than a 90 percent recovery rate, pretty good odds. Referring to the recovery rate, I would say how lucky we were, but in my heart I really felt that lucky meant Carol would never have gotten this terrible disease in the first place. Are there degrees of luck?

Many people would say how sorry they felt *for me* and how awful it must be for *me* and wanted to know how *I* was holding up. But I always thanked them for asking and told them I was doing just fine.

I never told them how often I would cry when I was alone thinking about what my beloved child was going through. There was no one there to say I shouldn't or that it wasn't good for Carol's morale. Sometimes the emotional pain was almost physical.

A few longtime colleagues from my previous office hadn't seen Carol for a long time. She used to visit me frequently. Now when some of my old friends saw her, they said they wouldn't have recognized her. Around that time it became apparent that the bridge of her nose had completely caved in, lying flat against her face. It had happened so gradually that, seeing her every day, I guess I hardly noticed.

But there was definitely a change. Oh, that it had happened the way she wanted, instead of the way it did! To me it was an improvement over the old nose even though the doctors called it a deformity.

In March we took a few days off to go to Carol's favorite ski resort, inviting John to accompany us.

Carol tired so easily, typical of chemo patients, so she skied only about a third of the time available to her. She slept a great deal. When she was awake and ready for quiet amusement we played board games. At least she was in her beloved snow-covered mountains.

Dr. Saxon and his team examined Carol with the rhinoscope again in April. When it was my turn to look, I could see that the blob was shrinking. What a tremendous lift that was after only two months.

The Cytoxan™ was working and although her hair had become a little finer and much lighter, she still had hair. From brown, it had turned to a honey color, roots and all. Acquaintances who knew nothing of her health asked me when she started coloring her hair and commented that it looked so natural.

When we moved into our new home in May, I asked Dr. Haring to recommend a local ENT just in case we ran into a problem and it wasn't practical to travel. He gave us a name and said he would let the doctor know that we would be in touch.

Just before we moved, Carol gave the computer back to Dr. Haring to give to his friend. Shortly after we moved into the new house, we bought one of our own. Besides working on the computer herself, Carol began teaching me how to use it.

Our move took place in the year and month that Carol would have finished college if she hadn't gotten sick.

All of Carol's college friends were graduating and Dick and I worried about how she would react to seeing them where she should have been.

"Do you think you can talk her out of going?" he asked.

"Not a chance," I answered. "Her plans are sealed in cement."

These were her friends, this was a momentous occasion, and she wasn't going to miss it. They would have been there for her; she would be there for them. Whatever emotions she had to deal with she kept to herself, like everything else.

In the middle of July, I made an appointment for Carol to see the local ENT Dr. Haring had recommended. She hadn't been feeling too well, which is expected occasionally with chemotherapy patients.

Since there wasn't an emergency, the appointment was set for later in the week. I hoped the new doctor could get to know her before a crisis arose.

I went to her room to check on her. She hadn't wanted lunch.

"My head hurts really bad," she moaned.

I'd gotten used to listening for words she wasn't saying, and had begun to read her signals this way: "OK" meant not great, but hanging in there; "crummy" meant some pain along with disgust and frustration; "really bad" usually meant excruciating.

"Have you taken anything?" I asked, dreading the answer, because when the medicine didn't work it usually meant a trip to the doctor or hospital. Carol administered her own pain medication. After all, she was twenty-two and responsible.

She had long since graduated from codeine to Percocet™. It didn't take a lot of figuring to learn how strong it was. In California the drug could only be obtained with a special prescription form in triplicate. If the prescription date was more than one week old, no pharmacist would fill it. Most drug stores didn't even carry it so we had to learn which ones did and patronize them.

"Two Percocet™."

"Shouldn't you only take one?"

"Yeah. But it's not working."

"Did two work any better than one?" I asked.

"No. I don't think I should take any more."

"I agree with you."

Then an idea occurred to me.

"Would you be willing to try acupuncture? Remember when I had treatments for my back a few years ago? It worked. Maybe it will work for your head. If the pain pills aren't helping, and we both agree taking more would be dangerous, we have to come up with something else."

There were times in the recent past when I'd asked Dr. Haring about the danger of addiction, knowing how strong the pills were. He had said, more than once, "As long as Carol is worried about addiction, I'm not. The day she stops being concerned, I'll start to worry."

"I'll try anything," Carol said. "My head hurts almost as bad as it did when I took the Septra™."

That had been bad. After phoning a couple of local offices, I found an acupuncturist who could see her immediately and took her there. Standing beside her as she lay on the examining table, I heard her explain where her pain was.

Bunches of skinny hair-like needles were stuck in different parts of her head and hands. When the treatment was over, she was no better than when we'd walked in. Unfortunately, either he wasn't too good or it just didn't work. When we arrived home ten minutes later we had accomplished nothing except relieving ourselves of $35. It was disappointing because acupuncture had worked for me.

I called the local ENT and told the receptionist what was going on with Carol. Although it wasn't an emergency, it seemed that it was bordering on one. She was very understanding and told me to bring Carol in immediately.

One of the nice things about our new home was that everything was very close, usually five or fewer minutes away.

When the new doctor examined her, he indicated that he was not seeing anything new or unusual from what Dr. Haring had told him to expect.

"What medications are you taking, Carol?" he asked.

Carol named them all.

"Are you seeing a rheumatologist?" he asked.

"No. Should I be?" she answered with her own question.

"I certainly think so. I would recommend you see one immediately."

He seemed a little intimidated by the fact that she was on chemotherapy.

"We don't know any here. Can you recommend someone?"

"Yes."

He gave me the name of a doctor whose office was right across the street.

"Let me call and see if they can take you right away," he said.

The doctor called the rheumatologist who agreed to see Carol immediately.

I paid the bill, made a return appointment for later in the week, and we walked across the street. The recommended doctor actually wasn't available but one of his associates was. We spent two and a half hours, and a couple of hundred dollars, with him. Even though he didn't do much, Carol did feel better when she left. Maybe telling her story one more time helped relieve some of her tension.

Basically, however, she was uncomfortable with the unfamiliar doctors. She saw both a few more times, but then decided commuting to Drs. Haring and Pryor was worth it.

Carol was still experiencing a lot of sinus pain and headaches. Insomnia and concern about how much medicine she was taking also troubled her.

"Sometimes I feel like a walking ad for the 'Pill of the Month Club,'" she remarked one evening.

"Well, you know the Cytoxan™ and Prednisone™ are necessary at this point," I said.

"I hate taking all the pain pills," she complained.

"I assume you wouldn't be taking them if you didn't need them."

"Yeah, but I have to keep taking more and more in order for them to work, and that's how people get addicted," she said. "I can't live with the pain, either. Something has to be done."

"Why don't you ask Dr. Haring about a pain clinic?" Dick suggested. "I seem to remember reading about one at UCLA."

When I asked Dr. Haring about it he said he would refer Carol to the UCLA pain clinic.

You can't simply walk into many pain clinics off the street. A doctor must refer you.

After Dr. Haring took care of the necessary paper work, I phoned for an appointment. The earliest date that could be scheduled was in two weeks. All Carol could do was hang in there. We all waited very impatiently.

The day before Carol's appointment, the receptionist called to say it was cancelled. The next available time, she told me, was eleven days later. Having no choice, Carol was scheduled for then. But I let the receptionist know how unhappy I was about it. That was a terrible mistake, equal to waving a red flag in front of a bull.

The receptionist called the day before the next appointment to cancel again, rescheduling Carol for eight days later.

When she called the day before that to cancel yet again, I was furious and became hysterical.

"Why do you think someone would make an appointment with your clinic unless they were in unbearable pain? How can you do this to someone who's extremely ill? It's been more than a month since my daughter has been needing and trying to get help. She can't continue like this. You've got to find some way of fitting her in. I can't take no for an answer," I screamed into the phone.

I can't ever remember being that angry with anyone else.

But coercion and threats made no difference; they did no good. Another appointment was scheduled. After hanging up, I thought of a dozen more things I could have told the woman, but it wouldn't have made any difference. These words always occur to me after it's too late.

Carol had been upstairs lying down. Coincidentally Dick had come home for lunch that day, something he almost never did. Again, no coincidence? I turned to Dick, fussing and fuming. He was well aware that something was wrong and I relayed the conversation to him.

"Now what are we supposed to do? How am I going to tell her it's been postponed for the third time?" I seethed. "If I had been in the same room with that woman I think I might have cheerfully strangled her!"

Dick didn't answer me but walked over to the phone.

"What's the clinic's number?" he asked.

"What good do you think you can do?"

"Will you please give me the number?" he asked again, calmly.

He dialed the number as I rattled it off.

"Who runs the pain clinic?" he barked into the phone after someone answered.

He jotted the name down on a piece of paper, and then ordered, "Put him on the phone!"

He apparently wasn't there.

"Then you'd better have him call me," Dick growled, "or you can tell him I'll call his boss."

Dick gave his name and phone number to whoever was on the other end of the line and hung up.

"I'm sure he won't call you," I said.

"Oh, he'll call all right," Dick retorted.

"What makes you so sure?"

"No one likes to be threatened without at least learning why. In these days of malpractice problems, he's going to have to find out what my beef is."

Within an hour, Dr. King*, the head of the pain clinic, called and Dick started to read him the riot act. He stopped Dick cold. This is the conversation Dick reported to me after he hung up.

"Tell me your problem," the doctor had said.

Dick told him of my exasperating experiences in trying to make an appointment and all the postponements.

"I listened to your problem," the doctor had said. "Now will you listen to mine?"

"Go ahead," Dick said.

"We have a receptionist who doesn't get along with anyone. She likes no one; no one likes her. It's impossible to get rid of her without documented evidence. They could get rid of me faster.

"When was your daughter's last appointment scheduled, Mr. Swart?"

"Tomorrow at 11:00 AM," Dick told him.

"Bring her in. We will manage to fit her in at that time," the doctor continued. "Now I'd like to ask a favor of you. If the person your wife has been dealing with presents any more problems, please write me a letter detailing exactly what transpired."

"You've got it, Doctor," Dick said. "Thank you very much for your time, courtesy, and patience."

"Believe me," the doctor added, "I understand your frustration, and that is not the purpose of the clinic. We'll do everything we can to help your daughter. Thank you for coming to me with the problem. You should have no trouble with our personnel tomorrow."

As Dick filled me in on the details of the conversation, I stood there with my mouth open.

"The squeaky wheel gets the oil," he reminded me. "Now go tell Carol what happened. It will give her something to think about and maybe take her mind off her pain."

Anticipating the cold shoulder when Carol and I entered the clinic, I wasn't disappointed. The woman in question was cold, but courteous.

Carol saw several different doctors at the pain management center, including two psychologists, a dentist, and a psychiatrist. She sometimes saw one at a visit; other times she saw as many as three. Dick and I were asked to consult with a psychologist who asked us to tell her about Carol, what kind of person we thought she was, and how we thought she was handling her illness. I had fun with that question. This is what I told the doctor.

"Carol was born on a Friday and I have frequently referred to her as Friday's child."

The doctor looked puzzled.

"Do you remember that age-old nursery rhyme that says: Friday's child is loving and giving?"

"Oh yes," she acknowledged.

"Having been raised in a large family," I continued, "she learned how to share at an early age and has never been possessive. Household chores have always been carried out with a smile. Carol's very organized and a good planner; she seldom loses anything.

"She's bright and eager to learn. She doesn't seem to have a shy bone in her body. She has generally conformed to my suggestions whether it's how to make a bed or how to apply make-up.

"Carol's hardly ever had a best friend and doesn't seem to confide in anyone. She's a private person, not greedy, and asks for very little.

"As a happy and creative person, she's displayed an interest in playing the piano and guitar and some sculpting in clay. She's also done some metal art, mosaic plaques, and textile art.

"When she was a young child, she was very fond of animals. Strays used to follow her home. Later, she was interested in horses and was given horseback riding lessons.

"We have only seen a disagreeable side to her nature since she's been sick. When she's in pain, she's more apt to be grumpy than to complain. Even though she's been through hell, and we all know there's probably more to come, I believe she will be well enough to live a normal life someday. I think she feels she will, also. She'll finish college because it's important to her, not because her father and I want her to.

"She's gregarious, charming, intelligent, self-assured, assertive, and classy. When she enters a room it's with an aura of poise and self-confidence. Usually, she's a happy person, laughs easily, and is fun to be around."

Dick filled in with his version of much of the same.

The doctor told us our stories matched those of Carol's, or things she said we'd say.

"Isn't that the way it usually is?" I asked.

"Not necessarily," she answered.

Carol went to the clinic several times a week, sometimes driving by herself, and sometimes with me, depending on how badly she felt. This continued for four or five months.

It would have been great to be more involved, to have sat in on other doctors' examinations or discussions. But it was handled the way the doctors wanted it to be.

Instead, I spent the time in the waiting room, doing embroidery. It was like going to a concert and listening to the performance from the theater lobby as the door opened occasionally. Now and then a doctor, on his or her way out to fight with the receptionist for another appointment, would stop and say to me, "She's doing just fine," whatever that meant.

We really weren't sure if the center was doing her any good, and if it were, just how much.

In the long run, though, it did enable Carol to do away with pain pills as a steady diet at that time.

She brushed up on techniques of relaxation and imagery. One of the doctors suggested taking L-Tryptophan and it did help her sleep.

Scheduling appointments was a constant us-or-her war with the receptionist, whom we came to know as Ginny Sue.* More often than not the doctor Carol was seeing had to accompany her to Ginny Sue's desk to actually demand that the next appointment be scheduled. It seemed obvious to me that the receptionist was the fly in the ointment at the center, as Dr. King had pointed out. She was always sickeningly sweet as we fought with her.

After one of Carol's visits to the center in August, she had also scheduled an appointment with Dr. Saxon.

15

The Chemo Is Working

Dr. Saxon allowed me a view through the rhinoscope this time. I could see that the green blob had been reduced by what seemed to be about 75 percent. What a wonderful sight that was. The Cytoxan™ was still working.

Dr. Fauci's research had shown that those patients who stayed on the medicine for a year after the disease is no longer active were the ones who had stayed into remission.

Carol still had all her hair, but was no longer having menstrual periods.

Dr. Haring said that the inside of her nose was definitely looking better to him.

Dr. Pryor, who was taking regular samples of blood and urine, and checking chest X-rays, said his tests were OK, also. Occasionally he would find some protein in Carol's urine, but not enough for him to be concerned. Too much protein could be a sign of reduced kidney function, a primary concern for Wegener's patients.

School had been an impossible undertaking during the winter and spring quarters of 1984. Fall of '83 had resulted in her withdrawal because of the lost time during the three hospital stays. During the fall of '84, Carol registered for and completed two out of three classes. She was very pleased with herself, and so were we. She was getting back on her feet and starting to live again. She called it "taking her life off hold."

Not taking a full complement of classes posed a new problem. Because Carol was an adult and still covered under her father's medical insurance, she had to be a full-time student. We discovered that she was no longer eligible for coverage as a part-time student.

It was the beginning of my learning to fight with medical insurance representatives regarding coverage of various professional services. I wrote to them and explained the situation. Carol was only a part-time student because she wasn't well enough to take a full load. I let them know that any of her treating doctors would be happy to write that she was disabled if that would do the trick and that they, the insurers, were penalizing her for trying to put her life back together. The long and short of it was her coverage remained in force.

Dr. Saxon wrote a letter stating that Carol was unable to attend college classes during the winter and spring quarters because of the ongoing treatment she was receiving. He stated that his hope was for her to return to normal activities once the disease was stabilized. That also helped to inform the medical insurance company of what to expect.

During the summer, she was feeling rotten on and off, and spending time at the Pain Management Center. Phil, the computer manager who worked at the same company Dick did, knew of Carol's software experience and needed someone to help out on various projects. She could work when she felt like it instead of during the regular nine-to-five workday. He offered her a job, which was just what she needed.

Since the pain center seemed to have done its job, the Cytoxan™ was doing its job, and Carol had completed two classes, we were finally beginning to feel like we were out of the woods, our heads were above water, and we could see the light at the end of the tunnel. Maybe our luck hadn't run out.

The plan for chemotherapy was to continue taking the Cytoxan™ at full strength for one year and nine months from the time she had first begun, and then taper the dosage for the last three months.

That year Ken was offered a job by a newspaper in Florida. He wasn't eager to leave California but it was too good an offer to turn down. We knew we'd all miss him greatly, but having your offspring move away is part of life.

I had mentioned to Carol the possibility of visiting a local Toastmistress club in our new hometown with the thought of perhaps becoming active in the organization again. She thought it was a great idea and wanted to go with me. I called a representative from the group and made arrangements for the two of us to go. Carol liked it so well that she suggested we join then and there.

When Carol gave her first speech, which by custom is autobiographical, she likened her family to the old television program, "The Brady Bunch," indicating a group that was intelligent and witty, genuinely interested in each other's comings and goings and pet projects. I wondered whether she would discuss her illness at all, since there were a number of people present who had no idea what she'd been through.

That night she invited a few women she had worked with at Dick's company who had become friends of hers.

"I won't be as nervous with familiar faces in the audience," she told me.

She handled the stages of her illness factually, including chemotherapy, and ended on an upbeat note stating that the disease would not win the battle—she would. I had always felt she was going to win and was glad she thought so, too.

It was the first time I heard her tell her story, instead of just giving her medical history. It was beautifully done with just a glimmer of emotion.

But there was more than a glimmer for me. I had been asked to evaluate her talk, as is always done by other members in that group. The evaluation kept me busy writing as I identified parts to commend and parts that could be improved for future speeches.

If I had been watching a videotape of the speech it would have been with tears streaming down my face. As usual, my feelings were kept in check until later and only released in the shower that night.

It didn't take long for Carol to become a valuable asset to the club. She learned a lot, taught the others a lot, and seemed to thoroughly enjoy performing. It felt so good seeing her beginning to savor life again.

There was new cause for concern, however. Carol was spending more and more time at her apartment in Riverside and seemed to be growing more distant toward Dick and me. I tried to ignore her apparent feelings of animosity, but sometimes she was downright hostile. It didn't occur to me that she was *sick of being sick*, and no one reminds you of that more than Mommy and Daddy with their constant admonitions to eat well, put on your jacket because it's chilly outside, or all the hundreds of things that parents tell their children—as if any one of those were going to make a difference in Carol's case.

In the fall, Carol went on the UCR All-Cal Winter Carnival ski trip. Unfortunately, she fell and broke her wrist. It was her first skiing accident in the nine years she'd be indulging in the sport. We didn't even know it had happened until Don told us. She had taken care of it herself.

"Why didn't she call and let us know?" I asked Don.

"I guess she was tired of your nagging and thought you might be mad at her," he answered.

It was Don's answer that made me angry.

"Why would she think that? Nobody plans to have an accident," I said.

I was also hurt. I had never been crazy about the idea of her going skiing, but would never be mad at one of my children for having had an accident. Did my kids really think that badly of me?

Both Ron and Don told me that Carol was trying to take control of her own life and stop being a burden to us. But at no time did Dick or I ever think of her as a burden.

The Cytoxan™ and the Prednisone™ that Carol was taking weakened her bones and made it easier for them to break. Those drugs also inhibited the healing process.

When Carol walked in with her wrist in a cast, Dick and I weren't sure how to handle our feelings. We decided to, as the kids say, play it cool.

"Yes, we knew you had a broken wrist," I told her. "Don told us. How did it happen?"

"It happened the first day on the slopes when I fell. I continued skiing for a while before having it tended to."

"Why?" I asked.

"I didn't realize it was broken," she answered.

Her threshold for pain must have become so high that she probably didn't recognize the wrist pain to be as severe as a broken bone.

"Is the cast heavy and uncomfortable? Are you having trouble shifting?" I asked, referring to her car which had a stick[24] shift.

"It's not heavy at all. It's fiberglass, not plaster. At the hospital they asked if I intended going back on the slopes."

"And you said 'yes'?"

"Well, I said I didn't know, so they decided to put on the lighter cast—just in case."

"And did you go back on the slopes?"

"I started to, and then I decided I'd had enough."

My heart started beating at a normal rate again.

"Did you tell them about taking Cytoxan™?"

"No one asked."

"Why should they? It's not a question they would have on their regular list."

"Don't worry about it, Mom. I'm handling it."

I cautioned her about not having the cast removed too soon, and then tried to act as if nothing had happened that was unusual. She didn't seem to want any sympathy, anyway. There was obviously no use dwelling on the accident, since all that could have been done had been. She was managing.

"The only real problem I have is washing my hair. I can't get this arm wet."

"How about using a plastic bag and a rubber band?"

"That sounds like a good idea. I'll try that," she answered.

A few weeks later we had a party in our new home, the first one Dick and I had given in a very long time, on December 30. As she'd always done in the past, Carol was there to assist, cast and all.

Instead of spending the night in Pasadena after the party, she drove back to her apartment in Riverside, promising to return the next day for our New Year's celebration plans. Since she was making progress and starting to live like a normal human being again, we felt we finally had something to celebrate.

But on the morning of New Year's Eve, 1984, the one thing the doctors were looking for but never hoped to find, came to pass, and our worst fears were realized.

Carol called from Riverside early in the morning. Dick had taken the day off and answered the phone. We were still in bed.

"Hello? Hi, sweetie. You're what? When did it start? How much?"

I sat bolt upright in bed. Dick's tone indicated trouble.

"What's going on?" I asked him.

To Carol he said, "Do you want us to come get you?"

To me he said, "She's urinating blood."

"Let me talk to her."

"Hold on a minute. Your mother wants to talk to you," he said.

"She sounds OK," Dick said as he handed me the phone. "She said she was not in pain."

I leaned across Dick and grabbed the phone.

"When did it start?"

"When I got up in the middle of the night. It must have been about 3:00."

"Did you call Dr. Pryor?"

"Yes. He said to stop the Cytoxan™, go to the hospital, and have them take a specimen. Then they're supposed to call and let him know what they find. I thought I'd come home and have it done in Pasadena."

"Can you drive?"

"Yeah, Mom. I feel fine."

She actually sounded fine, too—not nervous, upset, or frightened.

"Are you sure?"

"I'm sure. I'd tell you if I couldn't drive. I'll be leaving in about a half hour."

"OK sweetheart. If you change your mind, let us know. We'll come get you."

"I'll be fine," she tried to reassure me. "See you later," she said and hung up.

What she was experiencing was a condition known as drug-induced sterile hemorrhagic cystitis, a common side effect of Cytoxan™. The product information sheet in the PDR states that this particular side effect can be severe and even fatal.

Carol had the page Dr. Haring had torn out of his PDR with her. Had she read it? Did she understand what was going on?

I had awoken with a bad headache and after taking some pain pills, went back to bed. When Carol arrived, Dick took her to the local hospital's emergency room. The pain pills had put me in a fog.

"How is she?" I asked Dick when they returned.

"She seems to be fine but the specimen was extremely bloody. It was as dark as grape juice," he said. "She's not in pain and no one seemed worried."

Carol was resting so I went back to bed again. Later that day Dick had to make another run to the hospital ER, this time with me to get a shot for the pain of my headache. Tension was taking its toll.

Looking back now, I wonder if we should have had her hospitalized immediately. But Dr. Pryor had told her that unless she was having discomfort or pain he would see her on January 2, two days later, for an afternoon appointment. She kept insisting that she felt fine, so we made no attempt to have her treated further. We had no clue as to how serious that episode was.

All three of us stayed close to home that evening and retired long before midnight. The New Year's Eve celebration had been postponed.

We had plans to attend the Tournament of Roses parade in person for the first time. When she awoke New Year's Day, Carol still insisted that she was feeling fine.

The three of us walked to our grandstand seats, about eight blocks away, watched the parade, walked to a restaurant afterwards to have breakfast, and then walked home. We lived close to the parade route and getting around by car during the New Year's holiday was next to impossible in downtown Pasadena; everything is blocked off for the parade. We spent the balance of the day at home and then we all went out to dinner in the evening. We walked to the restaurant.

Dick and I must have asked her, separately, a dozen times that day, "How do you feel? Does anything hurt? Are you still bleeding?"

She answered, "Fine, no, and yes," respectively.

She didn't appear to be weak and helped herself to whatever she wanted in the way of food or drinks. She didn't ask to be waited on. Her color remained good. We still had no idea that she was losing blood in any appreciable amount, or that she might be in danger of bleeding to death.

The next day Dr. Pryor asked Carol to give him a urine sample when we got to his office. He and I saw it together when she came back into the examining room from the bathroom with the specimen cup.

The shocked look on his face probably matched mine. The specimen was dark red and looked like pure blood.

"I'm going to call in Dr. Floyd Katske, a urologist,[25] to evaluate the situation," he said to me.

"Fine," I answered. "Call whoever you think we need."

To Carol he said, "I'm putting you in the hospital."

Dr. Pryor is a low-key, calm, easy-going person. Seeing him that concerned made me realize just how serious the situation was. By 5:00 PM, Carol was on her way to surgery and Dr. Katske was going to perform a cystoscopy.[26] I was told that this procedure was the only way a urologist could determine where she was bleeding and what to do about it.

I had called Dick to let him know that Carol was going into the hospital, but didn't know at the time what would be done. By the time she was taken to surgery, he was already en route.

While I was waiting in Carol's room, in walked Dr. Haring with the classic comment, "We have to stop meeting like this."

It took every ounce of strength not to collapse into tears. Until you call upon the strength from your inner depths, you never know how much is buried there. I had become very proficient at keeping myself in check.

I wondered how he knew. Maybe Dr. Pryor had called him. I don't recall asking.

"You're a sight for sore eyes," I said. "What are you doing here?"

"I'd like to assist in surgery, if you don't mind."

Dr. Haring assured me that Dr. Katske was one of the best urologists around, and said, "I want to see for myself what's going on."

"Of course we don't mind," I said. "You know there's no one else we would rather have assisting."

He gave me such peace of mind by just walking in the door.

Dick arrived just as Dr. Haring was leaving Carol's room for the OR, and Don was a few minutes behind him. I had been unable to reach Ron at work.

Carol had been put in a two-bed room. In order not to disturb the other patient we went to the waiting area, just outside surgery, to wait. I didn't ask for a private room, which she usually preferred, because that could always be done later if necessary.

After a while, Dr. Katske, still in his surgical greens, came looking for us. He appeared to be a pleasant, short, thin, balding man. He explained Carol's latest crisis in an easy-to-understand manner.

"The hemorrhaging was quite severe," he said. "There were about fifty, more or less, lesions in the bladder that needed to be cauterized. There's no question that the cause was Cytoxan™."

Once again she had an illness not caused by the disease but by the treatment.

"What would have happened if we had done nothing?" I wanted to know.

"Does this sort of thing heal itself?" Dick asked.

I will never forget his answer and the vivid description he left in my mind.

"Picture this," the doctor said. "Suppose you took a razor blade and made cuts," he put his hand up to his face and circled his mouth, "all around here. What do you think would happen?"

"You'd bleed to death," I said.

"Exactly. That's the same situation we had here."

I felt like a bomb had just gone off underneath me. I began remembering that we *walked* to the parade, *walked* to a restaurant for breakfast, and later that day when we had gone out to dinner, once again we *walked* to the restaurant. *Carol was losing blood the entire time.*

"If nothing had been done to stop the hemorrhaging, she probably would have bled to death," he said.

I felt weak in the knees and could see the blood draining from Dick's and Don's faces simultaneously. They looked like they were in shock. None of us had realized the danger Carol was in!

While the Cytoxan™ seemed to be doing a great job on Carol's nose and sinuses, it had made an unholy mess out of her bladder.

My thinking was that when the Cytoxan™ was discontinued, the problems it might have caused would stop. How could I have been so wrong and so oblivious as to what she was experiencing?

"I have no way of telling at the present time," Dr. Katske continued, "if the damage ends with the bladder, or if the kidneys are involved."

How much worse can this get? I wondered how much more one small body could take.

"As far as I can tell right now," he went on, "it seems to be just the bladder."

"I was able to control the bleeding," the doctor added, "but only time will tell. I would recommend that the Cytoxan™ be discontinued immediately and indefinitely. Carol should be checked regularly for a while to determine the extent of the damage.

"She'll have a catheter flushing out the bladder for the next few days so we can monitor what's going on. I need to make sure she doesn't start bleeding again."

Then he asked, "Do you have any questions?"

"No, not at the moment," Dick said. "Thank you, Doctor," he added.

Don and I muttered, "Thank you," walked to where the chairs were and sat down.

The doctor left.

As we sat staring at one another, trying to sort out our thoughts and catch our breath, Dr. Haring came to talk to us. He didn't look nearly as solemn as Dr. Katske.

That's good, I thought.

"This is certainly serious," he said, "but I'm sure she's going to be OK."

Hearing it from him made all the difference in the world.

"The Cytoxan™ has done what we had wanted it to do," he went on, "which was to arrest the Wegener's. Hopefully, we've solved the present problem, too.

"At this point we have to hope and pray that nothing else goes wrong. She should be coming back from Recovery soon. I'll be looking in on her again later."

Then he left us.

Since Carol had wanted to continue seeing the doctors in Valencia, it meant that she would be staying in the hospital there. We would be traveling back and forth to visit her. It didn't matter; all that was important was that she was comfortable.

When they brought her back to her room, she had an IV tube coming from her arm and a catheter tube from her bladder. That meant she wouldn't be allowed off the bed. We watched her sleep until visiting hours were over and then went home.

This was the first hospital stay in which Carol was awake and alert during most of our visits. The catheter was uncomfortable and irritating, but she didn't seem to be in pain anywhere else as she had been the other times she'd been hospitalized. In order to take her mind off her condition, I brought a different game each day thinking it would give us something to do together.

She was still wearing the cast from the skiing accident. Almost everyone who saw her asked if she was in the hospital for whatever was broken under her cast. There was no choice as to which arm got the IV; she only had one free one.

We had discouraged visitors when Carol was in the hospital the other times because she wasn't up to company. But this time I said it was all right to visit when someone asked.

Sandy, my close friend and real estate partner, went to see her and later told me that Carol was concerned about all the trouble she had caused Dick and me because of her illness.

"I hate seeing the worried looks on Mom's and Dad's faces when they walk in the door, knowing I'm the cause," she told Sandy.

"Honey, have you ever seen the look on your grandmother's face when your mother has a headache?"

Carol nodded.

"Well, that never changes," Sandy told her.

I thought I'd done such a good job of hiding my concern.

"I don't know how she keeps her spirits up," I said to Sandy.

"She keeps them up for you," she said.

After four days with no further hemorrhaging, Carol came home. She had missed the registration deadline for school once again.

The catheter had irritated Carol's urethra so badly that urination was quite painful for her. It took several kinds of medication and a couple of weeks for that to clear up.

Ken had been in touch with us, of course. When he was able to get away from Florida for a few days, he flew in to see for himself that his little sister was truly on the mend once again.

Six weeks after the skiing accident, Carol expected to have the cast removed. I urged her to have it X-rayed first. Thank goodness she agreed because the bone doctor discovered that it was not yet healed.

It took twice the normal time frame for the healing to be complete, and then the cast was removed. Both the Cytoxan™ and the Prednisone™ were to blame. Chemo injures rapidly dividing cells such as those trying to heal the broken bone; and steroids cause a delay in the movement of the healing cells into the site in response to the injury signals.

Three weeks after the cystoscopy and the discontinuance of the Cytoxan™, Dr. Saxon examined Carol with the rhinoscope. I was amazed to see for myself that the green blob was *completely* gone. The tissue that was there looked mostly normal, with one or two reddish spots, like irritations. What a far cry it was from the first time I'd looked inside her nose. The Cytoxan™ had definitely halted the spread of Wegener's.

Dr. Saxon felt it would be wise to begin the chemotherapy again, but Carol was adamantly opposed. In view of the bladder problem, we all felt we'd better leave well enough alone for the time being. While we knew Dr. Haring would have preferred not taking Carol off Cytoxan™, he was aware that we felt there was no choice.

In touch with Dr. Fauci, who also wanted Carol to begin chemotherapy again, but understood our reluctance, Dr. Saxon acquiesced to Carol's will.

It turned out that we were only part way out of the woods when, just before the end of the month, the hemorrhaging began again.

Dr. Katske said Carol would need another cystoscopy, without even seeing her or a urine specimen. But was it necessary to put her through the same procedure again so soon?

"I think we should get another opinion before we have a repeat performance," I said.

It wasn't a matter of not trusting Dr. Katske. I just wanted to be sure there wasn't an easier way.

After hearing Carol's story and seeing the specimen, a local urologist sat down with Dick, Carol, and me and explained that performing the cystoscopy was the only way to stop the hemorrhaging that he knew of. That would be his recommendation, also, he said.

He added, "What we have in the specimen cup is almost pure enough to inject right back into her veins. You have no choice. She should be hospitalized immediately and the cystoscopy done as soon as possible."

Carol had faced so many difficulties with one problem after another for so many years with such bravery. When she was told she would have to be hospitalized again for another cystoscopy, it was only the second time I'd seen tears stream down her face.

"I'm so sick and tired of all this," she cried.

I wanted to take her in my arms and rock her like a child, but it wouldn't have helped. I sat in my chair while she sat in hers. How would she be able to keep up her morale? But she had to bear whatever came to pass; there was no other option.

Dr. Katske was the one Carol wanted to handle this episode again. He'd helped her the last time and she trusted him. We were on our way once more to the hospital. The cystoscopy was performed and she was hospitalized for another four days.

Several months before the initial hemorrhaging, Dick and I had made reservations for a trip. We'd planned to leave the end of March. Needless to say we were reluctant to go. We were discussing a possible change of plans with Carol when Dr. Katske came in to check on her.

"They're thinking of canceling a trip," she told him. "Tell them it's not necessary and I'll be fine."

"When are you scheduled to leave?" he asked.

"In about five weeks," Dick answered, "assuming we go."

"Where are you going?" the doctor questioned.

"The British Isles," I answered.

"I can't see any reason for you to postpone it. She'll be fine."

Then he looked at Carol and asked, "You weren't going, were you?"

"No," she answered.

"She was invited, but didn't want to."

"I'd rather spend the money on a ski trip," Carol said.

"I would definitely advise against Carol going abroad under the circumstances, but there's no reason for you two not to go," the doctor said.

"She'll get whatever care she needs whether you're in town or not. Doesn't she have brothers who live close?"

We both answered in the affirmative.

Dick and I knew, without question, we could count on Ron and Don to help Carol in any way possible.

"That's fine," Dr. Katske said. "There should be no problems."

"The care in Europe may not be what Carol is used to, and I wouldn't want any complications if she were to begin bleeding again."

"Then this could keep happening?" Carol asked as the color drained from her face.

"For this to have happened twice is extremely unusual, and I would feel confident that we won't see a recurrence, as long as you don't resume taking Cytoxan™.

"You must keep in mind, of course, that nothing in medicine is certain," he added.

We'd all heard that before.

"I was planning to go on a ski trip at the end of this week," Carol said.

"Would you please tell her how crazy it is to go that soon after what she's been through?" I asked.

But the doctor didn't agree.

"I see no reason why Carol can't go skiing if she wants to."

"You're kidding," I said. "Don't you think skiing would be too strenuous for her under the circumstances?"

"If she's not feeling up to it, she won't ski," the doctor said. And then he told us something that would serve as a guide for the rest of our lives: "Don't try to make an invalid out of her or you'll have a lot more trouble on your hands than you have now."

I suppose, without realizing it, that's probably what I was trying to do.

"I just want her to slow down so she'll get better faster."

"There's nothing she can do that will make a difference," he said. "Is she getting treatment when necessary?"

"Yes."

"Well, that's all she can do. Nothing else will alter her condition."

All the doctors kept telling me to let her do what she felt like doing. They wanted her to live as normal a life as possible. It was time to let go and step back—a very difficult thing for the mother of a sick child to do, especially under those current conditions.

She went on the ski trip at the end of that week and had no mishaps.

In March, Carol won our Toastmistress club's annual speech contest. I was one of the contestants that she beat, and was delighted. That meant she would represent our club at the council level in April.

Carol registered for two classes at college, which is all she felt she could physically handle. Her doctors concurred. So began the spring quarter at UCR. That meant she would again be living in the apartment in Riverside.

Simultaneously, she began working on another computer project in Pasadena. She would have to commute from Riverside two or three times a week. But Carol's enjoyment of both school and work made her feel like she was accomplishing something worthwhile. As she had said before, her life was no longer on hold.

At the April speech contest she placed third out of eight. She did a great job and made her club proud, not to mention her parents.

After school began and Carol was back at her apartment, she made the appointments with her various doctors on her own, going by herself. She had really taken control of her life.

The only way I knew who she saw was when the insurance explanation of benefits arrived. We would like to have known more about what was happening, but it was time to let her handle things. By now, she was twenty-three.

Against our objections, Carol got a part-time job to assist with her educational expenses. She agreed to work a specified number of hours a week. Interestingly enough, it was with the same company Dick had worked for when she was born.

The job and the commute seemed as if they would put too much pressure on her. The other jobs had allowed her to work when she felt like it. Dick and I had been handling her college expenses up till now and told her we would continue to do so for as long as it was necessary.

Perhaps though, she felt that because the illness had prolonged the years she was attending school it might be a financial burden for us. Maybe she just wanted to take care of it herself as she had done with so many other things in the past.

It never occurred to me that she may have wanted to prove to herself that she could take charge of her life again.

When Carol was hired, she didn't tell her employers about her health problems. As a part-time employee, she would not be covered under that company's insurance plan anyway. However, a physical examination was required for the job. When her blood was tested, Carol was told there were some abnormalities. She had expected that, since the chemotherapy had caused very definite changes. No follow-up on the blood test was ever pursued by the company.

The job went well and Carol enjoyed it.

"I'm the only one who understands the system," she told us proudly. "I frequently have to explain what's going on computer-wise to people who've worked there for years."

When worried about Carol's activities, I would discuss them with the various doctors she was seeing. They all kept giving me the same advice: "Let her do whatever she feels like doing. If she's not able to handle it, she won't."

In May we had good news and bad. The good news was that Dr. Katske said the bladder had healed and he didn't need to see Carol any more unless she had any new problems. The bad news was that Dr. Haring said it looked like the Wegener's was becoming active again. He wanted to talk to her about renewing chemotherapy to nip it in the bud before it got a good toehold.

Carol remained adamant about not wanting to start treatment again under any circumstances. As he had said before, he would not force anything on her, but he was very concerned.

"If the disease were to spread to the brain," he said, "there's no telling if anything would stop it. She has to make a decision."

What we hadn't realized was that she had already made one.

------

24.   Stick is slang for standard transmission which is what her car had.

25.   A urologist is a licensed physician who specializes in disorders and care of the urinary tract.

26.   Cystoscopy is the procedure for direct visualization of the bladder and urinary tract, removal of tumors and polyps, taking of biopsies, etc.

16

A Twenty-Three-Year-Old Teenager

A new friend, named Noreen,* from our Toastmistress Club, learned what Carol had been going through for the past seven years, and told us that she had worked for the City of Hope; she added that the doctor she worked for had a particular interest in Wegener's, and had collected a number of research papers about the disease, noting effective treatments.

The City of Hope, in my mind, was primarily a cancer treatment center, so I wondered why a doctor who worked there would be interested in Wegener's. Noreen told me, however, that the hospital and research center treated all catastrophic diseases, and Wegener's certainly fell into that category.

If her former employer were interested in seeing Carol, she asked if I would take her there. I told her I definitely would.

Then I told Carol about my conversation with Noreen.

"I think it would be a good idea to have an evaluation there."

"You won't be happy unless we do," she answered. "Go ahead and make an appointment."

Although she didn't usually employ sarcasm, I chalked it up to frustration on her part, and the nuisance of having to go through the same tests and stories all over again.

"Since the City of Hope treats so many cancer patients, and since the use of Cytoxan™ is primarily a treatment for cancer, maybe they have some way of using the drug without causing the bladder to hemorrhage," Dick said after hearing the details. "It's worth a try."

As usual, he suggested discussing it with Dr. Haring.

When I mentioned the City of Hope to the doctor, he thought it was a great idea.

"If they need any information from me, or even my file, feel free to offer it," he said. "Good luck, and have them send me a report."

"Noreen brought copies of several research papers about Wegener's for us to read. The most recent one was by Dr. McDonald, along with Drs. DeRemee and Weiland, our old friends from the Mayo Clinic. It seemed that they had found success using Septra™.

I called the doctor Noreen told me about and was informed that he was strictly involved with research and did not see patients. He offered to put me in touch with someone who did.

Within a short time a call came in from a Dr. Timothy Stevens.* After hearing an explanation of Carol's condition, he had his receptionist make an appointment for Carol. I pushed her to make the appointment as soon as possible. If this new doctor could assure Carol that chemotherapy could be administered without the threat of a bleeding bladder, it might give Carol more hope toward returning to treatment.

When the day of the examination arrived, Carol chose to meet Dick and me at the City of Hope instead of coming home and going to the hospital together. She was annoyed by the prospect of having to go at all, and acted as though she was actually doing us a favor.

"This is your idea, Mom, not mine. I know you won't be happy unless I have one more evaluation."

"This is not necessarily our idea of fun, either," I replied, "but since the subject of chemotherapy is being raised again, and the City of Hope treats so many cancer patients, maybe they have a way of dealing with the side effects that would cause fewer problems."

The aptly named City of Hope is an enormous complex, truly like a city unto itself. At that time, no one who went there for treatment or consultation paid a penny. We were told it was funded by donations or whatever patients' insurance paid.

Before we saw the doctor, we had a short conference with a social worker. I was a little uncomfortable anticipating that discussion because I had always associated social workers with the indigent.

But what these social workers do is emotional counseling, not only for the patient, but also for the whole family. That makes sense, since a catastrophic disease affects everyone involved and not just the patient.

Carol was reluctant to discuss anything with the social worker. But, accustomed to hostile patients, the woman was charming and patient.

The doctor we were to see was a kidney specialist. He was a little taller than average, slim and good looking. His youthful face belied enough years to account for his snow white hair. He had a soft-spoken, easy-going manner, and smiled a lot.

By the time we saw the doctor, Carol had become much more hostile, to the point of ignoring Dick and me when we spoke to her. We had to work around her attitude, since there wasn't a thing we could do to change it.

The examining room was small, but seemed to have an extraordinary amount of equipment on rolling carts and on the walls.

"What brings you to the City of Hope?" the doctor asked Carol.

She told her story so briefly that one would have thought it was nothing more than a hangnail.

I thought once again that keeping a journal of the happenings since the disease had first begun to change all our lives would have helped.

Dr. Stevens, like Dr. McDonald, asked Dick and me to step outside for a few moments so he could speak to Carol alone.

A short time later, the doctor came out and asked, "Is there anything either of you feel I should know that Carol hasn't mentioned?"

We filled him in on what we felt was important and then I added, "She's very unhappy about being here today."

"It's not at all unusual for seriously ill people to be angry and hostile," he said. "Thank you for the information."

He returned to the examining room and soon opened the door and said, "You can come back in now."

Like every other doctor, Dr. Stevens wanted his own set of blood and urine tests and X-rays. He arranged for the tests to be done immediately.

Then he said, "Carol should go back on chemotherapy. The disease has to be arrested. We have ways of administering the drugs that will fool the bladder, so the same problems she experienced earlier this year would be less likely to recur."

"Less likely?" Carol asked. "But it could happen again?"

"Yes, of course it could," the doctor said. "But it's our job to see that it doesn't."

Carol just scowled.

Dick and I liked Dr. Stevens and his manner. We also liked the City of Hope and the way things were handled. It reminded us a little of the extraordinary competence of the people at the Mayo Clinic. But it wasn't where Carol wanted to be treated so we never saw that doctor again.

Carol did go back a time or two for tests and consultations. She also received notifications of, and sometimes changes of, appointments. But which appointments she kept, which she changed, and which she ignored, was never brought up.

She refused to discuss anything at all about the City of Hope or what went on there. Perhaps she didn't want to begin all over again with strangers. I wondered if the doctor hadn't said anything about resuming chemotherapy if it would have made any difference in Carol's treatment decisions. Probably not.

For the next few months we saw almost nothing of Carol. Except for what we could find out from Don or Ron, we had no idea how she was or what she was doing. She avoided coming to Pasadena when she knew Dick and I would be home. If she happened to be there when we walked in the door, she disappeared quickly. If I was able to reach her by phone, the conversation went something like this:

Carol: "What do you want?"

Me: "We were all invited to a dinner party next Saturday and they'd like us to be there at 6:00" or "Dad's going to be out of town next week and you can use his car if you need to get yours serviced" or "I just had a call from Kenny and he'll be here for a week just before the July 4th holiday" or "One of the speakers can't make the next Toastmistress meeting and a new speaker needs to be assigned in her place."

Carol: "Is that all?"

And then the conversation was over.

I couldn't understand what was happening and it hurt. We'd always had such wonderful rapport. I loved hearing about what was going on in her life and she had enjoyed telling me. She had been interested in what was going on in my life also. If she ever had any doubts as to whether Dick or I would drop everything and run to her aid if she needed us, all she had to do was ask. She could have tested us in any way at all. But she had chosen to shut us out of her life.

I asked Ron and Don several times if they would please find out what the problem was. Both of them, separately and on several occasions, told me that she wasn't mad at us. She was just tired of my nagging.

That made no sense at all to me. I hadn't seen or spoken to her in so long that if inclined toward nagging her, I wasn't even being given the opportunity. It didn't take someone with a psychology degree to figure out she was building a wall between us, and I honestly had no idea why.

I was angry too. Although not physically feeling her pain, I had been through emotional pain with her in every other way. I would lie in bed at night, unable to sleep, frequently crying into my pillow so as not to disturb Dick, wondering what I had done to push her so far away from me.

Was this the same little girl that I carried inside me under my heart, fed at my breast, agonized over when she had skinned knees and sunburned shoulders? Was this the same little girl whose pony-tailed hairdo I combed so gently and tied with ribbons? Didn't she know how much it hurt me just to see her get an immunization shot some twenty years ago while holding her close, waiting to soothe the tears that never came? Didn't she know how just a scowl from her could break my heart? Didn't she even care?

When I was finished crying and my hurt feelings had abated, I would become angry and plot emotional punishments for her, which of course I would never carry out. She had been punished more than enough. There was no way I was deliberately going to add to her misery. I only wanted her to be healthy and happy, neither of which I had any control over.

I would have given her anything in the world that she wanted, including my life if that were possible. But she wouldn't give me the time of day. The wonderful relationship we'd shared was now in shreds.

The two things I wanted I couldn't have: the health and companionship of my little girl. I missed her so much it almost hurt physically, and I desperately wanted to feel her arms around me again.

After a few nights of sitting in the dark, licking my emotional wounds, I decided to put some thoughts and feelings down on paper. It relieved my mind of the moment's anxiety, and enabled me to go back to bed and possibly sleep. Before long, there were thirty pages and my night writing had become a catharsis.

My memory served me well while recounting, with pen and paper, the medical events that had led to the discoveries, treatments, and results of Carol's battle with Wegener's.

At that time, this wasn't intended to be a book; it was just the unloading of my mind and heart. Those pages were meant for my own personal recollections, and perhaps to keep the numerous details concerning her illness in some semblance of order. I had plans to recheck the facts with Dick and Carol to make sure my order was correct and nothing was forgotten.

The few people who knew the situation, Dr. Haring, Mom, two or three of our close friends, had some comforting words: "You've always had such a great relationship. She won't forget that. She knows where you are if she needs you. Just step back and give her some breathing room. She knows you're available. She's avoiding you because you remind her that she's been sick and right now she needs time and space to forget."

In other words, they were saying that she would come back to me, to us, in her own time.

We had been reminding her that the various doctors thought she should begin chemotherapy again, and that was the last thing she wanted to hear, or do.

One question arose with a couple of her doctors as to whether she was refusing treatment, setting herself up to defy death. Although the word was never spoken, my impression was that I was being asked if Carol might be contemplating suicide, even if subconsciously, by refusing treatment. That was never my fear. She valued life much too much to chance ending it, no matter what it cost to survive.

One evening Carol came to see one of her brothers, unaware that Dick and I were having a small dinner party. She was absolutely charming to all our guests, just as she'd been in the past. No one would have guessed there was a thing wrong in the family.

I stood there watching her, bursting with ambivalent feelings of pride and despair at the same time. How I wanted to give her a big hug and get one from her in return.

When Dick tried to put his arm around her, she squirmed out and made a quick getaway. I didn't even try to touch her.

Where did we go wrong? What did we do that was so bad?

Carol continued to come to Toastmistress meetings twice a month, where she treated me like she hardly knew me.

I hoped that my little girl was hiding somewhere inside that person who had become a stranger.

Before the hostility began, I had been nominated for President of the Toastmistress club.

"I think that's terrific, Mom," she'd said at the time. "You'll do a great job. Can I be program chairman?"

Later when I was elected, Carol volunteered to organize the installation.

She became program chairman, and began to carry out those duties, but still having as little contact with me as possible.

If you can't beat them, you have to join them. Since there wasn't a thing that could be done about her attitude, I had to accept it, and using one of Dick's favorite expressions from his old days in the private practice of law: govern myself accordingly.

I kept calling Mom again and again to ask for her advice and assistance. She kept telling me what I should have already known. Mom had a way of doing that.

"Give her time. Carol knows she's loved and when she's ready she'll come back to you."

Dick and I decided that the best course of action was no action at all. We would just wait it out, telling ourselves once again that we had no other choice.

I knew from receiving the insurer's explanation of benefits that Carol finally started seeing Dr. Haring again.

Phoning him for an update, I told him, "I'm just anxious to know how things are going."

"I'm happy to tell you," he said, "that Carol's nose and sinuses appear to be getting better again. It seems as if she made the right decision for her. There's no telling how long this present remission will last, but she knows where to get help if she needs it. And please feel free to call me at any time. I'm always happy to talk to you."

Ken was anxious to make a trip home. He knew the situation with Carol and wanted to see for himself if he could help. After he arrived from Florida, Carol seemed to be too busy to see him either in Pasadena or Riverside. He was hurt and disappointed when she didn't return his phone calls.

One night when I was up writing, Ken came downstairs, suffering from jet lag and unable to sleep either.

"I'm really sorry you're having so much trouble connecting with your sister," I told him, "but I'm glad Dad and I aren't the only ones. We were beginning to feel like outcasts."

"Well, I can't continue to take 'no' for an answer indefinitely," he said.

He had only a few days left before he had to go back to Florida and work.

"What are you writing?" he asked me.

"Some things about your sister. I think there might be enough for some kind of magazine article."

I said that with tongue in cheek, never before having written anything with the thought of publication.

"How would you feel about my reading it?"

There wasn't anyone with whom I'd rather share the story. All the years Ken was studying journalism, I was his editor. Now I might have the chance to turn the tables on him and get his opinion on whether or not his mom could write, too.

"I'd love it if you'd like to take the time."

"Hand it over," he said.

He read it without expression. When he was finished, he handed me back the pages.

"A lot of this is news to me. I moved out around the time Carol had the first biopsy. Getting settled in a new home and new job, and living two hours away put me somewhat out of touch on a daily basis."

Great. He found it informative.

"Is there enough for an article?"

"No!" he said emphatically. "You've got a book here, Mom. Expand it and go with it."

That was the validation I needed.

"I'm going to Riverside tomorrow," he announced, "and I'll camp on her doorstep if I have to."

We both went back to bed.

"Well?" I asked when Ken returned. "Did you see her?"

"It was really a strange visit," he said. "She says she's not mad at anyone. But she had very little to say altogether. I felt like a stranger instead of her brother. It was as if she didn't care if she saw me or not."

"Here I've come three thousand miles and she doesn't seem to give a damn."

We did our best to console one another.

"I guess we have to understand that being sick hasn't been easy for her. She's done so little complaining and has been so brave all along. It may have just caught up with her. Your father seems to have a pretty good description of the situation. He said we have a twenty-three-year-old teenager on our hands. She was too sick to have gone through the usual rebellious stage that the rest of you did, and that's what we're seeing now."

"It would be nice if that's all it is," Ken said. "I guess we'll just have to wait it out. So what are you doing to get through all this?"

"Well, I wanted to run away and hide until the whole thing blows over, but there's no place to go. I can only run away in my mind. My best bet is to go to work. It will give me less time to think about whether or not Carol's mad at me, and what to do about it. Your father has his work to occupy his mind during the day, and I go crazy with my thoughts because my mind isn't busy."

"I thought you weren't going to sell real estate anymore," he said.

"I'm not. Dad's tired of spending weekends by himself. I need a nine-to-five job. Then I can be home when he is."

"What kind of work are you thinking about?"

"I thought I'd try loan processing. I've had a job interview and hope to hear about it shortly."

Just before Ken left, I was offered the job and accepted.

Dick wasn't crazy about the idea but didn't protest. I was working for two months before Carol knew about it.

With one of my first paychecks, I bought her an answering machine and asked Ron to set it up for her during his next visit there. I put a funny note on it: "How come you never call your mother?"

After more time had passed, Carol started to become part of the family again. Each time she came home and stayed long enough to put five words together, I was overjoyed. We were making progress.

I was anxious to know how she was feeling and what was going on with her health. As long as we talked about school, work, dates, her car, clothes—anything but her health—it was OK. The minute I asked her anything like how she felt, had she seen Drs. Haring, Pryor, or Saxon, had they changed any of her medications, it was like the kiss of death, and she disappeared as quickly as if I had waved a magic wand. The message was obvious so I simply stopped asking.

Therefore, Dr. Haring was my best source. If there was any information to be gleaned from the other doctors she saw, he checked with them and let me know.

It became a habit to call him every so often to find out what was new with her. Information was never relayed through any of his staff; he always spoke to me himself.

"It's no problem," he said. "I'm happy to give you the latest news."

He gave me any information he had, either on Carol's physical well-being or sometimes just her state of mind.

"If she doesn't want to talk about her health," he said, "then don't bother her about it. Call me."

"It can't be easy for her," I said. "It's like living with the sword of Damocles[27] over her head."

"We all live with the sword," he answered. "The only difference with Carol is that hers is more pronounced."

Once he said, "By the way, I told Carol we've been having these conversations. I hope you don't mind."

"Absolutely not," I answered.

I had never suggested he not tell her.

Because Carol was now an adult, this might have been construed as an invasion of her privacy if he hadn't gotten her permission.

The doctor was very pleased to let me know that she had no objections.

Because Dick was traveling more for work, I found myself with more spare time and began to spend it with some of my single friends. One of my co-workers and I went out to dinner one evening and then came back to my house to visit for a while. She's an avid reader and seemed impressed with our extensive library.

She remarked, "Boy, you have it all. I wish I'd made it like you have."

Having told her about Carol, I said, "Would you like my grief to go along with it?"

Her silence was the answer.

Dick and I had become enamored with the idea of buying a vacation home. We made an offer to purchase one in the mountains. When that didn't work out the way we had planned, we switched our thoughts to the desert. We felt it would be an outlet and a chance to unwind from five days with our noses to the grindstone.

There was another reason for having a vacation home in the desert. Although my parents had talked about moving west for a very long time, they were beginning to sound much more serious. A house in the desert would give them a place to call their own if they did move to California. They could use our vacation home as a pivot point until they decided where they wanted to settle. We found a condo we liked in Palm Springs and bought it.

About the same time, Carol decided she wanted to have a party at our place in Pasadena. Because most of her friends were now people with whom she worked and who lived closer to our home, it was logical to have it there. Dick was going to be out of town again and I offered to get lost also, but she said that wasn't necessary.

Toward the end of the party, Carol's friend John arrived. I hadn't seen him in a long time and was delighted to have the opportunity to question him as to what was going on with Carol. Unfortunately, he was in the dark, too. They'd spent the time he was home from medical school playing telephone tag, and he knew less about what had transpired than we did.

After forty years in Florida, my parents finally sold their home and moved west. Carol now had a new excuse to visit home, just in case she needed one. When she knew they would be in Pasadena, she made it a point to stop by.

The first time Mom saw her after their move, she was shocked. She didn't recognize her own granddaughter.

"How could you not know her?" I asked.

"I was just getting out of the car and she was coming out of the house," Mom said. "I had no idea who she was."

"Who did you think she was?"

"One of Ron's or Don's girlfriends," she answered.

"When did you know it was Carol?"

"When she said hello and put her arms around me."

"Did she really change that much? I know she's cut her hair short. The last time you saw her it was longer, but ..."

"It's not her hair," Mom said. "It's her features. She looks like a totally different person."

"When was the last time you saw her?"

"1983, about two months after she got back from the Mayo Clinic."

"Oh. Now I understand. Telling you her nose had collapsed, and seeing it for yourself are two different things, aren't they? But I don't think she looks bad at all. Do you?"

"She looks adorable," Mom said. "But it's really a drastic change."

I actually had no idea how much she had changed. It was so gradual we had hardly noticed.

By that time, Carol was wandering in and out of our home and staying longer. Although still anxious to know how she was and what was going on, I knew better than to ask. As long as we didn't discuss her health, the visits went well.

---

27. From classical Greco/Roman history: to feel the sword of Damocles hanging over you is to have a sense of anxiety, of impending doom.

17

More Pain, No Gain

Back in school, hoping to graduate in June of the following year, 1986, Carol gave us all a silent indication that things were going along OK. Then one day, she sat down with me and let me know they weren't.

"The sinus pain and the headaches have been getting bad again," she told me.

Her voice was very matter-of-fact, but there was disappointment in her eyes. We both knew the direction in which we were heading, and neither of us liked it.

By this time I'd become a little wiser, and didn't jump in with both feet and start telling her what to do. Instead, I asked her what she wanted to do about these new problems.

I wanted desperately for her to come home again, but not for that reason—not because she was sick.

"I don't know," she said. "I'll see what Dr. Haring and Dr. Saxon suggest."

We both knew that if there was no improvement, treatments would have to become more aggressive. She had apparently decided not to discuss it for the time being.

If and when stronger treatment was necessary, we'd deal with it.

Carol began making more appointments with Dr. Haring and he was keeping a closer watch on what was going on inside her nose.

And once again the insurance papers indicated which doctors she was seeing. But she didn't see them that often. Dr. Haring, however, knew what was going on because she talked more to him. He continued to be unbelievably patient with my phone calls to him.

Carol only discussed her health with me if she brought it up. I tried to relate to her as though speaking to her brothers who hadn't had serious health problems and act accordingly.

One day she said, after a visit to Dr. Haring, "He wants me to have another consultation with Dr. Saxon."

"When are you going?" I asked.

"I don't know. I'll have to call him. I'd like to wait until exams are over," she answered.

"Can I go with you?" I asked.

"It's not necessary," she answered.

Not necessary to you, I thought.

"OK," I said, silently gritting my teeth. "If you need me, let me know."

Carol had little spare time. I was beside myself worrying about the combination of school, work, and commuting being too much pressure.

"If she's able to cope with discomfort, which could be anything from a minor annoyance to intense pain, I know that's what she'll do," I told Dick.

"She's twenty-three, a grown woman," Dick said. "We can't tell her what to do anymore."

Boy! Had he said a mouthful!

Carol was coming back home more and more. I felt it necessary to avoid talking about her health. It was like walking on eggshells to speak to her and I didn't want any to crack.

In the beginning of 1986, and towards the end of winter, I noticed, through the pharmacy bills, she was taking pain pills again. That has always bothered her since she likes to be in control, and feels that having to take narcotics takes that control away.

I began to think more seriously about writing Carol's story so that the rest of the world would know just how brave she had been. I also began to find that my job was becoming mundane and boring, so I quit and was now free to spend any time with Carol that she would let me.

Unfortunately, I couldn't dispel the feeling that she was going to be needing me a lot more.

By April the symptoms had returned in full force. Carol was taking more and more pain pills.

"I'd like to go with you next time you see Dr. Haring."

This time I didn't ask.

"OK."

She had agreed too easily. Now I knew we were in trouble again.

"I know I've told you this before," Dr. Haring said, "but I'm very concerned about the direction that the disease might take if it spreads."

"Then you think it's active again?" I asked.

"I can't see any other reason for Carol to be having headaches and sinus pain. Oh, we all know it could be a lot of other things. But I don't think so and I don't think Carol thinks so, either."

He looked at her. She lowered her head and nodded.

"I'd like to have you see Dr. Saxon for a rhinoscopy again," Dr. Haring continued. "Then we'll all find out what's going on inside your head."

"I've got some new symptoms," Carol said. "It's my ears. I think I have lost some hearing."

Damn! Why was she keeping these secrets?

"Let me have Randy, the audiologist, test you. I'll see how busy he is."

After Dr. Haring left the room I asked Carol why she hadn't said something about it.

"It's no big deal, Mom."

But it was to me.

The doctor returned and said the audiologist could see Carol in about five minutes. We walked to the other end of the building where the testing equipment was. Randy took her into the testing room while I waited in the reception area. It took about thirty minutes to complete the test.

"I was right," she said smugly as she emerged from the testing room. "I do have some hearing loss."

Dr. Haring said he thought aspirin might be the cause of her hearing problem.

"Do you still need pain pills?"

"Unfortunately, I do," Carol answered.

"Then let's switch to Tylenol with codeine and let me see you in a couple of weeks."

While we were there, I mentioned to Dr. Haring that I had watched the movie, "Anatomy of an Illness" based on Norman Cousins' book by the same name.

"The story fascinated me so I bought the book."

"It's a great book," the doctor said. "I think Carol should read it. There's a lot to be said about attitude in relation to getting well. By the way, I think Carol has a story to tell, too, if she ever feels like putting it down on paper."

That was very encouraging to me. If Dr. Haring thought it was important enough to tell others, I *had* to write a book.

"I'm a step ahead of you," I said. "I've started writing about Carol."

Then Carol had something surprising to say.

"I'd still like to have my nose fixed," she announced.

"After all you've been through, I didn't think you'd let anyone touch your nose unless it was a dire necessity," I said.

"I never stopped wanting to have it fixed, and now I think it needs it even more."

"What do you think?" I asked Dr. Haring who had been watching our interchange with an amused expression.

"I'm not really sure I would do anything about it. I don't think it looks bad," he said.

"I do," Carol said.

"What I'd rather see you do is get a prosthesis," the doctor added.

"A false nose?" I asked. "Wouldn't that stand out like a sore thumb?"

That was a dumb thing to say.

"Actually," he said, "it's fitted to her face and she might have to put a little make-up around the edges. But it's my understanding—although I've yet to see one—that no one would know the difference."

"That's amazing," I said.

"It's too premature to worry about. We have to get her cleared up first," the doctor added.

"So you still want to have your nose fixed," I said on the way home.

"Why are you surprised? I never changed my mind about that," she said.

Dr. Haring turned out to be right about switching to Tylenol because when she had another hearing test done two weeks later, the ringing in her ears was significantly less.

Even though we'd owned the Palm Springs condo for seven months, Carol had never seen it. One day she decided to have a party there and I was happy she was finally going to see the place. No matter how bad she felt, she always enjoyed having her friends around her.

Carol had told Dr. Haring that she would make an appointment with Dr. Saxon, but we knew she had other, more pressing, things on her mind. She was nearing graduation—two years overdue.

This was also the time of year that job recruiters were on campus.

"I'd like to get a summer job that could continue as a permanent one when I get my degree," she told us.

We all know how frustrating job hunting can be. But not for Carol.

She researched her field for salary comparisons before interviewing. Because of her Toastmistress training, public speaking experience, self confidence, and extensive work experience, she was definitely in the driver's seat and able to make higher demands. Everyone who interviewed her offered her a job, which was quite unusual.

Although her brothers kidded her, I reminded them that it was about time that something good happened to her.

Carol was able to negotiate a part-time job until school was over for full-time pay and benefits, except for hospitalization. Nothing that was pre-existing would be covered for a year. Fortunately, we were able to continue coverage through Dick's employer.

Carol chose the same company Don worked for. They were looking for someone with Carol's skills, and Don had made sure her résumé got to the right person. When the offers started coming in, some were lower than ones she had already turned down. When she mentioned that to the interviewer at Don's company, she was asked to give them a chance—that this was just a first offer.

Carol requested a final interview to question her soon-to-be immediate supervisor about what she would be doing. Since it appeared getting a job was not a problem, she needed to make sure that it was what she wanted to do.

Her future boss asked, "Don't you think the starting salary you've asked for is a little high?"

"Of course it is," Carol answered. "But who have you spoken to lately that's my age who has my qualifications, knowledge, and experience?"

She was hired under her own terms, initially as a part-time employee. She began working a specified number of hours per week, usually three to four days, but at her convenience and coordinating with her class schedule. Although she was commuting from her apartment near college one hundred fifty miles round trip, she was able to plan her freeway hours for times when traffic was light.

"I don't mind it," she would tell me. "It's relaxing."

But I was sure it had to cause some wear and tear on her body, since it seemed as though it would have done that even to a healthy person.

The company had agreed to hire her, full-time with benefits and a raise in pay, after college.

However, just before graduation, Carol was notified she needed two more classes to complete her double major of computer science and math. She would not be graduating in June. By this time, so much of her life had already been postponed, it was a disappointment—but minor compared to some of her other reasons for delay.

When she was hired at the full-time rate, the counselors at UCR told her she held the record for the highest starting salary of anyone in her field from her alma mater, and Don got $1,000 finder's fee.

Since Don and Carol were working at the same place, I wondered how they would feel about sharing an apartment. I broached the subject very carefully because, after all, it was none of my business. I didn't want it to seem like I was pushing them together or trying to interfere in their lives in case they didn't think it was a good idea.

They were way ahead of me, and had already started doing some apartment hunting. One thing was certain: since they'd grown up and gone to college together, they certainly knew that they could get along.

They found an apartment ten minutes from work in a security building with locked underground parking. That was one less reason to worry—something a mother never stops doing.

It was a perfect floor plan for them with two master suites, each with a private bath. Don moved into the apartment in June and Carol followed three weeks later. What a relief it must have been for her to drive ten minutes to work instead of two hours. And what a relief it was for me to know that.

Besides being ten minutes from work, it was also ten minutes from UCLA Medical Center and Dr. Saxon.

Carol finally got around to making an appointment with Dr. Saxon, and she let me come. He had a team with him as usual. I was not one of the people who got to see inside her nose this time since she was reluctant to have me look.

"The disease never left you completely," Dr. Saxon told Carol, "and I'm concerned about it spreading."

He and Dr. Haring were singing the same song again.

"I think we should do another CT scan," the doctor said.

"I had one," said Carol.

"When?"

"About ten days, maybe two week ago."

And I had thought the communication at UCLA had improved.

Not knowing which doctors Carol was seeing and when, I had no idea what tests were being done. The statements I received used codes, impossible for the layman to decipher. Although I was taking care of the bills, I didn't know what many of them were for. I had gotten so used to not questioning Carol; it was becoming a bad habit.

"I also had an MRI taken," she said.

"When?" the doctor asked.

"About the same time, give or take a few days."

"How come I don't have the results?"

Carol looked at him and shrugged her shoulders.

"That's a good question," I said. "Why do they keep these things to themselves?"

"Let's find out," he said and picked up the phone.

While the doctor was searching for an answer, I asked Carol, "What's an MRI?"

"It stands for magnetic resonance imaging. It's kind of like radio waves that are bounced off the person to form a picture."

"Why were they doing that?"

"There was supposed to have been a comparison made between the two tests to determine both the amount of destruction and whether there was a new recurrence of Wegener's."

"Are you aware of the results?"

"They said destruction was definitely continuing, which means the disease is active again. This time they used dye," Carol said. "It was injected into my veins before they did the scan."

Dr. Saxon said, "OK. Thank you," into the phone and turned to us.

"They're still looking for them and will call me back," he said. "The tests won't tell us anything we didn't already know," he added. "All they will do is confirm it.

"We're not facing an emergency at this time, but neither can we stand by and do nothing. If we ignore the situation, and the disease spreads," he continued as he walked toward Carol, "you could be in big trouble."

The phone rang. He turned back to the desk to pick it up. After listening for a moment or two he said, "Please send them to me immediately," and hung up.

"They had them both," he said. "They just hadn't bothered letting me know. They were sent to the warehouse after a week because no one picked them up. No one picked them up because I wasn't told they were ready," the doctor continued, shaking his head.

"It will take a few hours for them to be delivered," he added. "There's no sense keeping you waiting. We know what we have to do."

"You know," Dr. Saxon continued, "Tony thinks you should have never gone off the Cytoxan™," he said to Carol, referring to Dr. Fauci.

"In spite of the bladder problems?"

"Yes."

"Would it have made any difference if Carol had never had the scar tissue removed from her nose? Do you think it caused a reactivation?"

"Tony thinks so," he said.

"I wonder why this is the first time we've heard that."

"By the time we saw her, it was already done."

Of course. I'd forgotten about that. So much water had gone under the bridge since then. Pandora's Box had already been opened.

Almost as if he had read my mind, the doctor said, "It probably would have happened whether she had the surgery or not. Nobody knows what this disease will do for sure. You have to remember Wegener's is very rare and we're still learning about it."

Where had we heard that before—and how many times?

"Instead of Cytoxan™, I would like to start you on a drug called Imuran™," he told Carol.

He reached for the PDR and began to look for a guide to the dosage.

"What do you weigh now?" he asked Carol.

"About one hundred pounds," she replied. "Tell me about Imuran™."

"How is it spelled?" I asked.

"I-M-U-R-A-N," he answered. "It's an immunosuppressant that's usually used for patients recovering from kidney transplants. While Cytoxan™ is the most preferred drug for treating Wegener's, in view of what happened before, I think we'd better avoid it if possible. Even though Cytoxan™ has produced such a high percentage of remissions, there are others just as effective. It's just that when we find something that works, it makes sense to use it unless we have a reason not to, as we do in your case. We'll try the Imuran™ and see what happens."

"For how long?" I wanted to know.

"For about three months," he said. "We'll start her with a little lower than average dose and see how she tolerates it," he said to me.

"What are the side effects?" Carol wanted to know.

"About the same as Cytoxan™," he answered, "but there's less chance of bladder problems with Imuran™.

"You have to remember that this is an immunosuppressant, and by taking it, you're put in the same category as someone who has AIDS. You will need to be checked regularly to make sure you don't pick up an infection your body can't fight. If you pick up an infection that we don't know about while we're trying to keep the disease from spreading, and don't take care of getting rid of it, you could die from something as minor as a cut on your finger.

"If you think I'm telling you this to scare you, you're right. You must understand how important it is for you not to miss your blood tests.

"This is what's happened," the doctor continued. "Every time you had a crisis, we treated the crisis. For the year you were on Cytoxan™, we were really getting a good grip on stopping the disease. The unfortunate bladder incident panicked us, and when we stopped the Cytoxan™ what we really did was stop fighting the disease.

"It is imperative that we begin fighting it again and deal with whatever consequences arise when and if they happen. Perhaps that way, once and for all, we can lick this thing and you can get on with your life. Are you finished with school yet?" he asked.

"I need two more classes," she answered. "But I have a job."

"And she's living just ten minutes from here," I added. "So it looks as if you're stuck with her for the duration."

"Good," he said to me. "We'll take good care of her. This time we'll lick this thing."

I loved this man's attitude.

I then made a confession to Dr. Saxon that I'd had a registered astrologist do a life chart for me and a health chart for Carol.

"I'm not really sure just how much stock I put in that sort of stuff, but she said I'm going to live a long time and that Carol would outlive me."

"In that case," he said, with a twinkle in his eye, "all we have to do is look out for you, and Carol will take care of herself."

"I had another crazy idea and wanted to ask you about it," I said. "You're an immunologist. Tell me, if Wegener's is a result of an over-active immune system, why couldn't the blood from a Wegener's patient be given to an AIDS patient, since their immune system is under-active?"

"Great idea," the doctor said, "but it doesn't work that way. If we did that, the AIDS patient might end up with Wegener's also, and they've already got enough problems."

We took his prescriptions and had them filled; he'd also wanted Carol to take an antibiotic. The Imuran™ was less than half the price of Cytoxan™. It had become a standing joke in the family that the seriousness of one's illness was directly proportional to the cost of the medicine. Maybe that's why I wondered if the Imuran™ would work.

On the way home, Carol and I discussed what had been said about the surgery to remove the scar tissue.

"What do you think?" I asked.

"All I know," she answered, "is that I could hardly breathe before. It's much better now. I don't see how removing the scar tissue could have been avoided. In my opinion, it wasn't a mistake; it was a necessity."

It's her nose. We had to believe that her opinion had the most value.

Dick and I were in the midst of planning another trip, this time driving to Alaska, and were about an inch away from canceling the whole thing. It would be difficult, maybe impossible, to reach us if we were needed.

Dr. Haring understood our concerns. But he offered no advice in either direction, except to empathize.

"I'm happy that Dr. Saxon is going to be taking care of Carol. They get along well, and he's got the equipment and facilities to do the job. Besides, I feel I may have lost my objectivity," he said.

"If you have an old PDR lying around, would you mind sending me the page with Imuran™?" I asked.

When I got the page, it told me this about the drug: Imuran™, also known as azathioprine, turns off the cells that produce autoimmunity. It also blocks the inflammation that directly destroys joints and internal organs. It comes in pill or injection form.

The possible side effects were: nausea, vomiting, and heartburn; increased frequency of infections if the white blood count is affected; easy bruising and bleeding if the platelet count is affected; skin rash; loss of hair; and a slight, but definite, risk of developing cancer or leukemia after taking Imuran™ for an extended period. All too familiar, but the alternative to treatment, as we'd heard before, was worse.

The new chemotherapy started the beginning of June; we were scheduled to begin our drive to Alaska on the twenty-first.

Dick and I were very uncomfortable about leaving Carol when she had just started a new form of chemotherapy. This time, it was Dick who wanted to cancel the trip.

"I don't think it's going to make a bit of difference whether we're here or not," I said.

"Why don't we discuss it with Carol?"

At the next opportunity we sat down with her and told her our fears about being away.

"I think it would be ridiculous to cancel your trip," Carol stated, adamantly. "I'm going to continue with work and anything else I feel like doing. So far the side effects seem to be minimal, and Dr. Saxon doesn't expect a repeat of the bladder trouble. Even the PDR doesn't show that as a side effect. I can't understand what you're worried about."

"We're your parents. It says in the Parent's Handbook, which we were given when you were born, that we're supposed to worry," he said.

Carol scowled. "Very funny."

"But seriously, we don't want you to think we don't care enough to hang around in case you need us," Dick continued.

"I think she knows by now that we care," I said, grinning at both of them.

"There's no reason to stay home. I'm not going to have any problems this time."

From your mouth to God's ears, I thought.

"There's nothing that would be handled any differently if you were here, anyway."

"She's right," I said. "Promise you won't get into any trouble while we're gone?"

"Promise!" she agreed. "Besides, I'm counting on getting some new Alaska T-shirts."

"You're on," Dick said.

I told Ron and Don that we would call several times a week to find out how Carol was doing, and made them promise not to hold back any bad news. If there were a problem and we were too far away to turn around and drive home, one of us could fly while the other followed with the car.

We called every third day, once to Don's place and the other to Ron's. Ron and Don were in close touch with her; they told us all was going well.

Two weeks after we were on the road, Don told us that Carol had another biopsy taken. That was the fifth one.

"She what?" I yelled into the phone. "Why? What's wrong?"

"I don't think anything's wrong," Don said.

"How long was she in the hospital?"

"She wasn't in the hospital at all."

"How could she have a biopsy and not be in the hospital?"

"Well, she did, Mom."

"Where is she now?"

"Working."

It was evening. She couldn't be too bad off if she was working. I calmed down a little.

Don didn't know the details because he hadn't been there.

I'd had no idea there were plans for more surgery, and started telling myself that we should have stayed home. How could we have been so selfish as to have gone ahead with the trip?

"OK, Don, do me a favor. When Carol gets home from work, no matter what time it is, have her call us here. We're going out for dinner now, so wait an hour. But I want to talk to her tonight. OK?"

"OK," he said. "But she's fine—really."

"I believe you, sweetheart. I just want to hear it from the horse's mouth."

I had to speak to her, to hear her own voice tell me that she was OK.

Just as we were walking out the door, the phone rang.

"Hi, Mom. I hear you want to talk to a horse."

There was laughter in Carol's voice, and that settled me down somewhat.

"What in the hell happened?"

"What do you mean?" she said.

"Don said you had another biopsy."

"Oh, that. Well, I had an appointment with Dr. Saxon for my regular check-up and blood test. As I walked in the door, he said, 'Whatever your plans are for this afternoon, cancel them. I've made an appointment for you with Dr. Thompson to have another biopsy.'

"I was supposed to meet some friends at Disneyland," she added.

"What did you do?"

"Well, after my appointment with Dr. Saxon was over, I had lunch and then went to Dr. Thompson's office. After he examined me, he did the biopsy," she reported.

"Right there in his little examining room, as he had wanted to do the first time he saw you?"

"Yup," she answered.

"With no anesthetic?" I asked, incredulously. "Didn't it hurt doing it that way?"

"Of course," she said, "but he numbed it up first. He used Novocain."

"Did it bleed much?" I asked, remembering the last time he had performed the same procedure.

"Just a little. He took tissue from about five different places, and then said I could leave. So I went to Disneyland."

"You *what?*" I shouted into the receiver.

I was sure I had misunderstood her.

"I went to Disneyland. I was supposed to meet Sue and Scott there, along with some other people. There was no way to get in touch with them to tell them that I wasn't going, so I decided to go."

"What about the mustache bandage? How could you walk around Disneyland with a mustache bandage?"

"I didn't have one. I didn't feel great, but good enough."

I couldn't believe my ears.

"Well, what did the biopsy show?"

"Just what we thought. It's active again."

With the little bit of experience that Dr. Thompson seemed to have had with Wegener's, I wondered how he knew.

"Is the Imuran™ helping?"

"Not much."

"When do you expect to move in with Don?"

"We're going to do it over the Fourth of July weekend."

She rattled off a list of friends who were going to help her. It seemed that she had everything under control. There wasn't anything left for me to do.

Carol and I said goodbye and we continued our trip but also continued checking with Ron and Don several times a week.

When we returned, we were pleased that Don and Carol were settled in their apartment. Don told us that she seemed to be enjoying her job and that no one at work cared about the strange hours she kept.

"What do you mean by strange hours?"

"She prefers to work from late morning, somewhere between 10:00 and noon, to late in the evening, like 7:00 or 9:00."

"How are you and she getting along living together?"

"She's the perfect roommate, Mom. I never see her and she pays half the bills!"

In August I called Dr. Saxon for his opinion on the Imuran's™ effectiveness. He had always seemed to be so rushed. I'd been reluctant to bother him, and was also aware he was under no obligation to answer any of my questions because Carol was an adult and entitled to her privacy.

However, Dr. Saxon knew our family, how close we've been and how important it was for us to know about any progress Carol was making.

I was pleasantly surprised; he was more than friendly and answered my questions. He particularly assured me that, in his opinion, the Imuran™ was working.

"I've seen Carol several times and I can see her improvement through the rhinoscope."

"I wasn't sure if you'd mind my calling, but Carol doesn't like to talk about her illness and I never get any details from her."

"Don't bother asking her," he said. "I'm her doctor. It's my job to nag her."

Oh boy, I thought. I have a relief pitcher!

"Just ask me what you want to know. I'll be happy to talk to you any time."

What a relief it was to have two such understanding doctors. Whether it was because we got lucky or if being picky about whom we chose to treat her made the difference, I didn't care. I was so happy to be able to get information, which helped with my peace of mind.

So the Imuran™ was working. That was good news.

September 1986 was approaching, and with it the time for a decision about continuing Imuran™. The three-month probation for that drug was up.

As the month wore on, and we were getting more information from Carol, she was telling us the Imuran™ wasn't working. Reports from Don confirmed that. Her headaches were bad and she was once again experiencing a lot of pain in the sinus areas.

Dick asked me more than once, "Why don't you suggest to Dr. Saxon that he start her back on the Cytoxan™?"

"First of all," I said, "It's not up to us to tell the doctor how to conduct his business, and secondly, it's Carol's decision. She knows better than anyone what she went through with that drug before. It's up to her to make the choice."

18

Aggressive Therapy

Chemotherapy is frequently referred to as aggressive therapy. When something is fighting you long and hard, it stands to reason you fight back aggressively.

Dr. Saxon made the decision for us. Because Cytoxan™ was still the drug of choice, that was the one to be used. This time, however, it was to be administered intravenously. The protocol[28] called for the infusion of the drug followed by saline to flush out Carol's system with the hope that the toxicity would not affect her bladder.

The treatments were to be given once every four weeks, assuming there were no problems to inhibit the continuity, and she was to see Dr. Saxon once a week to have tests taken. The tests, which included blood and urine samples along with chest X-rays, were to make sure the therapy wasn't damaging other parts of her body and to see what results it was producing.

A few days before chemotherapy was scheduled to begin, she went to see Dr. Haring.

"She seems just like her old self," he reported.

But Janet, his receptionist, did not concur.

"She's really frightened," she said. "But I'd be, too, if it were me. I saw tears in her eyes as she told me about starting the treatment."

Listening to Janet, I had tears in my eyes, too, accompanied by a king-sized lump in my throat. If only there was some way for me to take the treatments for her …

"If it were me, I'd be scared to death," I told Dr. Haring.

"So would I," he said. "If she wasn't afraid of the possible consequences, I'd be sending her to a psychiatrist. I don't think I would handle her situation as well as she does."

"I want to be there with her," I told Dick, "but I'm afraid she won't let me come to the treatments."

"Tell her how important it is to you and insist if you have to," he said.

"I don't want to make this any tougher for her than it already is, especially if she doesn't want me there. But what if she doesn't feel like driving home?"

"That's a good point," Dick said. "Use that excuse and see if she buys it."

"I'd like to be there with you when you go for chemo," I told Carol.

As expected, she said, "It's not necessary."

"If I have to sit here inside these four walls wondering what's happening to you, I'll go out of my mind. Do me a favor and let me come. Then you won't be responsible for your mother going crazy. Besides, you might not feel like driving home."

"OK."

Good. She bought it.

"Don't you think I should be there, too?" Dick asked me when he learned Carol was going to let me come. I suggested he ask Carol.

"Suppose you ask her," Dick said. "She might be afraid of hurting my feelings if she doesn't want me there."

"I don't think it's necessary for either of you to be there," Carol said when I brought it up. "I'm sure I can handle it."

I hoped I wasn't losing ground.

"We've already decided that I'm going with you, but I'll tell Dad one of us is enough."

The night before the first treatment, we were all apprehensive.

Carol finally let someone know how she was feeling, in a long discussion with Ron. She definitely was afraid. But she wasn't going to complain or carry on. Her paternal grandmother had "enjoyed" poor health, and for many years that was her only topic of conversation. Carol had decided she wasn't going to be like her grandma. If people were going to point their fingers at a complainer, they would have to look elsewhere.

When the scheduled day rolled around, I was up and out bright and early, not even needing the alarm.

Carol, by nature, wasn't the happiest of people in the world in the morning. But she seemed a little testier than normal, not unexpectedly.

If she weren't scared that morning, though, she would not have been of sound mind. The first day of an IV chemotherapy treatment cannot possibly be compared to the first day of almost anything else on the same emotional level.

"I think we ought to take my car in case you don't feel like driving home," I told her.

"OK," she answered. "Can I drive there?"

After the car was parked, we went into the medical center.

"Where do we go?" I asked Carol, who had all the details.

She pulled a slip of paper out of her pocket.

"The Jonsson Comprehensive Cancer Center in the Louis Factor Building. Eighth floor. Bowyer Clinic."

There were signs to follow and it was a much longer walk than the other places we'd been to at the medical center. We wound our way through the maze of halls, then outside through a courtyard and into the Factor Building.

There were automatic black glass doors that opened as we approached the building. The lobby was done in black marble and looked more like an office building than a medical treatment center. It lacked the hustle-bustle of the rest of the medical center. No one goes to the Cancer Center unless they have business there.

In the elevator, for one of the few times in my life, I couldn't think of a thing to say. Wishing her good luck didn't seem appropriate. I was hoping for much more—for her, for us all.

The elevator door opened and we stepped into a small reception area with a few gray tweed upholstered chairs, a soft-drink vending machine and a drinking fountain. We walked though an open glass door and entered a hall. On the other side of the hall was a larger waiting room.

The atmosphere in the Bowyer Clinic seemed altogether different from the rest of the medical center—decidedly, and surprisingly, more cheerful.

Carol gave her name at the desk and we sat down to wait. She didn't seem to feel much like talking, so I tried not to chatter as is usual when I'm nervous.

I had brought a book, some knitting, and a note pad. Like a good Girl Scout, I was prepared with more than enough stuff to keep me busy through a rainy weekend in the country.

Carol had brought her backpack and, along with the usual stuff one carries in a purse, she had last night's pizza—possibly for lunch—and a couple of magazines. As ridiculous as I thought the cold pizza seemed to me, I decided not to do or say anything. Whatever was going to make her happy would have to be all right.

"Did they say how long it would take?"

"All day. After they run the Cytoxan™ through, they want to flush out my kidneys and bladder with saline. They can't put the saline through too quickly or they'll run into trouble."

Her name was called shortly and the man at the desk asked her to pay for her blood test. Then she was instructed to sit down again and wait.

A pretty blond woman came looking for her and introduced herself as Melinda. She was to be Carol's nurse that day and explained the procedures.

"Each time you come here," she said, "you'll have to have a blood test to make sure your platelet count is all right. After your blood is checked, and if it's OK, the pharmacist will mix the Cytoxan™ mixture specifically for you. Then you can purchase a cold cap.[29] Let me show you where the blood tests are done."

Melinda and Carol disappeared down the hall and returned in about five minutes.

While they were gone I looked around the waiting room. There were people of all ages, and it was impossible to tell the patients from those who accompanied them. No one in the room looked like they were dying. No one was bald. Those whose names were called, obviously patients, didn't even look particularly sick. It was such a pleasant surprise to me.

I recalled Carol's high school friend who had died. He looked skeletal and had lost all of his thick, curly hair.

Chairs upholstered in the same soft gray tweed were placed around the room near low tables. Magazines were plentiful. Against one wall was a hot plate with free coffee and tea.

Carol returned holding a piece of cotton in the fold of her arm where blood had been drawn.

"How were they?" I asked, knowing she had become an expert on the competency of phlebotomists.[30]

"OK," she answered.

That was good. She certainly would have had a lot to say if the technician wasn't proficient.

Melinda was back again in a few minutes.

"Your blood checked out OK," she said. "Take this authorization to the pharmacist for the Cytoxan™ mixture and you can purchase a cold cap."

Carol complied and I followed her to get a glimpse of what was going on. The pharmacist had his own little corner, and the pharmacy appeared to be very well stocked. He sat on a high stool behind a half door that had a little counter suitable for writing.

She paid for the mixture and the cold cap. Melinda was at her side again, guiding her to where the IV would be inserted.

"Couldn't this all be done at the same time instead of going back and forth from here to there and paying for everything separately?" Carol asked.

"No," the nurse said, "because if we find that your platelet count is too low, then we won't do the therapy that day. That would mean the Cytoxan™ would have to be discarded and you would have paid for nothing. Then people want a refund and we don't do that. I know it's a pain in the neck, but we have found that it works better this way."

I thought the clinic was much better organized than the rest of the medical center, and the people working there seemed to care more about the patients.

Melinda took Carol into a combination office/treatment room called the Chemotherapy Infusion Room. It adjoined what looked like an ordinary three-bed hospital room. All three beds in the next room were filled with patients hooked up to IVs. Someone was sitting in a chair beside each bed. The patients and their companions were chatting quietly, reading, or dozing. No one was retching.

Both rooms had very large windows looking out on the city. The blinds were opened wide, making the rooms appear bright and cheerful. On one large windowsill there was an old-fashioned glass IV bottle filled with hard candy and turned upside down in a holder.

Carol was shown to a light brown recliner-type chair with a footrest and swing-away arms. I was surprised that she wasn't put in a bed.

The room was sectioned off with partial walls. In the first section, which resembled a stall, was a desk. Carol's chair was in the second, and there was a similar chair in the third section. Atop the walls were plants and knick-knacks. A crocheted nurse doll, holding a syringe, was on each wall.

"Is this where she is going to have her treatment?" I asked.

"Yes, it is," the nurse answered cheerily.

Melinda was obviously very adept at inserting IV needles, for it quickly went into Carol's forearm. Unfortunately, it wasn't painless. She attached the other end of the IV to a small bag of saline solution and hung it from a pole on wheels. There was a large cylinder, about the size of the cardboard core of a bathroom tissue roll, in the middle of the tubing, with a window for viewing the contents.

After regulating the flow of the saline, Melinda unpacked and unwrapped the cold cap, manipulated it with her hands, and placed it on Carol's head. She fastened it securely and wrapped it all with an Ace™ bandage to make sure it would stay put.

"When the cold cap is unfolded and the chemicals are mixed," Melinda explained, "it's as if it was filled with ice. It fastens around the scalp and the coldness is supposed to restrict the flow of blood to the roots of the hair. The purpose is to prevent hair loss."

"Does it work?" Carol asked.

"Sometimes yes and sometimes no," Melinda answered. "Everyone's body reacts differently to the treatment."

She put little paper-thin plastic foam caps around Carol's ears so the coldness wouldn't make them uncomfortable.

"How does that feel?" she asked.

"Awkward, but I can handle it," Carol answered.

"We'll give the cold cap twenty minutes to freeze your scalp, and then I'll start the Cytoxan™," Melinda said, as she checked the flow of the IV again.

She left us for a few minutes. When she returned she was carrying a large hypodermic needle containing the Cytoxan™, a five-hundred-milligram dose.

When twenty minutes had passed, the nurse injected the Cytoxan™ solution into the top of the cylinder. It was crystal clear. The saline dripped in and mixed with it.

This was it—the first dose of two years' worth of poison. I felt a strange sensation come over me, remembering a movie I'd seen and likened this scene to it. It had depicted a gas chamber used for the executions of criminals. But this is different, I told myself silently. That took lives; this is supposed to give life back to us.

How was Carol feeling? What was she thinking? She shared no thoughts, however, and seemed to have no fear.

"The Cytoxan™ might burn a little going in," Melinda said, "and it might make your eyes water or your nose stuffy."

None of those occurred.

While the Cytoxan™ was being infused, Melinda took Carol's blood pressure and asked how she was doing several times. She also offered us coffee.

"Will this make me sick to my stomach?" Carol asked.

"Not everyone gets sick," the nurse answered. "If they do, it's usually the next day."

"Will I be able to go to work, drive, or bathe?"

"It depends on how you feel," Melinda said. "Usually people plan to hang around home for a day or two after their treatments until they're able to determine just how their body will react."

Then she handed Carol a sheet of paper to read that explained what to expect from Cytoxan™.

"You may find this interesting," she said.

Carol read it and chuckled.

"This was written for laymen, Mom," she said as she handed the paper to me.

The print was very large, and it looked as if the wording was meant for a fourth-grader. It told us this:

"Cytoxan™ is a clear fluid after it is dissolved. It also comes in tablets, white with blue specks, and in doses of twenty-five and fifty milligrams. It can be taken by mouth or be injected into the vein. Common side effects are nausea and vom-iting, usually occurring about six hours after the drug is given through the vein, which may last eight to ten hours. When the tablet is taken, nausea may occur throughout the entire day. There may be general thinning of the hair. Nasal stuffiness, sinus congestion, sneezing, watery eyes, and runny nose may occur during or immediately following injection of the drug. Reduced blood count may occur one to two weeks after treatment.

"Less common side effects are bladder irritation, and the drug may produce burning on urination or bloody urine. Adults should drink at least three quarts of fluid of any kind during the day of the injection and two days after receiving it, forcing frequent emptying of the bladder. When taking the tablet, it should be taken early enough in the day to allow for drinking large amounts of fluids and frequent emptying of the bladder. If unable to drink fluids or pass urine, call the doctor. Children between the ages of two and twelve should drink two quarts of fluid, and children under two years old should be given one quart of fluid during the day of the injection."

The paper didn't tell Carol anything she didn't already know, and was a far cry from the page Dr. Haring had given us from his PDR.

Melinda checked the flow again and asked Carol, "How do you feel?"

"OK," Carol said, "but I'm freezing."

"Oh, the cold cap does that," Melinda said. "I'll get you a blanket."

She left the room for a few moments and returned with a blanket. She spread it over Carol and then she gave her a sample of Compazine™.

"If you feel nauseous later, this might help," Melinda said.

"Thanks. Dr. Black* also gave me some prescriptions for Compazine™ sup-positories and dexamethasone. I guess I'll have to see what I need and what works."

"Who's Dr. Black?" I asked. I'd never heard of him before. "Is he a resident?"

"No," Carol answered. "He's a real doctor. He graduated from Yale, and he's one of the doctors working with Dr. Saxon. He's been assigned to me for quite a while, but Dr. Saxon is still making all the final decisions."

I'd been so left out of things lately. As usual when this happened, I was stew-ing over having been kept in the dark and putting my own interpretation on these things.

After about forty minutes, the solution had been absorbed. Melinda was with Carol almost the entire time. If the nurse left, it was never for more than a minute or two. She took Carol's blood pressure again and asked how she was doing several more times. Melinda made it plain that guests were not only permitted to sit with the patients, they were encouraged.

"It's a good idea for someone to be with the patient. One never knows how chemotherapy will affect them, physically or psychologically. We really welcome guests. The patient may need help and/or moral support."

I liked this woman: She reinforced my being there. Carol and I explained why she was getting chemo. Melinda had heard of Wegener's but to her knowledge no other patients at the clinic were being treated for it at that time.

When the Cytoxan™ had been completely absorbed and Carol was showing no ill effects, she was to be transported to DMPG, on the third floor of the medical center, for hydration.

"What's hydration?" I asked.

"Because of the toxicity of the Cytoxan™, it's necessary to flush out her system as much as possible," Melinda explained. "They'll be giving her a saline solution to accomplish that."

An escort was summoned and arrived with a wheelchair. Melinda suggested that Carol not fight the use of the chair, even though she said she felt good enough to walk.

"You wouldn't want to catch the IV on anything and dislodge it," Melinda said. "Then they'd have to start a new one."

Carol got into the wheelchair, I gathered up all my "toys," as Carol called them, and followed her and the escort to the medical center's third floor for the next step in the therapy.

It's necessary to check in with the receptionist upon arriving at DMPG. She checked her schedule and reported to Carol, "You're not on my list. Who is responsible for making the arrangements?"

"Dr. Henry Black."

"I'll see if I can track him down," the receptionist said.

The escort left Carol in the wheelchair in the reception area.

Just then, Dr. Black walked in the door, told the receptionist what was needed, nodded to Carol, and left. With that detail squared away, Carol was taken to what appeared to be a large supply room with bags and boxes of all kinds against the walls. There was an examining table in the middle.

A nurse who introduced herself as Amy came in, checked the chart we had brought with us from the Bowyer Clinic, and procured the necessary equipment from the cabinets: a liter of saline and a tube to attach it.

Michael, the head nurse, entered to check on Carol as Amy was hooking her up. He explained the hydration procedure.

"We'll be giving you two liters of saline today, and checking on you periodically. If you have any shortness of breath, notice any swelling, or feel in any way peculiar, please let us know as soon as possible."

After the flow was adjusted, we were taken to a small examining room where Carol was able to lie down and relax, as much as anyone could under the circumstances.

By this time our tummies were telling us it was time for lunch. After the nerve-wracking morning Carol had just gone through, she said the cold pizza didn't sound all that interesting. I hadn't brought any cold pizza for myself and I was starving. While she was hooked up to the saline, Carol couldn't go anywhere, except to the bathroom.

"I'll get something for lunch," I said. "Is there anything special you'd like to eat?"

"Surprise me," Carol answered.

"OK," I said. "Don't go running off while I'm gone."

She nodded in the direction of the pole hung with the bag of saline.

"I don't think you have to worry about that."

She was in a much better frame of mind than when she had walked in that morning, and no wonder. Fear of the unknown can play havoc with someone's mind. I felt better, also. She had been given the infusion and weathered the storm. The unknowns were out of the way. She wasn't in pain and, so far, wasn't nauseous. We both felt it had gone well.

She had taken the first step toward getting rid of Wegener's once and for all. We were no longer sitting with our heads in our hands wailing: "What do we do now?" We were doing it.

As I was en route to find lunch, it seemed like a good time to phone Dick to let him know what had gone on that morning and how Carol had handled it. I was so proud of her.

"You don't need to feel guilty about not being here. The rooms she was in weren't that big. Two of us would have been in the way."

While on my way down to the cafeteria, it dawned on me that the shops and restaurants in Westwood[31] were close enough to walk to, and there were lots of unusual places to eat nearby. I decided not to get hospital food, but something different from the outside.

"Swart Catering Service," I announced, re-entering the room with my arms laden with goodies.

"They're using some pretty old delivery people," Carol teased as she grinned at me.

"Be nice," I told her, "or I'll eat all this by myself, including the chocolate chip cookies, your favorite."

I spread out the feast.

"Bringing you along wasn't such a bad idea after all," Carol said, smiling. "It looks as if once a month we're going to have a gourmet pig-out day."

It felt good finally being able to do something for her. I'd had felt so guilty for so long not being able to help her. Maybe getting lunch on her treatment day wasn't a big deal, but at least I would be able to do *something* to make her feel better, something that she couldn't do for herself.

Since drinking was so important, I was also able to bring her drinks during the day.

The saline has to drip slowly or the body will experience the same effects as if a person were drowning. Pediatric needles had to be used on Carol because of her small veins.

Although both Michael and Amy checked on her frequently, when it was time to change the bag, we all let it go too long. Carol and I noticed at the same time that the saline had run out, and blood was starting up the IV tubing. We hadn't been aware that when there's no fluid going into the vein, the IV tube then acts like suction.

I ran looking for a nurse and spotted Michael.

"The bag's empty and blood is going up the tube," I cried.

He broke into a run and beat me to the room, but he walked in calm and smiling. Amy had left the next bag close by, and Michael exchanged the empty for the full one.

"We'll have you all fixed up here in a minute," he told her. Referring to the blood in the tube, he added, "You didn't lose much."

"It doesn't seem like much to you because it's not your blood," Carol barked at him.

"Don't worry," he said. "I'm giving it all back to you."

He stayed with her until the blood was reabsorbed and the IV was flowing properly again.

By the time she had been completely hydrated with the two liters, it was after 5:00 PM. We had been there all day and it had been a grueling one.

"Before you leave, Dr. Black wants to see you," Michael told her. "I'll page him and let him know you're finished with hydration."

"I'd like to get out of here," she said. "I've had enough of this place today."

"How old do you think Dr. Black is?" I asked her. "He looks like he's about Kenny's age."

"I'll ask him," she said.

As he walked in the door and before he had a chance to open his mouth she asked, "How old are you?"

"Thirty-two," he answered with no hesitation.

Being flushed with poisons gave her a lot of nerve. But the doctor didn't seem to mind.

"How do you feel?" he asked.

"Tired," Carol answered, "but OK. How am I going to feel tomorrow?"

"We'll just have to wait and see," he said. "You have your prescriptions?"

"Yeah," she answered.

"Let me know if you have any problems," he said.

At that point, I let Dr. Black know we'd already had problems.

"They didn't even have her on their list here this morning. I can't believe how disorganized things are. When Carol was at the Mayo Clinic a few years ago, she was treated with much more care and concern than what usually happens here, and everyone there knew what was going on."

"That's a private operation," he said. "This is run by the state."

"Why should that make a difference?"

"For one thing, there's a big difference in the money allotted, and for another, there's greater control over the employees. On the other hand, at a state-run institution, the latest and most up-to-date treatments and equipment are more readily available. So there's a good side to doing it here."

"Well, that's something to think about," I acknowledged.

Then to Carol he said again, "Let me know if you need me."

I was beginning to feel better about him.

The first chemotherapy treatment came and went, and Carol's stomach was none the wiser. Perhaps it was because she was given a lower than normal dose of Cytoxan™. Afterward, I took her to her apartment.

"There's no sense staying with me. I'm just going to sleep," she said.

Nevertheless, I waited until Don came home before leaving.

The second treatment didn't go quite so well. To begin with, Carol was feeling rotten that day.

"We have to stop at 7–11 on the way," she said. "I'm only getting one liter of saline today and I promised Dr. Black I would drink the other liter."

The dosage of Cytoxan™ was increased to seven hundred fifty milligrams. The reclining chair was used again, with Melinda administering.

When the infusion was completed, Melinda wheeled Carol down to the third floor.

DMPG had never heard of Carol when she arrived—again. The receptionist spent some time tracking down Dr. Black so that she could complete her admittance forms.

As before, Carol was placed in a supply room where the lights were bright enough to do brain surgery, and very annoying. But they had to remain on because there weren't any windows in the room. The noise from the people constantly coming in and out for equipment was also unnerving.

She tried to sleep through the hydration, and we never had our gourmet feast.

I was also uneasy about Carol being given only one liter of saline, feeling that it was too soon into the therapy to know if her bladder would be angry at not being flushed properly. Since she had slept through most of the therapy, I didn't think she was drinking enough, either.

There were frequent checks on the flow of the saline, as had happened last time.

I called Dick halfway through the therapy and told him about my trepidations.

"The doctor should know what he's doing," he reminded me.

"I certainly hope so."

"I need some new prescriptions," Carol told me when I returned from my phone call. "Would you go up to Dr. Saxon's office with me?"

"Of course. But how are you going to go and do you know where his office is?"

"It's on the fifth floor. I'll take the pole."

We were on the third floor.

"Isn't the bag getting too low?" I asked.

"We won't be that long."

After telling her nurse where we were going, we walked the IV pole down the hall, around the corner, and into the elevator.

As we were getting off, someone caught the IV tubing and almost pulled the needle out of Carol's arm. We must have really scared him when we both screamed, "Wait!" Fortunately, he was moving slowly enough and stopped in time. We unwound him and took off for Dr. Saxon's office.

The doctor was on the phone and motioned for us to come in. We had to wait a few minutes for him to finish, and then we chatted a while about how Carol was doing. The poor man had laryngitis and could hardly speak.

"Why aren't you home in bed?" I asked.

"I feel OK," he said. "I just sound terrible."

"Is this going OK?" he asked, pointing to the IV pole.

"So far, so good," Carol said.

"You know, a few years ago all we could offer Wegener's patients were prayers," he told us.

I had read about the mortality rate prior to Dr. Fauci's research, but never cared to discuss it with anyone. Hearing Dr. Saxon say it out loud gave me the chills.

"At least, thanks to Dr. Fauci, we now have this treatment," he said, then added, "You don't look so good, Carol. How are you feeling in general?"

"I'm having a lot of pain in the sinus area," she told him. "I need some more codeine and another prescription for Prednisone™."

"How much are you taking now?"

"It varies. I get both ten- and five-milligram tablets and take different amounts according to a decreasing or every-other-day schedule."

"I'll give you prescriptions for both."

The twinkle in his eyes was there again as he looked at me and said, "I don't think we have to worry about Carol overdosing on Prednisone™."

He wrote the prescriptions and, sticking out my hand for them, I said I'd have them filled for her.

"I think it would be a good idea for you to see Dr. Thompson. You may have a pocket of infection," Dr. Saxon said to Carol. "Do you want me to call down there and see if he can see you today?"

"No," Carol said. "I'll make an appointment. I just want to go home and go to bed as soon as this is finished."

As she said that, we both looked up at the bag hanging from the pole and discovered it was empty. Not again.

"We have to go," she said, grabbing the pole and heading for the door.

We barely had enough time to get back to the third floor. We both yelled, "Goodbye and thank you," to Dr. Saxon and made a mad dash for the elevator.

Fortunately, it was quick in coming. Otherwise we would have had to brave the stairs while carrying the pole. We made it back down to DMPG just as her blood was starting back up the tube.

As we passed Michael's office, Carol held up the IV-attached arm and pointed to the blood at the end of the tubing.

"Guess what?" she said.

"Not again," Michael said, as he quickly escorted us back to the supply room and disconnected the IV. "I hope you're not going to make a habit of this."

When we were leaving, two more employees I had never seen before spoke to Carol, calling her by name and inquiring as to her well-being.

"Are you becoming recognized or notorious?"

She just grinned. "I guess I'm here a lot."

That was an understatement. She had friends all over that institution. I hoped her doctor was one of them.

I had talked her into spending the weekend with us, and brought her home.

The Compazine™ Carol had been given for nausea didn't seem to be doing the job. Besides being nauseous, she felt over-stimulated. When she didn't feel she could sleep, she parked herself on the living room couch with the television going.

At least she ate and drank during the weekend. On Sunday evening, Ron drove her home, but not before she thanked Dick and me for taking care of her. It was very touching, and the last thing we expected.

Later in the week, Carol complained again of feeling over-stimulated, as if she couldn't sit still and her body was racing a mile a minute. But she was too weary to do anything. She did, however, work that week in spite of it all.

Thanksgiving was approaching, and Bea was coming in from New York to spend it with us. Then Ken called and said he would be joining us, too.

One evening when I was finalizing plans with Bea, her daughter—my niece, Peggy—got on the phone. She told me she had come across a magazine article about chemotherapy and wanted to know if Carol might be interested in reading it. Unfortunately, it was all about cancer and not about Carol's disease.

Everything I'd read about chemotherapy also pertained to cancer. I had recently purchased a book called *Coping with Chemotherapy* by Nancy Bruning, hoping to find something in it that would benefit Carol. Wegener's was never mentioned in that book, either. But if Peggy thought the article might do Carol some good, I asked her to send us a copy.

She sent the article and, among other things, it discussed hair loss and how to handle it.

I passed it along to Carol, but Carol wasn't interested in reading it. She had something more exciting to think about.

"Guess what? My old UCR counselor called and asked if I would speak to the seniors next week about my job."

"That's really flattering. What does she want you to tell them?"

"Anything I want to. I'm open to suggestions."

"I'll come up with a list for you and ask Daddy for ideas if you'd like. He always has opinions. Will it be a problem taking off work that day?"

"Oh no. My boss thinks it's great, and it's good publicity for the company."

She was thrilled and so was I.

Her presentation went well and she got positive feedback. It was great to see good things finally happening to our little girl. It was certainly about time.

About a week before the next treatment, I asked Dick for his opinion about one of my worries.

I'd read that hair loss, if it occurs, usually happens around the third treatment. Carol's third was coming up.

"If it happens to her and she's not prepared, going to work will be a real problem. I don't know how to approach her about it. I don't want to upset her or cause her to worry about something that might not happen. On the other hand, she needs to be prepared. What do you think I should do?"

"Ask the chemo nurse. You say she's friendly and sympathetic. She must have had a lot of experience with this sort of thing. She may have some suggestions."

"That's a great idea," I said.

A few days before treatment number three, a blood test—CBC and platelet count—left Carol with an enormous bruise, about the size of a coffee cup. One of the side effects of chemo is easy bruising. Carol looked as if someone had punched her. In fact during much of the time of her IV chemo treatments, she often had spots that looked like bruises, sometimes as large as a saucer.

"Oh well," she remarked when we discussed it, "the office is usually pretty cold. I'll be wearing long sleeves anyway."

She was learning to cope in so many ways.

On the day of the treatment, Tuesday before Thanksgiving, we arrived at the clinic at 9:00 AM. Carol had her blood test, and Melinda approached us with a slip of paper in her hand.

"Your white count is very high, approximately twenty-four thousand," she said. "I have to call the doctor to get an OK before we begin treatment."

"What's the normal range?" I asked.

"About five to ten thousand," Carol and Melinda answered in unison.

"Below two thousand is dangerous," Melinda added. "I'll check with—who's your doctor?"

"Dr. Black," Carol answered.

"OK. I'll be back soon," she said and left.

She returned a few times to let us know she was still trying to reach the doctor. After an hour, Carol suggested, "Try Dr. Saxon. Dr. Black may have left town for the Thanksgiving weekend."

"Do you know if anyone is taking Dr. Black's calls over the weekend?" I asked Carol.

She gave me the name of a doctor.

Melinda must have had no trouble getting through to Dr. Saxon. She returned shortly.

"He says it's OK. We can get started," she said, sounding relieved.

Carol went to the pharmacy, checkbook in hand, and when she returned Melinda quickly took her into the infusion room. It was 11:00 by this time. We'd been waiting for two hours.

After things settled down I asked Melinda, out of Carol's hearing range, "What percentage of people lose their hair while undergoing chemotherapy? I've read that it frequently happens around the time of the third treatment, and this is her third."

"Most do lose their hair," she answered. "But if Carol hasn't by now, it's possible that she'll just have a general thinning. It could also be that we're not giving her full strength yet. We started with only five hundred milligrams of Cytoxan™ and increased to seven hundred fifty milligrams the second time."

"What's she getting today?" I asked.

"One thousand."

"How high a dose will she get?"

"That depends on Carol and her doctor."

"They're probably keeping it low because she had hemorrhagic cystitis when she was on oral Cytoxan™," I said.

I'd told Melinda that before, but with the volume of patients she probably saw it seemed unlikely she'd remember anything that might not be in Carol's chart, or that hadn't happened during their association.

"We might have to wait and see what happens with Carol's hair after the dose is stepped up. It could be that the cold cap is working," Melinda said.

Although all the literature said the hair loss took place by the third treatment, Carol's dosage this time might not be the same equivalent as a normal third treatment. Now there was one more thing to worry about.

"What are you two plotting over there?" Carol called to us.

I told her, referring to the things I'd read, that we were discussing hair loss.

"It's not a true test," Carol said, "because I'm getting a lower dose of Cytoxan™ now. It might happen when I start getting higher doses."

She didn't miss much.

"You might want to consider getting a wig while you can match your own hairstyle," Melinda suggested. "Some people like to do that. Then if they lose their hair, they're prepared. You won't have to go out wearing a hat or a scarf."

"That sounds like a good idea," I said. "If you need help shopping for a wig, I'll be happy to go with you."

Melinda gave Carol the names and addresses of two wig shops patients had told her about.

We had our gourmet feast after Carol was settled in for hydration. I found a restaurant that had unusual food and even brought back some French pastry.

After lunch Carol said, "I need to see Dr. Saxon for some prescriptions again."

The saline bag was half full. We had plenty of time. There was not going to be a repeat performance of last time.

As if she had read my mind she said, "There's plenty of time."

We watched very closely as we entered and exited the elevator, holding on to the tubing so that no one else could get caught in it.

"Dr. Saxon says he's treating my 'twin,' a sixteen year old girl with Wegener's"

"No kidding. How's she doing?"

"She's on oral Cytoxan™ and apparently responding well."

"I hope someone's telling her to keep drinking," I said. "Maybe we ought to tell him to give her our phone numbers in case she would like to talk to someone who's 'been there.'"

"That's a good idea. I'll mention it to him," she said.

Dr. Saxon appeared to be in much better shape than the last time.

"I need some more codeine and Keflex™," Carol told him, "and the Compazine™ isn't working. What else can I take?"

"Have you ever tried the Scopolamine™ patches?" the doctor asked.

"The stuff they use for sea sickness?" I asked

"Yes. I've been told they work pretty well."

"I'm willing to try," Carol said.

"How's your other Wegener's patient doing?" I asked him.

"Coming along nicely," he said.

"If she would like to talk to me, you can give her my phone number," Carol offered.

"If her parents would like to talk to us, you can give her ours, too," I added.

"That's a good idea," he said and turned around to the huge stack of files on a credenza behind him. He pulled one out and said, "Give me your numbers."

He wrote them right on the front of the file.

When Carol had first started taking oral chemo, Dr. Pryor had given her the name of a man who was a Wegener's patient. But she had chosen, at that time, not to get in touch with him. Perhaps she thought she didn't have a lot in common with a married man in his forties.

But this was different. This was a girl who was the same age as Carol had been when she was first diagnosed eight years ago. They might have more in common.

Dr. Saxon asked Carol if she'd seen Dr. Thompson.

"Not yet, but I'm feeling better."

"Couldn't Carol see Dr. Haring instead, or would it pose any problems for you because he's not here at UCLA?"

I knew that Carol had failed to keep an appointment with Dr. Thompson because the office had called my home looking for her.

"She can see whoever she wants. It's no problem for me. I think she should be checked periodically but it doesn't matter by who."

"Dr. Haring told me he was glad you were treating Carol because he felt as if he had lost his objectivity."

He smiled, looked at Carol and said, "She does sort of grow on you."

After we left Dr. Saxon I asked her, "Are you going to see Dr. Thompson?"

"Don't worry about it, Mom."

That meant mind my own business. I got the message and didn't pursue it.

During hydration that afternoon, not much voiding was taking place and Carol was feeling very puffy, as she termed it. We had a different nurse named Anne. She and Michael were concerned about Carol's all too few trips to the bathroom.

"I'll call Dr. Black and try to get an OK for a diuretic," Anne said.

After two hours, she was having no luck at all. We hung around the hospital until 6:00 PM, but Dr. Black never answered his page.

I wasn't happy with the situation.

"I'm OK, Mom. Stop worrying."

I took her home and she kept insisting that a few trips to the bathroom would solve her problem. After we arrived at her apartment, she was finally able to go and said she felt better.

---

28. A protocol is a written plan specifying the procedures to be followed in providing care for a particular condition.

29. A cold cap is a helmet with a thin, paper-like fiber on the outside and a chemical compound inside which turns cold when the helmet is taken out of its wrap and manipulated by hand so that the chemicals mix.

30. A phlebotomist is a laboratory technician who draws blood from veins for testing.

31. Westwood is the Los Angeles suburb in which both the UCLA Medical Center and University are situated.

19

Treatment Aftermath

Our Thanksgiving plans called for Dick and me to go down to Palm Springs with Bea on Tuesday after Dick finished work. One of the boys was to pick Ken up at the airport the next day. They all, including Carol, had expected to work on Wednesday.

Upon arriving home from UCLA, I discovered that Dick and Bea had waited for me to have dinner. We walked to a nearby coffee shop. During the meal, I wanted to discuss what had happened to Carol that day, but no one seemed to want the details. I felt so alone and really needed to talk about it.

The three of us drove down to Palm Springs, arriving after midnight. I wanted desperately to know how Carol felt, but thought it was too late to call.

The next day I called her at work twice and no one answered her phone. It was not unusual for her to be away from her desk, but I was apprehensive anyway. Two calls to her apartment got no response. I had left a message on her answering machine each time, hoping for a return call when she got home from work. We didn't hear anything from her until that evening. She had not gone to work, but had spent the day half in bed and half in the bathroom, vomiting. Chemo had finally caught up with her.

"Are you going to be well enough to make the trip to Palm Springs?"

It was a two-hour trip from her apartment. It was important for us to be together, but not at the expense of her comfort.

"Don's bringing me down tonight. We'll be there late."

They arrived about 11:30 PM and Ron and Ken, coming from the airport, were a few minutes behind them.

Carol looked pale and worn out, exactly what I had expected. She said hello and then moments later, good night.

The next day, Thanksgiving, after having slept most of the day, she was able to enjoy dinner, since her stomach had settled down and even did some socializing afterward.

We attempted some shopping on Friday, but after a couple of hours her head hurt. When we got home she rested for a while and then made preparations to leave the desert.

"I was hoping you could spend the whole weekend resting."

"I have to work tomorrow," she said.

On Saturday she worked for seven hours even though her stomach was upset and her head hurt. Through the grapevine she heard that her boss was upset at her absences. Of course he was totally unaware of her health problems.

"I'm going to talk to my boss tomorrow about my being gone so much," she informed me.

"What are you going to tell him?"

"I don't know yet," she answered.

After Carol left Friday, Ron called to tell me that Sharon, the mother of Dr. Saxon's other WG patient, had phoned. He gave me her number and I returned the call. We exchanged symptoms and treatments, shared thoughts and feelings about doctors, and made tentative plans to get together so that the girls could meet. I told Sharon about the WG research papers and that I would duplicate them for our meeting.

The next time I spoke to Carol, I asked, "What did you tell your boss?"

"Nothing," she said. "He never brought up my absences and neither did I. They get more than the forty hours a week they pay me for, and he knows it. They were upset because they couldn't reach me to ask a question, and would like me to be there when the other employees are."

"Then your strange hours are the problem more than your absences?"

"That's what it seems to be."

There had long been a difference of opinion among those who knew Carol's story as to whether or not she should tell the people with whom she worked. Her doctors felt it would be advisable for co-workers and employers to know. Dick, looking at the situation from a management standpoint, felt that her chances for promotion were slim to none if any boss thought her health problems might be a handicap. I wanted her to do whatever was going to cause the least stress. But in the end, Carol did what she felt was the appropriate thing to do, whenever she needed to make that choice.

A few days after Thanksgiving there was a TV movie about Senator Edward Kennedy's son who'd lost a leg to cancer. Bea was still there and all three of us watched it. One of the scenes depicted a chemotherapy treatment.

"Is it like that when Carol goes for hers?" Dick asked.

The scene was very authentic.

"Yes, except Carol sits in a recliner-like chair instead of lying down in a bed.

That was all I could say. Then I went into the bathroom and had a good cry to avoid disturbing either of them.

Watching that scene had brought all my pain to the surface again. Oh, why did I have to hide my tears? Why couldn't I weep in the living room in front of the television set? Why couldn't I cry that it wasn't fair for her to have to go through this? This was my baby who was suffering.

But I would have felt guilty making everyone else uncomfortable. Finishing my crying and drying my eyes, I returned to the living room and never said a word. Since my eyes never get red and puffy when I cry, no one ever knew.

At Carol's next treatment, the dosage of Cytoxan™ was increased to one thousand two hundred fifty milligrams. This time Lesley was her chemo nurse.

"She's the best one with needles, so far," Carol commented after the treatment began. The cold cap chilled the rest of Carol besides her head, and she needed warmer clothes and a blanket.

When we arrived at DMPG, the receptionist checked her appointment list. Noting that Carol's name was missing as usual, she said, "Give me your ID card, go on in, and get started. I'll do what I have to do here and bring your card to you."

Carol had developed another ally.

"Who's supposed to take care of getting Carol's name on the list?" I asked the receptionist.

"Dr. Black," she answered.

"Hasn't anyone filled him in on the procedures here?" I asked.

She just shrugged her shoulders. I didn't really expect an answer.

"The next time you see Dr. Black, I wish you'd tell him about this." I suggested to Carol.

"Don't worry about it," she said.

I knew that meant mind my own business.

It takes having children of your own to realize that your progeny are always your own business. I wondered if Carol would ever know that.

"I'd like to go with you to your next appointment. I haven't had an update in a while."

"OK."

Wow, that was easy, I thought. Maybe she had decided fighting me on some issues wasn't worth it.

Christmas Eve meant a clan gathering at our home. We were once again entertaining out-of-town relatives. From the time the children were very young we'd always gone out for dinner that night. Carol was feeling well enough and it was nice to have most of the family together.

Carol spent all of Christmas day in bed; she needed the rest.

After all our guests left, Ron came to me for a hug. It was the first time in a long time that one of the boys expressed great concern out loud for Carol.

"I'm so afraid for her," he said.

Our tears were so close to the surface we could hardly speak. We just sat and held each other for a long time.

Finally I said, "The doctors all say that she's going to get well. We have to believe that. You do believe that, don't you?"

He nodded.

"Does she believe that?"

I knew they'd been talking a short time earlier, and wanted so much to know what had been said. But the children have never betrayed one another's confidences, and I wasn't about to ask one of them to start.

"I don't know. I guess so," he said.

"Well, she is," I vowed. "We'll make sure of that."

He seemed to feel better. I felt like I had deserved an award for being able to keep my composure.

Carol's fourth treatment was scheduled for December 30th. 1986 was almost over.

From start to finish there were no significant problems with the fourth treatment. Two liters of saline were used, and we didn't leave the medical center until 6:30 PM. It was another long day.

As we left the hospital, Carol was telling everyone, "Only twenty more treatments to go."

What a kid I'd raised!

If one lives in Pasadena close to Colorado Boulevard, the route of the Tournament of Roses Parade, it's a good idea to leave town before New Year's Eve. Lots of streets and freeway exits are blocked off, making it difficult to get around town. We planned on spending the holiday in Palm Springs, hoping that Carol would come with us so I could care for her again. But she had other plans.

"I'll be sleeping most of tomorrow," she said. "If I feel OK, I'm going to a party."

"Will you be well enough to drive?"

"Probably, but Ron and Don offered to take me wherever I want to go."

"Dad and I can stay in town if you need us."

"I won't need you." Then she added, "Thanks for coming with me, Mom," and gave me a big hug and kiss.

I left Carol at her apartment.

Later, she told me that most of New Year's Eve was spent hanging over the toilet bowl, with the worst episode of nausea and vomiting she had experienced yet. Thinking she would probably spend the evening at home, she'd told Ron and Don she wouldn't need them, and they took off for parties of their own.

About 8:00 PM, she decided she had enough of being sick, and that it was time to have fun. She got cleaned up, dressed up, and drove herself to a party.

"How did you decide you were in good enough shape to go?" I wanted to know.

"I took it a few steps at a time. When it seemed as if I was finished vomiting, I took a drink and waited a half hour. Then I took a shower and waited another half hour. After I got dressed, I waited a half hour again. Then I decided I would try to go.

"The worst that could happen was that I wouldn't feel well after I got there. The party was close enough to your house to have someone drive me there. I could always pick up my car the next day. But it worked out OK. I didn't feel great, but it was better than staying home alone on New Year's Eve."

When she told us about the day she'd had, we had to admire her intestinal fortitude.

Shortly after the holidays were over, Carol went on a ski trip to Oregon. She came back elated and quite rested, or so she said, although she looked tired to me. One of her friends told us later that she had spent a good deal of the time in bed. I was glad to hear that because Carol's fifth treatment had been arranged for the following Friday.

Having the treatment on Fridays instead of Tuesdays seemed to be a good idea. Dick had actually suggested that months earlier, but until it became a problem for Carol at work, there was no reason to make the change. For those patients who worked, it was probably the best day to have chemo. But that also meant the clinic would be crowded. Since the post-chemo days had been workdays, that had left Carol no recuperation time.

She still had not told her boss anything about her health situation. With the weekend to regain her strength and settle her stomach, maybe she wouldn't have to.

Susan, whom she hadn't met before, was to be her chemo nurse at that treatment. Melinda was no longer working in the clinic, having been assigned to research. Susan was also blond, pretty, cheerful, and vivacious. She had just come back from maternity leave and we enjoyed hearing about her new baby.

Carol had gotten to know Lesley, the third chemo nurse, a pretty brunette, who was a little more reserved than the other two. Those ladies were a special breed of nurse. They were caring, compassionate, concerned, knowledgeable, and exceedingly competent, particularly when it came to finding veins.

The fifth treatment was done in a small examining room because the infusion room was already full.

As Susan was inserting the IV needle she began to ask Carol how old she was and what kind of work she did.

When she left the room, Carol said, "Did you notice she asked questions about me?"

I nodded.

"That's to take my mind off the needle. People feel good talking about themselves, and psychologically it might make the insertion go easier."

She had learned a lot from her chemo experiences.

"Well, she must have been right," I said. "It worked. I've never seen nurses as efficient at inserting IVs."

"They'd better be," Carol said.

Number five treatment was a smooth one. We explained what Wegener's was to Susan, who hadn't heard of it before. To her knowledge, there were still no other Wegener's patients receiving IV chemo at the Bowyer Clinic.

"How are you doing, Carol? Is it working?" she asked.

"We certainly hope so," I said. "The research papers I've read from NIH show a 90 percent remission rate."

Upon Carol's arrival at DMPG, we learned she was not on the appointment list again, but at least Dr. Black was there. The receptionist didn't have to go far for her information this time.

"Hi, Carol. How did it go last time?" he asked.

"I was pretty sick for a couple of days."

"Nausea?" he asked.

"And vomiting," she answered. "I think I need something different instead of Compazine™. What can you give me that will work?"

"You just have to get used to it. My wife went through that with both pregnancies. It's good preparation for you."

I was appalled at his remark. What an insensitive oaf! How dared he compare a natural happening with what was taking place in her life then? Didn't he realize that a young woman of twenty-four would probably want to have children someday, but with her past health history would find that it was too risky? Or even impossible? Wasn't she going through enough hell, mentally, physically, and emotionally without his rubbing it in? His comment was a classic example of someone sticking his foot in his mouth. A doctor, more than anyone else, should be aware of the mutagenic[32] potential that Cytoxan™, or any other cytotoxic drug, has.

If, or when, the time came for Carol to consider bearing children, the negative considerations were many. Her eggs might have been destroyed by the Cytoxan™. If it could be determined that her eggs are intact, it might not be possible to know if they are damaged, something that could result in a less than perfect baby.

Since hormonal changes take place during pregnancy, she might be advised against conceiving because of the harm those changes might do to her system, maybe even causing a recurrence of the Wegener's if she were in remission. It was all a moot point anyway because Carol hadn't had a menstrual period for several years.

Questions concerning these issues still cannot be answered, and no one knows what the future will hold.

I wish I'd the guts to tell him off—or even push his face in. But I felt it was important to keep my mouth shut and not do or say anything to hurt any rapport he and Carol had established, not to mention jeopardizing my chances of getting information from him in the future. Nevertheless, his remark would not be forgotten.

"I don't think it's quite the same thing as morning sickness," Carol answered sarcastically.

The remark hadn't gotten by her either.

"Throwing up a dozen times a day is simply not acceptable. I have to have something to combat the nausea and stop the vomiting," she emphasized.

Atta girl! I thought. Don't let him get away with sloughing you off.

I couldn't tell from his expression whether or not he had gotten the message. But making no further comment than, "Maybe this will help," he wrote her a prescription for Reglan™.

After hydration, we'd had the prescription filled, picked up Carol's clothes for the weekend and she came home with me.

On the way home I asked her, "Did you know that I had taken Reglan™ for a while?"

"For what?"

"Esophogitis.[33] When the doctor prescribed it, I looked it up in my paperback drug book and remember reading that the primary use of Reglan™ was to combat nausea due to chemotherapy. I wonder why it wasn't given to you originally."

"Probably because Compazine™ is more popular. Did I tell you what John said they do to chemo patients at NIH?"

"How does John know about NIH?"

"That's one of the places where Hopkins med students are taught. Anyway, he said that they admit them …"

"As inpatients?"

"Yup, and hydrate them the day before chemo. After the chemo they hydrate them for twenty-four hours. The patients sleep through most of it and never experience the nausea and vomiting. He's going to send me the protocol."

"That should be worthwhile," I said.

When we got home, she was feeling well enough to go out for dinner before we drove down to Palm Springs. She took the trip well and went to bed shortly after we arrived.

She spent all day Saturday in bed except for meals. She sat up long enough to drink whatever I brought. She got food if she asked for it. There was no vomiting so it appeared as if the Reglan™ was doing the job.

"Do you know if Carol's using the Scopolamine™ skin patches to combat the nausea?" Dick asked.

"I don't know."

Later she confirmed that she was.

She slept most of Sunday, but was a little nauseous toward evening. She had cut down on the Reglan™, and felt that taking it once she was already nauseous wouldn't help.

I had asked her about using the Compazine™ suppositories, which at least wouldn't have to be ingested orally.

"That's a good idea," she said.

After using one, she went back to bed and slept for a while again. We left Palm Springs late, but Carol felt well enough to stop on the road for pasta. The entire weekend passed with all the food going in the right direction only.

A medication called Procrit™ was then being advertised on television. It was supposed to give people who were on chemotherapy the strength that the cytotoxic drugs were sapping.

After seeing this ad I asked her, "Do you find you're more tired or weak since you've been on chemo? Or is it something that comes and goes?"

"Mom, I have to push myself just to get out of bed every single morning!"

Still, she never complained. But she did report to me, "I've been ravenously hungry the week after chemo."

"Your body is probably trying to rebuild energy to fight what it perceives to be poison."

The day of Carol's sixth treatment she told me, "I've had a lousy month."

"Have you gone to Dr. Thompson to see if he can do anything?"

"No."

"Why?"

"I don't want to. I'm not comfortable with him."

"Why don't you try to see Dr. Haring?"

"It would take too long. I can't take the time off work. They're beginning to notice my absences, and I've had to start keeping normal hours there."

"Would it help if your boss knew you had health problems and were really not a flake[34]?"

"That's what I've been thinking. I'm going to talk to him."

---

32.   Drugs with a mutagenic potential have the ability to induce genetic mutation which might lead to birth defects.

33.   Esophogitis is an inflammation of the mucosal lining of the esophagus.

34.   Flake is slang for an irresponsible person.

million Americans per year. In 1981, Mayo Clinic had treated fifty patients. In 1983, eighty-five patients were studied for twenty-one years at the National Institutes of Health in Bethesda, Maryland.[35]

A rough estimate would be in the United States there are probably five hundred new cases diagnosed each year.

You mentioned having others getting an early diagnosis. That is the key to a successful remission. As we become known through our support group, more doctors will be aware of the disease and begin early treatment.

The other key to remission and survival is an active participation on the part of the patient. That is understanding instructions by the doctor—following them exactly and fighting with all you have with a positive mental attitude. I might add drinking plenty of water—I drank one gallon per day each time I was put on Cytoxan™.

I forgot to mention that I have Dr. Nabih Abdou from Kansas University Medical Center, Kansas City, Kan. and Dr. Thomas McDonald from Mayo Clinic as my sponsors, as well as my ENT specialist Dr. Thomas Cotton—Kansas City, Mo.

Myrna and Carol, I want to be your friend. I want you to know that I am here anytime if you need anything or need someone to just vent your frustrations.

You know I have been through it all too and I understand everything you are going through and all the frustrations that you feel. You are not alone, and you are not the only one in the world that has Wegener's granulomatosis, like I thought I was, AND you can lick it and you can be a survivor.

Carol, I want to give you hope—I want you to fight with everything you've got. I want you to know that you must believe and know that you can lick this and survive.

Enjoy the enclosed articles I have collected over the years and do write to me. Let me be your shoulder to cry on and your ear to listen, when you need to talk. You know I've been through it all just like these others and we understand what you are feeling and what you are saying.

If you feel down and feel like no one cares, just know that I love you and that you must believe that you will feel better. Maybe you don't feel like reading the articles right now and that's OK. Maybe later you will. Keep them and re-read them and know that when you feel alone—I am there with you with my love and prayers.

You might enjoy writing to the other girls your age. We criss-cross letters and phone calls across this nation.

I might add that I am in remission and have been for some time now. My only problem now is fluctuating hearing loss and I am having some very new treatment for it and it is helping. It is a new theory that hearing loss is caused from the autoimmune disease itself. I feel well and exercise daily.

I do hope to hear from you soon. Myrna, Julie's mother's name is Barbara, and Michelle's mom is Pat. You might get a lot of support from them.

Keep your spirits up. Be positive and read any positive books you can. Until I hear from you, God bless you and remember you have a full life ahead of you.

She signed the letter with "love and prayers." I felt the love come right off the paper.

By the time I finished reading it, tears were streaming down my face. It was one of the most loving and compassionate letters I've ever received, and I'll cherish it as long as I live.

She had started a support group with two other patients at her home in Kansas City, MO. They met at her kitchen table. I had yet to meet her, but loved her anyway.

Three weeks after my conversation with Sharon, the mother of Dr. Saxon's other WG patient, she, her husband, Bob, and their daughter, a young lady we came to know as Collette, spent an evening with Dick, Don, Carol, and me at our home. We exchanged details about what had happened to the girls and how it had been handled.

The girls sat down on the couch and exclaimed, almost in unison, "Oh my God. Your nose looks just like mine!"

They both had experienced saddle-nose deformity.

Besides having seen Dr. Saxon, whom we all agreed was a terrific doctor, Collette had also seen Dr. Thompson. Bob told us that before her sinus surgery, no hint of WG had been mentioned. Since a biopsy is the only definitive way to arrive at a diagnosis, that sounded reasonable. Both of Collette's parents said it was their understanding that Dr. Thompson's job was teaching as well as treating, which may have been the reason for his lack of bedside manner.

Collette told us she was presently taking oral Cytoxan™, and related how she carried a water bottle with her everywhere at school so she could drink all day. A teacher had given her a hard time about bringing it into the classroom. It made me angry to think that there are people with such lack of compassion that a student fighting for her very life can be made to feel guilty over carrying a bottle of water to class.

Sharon had brought a copy of a recent article from People[36] magazine which told the story of another young lady who was a WG patient, one of the people Marilyn wrote about. She was nineteen. In one of the pictures the caption said the girl, Michelle, was wearing a nose prosthesis and that a doctor in Chicago had devised a way to put magnets under the skin to hold it on. The article told that

Michelle was misdiagnosed and treated for Lethal Midline Granuloma instead of WG. Although these two diseases have a number of common symptoms, the treatments are vastly different and had caused her to lose her nose altogether.

I was finally beginning to feel as if we weren't alone in the world.

I gave Sharon the duplicate copies of the papers and Dick proudly told them, "Myrna's writing a book about Carol and what she's been through."

Somehow I thought their reaction would be something like, "big deal" and was very surprised when all three expressed opinions that it was a wonderful thing—sharing Carol's story. Their indication was that it might help others, particularly those who might be diagnosed earlier because they'd now heard of the disease. They also felt it was important for others to know what had helped Carol, because it might help them.

Up until then, I thought my family was just humoring me when they saw me writing. I knew putting the story down on paper was very cathartic for me. It was encouraging to hear strangers' views, considering they hadn't read a word I wrote.

"We ought to get together in a couple of months," I suggested.

Collette and her parents thought that was a good idea and we promised each other we would keep in touch.

After everyone left, Carol joined me in the kitchen as I was cleaning up.

"Her nose looked just like mine, Mom," Carol said.

She was right. Collette's nose was flat against her face from the bridge most of the way down to the tip, the only portion that stuck out.

Then Carol added, "It didn't look bad at all."

"That's what I've been telling you. I hope we did them some good and gave them useful information."

"I'm sure we did," Dick added as he joined us in the kitchen. "They were able to see that Carol had finished high school, went to college, had a job, and maintained an active social life. She was not sitting in a corner somewhere feeling sorry for herself but out there in the world—living."

We enjoyed the visit and have kept in contact with them ever since. Carol often refers to that get-together as the first Los Angeles support group meeting and to Collette as her little sister.

About two weeks after meeting Collette, Dick referred Jim, his right-hand man at work, to an optician we had used. The shop was run by a father and son, but we'd only seen the son when we purchased our eyeglasses. Jim saw the father, Hubert, who told Jim that he'd just been released from the hospital.

When Jim asked what for, he almost fell off his chair when the optician said, "Wegener's granulomatosis."

Jim told the optician about Carol, and that it was Carol's father who had referred him.

When Jim returned to work, he could hardly wait to relay the events that had just taken place. Dick called me to fill me in. About an hour later, Hubert called Dick's office. He was desperate to talk to someone who knew something about the disease. He told Dick that a doctor from Kaiser Hospital had saved his life and that he had only one kidney.

"What did you tell him?" I asked, excited that we had found someone else to exchange information with.

"I told him I thought he ought to talk to you, that you have a lot more information about WG because you've gone to all the doctors' appointments with Carol. Why don't you give him a call? He's very anxious to meet with us."

I was excited, too, thinking that it would be great if the three families could meet and exchange information.

I called, but Hubert had already gone for the day. However, his son and I had an interesting conversation exchanging information about his father's and my daughter's experiences with WG.

"I have some information that I'll duplicate for your Dad," I said. "You'll probably find it interesting."

Carol's response to the latest find was, "It looks like fate is finding us a support group."

"What a coincidence that our optician's father is a WG patient."

"There are no coincidences, Mom."

Although Dr. Fauci's letter didn't point me to a support group, he had a particularly interesting comment that I usually share with new members regarding my inquiry about the life expectancy of WG patients.

The letter came around the time Carol began earning a substantial income.

Dick and I had taken her out for dinner, and the discussion afterwards at her apartment led to finances. Dick was explaining the benefits of opening an IRA beyond the usual savings accounts he had always encouraged the kids to maintain.

Then she asked, "How old do I have to be in order to take the money out?"

"Fifty-nine and a half."

Dick's response was met with silence rather than her usual manner of asking questions.

"You're wondering whether or not you'll live to be fifty-nine and a half, aren't you?" I asked.

"Yes," she said softly as she nodded and bowed her head.

"I brought a copy of a letter from Dr. Fauci that came yesterday. I think he has the answer for you."

This is a quote from the letter to me dated March 30, 1987:

"The average life span of Wegener's patients can be normal if they are put into an early remission and do not have significant residual renal function impairment."

As she read it I could almost see the relief she was experiencing.

"What do I have to do to open an IRA?" she asked.

Dick gave her the necessary information, and the next time we spoke she had taken steps to set up such an account.

A week later as I was trying to organize all the research papers I had collected, I came across the article from People magazine and began to wonder if Michelle's parents might have information that we didn't. I wanted to talk to them. The article said they lived in the South and the article's author was listed as a staff writer working out of Chicago. The magazine's home office was in New York, which was the only address available on the masthead.

I composed a letter to the author telling her briefly about Carol and asking her to either give me the address of the family in the article, or forward my letter to them, not really knowing if they would respond. Carol agreed that it might be interesting to exchange information.

A few weeks went by without any word from the author. However, the article mentioned the names of Michelle's parents so I decided to check the phone listings and met with success.

My call resulted in a nice conversation with Michelle. She suggested calling her mother at work and gave me the phone number.

Michelle's mother, Pat, and I had a lot of information to share about our girls. She was pleasant and friendly and told me about a call she'd had from a woman in California named Arlene.

"Her husband is a Wegener's patient and they live in a Los Angeles suburb."

She gave me the phone number for Arlene, whose husband, Fred, was the patient. They lived in a neighboring town, fairly close to our house. The two of us met for lunch and she was very excited about getting a support group started. She even offered her home for the meeting.

I contacted all the people whose names were on my list and asked them if they were interested in forming a support group. Each one said they were. However, I had no idea where to go or what to do for information on how to get one started.

There was a phone number posted in the Bowyer Clinic offering counseling for cancer patients. Since Carol was being treated there, and no number was given for anyone who wasn't a cancer patient, it seemed as if it might be a good place to start.

I made three phone calls before anyone called me back, and was referred to a cancer support group in a neighboring town. My thinking was that by attending a meeting and talking to the leader, I might know how to proceed.

I left my name and phone number on the group leader's answering machine and received a call that evening. I was so excited about getting a WG group going. The lady who called me was pressed for time so I briefly explained about starting a group and she said she would call me back the next day.

After several days without hearing from her, I tried again, thinking that perhaps she might have misplaced my number. Again I didn't hear anything, so after waiting several more days, tried again. When there was still no return call, I wrote a letter explaining my mission and asked to be steered to someone who could help if she couldn't.

In spite of all these efforts, no one from that group ever called or wrote.

After finding a phone number in the yellow pages called Hospital Helpline, I tried that. A friendly woman referred me to the California Self Help Center at UCLA. It seemed strange that we'd never heard of that service considering all the times we had been to the medical center.

A friendly man spoke to me and said he would send me information from the center. What arrived was a form to fill out details for an already formed support group to add to their master list, and a catalogue of booklets to order about starting a group. I ordered two of the booklets, but it was several months before they arrived. They were definitely helpful, but we needed more than the printed word; we needed a real live person.

By this time another letter from Marilyn arrived along with one from Anne who said if there was going to be a group, to count her in.

During one of Carol's treatments, I discussed my idea to start a group with one of Carol's chemo nurses.

"There's a social worker here at the clinic who might be able to help," she offered, and gave me the phone number.

After two attempts to reach the social worker, she returned my calls. She suggested trying the Self Help Center and indicated that she was too tied up with cancer patients to spend any time helping others. It was disappointing. I had read about cancer patients who were on chemotherapy for six-month periods. Didn't it mean anything that someone was undergoing the same treatment for two years?

Some time later, a second mailing from the Self Help Center arrived with the name of a person to contact if someone was interested in starting a group. That was my cue.

Three phone calls later I was finally able to speak to a woman who referred me to a doctor whose job it was to help groups get started.

After three more phone calls, the doctor's secretary called to get preliminary information from me. I gave her my ideas of topics to discuss at the meetings and she indicated she thought they were good. She told me to hang in there; the doctor was very busy, but he would get back to me. I never heard from him.

At that point, I decided to just pick a date and let others know. Almost every one contacted said I was the first person they'd spoken to who'd had experience with Wegener's. I also contacted the man whose name had been given to me by Dr. Pryor a couple of years earlier, and sent a letter to Anne. In December, a few weeks before Christmas, six Wegener's patients, including Fred, Anne, Collette, Hubert, the optician, Dr. Pryor's patient, John, and Carol, along with assorted family members, met at Arlene and Fred's home.

I'd also sent Marilyn an invitation and was overwhelmed and overjoyed when she and her husband Sam walked into our meeting. I couldn't believe that she had taken the time, inconvenienced herself, and spent the money just to lend support to our first meeting. In person, Marilyn was even more friendly and loving than she was in her letter.

Everyone had a chance to tell his or her story and we truly bonded.

Marilyn and I began to correspond regularly and exchange names and addresses of everyone we picked up along the way. Before long we had twenty names on our list, including one in Canada and one in Mexico.

With two patients living outside the United States, Marilyn and I decided we could call ourselves an international organization, and began using that word in the title of our members list. At that time we identified those who were patients, those who were family members or friends, and those who, sadly, had lost a loved one to the disease but still wanted to be part of our group.

Anne worked for the AMA and offered to get the Los Angeles directory of doctors for me which she sent shortly thereafter. Because it hadn't been invented yet, or perhaps because I had just never heard of the mail merge[37] program, it took literally months to write separate letters to every doctor whose discipline would afford them the opportunity to treat a WG patient. That included family physicians, otorhinolarngologists, rheumatologists, nephrologists, urologists, pulmonologists, and immunologists.

I told them that as the mother of a Wegener's patient I was in the process of forming a support group, and asked that they pass along my name, address and phone number to anyone who might be interested. In case they didn't presently have a WG patient, I asked that they save the information in the event they acquired a patient at a later date. I couldn't think of a better cause for my time, money, and energy and that has never changed.

Very few answered but that didn't bother me. I had put the information out there and had to hope that whoever had it would pass it along when the occasion arose.

Never having been involved with a support group of any kind, I had no idea how to conduct one so I had to wing it.

We muddled through and began having meetings every so often. Free places to meet were difficult to find. Sometimes we met in one another's homes, sometimes in a church meeting room—I paid for that one—and sometimes in a nursing home. I was determined not to charge anyone who wanted to meet with us.

Many months and meetings later, Marilyn came to California and surprised me again by showing up at our meeting place. I was delighted to see her. I had made it a habit to include her in all my correspondence so that she would always be aware of our activities and meeting schedules. At that particular meeting we were using the conference room of a nursing home we had been lucky enough to get without charge.

Dr. Steven Weiner, a rheumatologist who had done research on and treated a number of WG patients spoke to us for the first time. I asked him for statistics as to how many WG patients there might be at any given time, which unfortunately he didn't have. His answer was very thought-provoking, however.

He told us that half of all the people who have Wegener's, at least at that time, were walking around undiagnosed. They were probably being treated for sinusitis, bronchitis, or similar symptoms of upper respiratory distress. Only the most conscientious doctors look beyond the ordinary when the patient is not getting well.

Marilyn had flown into LAX and taken a taxi to our meeting in Pasadena. It was a long ride and probably an expensive one.

As our meeting was finishing up, she asked me, "Do you know of a pay phone nearby?"

I didn't but my house was five minutes from the nursing home.

"Why don't you come home with me and use my phone? Who do you want to call?"

"I just wanted to call a taxi," she answered.

She was staying at a hotel near the airport.

"You're not calling a taxi. I'll drive you back."

She protested, but I insisted.

On the way to her hotel we had the better part of an hour to visit with each other. She related what she had gone through as a patient; I told her what Dick, the boys, and I had gone through as family members. After that, she told me, "You know, all the while I've had this disease I never once stopped to think about how my family was handling this."

I believe the information and experiences we shared that evening changed both our outlooks in many ways. We knew we would be friends forever.

---

35.   In 1983, research papers were published by both the National Institutes of Health, authored by Drs. Fauci, Haynes, Katz and Wolf; and the Mayo Clinic, authored by Drs. McDonald and De Remee. Both papers discussed patients followed for over twenty years.

36.   Refers to People Magazine Issue dated December 8, 1986.

37.   Mail merge is a feature supported by many word processors that enables the user to generate form letters.

21

Conflicting Responsibilities

I don't know if it was psychological or physical or both, but by the time Carol went for her next treatment, a week late because of a ski trip, she was not feeling tip-top.

Lesley was her nurse again. She put the cold cap on before she put the IV in, and when she went to insert the needle she couldn't find a cooperative vein. After two unsuccessful tries, Carol was in tears and Lesley was pretty apprehensive, too. I stayed way in the background, out of the way. If there was nothing I could do to help her, at least I wasn't going to get in the way and cause them any trouble.

Lesley apologized several times. Carol told her, half serious, half teasing, "Three strikes and you're out. You'd better get it next time." Then she said, "If this is the fault of putting the cold cap on first, would a hot pack[38] on my arm help?"

"That's a good idea," Lesley said, and tried one. It worked and on the third try the IV was finally inserted. The rest of the treatment day was uneventful; the morning had been bad enough.

Carol spent the weekend at her apartment with Don taking care of her. Although some people who are sick seem to have a fear of loneliness, Carol would have preferred to be alone.

A few days later, as I was halfway out the door, Carol phoned, sounding awful.

"My knees really hurt bad, Mom. I can hardly get out of bed to go to the bathroom."

The distance from her bed to the bathroom wasn't five feet. She had experienced joint pains before, but never this bad. I asked if she'd spoken to Dr. Black.

"Yes. He wants me to come down to the hospital and get X-rayed. I'd like to take a shower, but I'm afraid to get into the tub. If I fall, I can't call you from the bathroom."

"Hang in there," I said. "I'm on my way."

When I arrived, she didn't seem to be any better. She said she had taken codeine but it hadn't helped much.

"When are you supposed to be at the hospital?"

"Whenever I get there," she answered and went to take a shower.

"I have to make a phone call before I leave. I have a job interview today and I'll have to reschedule it."

"I didn't know you were looking for another job."

"Actually I wasn't. It's kind of an interesting story. I'll tell you later."

"What are you going to tell them on your interview call? Something like the flu?"

"Yeah. I guess so."

Carol made her phone call and we left. She walked slowly and used the elevator instead of the stairs. In the hospital parking lot she declined my offer of a wheelchair.

In the hospital, she told me about the job interview.

Harry,* a former co-worker who had gone to another company was trying to recruit Carol for a job opening there, and sent her an application. Since she wasn't looking for another job, she put it aside until it became easier to fill it out than to put Harry off. Harry's boss must have liked what he read. He soon called Carol for an interview, which had been scheduled for today.

After the X-rays were taken, Carol was given her file and a stack of previous X-rays to take to DMPG where she was to leave samples of blood and urine to be tested. Then the results would be sent to Dr. Black—we hoped.

"I gave them blood, but no urine," she said.

That didn't surprise me. She hadn't had anything to eat or drink since I'd been with her.

When we got back to her place, I fixed her lunch and sat down with a book while she went back to bed.

"You don't have to stay, you know."

"I know. I want to. If you're able to produce a specimen I can take it to the hospital."

Later that day Harry called to let her know that rescheduling her appointment would be no problem, even if it was a week later.

During the afternoon Dr. Black called.

"Her blood test and X-rays showed nothing new or different."

"What does that mean?"

"That there are no new problems."

"What about her knees?"

"Joint pains are a part of Wegener's."

"This bad?"

"She's never had it this bad before, has she?"

"No."

"Maybe it's because she delayed her treatment. We'll just have to deal with the pain now. She has pain pills, doesn't she? And she should get some relief in a day or two as the chemo kicks in. I'm not happy that she's having pain, but I'm pleased that the tests did not show a worsening of the Wegener's."

I waited until Don came home, and then left.

Carol had three interviews with Harry's bosses in multiple levels of management within the next couple of weeks. Even though she had no plans to make a career change, she did finally accept an offer. She gave notice at her old job and was to begin the new one the day after her twenty-fifth birthday.

Then she was faced with a new dilemma.

In preparation for Carol's quarter-century celebration, her friend Pam arranged for a surprise trip for Carol and their friend Sue. Carol didn't know any of the details other than she would be traveling by plane and what sort of clothes to pack according to the weather information she had been given. The week before the trip Pam arranged a treasure hunt for Carol with clues as to where they would be going. Carol's always been great at those sorts of games, but this time she was stumped and didn't figure it out until they were waiting to board the plane.

The eighth treatment was to be the week before she left on her trip with three days to recover from the effects, so getting on a plane a week later should pose no problems.

A few days before the treatment, Lesley called and told me that the entire chemo staff would be meeting Friday morning, so Carol's treatment would have to be rescheduled. I told her about the trip, the new job and how close to impossible another day would be.

"I'm really sorry," Lesley said, "but we have no control over this. It's an administrative decision."

I thanked her for calling and added that Carol would get back to her.

When I told Carol she was annoyed, but determined to go through with her original plans.

"They can't change this one. I promised my boss I would give them a full two weeks of work before I left. I can't have therapy next week because I won't be in any shape for the trip to wherever I'm being taken. If the tickets are cashed in, 50 percent of the money will be lost because it was a special deal, and Dr. Black won't let me put off therapy for two weeks. Besides, that would be the first week of my new job. I'm already taking Monday off to recuperate from the trip. It's totally out of the question to change the treatment that's scheduled. They have to take me Friday."

"Well, sweetheart, tell that to Lesley and good luck. Let me know what happens."

In a short while Carol called back.

"I'm going for therapy on Friday, as scheduled, but at 2:00 PM instead of 9:00 AM."

"How did you manage that?"

"I spoke to Lesley and she couldn't do a thing. Then I called Dr. Black and told him the situation. He agreed to let me forgo hydration if I would drink a liter before and after the treatment. I promised I would. Since the staff meeting is in the morning, they'll do the chemo in the afternoon and I'll work half a day."

The clinic was extremely busy that afternoon. I sat in the waiting room while Carol was infused. Lesley called down to DMPG to make sure they had the proper orders. Carol was to be released through them.

"What do I do about the IV?" Lesley asked.

"Take it out," Carol said. "It's four o'clock. There's no way they're going to hydrate me."

Lesley agreed and removed the IV.

Without Carol's being connected to an IV, there was no need for a wheelchair, so she and I walked down to DMPG unaccompanied.

"Where's your IV?" Michael asked, as Carol checked in.

"I told Lesley to take it out, and you're not putting it back in."

"I understand what you're telling me, but we have written orders. Unless we can reach Dr. Black for an OK, we have to give you a liter of fluid."

"Then call him," Carol said. "He's the one who came up with the idea of my drinking a liter before and after the infusion."

"We're trying," Amy said, "but he's not answering his page."

"Try Dr. Saxon," Carol suggested.

"He's out of town."

Amy and Michael explained again that nurses had to comply with written instructions from doctors or they could lose their jobs, even though they knew Carol wouldn't have purposely misled them.

"Couldn't I drink the liter while you watch?" Carol asked.

"We'll be right back," Amy said as she and Michael left the room.

Shortly they returned with a pitcher filled with ice water. The pitcher had measurements on it and was filled to the liter mark.

"If you can drink this while we watch," Amy said, "then we can honestly say we gave you a liter."

"I knew there was a way to handle this and make everyone happy," Carol said, smiling.

They began taking turns watching Carol drink.

"This is a lot easier," Carol said. "I wonder why I can't do it this way all the time."

"Ask Dr. Black."

"I think I will."

It took about an hour and a half to drink the water. By the time she was three-quarters done, she remarked, "Now I know why they don't normally let us drink our hydration."

"Why?"

"I'm getting nauseous."

When she was finished, we drove home, very slowly. Don was already there.

Carol didn't want to come home with me, and was hoping not to have to bother Ron or Don over the weekend. Both had offered to be on call in case she needed either of them.

"I feel guilty about asking them to do things for me."

I had to clear this up and started to explain: "You've been fighting this thing for nine years now."

"Eight and a half," she interrupted.

"OK, eight and a half years. Every one of us loves you very much. I'm sure you know that."

She nodded.

"What you may not know is that we've spent a lot of the last eight and a half years feeling guilty because we're healthy and you're not. I know it's illogical, but that's the way it is.

"We can't change what's happened to you, and we can't give you our good health, no matter how much we would like to. So in order to assuage our guilt feelings, we want to do things for you to try to make you feel better. It's all we can do to help.

"I never once asked your brothers to hang around and help you after chemo. It was their idea; they volunteered on their own. By your not calling them when you need someone and by your not letting them do something to help you when the occasion arises, you're taking away the opportunity for them to alleviate their guilt and feel better about themselves. You must give them that chance.

"We do what we do for two reasons: we love you and want to help you because that's what families are all about, and it makes us all feel less guilty about being healthy. It's not fair for you to take that away from us.

"Now shut up and eat your pizza."

"And drink your beer," Don added. "By the way, can you have beer?"

"I can have anything I want," Carol answered.

"I thought you weren't supposed to have any alcohol the week after chemo," I said.

"That was just the first few times, to see if it would make any difference."

"Did it?" I asked.

"Who knows," Carol answered.

On the specified date and time Pam and Sue blindfolded Carol, drove her to the airport, led her through the terminal and the security gate, each holding an arm and giving her directions such as walk straight ahead, make a right turn, etc. until she was waiting to board the plane. She had no clue until the flight attendants announced where they were going. What she didn't know was that Kenny would meet them—in New Orleans. That scenario would be impossible today. I can't imagine security personnel allowing someone wearing a blindfold to be led through the sensors.

Carol had now completed twelve treatments and was starting on her second year. I wanted to do something to show her how much we admired her courage and found the perfect gift: an emerald pendant and earrings, her birthstone. I presented her with the pendant, expecting to give her the earrings some time in the future. She was thrilled with her gift.

After one of Carol's subsequent treatments, Ron and Don had offered and expected to be on call for her as they had done before. Previously Don had woken her up frequently during the weekend, offering her drinks to keep her system flushed out, and made sure that she had something to eat.

This particular weekend he was called in to work, and she couldn't reach Ron. Carol spent most of the weekend sleeping and by the time Sunday evening rolled around the drug had not been flushed out of her system properly. She felt lousy and was unable to go to work the next day.

Thereafter I insisted she come home with me after treatments. Friday and Saturday nights I would wake her up several times during the night to drink. Sometimes she came downstairs for meals; other times I brought them up. It worked well because I knew she was being taken care of and made sure she didn't feel guilty about keeping Dick and me from doing something we might have planned that one weekend a month. I convinced her that nothing was more important to us than seeing her through those few days and she finally came to believe that.

Carol learned to help the health professionals help her. At one of the treatments, Susan was having trouble finding a good vein.

"Try a hot pack," Carol suggested. "It worked for Lesley."

"You've used that arm a lot," I mentioned to Carol. "I read recently that the veins can get scarred from too many IV's. Is once a month too many times?"

"It certainly is," Susan answered. "Let's try the other arm."

She put a hot pack on the other arm and left the room.

When she returned, I had left the room. The IV was in when I came back.

"That was quick work," I remarked.

"Carol found the vein for me. She said try this one, and it worked."

Carol was happy that she was able to help and only had to get stuck with the needle once.

Lesley was Carol's nurse for treatment number thirteen.

"Today is going to be a good treatment day," I said. "I can feel it."

I couldn't have been more wrong. Actually my feeling about the physical part of the treatment wasn't far off. But a new problem got in the way.

Carol's new job carried a lot more responsibility than the old one. She was part of the Global Trading Department of Security Pacific Bank, which supported computer systems for domestic securities trading. It was her job to see that the computers ran smoothly and to fix problems as they arose. Because computer trading was still in its infancy, there were many technical problems and she was the go-to person for the solutions.

When she was hired, she told her new boss she would need one day off a month for medical reasons. The time off was approved as long as she wore a pager and could answer questions.

It was during her thirteenth treatment that the pager began to beep. A man who was going on vacation for the next two weeks needed information before he left.

"Can I use the phone here?" she asked Lesley.

As she completed her call, the cold cap fell off and Lesley was upset at having to redo it. Just as Carol was settling in once more, the pager beeped again.

"It's my boss. I'd better call."

Lesley told her to use the phone down the hall this time and I went with her as she pulled the IV pole along. Her boss had her on the phone for what seemed like an interminable period of time.

I stayed close by and kept a watch on the IV in case something went wrong. Then Lesley reappeared.

"You cannot stay here and be watched," she barked at Carol. "You're not the only patient I have and I cannot continue to run down the hall ..."

Continue? She's only done this once.

"... and leave my other patients just to check on you."

She had a valid argument. Carol completed the phone call as soon as she was able.

Apparently the whole system at work crashed. While Carol talked her staff through the details of how to get it up and running, Lesley came looking for her a few more times.

Upon our return to the infusion room, Lesley jumped on her again.

"You're not my only patient. I can't check on you when you're down the hall and I can't keep running back and forth between you and my other patients. I can't leave all my other patients for one. This will not work. I hope you're not going to make a habit out of this."

I was tempted to point out it was the first such occurrence, but I kept my mouth shut.

"It's not a social call," Carol replied. "My job depends on my being available."

"Well, you have to be available to me," Lesley said. "You're my job."

Then she said to me, "This room is much too crowded. You'll have to wait in the waiting room."

Without saying a word, I picked up my things and went to the waiting room. I wasn't insulted about being moved; the nurses' first obligation is to tend to the patients' welfare and I was excess baggage. It was the way I was ordered out that annoyed me.

During the remainder of time Carol was there, I checked on her three times. Each time she appeared to be resting and had her eyes closed, so I didn't disturb her. After a while the infusion room had emptied out, but there was no way I was going to go back in.

Later Susan came looking for me.

"Your daughter is going to DMPG. Would you like to accompany her?"

I thanked her, gathered up my things once again and met Susan, Carol ensconced in a wheelchair and the escort in the hall.

"Lesley's mad at us," I told her. "I didn't want to cause any more trouble by hanging around where I wasn't wanted."

"Oh, I'm sorry," Susan said.

"You don't have to apologize. It's not your fault," I answered.

I knew when Carol left the clinic there were bad feelings between Lesley and her.

When we got down to DMPG I told Carol, "I came within an inch of telling her off."

"Me, too," she said.

"I would appreciate a room with a phone when you have one available," Carol requested.

I left to get lunch and by the time I returned, Carol's room had been changed. Besides having a phone, the larger room also had windows and was much more cheerful.

It's impossible to tell if it was the lunch or dinner she ate, the aggravation of the day, or if she took too few anti-nausea pills, but Carol spent the next thirty-six hours with her porcelain buddy.

When it was all over and food was going the correct way through the alimentary canal again, I reminded her, "I know what the problem was. That was treatment number thirteen, the unlucky one. From now on, it should be smooth sailing."

"You're probably right. I never thought of that."

During the weeks after the thirteenth treatment I became more and more upset with regard to Lesley, and told Dick about it.

"Why don't you call or write to her boss?" he suggested.

"I'd just as soon stay on good terms with someone who's sticking needles in our daughter's arms."

I stewed about it until one day when I was listening to one of Carol's motivational tapes which stated that successful people always look on the positive side of things. I began to realize that I needed to explain things to Lesley and keep the peace. After all, she was only doing her job.

When discussing the episode with Carol, she said, "A Cytoxan™ infusion could be dangerous and has to be watched very carefully."

"But when you couldn't get off the phone, you had no choice," I said. "You can't ignore your boss's page when you said you would be available."

"I should never have let them know I'd be available in the morning. During hydration there's not as much possibility of problems," Carol said.

Upon our arrival at the clinic for the fourteenth treatment, I was apprehensive about confronting Lesley. It seemed as if she was avoiding me, also. I knew we had to clear the air but wasn't sure how. Then the thought came to me: I'll ask Susan if she could act as a go-between.

The infusion room was crowded and Lesley kicked me out as soon as I walked in. Sensing my frustration, Susan made three trips to the waiting room to try to ease the friction. Finally she said, "I don't think I should get involved. I'd hate for my co-workers to think I'm talking about them behind their backs. She's a take-charge person and so are you. Perhaps she's intimidated, but I really feel you should try to talk to her."

I watched and waited until there was a break in the action.

"When you have a minute, I'd like to speak to you, Lesley," I said.

"I have to record something in a file and I'll be right with you," she answered.

When she stepped into the hall where I was waiting, I began, "I know you were upset with Carol last time and I wanted to explain what happened. She's twenty-five years old and although she still looks like sixteen, she has a job that carries a lot of responsibility."

I proceeded to explain what the job entailed.

"When Carol was beeped, it was her boss calling. One doesn't ignore that. There's a project for several hundred thousand dollars for which she suggested an independent contractor. The company is in the process of making a decision and her boss needed her input.

"She has since made it clear to her boss that during her one day a month medical leave she will no longer be able to answer pages immediately, but will make sure she gets back to them as soon as possible on the same day. That way she'll be where you need her to be and you won't have to go looking for her like you did last time. I don't want there to be any hard feelings between you and her and neither does she.

"The people she works with have no idea what health problems she may or may not have. When she hired on, she said she needed one day off a month for medical reasons. No questions were asked; no explanations were offered. For all anyone knows, they may believe she has female problems once a month.

"We've discussed whether her boss and co-workers should be told, but it's Carol's opinion that as long as she can keep it from them, the better. It's no secret that if the truth be known, her chances for a promotion would be severely limited. Those in charge would likely promote someone they deem to be in good health.

"Carol has arranged not to be disturbed during chemotherapy again, and there won't be a repeat performance."

Lesley thanked me for taking the time to explain Carol's circumstances and promised that as long as Carol stayed where she was supposed to be, there wouldn't be any more problems where she was concerned.

"You know we can't have her down the hall when we're trying to watch her and we must keep close tabs on our patients during infusion. I'm glad you have things worked out."

"We've felt that Carol has had such fantastic care here at the Bowyer Clinic that we'd hate to have anything upset the apple cart. We also don't want to be on unfriendly terms with anyone."

"Thank you for telling me," she said.

I felt better having the air cleared and Carol approved of the way I handled it too.

When we went for the fifteenth treatment, we were all friends again. Melinda had been replaced by Lisa. We had spoken briefly that day and I told her our feelings about Dr. Thompson.

"He's a marvelous surgeon," she said. "He's the one who operates on all the movie stars."

When I discussed Wegener's with Lisa, she seemed to be knowledgeable about the disease.

After observing the hectic schedule Carol kept, one of her newer friends remarked, "I don't know how you accomplish all you do while on chemotherapy. I can't imagine what you'd be like if you weren't."

I hope she gets the chance to find out one day.

Carol's new job was in downtown Los Angeles, which meant a long drive on a busy freeway. She and Don discussed buying a place of their own but about the time Carol began working downtown, Don got a job in the next county just south of Los Angeles. It would have meant an even longer commute for him. They decided to split up and kidded about it being a friendly divorce.

Dick and I went apartment hunting with Carol again and found a spectacular one with four levels and a secured parking area. She bought new furniture and Don took what they had been using. Because there were stairs galore, she got all the exercise she needed just going from room to room.

As Carol continued to have monthly treatments, we began the day by stopping for something to eat before she reported to the Bowyer Clinic. I noticed that her dawdling time was increasing.

"Now that you have so many treatments behind you, do you feel like it's getting easier?"

"Absolutely not. That's why I'm not in any hurry to get there."

Although it had become routine for me, it became an aversion to her.

Listening to comedy tapes on the way home delighted her and helped to take her mind off what was to come in the next few days.

The Scopolamine™ patches worked well and gave her relief from the nausea. Unfortunately she had trouble sleeping because the anti-nausea drugs also acted as stimulants.

A few months and several treatments later, when we thought everything was under control, the bottom dropped out of our world once again.

Carol called me. "I have some bad news."

---

38. A hot pack is similar to a cold cap. When it's unwrapped and manipulated by hand the chemicals mix and it produces heat.

Pam, Carol with blindfold, and Sue, 1987

22

The Disease Spreads

"What kind of bad news?"

"There's a spot on my lung."

I detected trembling in her voice.

I felt the room sway, the walls start to close in, and my knees turn to rubber as I grabbed for a chair and fell into it. For a few moments I was paralyzed with fear.

What was going to happen to her now? During the eight years Carol had been fighting Wegener's we'd been told that she was lucky because the disease was confined to her nose. It hadn't spread elsewhere. Dr. Haring had been concerned about a spread to the brain; Dr. Saxon had been concerned about spreading anywhere. Should chemo have been started sooner? The doctors thought so. Had she lost any ground by waiting? Had the prognosis changed?

I had been shopping with my parents and my biggest worry that day had been what to make for dinner. How complacent I had become.

My composure returned, but my heart was still beating a mile a minute.

"How do they know?"

Mom walked in the door with an armload of bags, took one look at my face, and froze in her tracks.

I put my hand over the mouthpiece and told her, "There's a spot on her lung."

The look on Mom's face mirrored what I was feeling: panic!

"I was really furious when Dr. Black said it was on a scan that was taken in June, several months ago. I asked him why they waited until now to tell me."

I was glad she was angry. That meant she would fight like she had in the past.

"What answer did you get?"

"He said they needed to take another CT scan and compare the two in case it was a spot on the film."

"What are they going to do?"

"They want to do a bronchoscopy[39] next week."

"What's a bronchoscopy?"

"They stick a bronchoscope[40] into my bronchial tubes and take a piece of tissue from the spot. Then they'll examine it to see if it's Wegener's or something else. I'll be awake and they'll use a local anesthetic."

"I would like to be there," I said.

"It really isn't necessary, Mom," she stated.

"Humor me. I'll go bananas if I'm just sitting here waiting for news and wondering what's going on. Besides, you might not feel like driving home."

"OK. I'll let you know what time and day they want me."

I hung up the phone and gave my parents the news. Then I called Dick at work to tell him.

I don't know how I got through the details without breaking down, trying to be cheerful and hopeful while my heart was breaking.

As soon as I was able, I snuck away to the bathroom to cry although I felt like screaming: she's had enough; don't test us anymore!

When the scheduled day rolled around, Carol made a few phone calls to friends, telling them about the bronchoscopy, and asking for their moral support, good wishes, and prayers. I had no idea that many people knew about her illness and treatments.

Dick had wanted to be with us, but Carol, as usual, was determined not to make a big deal out of this. We worked it out this way: there was no need for Dick to take the whole day off work, since the bronchoscopy wasn't scheduled until 2:00 PM. As soon as I had enough details, I would call him at work and he'd meet me at a designated place in the hospital.

Carol had to have a CT taken first thing that morning and went to the Nuclear Medicine section in the basement. Carol had gotten to know her way around the huge medical center, while I frequently had no idea where I was or where I was going and felt like a rat in a maze. Every time I told her that, she would jokingly inform me that there really was cheese at the end.

The instructions she had in hand were for an MRI.

"But the doctor said, scan," Carol told the receptionist.

"The paper you have here doesn't say that," the woman told her.

"Why don't you check your schedule?" Carol asked.

To me she said, "I was standing there when Dr. Black made the appointment. He must have absent-mindedly put something else on the instructions."

Great. And this is the expert who's responsible for my daughter's life.

"You're on the schedule for a scan," the receptionist told Carol. "I'll call upstairs and confirm it."

Shortly thereafter Carol's name was called and she was taken into the room where the scan was to be done. Moments later Dr. Black came to the receptionist's window.

"I'd like the scan for Carol Swart to be sent to me immediately. The results are needed for a bronchoscopy this afternoon."

I couldn't hear what the receptionist was saying, but it didn't take long to realize the man was asking, pleading, cajoling, and then insisting that he have the scan in hand by 1:00 PM. It was currently 10:00 AM.

I heard a little more from the receptionist, who had now raised her voice, telling him that there was no way he was going to get what he wanted. Apparently he had no intention of taking no for an answer, and decided to go over the receptionist's head.

"I have to check in at DMPG on the third floor," Carol said when she returned.

Since her joints hadn't been bothering her for a while, Carol had gotten back into the habit of walking upstairs rather than taking the elevator whenever there was a choice. Maybe that was one of the ways she kept her weight down. I followed her to the stairs and climbed with her, puffing and panting all the way.

"What do you have to check in for?"

"The bronchoscopy is considered a surgical procedure and I have to find out where to go."

Unfortunately no one had given the receptionist information to tell Carol.

Doesn't anyone at UCLA talk to anyone else?

The note that the receptionist pulled up on the computer read, simply, "Call Dr. Black."

She tried, but he was nowhere to be found. No information was available for me to pass on to Dick.

It appeared that the easiest thing to do was to steer him to a spot, and then go there and get him at an agreed upon time.

No food was supposed to be ingested prior to the bronchoscopy, so Carol and I walked around Westwood for a while and window-shopped. If she was upset, or apprehensive, it didn't show.

When it was time, we reported back in at DMPG.

"Where do we go from here?" I asked the receptionist.

She had finally gotten some details.

"A doctor from the fourth floor will come and get you," she told us.

In about five minutes, one did. He introduced himself and asked us to follow him. I followed along around the corner, in the elevator, and down the hall, until

I could go no further. A nurse directed me to a small waiting room. I sat down for a moment and looked at my watch. It was just about time for Dick to arrive. Back I went to the third floor to search for him. He had just walked in the door, and accompanied me back to the fourth floor waiting room.

A doctor we had never met or heard of before came into the room looking for us and introduced himself.

"I'm the one who is going to do the bronchoscopy," he said.

I learned later that Carol had sent him out to speak with us.

"Will the bronchoscope be inserted in her throat?" Dick asked.

The doctor assured us that, "Even though it is usually done through the nose because the patient is awake and it's much less uncomfortable, in Carol's case we will not bother the nose, but go through the throat."

I was surprised that he called her by name, and we were both pleased that he knew something about her situation.

"After anesthetizing the area, which takes about thirty to forty-five minutes," the doctor explained, "the bronchoscope will be inserted into her bronchial tubes.

"We'll try to get a tissue sample for examination under a microscope," the doctor continued. "We will then try to determine whether the spot is an infection or a spread of Wegener's."

It seemed that he knew something about Wegener's. That was also comforting.

"I will see you afterward to let you know what we have found," he added. "Carol told us she has not eaten. Is that correct?"

"Yes, it is," I confirmed.

"Well, I'll see you in a little while," he said.

"Good luck," Dick and I said, together, as the doctor turned and left the room, heading down the hall to where I had left Carol.

I left to get some soft drinks and something to munch on. An hour and a half later the doctor came looking for us.

"Unfortunately, very little tissue was obtained," the doctor informed us, "and there is almost no way of telling what we are dealing with here."

"Why?" Dick asked.

"As we suspected, the spot we saw was not inside the bronchial tubes but in the lung tissue. We had no way of knowing that for sure and felt we had to try this procedure first. It could have told us something we could work with, and it's the least dangerous for the patient.

"Carol tolerated the procedure well, although she was just a little uncomfortable towards the end.

"She will be taken up to the out-patient recovery area on the seventh floor shortly. If you like, you can go up there and wait for her," the doctor concluded.

We thanked him and went up to the seventh floor.

A young nurse, who introduced herself as Cindy, was a perfect recovery room attendant. She was friendly, cheerful and helpful.

About ten minutes later, Carol arrived. While she snoozed for a while, Cindy took her vital signs several times and chatted with us.

A few hours went by and the doctor who had escorted Carol and me from the third floor earlier that day came up to see her. By that time she was awake.

"He assisted," she explained.

"When can we expect to get answers from today's procedure?" I asked the doctor.

"Why don't you contact Dr. Saxon in a couple of days," he suggested.

Pleased with how Carol seemed to be, he released her, and she was escorted downstairs in a wheelchair. As usual, Dick had gotten a better parking spot than I had. Carol rode with him and we met at her apartment.

Several times within the next few days, I asked Carol if she had heard from Dr. Saxon.

"Why don't you call him yourself and see if he has any results yet," she suggested.

That was a green light if I ever saw one. I didn't waste a minute getting to the phone, but Dr. Saxon wasn't available. I left a message for him, but it was Dr. Black who returned my call. I wasn't even sure he would tell me anything. After all, Carol was now an adult and he was under no obligation to answer my questions.

Fortunately, that didn't seem to be a problem.

"I've just spoken to Carol and she said it was all right to give you this information," he said.

"There was not enough tissue obtained during the bronchoscopy to draw any conclusions. The spot in question was outside the bronchial tubes, in the lung tissue. That couldn't be determined by the various films."

"How big is the spot?" I asked.

"About the size of a quarter," he answered. "By the way, I went looking for you after the bronchoscopy, but you must have already gone up to recovery. I was there during the whole procedure," he said.

"I wish we had known," I replied. "Carol's father and I would like to have spoken to you."

In a few days we saw Dr. Saxon.

"What do we do now?" I asked.

"There are two alternatives," Dr. Saxon explained. "We can do a needle biopsy, which entails sticking a needle into the spot in her lung and withdrawing tissue to analyze, or we can operate on the lung. We would actually go in and cut out a piece to examine."

"I'd prefer not to have an operation on my lung," Carol informed us.

"I don't blame you," the doctor said. "From our point of view, we try to find out what we can in the way that's least damaging to the patient. That's why we did the bronchoscopy, even though it was pretty certain that it wasn't going to tell us much. But we had to try that first. Now the needle biopsy is the next, least dangerous step.

"If the spot turns out to be an infection, the drugs we give you for Wegener's could open your body up to the equivalent of an explosion of infection. We must rule out that possibility before we begin to treat the spot as Wegener's."

"What are the dangers of a needle biopsy?" Carol asked.

"The lung could collapse," he answered. "But we have to know. If an infection runs rampant, it could kill you."

He gave Carol another prescription for an antibiotic.

"I think I can do the needle biopsy on Wednesday," he continued. "I'll let you know."

That was two days away. They were moving quickly. There was no time to waste if the Wegener's was spreading or if Carol had an infection.

"I'll get the prescription filled for you if you like," I told Carol on the way home.

"You'll be sorry," she said.

"Why? Is it expensive?"

"Very."

I had the prescription filled for her and she was right. One hundred pills of Ceclor™ were $237. The cashier was apologetic.

Carol called me the next day.

"Wednesday is OK," she told me. "They'll do it first thing in the morning."

Later that day she called again.

"They've changed their minds. The needle biopsy is off. They're certain it's Wegener's because I don't have any symptoms of an infection."

"If they're sure the spot is not an infection, do they want you to continue taking the Ceclor™?"

"No."

"It figures," I said.

I was busily emptying the dishwasher when the phone rang. The voice on the other end was the voice of terror, but covered by a layer of sarcasm.

"Mom, I just spoke to Dr. Black and he says the spot in my lung is larger. Isn't that a drag?"

The paralysis of fear gripped me again. Then the mother-has-to-make-it-all-better complex took over. Quick! Say something encouraging.

"It probably hasn't been long enough for the chemo to do the job. How do they know?"

"I had another a chest X-ray."

"Remember the odds are on your side. How have you been feeling?"

"No different until now."

"Are you having any trouble breathing or pain in your chest, any indication that something's wrong there?"

"No. Nothing. Why? What are you thinking?"

I had been going merrily about my day-to-day business, emptying the dishwasher, thinking that everything was on an upswing. I wasn't ready for this turn of events. But I had to be positive. She was looking for hope and she was going to get it.

"Remember when the astrologist did our charts and we were amazed at how right she was about all the things she couldn't possibly have known about us any other way?"

"Uh huh, but what does that have to do with this?"

"She said, specifically, that you were going to outlive me, remember?"

"Yes."

"I don't see how she could have hit the nail on the head about all those other things and missed on this one. I believe the chemotherapy is going to work. The doctors believe the chemotherapy is going to work. You have to believe it's going to work. We just have to give it some more time. I'd like to talk to Dr. Black. Do you think he'll tell me anything?"

"I told him you'd probably be calling and he said he'd be happy to talk to you."

"Good. I think I'll call him now and let you get back to work. OK?"

"OK."

"Chin up. I love you."

"I love you, too."

Telling her that had become a habit. In fact, I'd been telling a lot more people how I felt about them. It had become very important to me to let those I cared about know it in no uncertain terms.

I immediately put in a call to Dr. Black and asked to have him paged. He must have been sitting by the phone because he called me back in less than ten minutes. I was pleased that I didn't have to wait hours for someone to track him down.

"I just spoke to Carol," I told him, "and she tells me the spot in her chest is larger. How much larger?"

"About the size of a half dollar," he said. "Did she tell you that there were also blood cells in her urine?"

"No, she didn't. How much trouble are we in?" I asked him with no beating around the bush.

"Well," he said, "we're not happy about it ..."

I should hope not, I thought.

"... but I don't feel it's out of control," he said. "The blood cells are microscopic and the increase of the size of the spot in the lungs we feel hasn't been affected by the chemotherapy as yet."

"What was Carol's reaction when you told her?" I asked.

"Well, she was very frustrated, of course," he answered, "and asked what we intended to do now."

"What did you tell her?" I asked.

"We intend to push the Cytoxan™ higher," he answered. "I'd like Carol to see a rheumatologist, a Dr. Bevra Hahn.[41] I want to know if there are any new problems we're not aware of."

Good, I thought. He had a plan and seemed to be in control.

"Are you aware that Carol has plans to go skiing next week in Oregon?"

"Yes, she mentioned that."

"Should she postpone the trip?"

"No. We want her to continue with whatever she has planned, as long as she feels up to it."

"For your information, Dr. Saxon suggested that Carol see Dr. Thompson a couple of months ago. She doesn't like him and she's not going to. If you think she should be seen by an ENT, I think she'd be happier going to Dr. Haring, the doctor in Valencia who first diagnosed the Wegener's and has been involved in her care ever since."

"Was there a problem with Dr. Thompson?"

"No. It's not a question of his competence at all. Carol feels that he just doesn't care if she lives or dies. It's strictly a personality thing."

"Of course she can see anyone she chooses. There is a doctor here who she might be happier with. Tell her to let me know what she'd like to do."

I called Carol back.

"I just spoke to Dr. Black. He doesn't think you should cancel your trip next week."

"I wasn't going to anyway."

I should have known.

"If you were in real trouble, I think they'd hospitalize you and would certainly suggest you not leave town."

"I guess so," she said.

I can't remember hearing such depression in her voice.

"I hope you're not going to be mad at me, but I told him you don't like Dr. Thompson and would prefer seeing someone else. I told him about Dr. Haring and he said that was fine. There's another ENT at UCLA who he thinks you might be happy with if you don't want to travel to Valencia. But he stressed that anyone you want to see is OK with him."

"Did he say who it was?"

"No."

"It's difficult getting out to Dr. Haring during the day."

"I'll bet he'll see you after hours if necessary."

"Maybe I'll call when I get back," she said.

I hung up the phone thinking I have to tell Dick. Then I picked it up again. After dialing most of his number at work, I replaced the receiver, remembering I had taken him to the airport yesterday.

He was in Florida, damn it. I wanted to talk to him. I needed to talk to him. I checked the time. It was 2:30 PM. That meant it was 5:30 in Florida. Was he still at his meeting? Was this the night he was leaving the hotel and staying with Kenny? Maybe I should call him there. Damn the three-hour time difference. I decided to wait till later.

---

39.   Bronchoscopy is the visual examination of the tracheo-bronchial tree using the flexible fiberoptic bronchoscope.

40.   A bronchoscope is a curved flexible tube for visual examination of the bronchi.

41.   Dr. Bevra Hahn is the Chief of Rheumatology at UCLA Medical Center.

23

Educating Myself

I finished putting the dishes away, picked up a notepad and drove to the library. Maybe there would be some specific literature available about how Wegener's can be stopped. It was high time I got more education about this insidious disease. There might even be some personal accounts of people who'd had it, how they coped, and what made them well again. It wasn't that I didn't believe what the doctors said. I did believe them. I just wanted more details.

The librarian was helpful. But there were no personal accounts. The only information I was able to find was in *The Merck Manual* from 1982. It was already five years old. The following information was gleaned.

The cause of Wegener's granulomatosis is unknown, although the disease resembles an infection process. Chest X-rays look like malignancies. Hypersensitivity has been thought to be the basis for the disease. Men are affected about twice as often as women. The disease can occur at any age.

Complaints usually begin in the upper respiratory tract, and include infections of the nose and sinuses, with nasal ulcerations. Secondary bacterial infections follow. Other symptoms include ear infections with possible hearing loss, and coughs with the sputum containing blood. The nasal infection is often mistaken for sinusitis. The mucus membranes of the nose bleed easily, are red and raw, and have the appearance of grains of sand.

Additional symptoms can be fever, general fatigue, weight loss, joint pain, skin sores, obstruction and bulging of the tear ducts, blockage of a coronary artery caused by inflammation of the blood vessels, localized, that may progress to generalized, inflammation of the blood vessels of the kidneys, with subsequent high blood pressure and excessive amounts of waste products in the blood. Kidney involvement is the symbol of generalized disease with the urine containing large quantities of protein and blood. Without quick and proper treatment, the kidneys will cease to function properly.

Sufferers of Wegener's also have an abnormal increase in the number of circulating white blood cells.

A biopsy is necessary for a definite diagnosis. The disease may improve spontaneously.

Wegener's granulomatosis usually progresses rapidly to kidney failure once the scattered blood vessel stage begins. Those with limited forms may only have sores in the nose or lungs with little of their entire systems involved. The sores may improve or get worse for no apparent reason.

Early diagnosis is imperative and treatment stressed because of the possibility of success with chemotherapy using cytotoxic drugs. Limited Wegener's may respond to adrenocorticosteroid therapy.

Once consistently fatal, the prognosis has improved by treating with immunosuppressive cytotoxic drugs. The full-blown disease requires chemotherapy, with cyclophosphamide (one to two mg/kg/day) being the agent of choice, although azathioprine (two mg/kg/day) and chlorambucil (0.1 to 0.15 mg/kg/day) have also been used successfully.

The length of therapy depends on the patient's clinical response. White blood cell counts are monitored closely, and doses of the preferred drug are gradually lowered. The drug must be effective in halting the disease without causing an abnormal decrease in the white blood cells. When no sign of the disease has been found for one year, the therapy is discontinued.

Complete long-term remission can be accomplished with proper treatment, even though the disease may be advanced.

Kidney transplants have been successful in treating cases of functional failure. Corticosteroids are used intermittently for symptoms not involving the kidneys in addition to the cytotoxic drugs.

For use by a city of about one hundred eighty thousand people, the main library in Pasadena is large and well-stocked. I was disappointed that I could not find case histories, statistics, suggestions for coping, and personal accounts. I was also curious about who Dr. Friedrich Wegener was.

I asked the librarian to suggest where answers to these questions might be found.

"Have you tried the CHIPS librarian?" she asked.

"The who?" I asked

"Just a minute and I'll look up what the letters mean. Here it is: Consumer Health Information Program and Services. It's an agency that serves the entire county."

She gave me the name and phone number of the library where this information might be available.

The CHIPS librarian I spoke to was friendly and helpful and promised to research Wegener's. The library system in California at that time offered this service free of charge.

The material I received from the CHIPS librarian was not dated, nor do I have any idea where the librarian found it. Sources cited were from the years 1931, 1936, 1968 and 1976. The prognosis given was frightening, to say the least: ... progressive, with death occurring usually in a month, occasionally in two to three years. The death is caused by uremia and arteritis, with spontaneous remission of two or three months being observed that temporarily interrupt the fatal course of the disease.

I'm so glad I received that information when I did instead of when Carol was first diagnosed in 1978. She was very much alive, after having fought the dragon for eight years, and by now my optimism had taken over again. I was convinced she would stay alive.

I needed to search for further answers.

Don and Carol had gone to college with a lady named Linda who was working as a reference librarian in Riverside. I called her and told her about the CHIPS librarian for our county and the information I'd received.

"We have that here, too," she offered.

"I wonder why I never knew about it before. Lack of publicity or communication, I suppose. What are my chances of getting more information?" I asked her, "and how much trouble would it be?"

"I'm a reference librarian," Linda told me. "It's my job to dig for that sort of thing."

She was able to get me quite a bit of material that included case histories, magazine articles, and information on Dr. Friedrich Wegener.

"If that's not enough, I can keep digging," she said. "You might also want to try the hospital library."

I had no idea that hospitals had libraries that were open to the public.

When I sat down to read the information she sent I discovered I was in need of a medical dictionary. I could only understand every fifth word. That was my next purchase; in fact I purchased two of them because I found information that one had and the other didn't.

Besides information about the disease, I learned something about Dr. Wegener. He was a pathologist and the son of a doctor. Born and educated in Germany, he was the chief physician at a pathological institute. Between 1936 and 1939 he is credited with the discovery and research into the Wegener Granumatologue Pathology of the Kidneys and Blood Vessels. Although Dr. Heinz

Klinger was the first to report the disease in 1931, Dr. Wegener was the first to define it as separate and distinct.

Research papers revealed success with various cytotoxic agents, with a large majority of patients alive and well from months to years beyond treatment. Studies had been done in universities and medical centers all over the globe. After reviewing the research, there seemed to be little doubt of the effectiveness of the drugs, with cyclophosphamide being the drug of choice.

My research proved to me that Carol was being treated properly today, and that was comforting. In the back of my mind a nagging voice kept asking: What about tomorrow? I kept pushing it away with the thought: one day at a time.

I had spent more time at the library than I had intended. There was barely time to eat and dress for a civic meeting I had planned to attend that evening. I still hadn't called Dick. The more I thought about it, I felt the bad news could wait. There was nothing he could do about it anyway. He had really been looking forward to visiting with Ken and it would cloud their time together. I decided to tell him when he returned. At least I could give him an extra two happy days there.

I thought of calling Mom and a few of my friends, but I changed my mind. There was no one I felt like talking to anyway—unless they could work miracles.

Dick was scheduled to arrive Sunday in Palm Springs. For the next two days I was alone in the house most of the time, with every opportunity to cry. But I did my chores like a zombie; the tears would not come.

This disease was relentless. My heart was breaking for her but my eyes were dry.

On Friday I packed my car and began the two hour drive down to the desert. Partway there the dam broke and the tears finally flowed. I screamed and wailed and let it all out with the radio blaring and the traffic racing by all around me.

Where does it all end? When does the poison start to work? I knew it had to work. It was not possible to think she might be one of those for whom it didn't. She's supposed to outlive me, damn it. The stuff is supposed to work.

By the time I told my parents I was in much better shape. In front of them I was hopeful. Perhaps I'd convinced myself.

On Sunday when I picked Dick up he was brimming with news of Kenny. He didn't even notice how quiet and sullen I was at first.

Finally he said, "So what's new here?"

I told him. It was like watching the air go out of a balloon. He was devastated. "What are they going to do?"

I told him about my conversation with Dr. Black.

"How is she taking it?"

"She's depressed and frustrated, and I think angry, too. But she's going on her trip to Oregon. I think that will do her good."

24

Treatment Continues

At the next treatment, the dosage of Cytoxan™ was increased to one thousand five hundred milligrams.

"I'd like to go with you to your next appointment. I haven't had an update in a while."

"OK."

Her appointment was the tenth of March. Dr. Black had just finished Carol's uneventful examination when Dr. Saxon entered the room.

"So, how are we doing?" he asked.

"OK," Carol answered. "Actually, maybe better than OK. In fact this last month has definitely been better."

"It ought to be," Dr. Black said. "The spot is smaller."

"That's great news," I said. "It was certainly worth the trip today."

"How do you know?" Carol asked.

"From your chest X-ray," Dr. Black answered. "Don't you remember I told you when I spoke to you last week?"

I looked at Carol, puzzled. She wouldn't have kept news like that from us.

"You never told me that," she said.

I could tell she was annoyed. That was too good a secret to keep.

Dr. Saxon seemed to sense her annoyance, and stepped into the conversation. "It's nice to know it's working," he said. "I'm pleased."

He didn't have to tell us he was pleased. We could tell from his broad grin and the twinkle in his eyes.

"I'm so relieved," Dr. Black said. "I can tell you now, we were getting pretty worried."

"Wait till your father hears this," I elatedly told Carol.

"What are my chances of getting cancer in the future because of the chemotherapy?" Carol asked.

There was no squirming out of this one.

"There's no question," Dr. Black answered, "that the chances are greater. But we're not talking about large percentages. Of course I can't give you figures because everyone is different. But let's say you had a one percent chance of getting cancer; chemotherapy might make it three percent."

Then he looked at me.

"Has anyone in your family had cancer?" he asked.

"Yes. My grandmother had cancer of the uterus and the esophagus. She was cured of both and died many years later at the age of eighty-six from something else connected with old age. My mother and her two sisters had uterine cancer. All three were cured and are alive and well today, fifteen to twenty years since their surgeries. No one in Carol's father's family died from cancer and most of them lived well into their nineties."

Dr. Saxon picked up the conversation and turned to Carol.

"It sounds like you have pretty good genes. If I had a choice of medicines as opposed to good genes, I would choose the genes every time. You couldn't have better odds."

He turned back to the desk and Carol's file.

"I'm so relieved that it's shrinking," Dr. Black said.

"If things are going well, can I postpone my next treatment for a week?"

"Why?" the doctor asked.

"I want to go skiing. The week that my friends can get away is the week of my treatment."

"Well, under the circumstances," Dr. Black said, "I suppose it will be OK. But only a week—no more."

"I don't like the idea of cold air in your nose. You have nothing inside, no chambers or little hairs to warm it first. It will hit straight back in your throat," Dr. Saxon said. "This might cause trauma to the inside of your nose."

"Can you wear a mitten on your nose?" I teased Carol.

"How about a scarf?" Dr. Saxon asked.

"I'll come up with something," Carol said. "I was thinking about going snorkeling this weekend. Do you have any problems with that?"

"Water is fine," Dr. Saxon said. "That not only won't hurt, it will help. But I'm not crazy about the cold air."

"Don't worry," Carol said. "I'll stuff my nose with cotton or something."

Again, Dr. Black, referring to the X-ray, said, "I'm so relieved that it's shrinking."

Maybe he's not so bad after all, I thought. He does seem to care, and that's important.

About that time, it was suggested that Carol have a bone density test. She had taken Prednisone™ on and off for years, and her doctors wondered if that drug had caused any damage.

Dr. Black's wife was an orthopedic specialist, so Carol was sent to her. The test showed she had the bones of a sixty-five-year-old woman. She was twenty-six.

It was Saturday morning, December 12, 1987. Dick and I had arrived home from La Jolla[42] the night before, from another of Dick's business trips. Don was at our place with his friend Gilbert, Linda's brother, doing some work on our computer.

"I'm going over to Carol's in a little while. She wants me to bring some medicine from the pharmacy. I guess she doesn't feel well," Don told us.

"Why don't you call and see if she needs us?" Dick asked.

I already had the receiver in my hand and was dialing. She answered quickly.

"Hi, sweetheart. Daddy and I are back. I hear you're not feeling well."

"No," she answered.

"Have you had anything to eat?"

"Not much. I've been taking codeine and my stomach's a little queasy."

"You're in pain?" I questioned, all the while thinking that was a dumb thing to ask. Taking codeine isn't like eating bon-bons.

"Yeah."

"Do you want me to bring you something or make you something to eat?"

"No, I don't want anything."

"Have you called the doctor?"

"I spoke to Dr. Adelman and he called in some more codeine for me. He said he'd be around this weekend if I got worse."

"Who's Dr. Adelman?"

"A new doctor working with Dr. Saxon. He's OK. You'll like him."

"Don's on his way. If you need anything, let us know. OK?"

"OK."

I hoped he'd be able to help her even if it was only psychologically.

Dick and I went about the rest of our business that evening with an uneasy feeling.

"I wish she'd let us come over and feed her—or something."

"You know your daughter. She likes to handle things her own way. If she needs us, she knows where to find us."

The next day, Sunday morning, she called me. Dick had taken off early for Florida—another business trip. By this time he was meeting himself coming and going, and it seemed like he was gone more than he was home.

"I called Dr. Adelman and he said to go down to the emergency room."

"You want me to take you?"

"Yeah, please."

"I'll be on my way in a few minutes."

Although we'd been in ERs before, this was to be our first time at UCLA.

The ER clerk said, as Carol signed the register, "I need to get some information from you," and proceeded with the usual questions. She paused long enough to hand me a sticker for my car so I wouldn't be ticketed in the ER parking lot.

"I'm on chemotherapy once a month and I'm being treated for Wegener's granulomatosis," Carol told the clerk.

We both watched as the clerk's head arose from her typewriter with the same blank stare we'd seen so often in the past.

Carol gave me a knowing smile and nod and I could see that here-we-go-again look in her eyes. She turned back to the clerk.

"That's a new one for you, isn't it? Would you like me to spell it for you?"

"Yes, please," the clerk responded. Then, after writing the name down as Carol spelled it, asked, "What is it? What does it do to you, and why are you here now?"

Carol offered a brief explanation and added, "I have a bad sinus infection now and I've had some pains in my back."

"Which sinuses? Do you know?" the clerk asked.

"Here," Carol said and pointed to her forehead above her right eye, "Frontal."

"Are you on any medication right now?" the woman asked.

Carol offered the names of her current prescriptions.

"If you'll have a seat ..."

"Dr. Daniel Adelman from immunology wanted to be paged when I arrived," Carol told her.

"Dr. Who?" the clerk inquired.

"Dr. Adelman," Carol answered, and then began spelling again, "A-d-e-l-m-a-n. He's from immunology. I spoke to him just before I came. Do you want his pager number?"

"That won't be necessary. I have it. Just have a seat."

"Is there a place where I could lie down?"

"No, but if you'll just have a seat, it won't be too long."

As we walked through the doors to the waiting area, I couldn't help chuckling as I remembered a comedy routine from a recording the boys had. It depicted an emergency room. The patient was given a number, like in a butcher shop. As the comedian read the number out loud, number ninety-seven, the loud speaker boomed out, "Number three, now serving number three." I reminded Carol of it and got a chuckle from her, too.

"We have to laugh," I said. "It keeps us from crying."

The waiting room had half a dozen people in straight-backed, plastic uphol-stered chairs. No one was bleeding or gasping for breath. For all we knew, per-haps none of them were patients—just friends or relatives. We waited about ten minutes and Carol needed a drink. Pain medicines are notorious for drying out your mouth.

I searched the nearby halls and found a drinking fountain, devoid of cups.

Returning to the receptionist to request cups, I found her with another patient who was telling her sad tale of woe and getting no sympathy whatsoever. After the clerk repeated procedures and instructions—no less than four times with the patient arguing all the while—I began to feel sorrier for the clerk than the patient. Finally, the patient turned to me and started recounting her problems.

"I don't work here," I said. "I'm with a patient myself."

She apologized and stepped aside.

I asked the clerk for a cup and she murmured something like there should have been some there. She whipped around a corner and returned in moments, handing me a stack. I put the rest where others would have access to them, and returned to Carol with a full cup of water.

Soon thereafter she was summoned and we entered a small examining room. A nurse appeared and took additional information.

"Dr. Adelman wanted to be paged when I got here," Carol told her.

"OK," she said. "I'll get on it."

During the next two hours the nurse returned twice to inform us that the doc-tor had not answered the page.

"I don't think they know what to do with you," I said.

It was chilly and I asked for a blanket for her. The examining table was far from comfortable but it was better than sitting up in the waiting room.

Finally the nurse returned and said Dr. Adelman had answered and given instructions to another doctor who would be in shortly.

"They didn't get around to telling me," she said, and apologized.

I wondered once again, doesn't anyone at UCLA talk to anyone else?

A young doctor from immunology appeared, introduced himself, and began with his questions.

Carol filled him in on the happenings of the past week along with a brief run-down on her present medications and treatments. He suggested a strong antibi-otic and pain pills, said he needed a prescription pad, and left.

Before he returned, in popped Dr. Saxon. It was as if the sun had just come out. We were both so happy to see him.

"Drs. Adelman and Macy were at my house this morning for brunch when your call came. I figured I'd come down here and see what was going on with you myself."

"I thought maybe you were doing ER this week," Carol teased.

"They don't even know who I am down here," he said. "So what's going on?"

"I've got this really bad headache."

"Where?" he asked.

"Here," she pointed to her forehead, "and I've had some pains in my back and chest. But that doesn't hurt today, only my head."

"Let's get some sinus X-rays and see if there's anything new," he said, and left the room to arrange for them.

"Who's Dr. Macy?" I asked, hoping Dr. Adelman wasn't leaving us already. I'd hardly gotten used to him and liked him much better than Dr. Black. I felt he was much more professional in his speech and manner.

"He's working with Dr. Saxon, too," she said.

The nurse appeared to take Carol to have the X-rays done.

"Do you need your jacket or blanket?" I asked, assuming she'd have a long way to go in the huge medical center.

"We're just going down the hall," the nurse said.

"Not to X-ray?" Carol asked.

"We have our own here in ER," the nurse said.

"Oh, that's great," I said. "I thought she'd have to go much further."

Carol was back in a few minutes and climbed back up on the examining table. Dr. Saxon reappeared.

"There's not much new on the X-rays. The region of your frontal sinus is opaque."

"What does that mean?" I asked.

"That something's in there," Carol said.

"We already knew that," Dr. Saxon agreed. "I wanted to see if anything was different from the last set, and there's nothing new. Where does it hurt, Carol?"

"Here," she said, touching her forehead on the right side again.

"Right here?" he asked as he lightly pressed the spot she had indicated with his thumb.

"Ooooh, that's it," she moaned.

"The problem is," he explained, "you obviously have a pocket of infection in that sinus cavity."

"Tell me something I don't know," she said, feigning sarcasm.

He glanced at me with mock exasperation.

"She's the one patient who gives me gray hair," he muttered, smiling. "The normal drainage that most people have in their heads—that I have, that your mother has—you don't have anymore. It's either non-existent because so much has been eaten away, so to speak, by the disease, or perhaps blocked. In other words, it's all screwed up."

He glanced at me and smiled. "That's a medical term, you know."

I nodded. "I thought so," and smiled back.

"Anyway, Carol, when you get an infection it has no place to go so it just sits there and festers. We've got to get rid of it. I can do one of two things. I can admit you to the hospital …"

"Noooo," she moaned.

Before I had a chance to interject my opinion, he jumped back into the conversation.

"I said I *could* admit you. I didn't say I was going to. I could admit you and have them pump antibiotics into you, or I could give you something strong, maybe Augmentin™, which is amoxicillin plus a buffer to make it a broader-spectrum antibiotic …"

"And something for the pain?" Carol asked.

"And something for the pain," he agreed.

"You're not an emergency," he said, glancing at me again.

I was reassured. I trusted this man.

"If this were an emergency, I wouldn't be giving you a choice."

"What about work?" Carol questioned. "I've used up all my sick leave and all my vacation days for this year."

"You can go to work," he said.

There's no use saying anything, I thought. She's no longer just your little girl, Myrna. Whatever it is, she's going to do it her way. You raise a child to become self sufficient and conscientious, and look what they do. They begin to take care of themselves.

"If she goes to work or stays in bed," he said to me as if he was reading my mind and sensing my frustration, "it won't make a bit of difference. If I can keep her on her feet and she takes her antibiotics …"

Then he turned back to Carol. "How does this sound? I'll give you a couple of days to see if the Augmentin™ will do the job. If we can't get a grip on this, then we'll have to admit you."

"What about the pain?" she asked.

"What are you taking now?"

"Tylenol with codeine, but it's not working."

"How many?"

"Three or four number threes at a time."

"OK, I'll give you Percocet™. Have you ever had it before?"

"Yeah, a few years ago."

"Which doctor did you see a while ago?" referring to who she had seen here in the ER.

"We can't pronounce his name. He's young and from immunology."

"OK, I'll go tell him. I'm not allowed to write prescriptions down here. Bureaucracy, you know." Then turning to me he said, "We'll get her fixed up, Mom."

"Do you have any children?" I asked.

"Two little girls."

He understood.

"Call me, and let me know how you're doing. OK?"

"OK," she said.

We both thanked him. His presence was so reassuring.

While we were waiting for the prescription, I asked her, "How do you feel now?" forgetting for the moment that nothing had changed. The fact of the matter was that I felt better, probably because something was being done. We were no longer sitting on our hands.

"I think I'm getting hungry," Carol said.

"A mother's favorite words. We'll get you something as soon as we leave here."

"I feel like turkey," she said. "I've been feeling like turkey ever since Thanksgiving."

"You had your turkey on Thanksgiving," I reminded her. "You took it with you."

She had taken off that afternoon for a few days of skiing. Our turkey had been ready early enough for Dick to have carved some slices and for me to make sandwiches for her to take.

"Yeah, but I never got any leftovers."

"So you didn't. Turkey it shall be."

We had been in the ER for three and a half hours. She had not had anything to eat or drink since I'd been with her, except for a couple of swallows of water. I was glad she was hungry. So was I.

The young doctor reappeared and explained what Dr. Saxon had already told us. We listened politely; neither of us interrupted him. It was his job. He handed Carol the prescriptions which she in turn handed to me, and we were on our way.

We stopped on the way home and had our sandwiches, arriving in time to meet Don and Gilbert again. Carol and I had half-sandwiches left, which they polished off. Carol climbed into my bed, which I hadn't even bothered to make that morning, and I had her prescriptions filled.

"I'm sorry the Augmentin™ is kind of expensive," the pharmacist apologized as I took out my checkbook.

"What do you call expensive?" I asked him.

Thirty pills had been prescribed; the price was $46.

"We've had some that were over $2 a pill," I said. "I don't think these are expensive at all. If they do the job, we'll be happy."

When I returned, I tried Dick's hotel. He had just arrived and was unpacking.

"I wish she would stay in bed for a few days at our place," he said.

"So do I," I answered, "but Dr. Saxon doesn't seem to think it would make a bit of difference. You and I can't get over the feeling that plenty of bed rest and chicken soup …"

"I know," he said. "Well, keep me posted and give her a hug and kiss for me."

"I won't call you unless there's some drastic change, which no one is expecting."

We said our goodbyes, and I delivered the hug and kiss from Daddy.

Later that evening I drove her home, offering to stay.

"I'm just going to sleep," she said, and thanked me for taking care of and being with her that day. I just told her she was welcome and silently thanked whatever fate or gods had made me available.

Monday and Tuesday I phoned her at work, pleased when she answered. Good, I thought, as I heard her voice on the other end. She's on her feet and holding the dragon at bay.

"How do you feel?"

"Not great but getting better."

Wednesday I left her alone, keeping the thought that no news was good news. What a dreamer I had become.

Thursday, the day before the next chemo treatment, I thought I'd better check to see if arrangements had been made. Dr. Adelman returned my call quickly and explained that there was no standing order. Arrangements had to be made for each treatment, and Carol was to remind him.

A short time later, a lady called from DMPG and told me, apologetically, "I wanted to let you know they're expecting Carol in the Bowyer Clinic tomorrow morning at 9:00. I'm sorry it's such short notice."

Trying to put her mind at ease, I said, "There's no need to apologize. I'm tickled Carol's on your schedule because chemo is on ours."

There was a sigh of relief on the other end and she said, "That's good. Some people aren't as organized as you, and they get really mad when we don't give them a lot of notice."

If someone is getting chemo on a regular basis, how can they not know when their next treatment will be?

Friday morning, Carol didn't seem to be dawdling as much, or was it my imagination? She was almost packed and ready. We drove around Westwood after battling the usual early-morning freeway traffic, looking for an open restaurant that was serving breakfast. We found only fast food places and chose one. With some time to rest and catch my breath, I observed she wasn't in any particular hurry to get to the clinic again. Oh well, I thought. There is no use pushing her. She knew enough about it by now to have built up apprehensions. And, by God, she'd certainly earned them. If she wanted to put it off ten more minutes, let her have that time. They couldn't start without her and usually kept us waiting long enough. When she'd stalled as long as she felt she could get away with it, she readied herself and we left for the hospital.

"I thought this would get easier," she said. I'd heard that the last five or six times. "But it hasn't."

"It's not going to last forever," I answered. "There'll be an end."

"Will there?" she questioned as she gave me a heartbreaking look, and I felt the familiar lump forming in my throat.

"Yes, there will. Remember what one of the nurses that attended you during hydration had said that day?"

I reminded her. "Everything has a beginning, a middle, and an end," one nurse had told her. "Before your treatment started, that was the beginning. What you're going through now is the middle. When you're finished, it will be the end. This does not go on forever.

"Onward and upward," I told her. "We're more than halfway through. We can't slow down now."

When Carol checked in at the clinic and had her blood test, Sharon, the head nurse with whom we'd had no prior contact, came looking for her.

"Dr. Adelman asked us to page him when you arrived. He wants to see you before you begin your treatment. If you'll follow me, you can wait in an examining room."

We both got up and proceeded down the hall and around the corner.

"Have you had your blood test done?" she asked.

"Yes."

"Good," she said. "I'll let the doctor know you're here."

A short while later, Dr. Adelman came through the door and approached the table.

"So, what's new today?" he asked.

"I feel lousy," she answered. "My chest and back hurt again."

He pulled his stethoscope from his pocket and placed it here and there, listening at places Carol pointed out, and places that she didn't. Then he tapped his finger against the hand he had placed on her chest as he listened for sounds again. Once more he put his stethoscope to her chest, turning it back and forth from the rubber side to the metal side. From her childhood asthma days, I surmised he was hearing something.

"There are some squeaks and rattles in there," he said, then asked, "Did you have a chest X-ray last Sunday?"

"No. Just sinus X-rays."

"I want a chest X-ray now. Then I'll be back."

He left and Sharon reappeared. I began gathering up our jackets and books.

"You can leave everything here if you like," Sharon said.

"I thought you might want to use the room," I said. "It's such a long way off and they may keep her a while."

"She's only going down the hall."

"You have X-rays here, too?"

"Oh, yes. We have our own."

I settled back down to wait as Carol followed Sharon out the door and returned in a short while. She climbed back on the examining table and we waited for the doctor again.

He appeared with a large envelope in his hands.

"We have some spots ..."

"Can I see?" Carol asked.

He pulled the X-rays out of the envelope and started to hold them up to the light.

"Come on down the hall," he said, as he replaced them in the envelope.

We followed him into a small room with light boxes on the wall. He pulled two X-rays out of the envelope, affixed them to the light boxes and turned the light on. We were looking at one side view and one front view of Carol's left lung. The doctor pointed out three spots, one near the breast and two at the bottom. They were about the size of a teacup, elliptical in shape, with ragged edges and a border somewhat lighter than the center.

The familiar kicked-in-the-stomach feeling returned. Dr. Black had told us the spot was getting smaller. I was under the impression there was only one spot. But now I was seeing three, all much larger than a half dollar. I couldn't begin to imagine what Carol might be feeling. I didn't want to look at her and give my feelings away.

"We have no way of knowing whether this is infection, a spread of Wegener's, or cavitation.[43] In any event, I want you in the hospital and, by the way, Dr. Saxon concurs, until we can determine what it is and what to do about it."

"The Cytoxan™ didn't do a damn thing," Carol murmured softly.

She didn't have to say the rest. I could hear her thinking, "I've been through hell and for what!"

"I'll make arrangements to have you admitted," Dr. Adelman said.

We all returned to the examining room.

"What about chemo?" Carol asked.

"We're not going to do it now. Maybe tonight, maybe tomorrow. We'll see. We need to get you hooked up to an antibiotic. I'll be in to see you this afternoon."

There was more waiting. It was 11:30.

After Dr. Adelman left, Carol resumed her resting position on the table.

"Are you hungry?" I asked.

"No."

Neither was I.

Shortly thereafter, two men knocked and I bid them enter. The spokesman of the pair introduced both of them, his colleague as an intern, himself as a resident. He had several three by five cards in his hand.

"May we ask you some questions?"

It turned out to be the editorial we because the intern never opened his mouth.

"It's guinea pig time," I joked to Carol; then to the doctors, not wanting them to think me sarcastic and uncooperative, I explained, "I'm just teasing. We understand this is a teaching hospital and that Carol is an unusual case. If she's not feeling up to answering, I'll try to help."

"That's OK, Mom," and then to the doctors she said, "Fire away."

The resident, who we came to know as Scott Denardo, asked the "when did it start, what were your symptoms, and what happened next" questions, and Carol answered. By the time they were finished, it was one o'clock.

"I'm getting hungry," Carol said.

Just then a woman in a white uniform stuck her head in the door. I told her what we were doing there.

"We've been here an hour and a half since being told she was to be admitted. Can you find out what's going on?" I asked her.

"The procedure is to hold you here until they have a room. I guess there's no room available," she answered.

"In the whole medical center?" I asked. "Maybe we should find another hospital."

"I'll see what I can find out," she offered.

"My God," I said turning to Carol when the woman had gone, "did that come out of my mouth? I'm beginning to sound like your father. I'm usually not as impatient as he."

"I don't think patience has anything to do with it," she said. "We've spent half the day here."

"According to Murphy's Law," I said, "if I get you something to eat, you'll be gone when I get back and I'll wander around the medical center for days searching for my lost lamb."

"Probably." she answered. "I have some snack bars with me. Would you like one?"

"Never mind," I said. She liked to carry various kinds of health food bars. They all tasted like sawdust with glue to me.

The nurse poked her head back in.

"I just checked with Richard. He makes the arrangements. They have a room for you and he's called for an escort."

"I'm really surprised that she had bothered to check," I said. "I guess I'm getting cynical in my old age."

"We're at the Bowyer Clinic, Mom. Remember, you said they were more efficient here."

Another half hour had passed. I decided to ask if we could walk over to the medical center. Carol was able and we both were ready. I walked down toward the infusion room, figuring the head nurse would be the one to ask. Susan was talking to Dr. Denardo and his cohort.

I asked Susan, "Where's Sharon's office? I was wondering if we could just go on over to the medical center instead of waiting for the escort. It's after two and Carol hasn't had anything to eat for quite a while."

"I was just getting ready to take you myself," she said.

---

42.   La Jolla is a small seaside town north of San Diego.

43.   Cavitation refers to the formation of cavities within the body such as those formed in the lungs.

25

Educating the Staff

As she started toward a wheelchair, the escort appeared and we were finally on our way. Carol was taken to the oncology section probably because they would be better equipped to handle her treatment when it was scheduled. I immediately asked about lunch and explained where we'd been to the nurse.

Carol and I chatted a few minutes about the view, whether she should get undressed, whether I should bring up the clothes she was planning on taking to my house for the weekend, and other small talk.

Her vital signs were taken and charted.

"I'd like a drink."

The nurse brought Carol an empty pitcher and no cup.

"Are you on any special diet?" she asked.

Carol answered, "No," and offered a brief explanation of why she was being admitted.

The nurse said, "I'll order a tray right now."

"I'll get some water and a cup," I offered, and set off down the hall. Upon seeing the nurse who had been with us, I asked her for a cup and where I could find ice. She gave me a cup, directed me to the ice machine, and then said, almost absent-mindedly, "I'd better call for a tray," as if it was a new idea.

When I returned with the water and ice, Drs. Saxon, Adelman, and Macy were with Carol; Dr. Saxon began filling me in.

"We're going to start an antibiotic and probably do her treatment this evening. I'd like to call in Dr. Bevra Hahn. I think she saw Carol before. She's a rheumatologist. Then we'll decide what to do," Dr. Saxon told me. "Dr. Hahn indicated that she wasn't sure how you felt about her," he said to Carol. "Did you two get along?" he asked as he glanced in my direction.

"I never heard any negative comments about her," I said.

Carol shrugged and said, "No problem."

"We may want to get Dr. Thompson involved, too. He might want to stick a needle in your head," he pointed to his own forehead, "and drain this thing."

When Dr. Thompson's name was mentioned, Carol looked at me and I shrugged. If Dr. Saxon felt that Dr. Thompson was competent, I certainly wasn't going to fight with anyone about using him. I remembered that one of the nurses in chemo had recently told me that he was an outstanding surgeon.

"When any of the show business celebrities have problems from the neck up, he's the one they call," she had said.

"We'll get you started on the antibiotic and go from there," Dr. Adelman said.

A nurse came in, started an IV, and Carol was given her antibiotic.

Drs. Saxon and Macy left, but Dr. Adelman stayed.

"I don't have your file with me," he said. "Fill me in on what you've taken and when you've had surgery."

Carol gave him years and corresponding medicines. I filled in a place or two when she was uncertain.

"He should read the book," she muttered, referring to the manuscript I'd written about her.

Although Dr. Saxon had read it, I had asked him not to share it with anyone. A decision had not yet been made about using real names.

"Don't forget to include pain meds," Carol reminded him. "Also, after chemo I'd like to have control over what anti-nausea pills I take and when. That way, if they make me too wired, I can cut back."

"OK," he said, and read aloud what he was going to put on the orders, adding the words, "at patient's discretion."

"And can I have something to help me relax?"

Ativan was added to the list. As Dr. Adelman left to give the orders to the doctor on call, the lunch trays arrived.

As we each ate from our trays, Carol said, "I know why Dr. Hahn might have thought I didn't like her. When we met, it was right after I found out I had a spot in my lung. The doctors knew about it for months and never told me. I was feeling rotten, betrayed, and in a pretty bad mood. She may have taken my disgust as a personal affront. But it's been a while; I'm surprised she even remembered me."

Another nurse came in and said, "You'll be having your chemo later today. An IV team will be down to start your saline, and I've ordered a cold cap."

We both thanked her and she left.

"It's four o'clock. I'll be leaving soon to get Daddy from the airport." He was returning from another business trip. "I think I'll bring your overnight bag up in case you want anything from it."

When I returned from the parking lot, Dr. Hahn was sitting on Carol's bed and they were talking. Carol introduced us and I shook hands with a lady of medium height with short brown hair, conservatively dressed in a pleated wool skirt and tailored blouse, wearing loafers. She was friendly, personable, and asked Carol numerous questions about her present symptoms while taking notes.

"Dr. Saxon and I are thinking of changing Carol's treatment. We're thinking that Cytoxan™ may have run its course, and we're considering changing to Leukeran™.[44] There's evidence that it's been effective with Wegener's."

I noticed she used the European pronunciation with the W sounding like a V.

At that point, Dr. Saxon, along with his shadows, returned.

"I think my mom has research papers that discuss the use of Leukeran™ for the treatment of Wegener's, don't you, Mom?" she asked turning toward me.

"You do?" Dr. Hahn asked as all heads swung in my direction.

"Yes, I do."

I wasn't going to offer it. First, I thought it would be presumptuous, and second, I assumed the doctors would have access to more and better information than I had.

"Do you think you could lay your hands on it in the next few days?" Dr. Hahn asked.

"Oh, yes," I answered. "I know exactly where it is."

"Mom has quite a large collection of research papers, maybe the largest private collection," Carol said, proudly.

"I hardly think it's the largest, but certainly I have quite a few and if you'd like, Doctor, I'd be happy to bring them all in."

Dr. Hahn's face became quite animated.

"Would you really? Oh, I'd appreciate that if it's not too much trouble."

"You're trying to make my daughter well, and you're asking if it's too much trouble for me to bring you information that might help. It's not only no trouble, it's my extreme pleasure. It never occurred to me that any of those papers might help Carol. I must tell you, Doctor, that particular paper about Leukeran™ was written over twenty years ago. Would it still be pertinent?"

"Mrs. Swart," she said, "the disease has not changed, nor the results from the treatment. I think it would be very pertinent. I won't be here tomorrow," which was Saturday, "but I plan on being here the day after."

"I think I'll give Tony a call," Dr. Saxon said, referring to Dr. Fauci, "and see what he thinks."

"I have someone at the Mayo Clinic I'd like to check with," Dr. Hahn added.

"Will you be talking to Dr. McDonald?" I asked her.

"No." She mentioned a name but it was unfamiliar to me. "Would you like me to call Dr. McDonald?"

"I only mentioned his name because he had seen Carol in 1983 and I have several papers that he has co-authored. Wegener's seems to be one of his special interests. I'm certain that your contact would have access to the same information."

"I won't be here tomorrow," she reminded me, "but I will on Sunday."

"The papers will be here, too," I said.

"Thank you," she said. "That's very nice of you. I'd appreciate that."

"My pleasure, Doctor," I said.

She had no idea how much pleasure I derived. I would finally be able to do something myself that would help my little girl.

After all the doctors left, I went to LAX to get Dick.

"So what's new here?"

"As of a couple of hours ago, your daughter is an inpatient at UCLA. They're thinking that the Cytoxan™ may have run its course."

"What are they going to do?"

"They're talking about changing her treatment, possibly to Leukeran™. Dr. Saxon is going to call Dr. Fauci, and Dr. Hahn has someone at the Mayo Clinic she wants to talk to."

"Who's Dr. Hahn?"

"A rheumatologist Dr. Saxon called in for a consultation. Carol saw Dr. Hahn before, but doesn't remember that much about her."

"How is Carol taking it?"

"She's depressed and frustrated, and I think angry, too. She feels like she's gone through months and months of hell for nothing."

We went directly to the hospital. Carol was happy to see Dick and, as usual, he had a little gift for her.

That evening, the intern came to tell us that the chemo would be started shortly. We left at 10:00. No treatment had been started.

Saturday morning when Dick and I arrived, the chemo had still not been administered.

"They're going to do it this morning," Carol told us.

A nurse and Dr. Denardo arrived with a tray. On it was a syringe, vials of liquid, probably the Cytoxan™, and tubing.

"We're going to start a new IV," Dr. Denardo said.

"I don't want another IV. Why can't you use this one?" Carol asked pointing to the one already attached to her arm.

"We always use a separate one," the doctor said.

"They don't use a separate one at the Bowyer Clinic," I told him.

I could tell by the looks on their faces that they didn't much care what was used at the Bowyer Clinic.

"Where's the cold cap?" Carol asked.

"We don't use them here," the nurse was adamant. "They don't do any good."

"I think it does a lot of good!" Carol was just as adamant. "I've had seventeen treatments so far and haven't lost my hair. I'd like not to take that chance."

"Well, we don't feel it's necessary. We don't even have them here," the nurse said.

It looked like a line had been drawn with them on one side and us on the other.

"One of the nurses told us last night that one had been ordered for Carol," I said. "*She* must have thought it was necessary."

"Hasn't one been ordered for me?" Carol asked.

"I'll check," she said.

"Please also check about using the same IV," Carol asked.

"I'll do that," Dr. Denardo said.

In a few minutes the nurse returned with a small cardboard carton.

"We have no cold caps in this section," she told us. "I'll have to make you one."

She tore open the carton and proceeded to tape several small cold packs together. "This should do the job."

Carol looked at me, smiled, and shrugged. I nodded. Several cold packs are as good as a cold cap. As long as we had something that would work, we were happy. The nurse attempted to place the makeshift cap on Carol's head.

"Wait a minute," Carol exclaimed. I have to have something for my ears. The cold cap freezes my ears. They use little foam caps …"

"At the Bowyer Clinic," the nurse said with an exasperated sigh. "Of course they do."

I began to wonder if Carol was going to have her treatment at all.

The nurse got some paper towels from the bathroom and folded them a few times. Then she placed them on Carol's ears and pulled the makeshift cold cap over them. She didn't even ask if that was all right. I think she figured by now that someone would tell her if it wasn't. She was now following orders instead of giving them, and it was apparent to me that she was not happy with the patient being in control. But Carol got what she needed and that was the most important thing.

"Could I have another blanket or two, please?" Carol asked. "I get chilled when this is on."

The nurse didn't even answer; she just left the room and returned shortly with two warm blankets. Apparently hospitals have places where they warm the blankets—a great idea.

Dick was watching us with an amused expression. When we were alone he said, "You two are real trouble-makers."

"We had a good teacher."

"I'm not about to lose my hair because it's too much trouble for her," Carol remarked.

"I can't believe they don't have cold caps in oncology," I said.

Dr. Denardo returned.

"You're right," he admitted. "We can use the same IV."

Carol heaved a big sigh of relief. No second IV. Hooray!

The doctor filled the syringe with medicine from the vials.

"The cold cap is supposed to be on for twenty minutes before you start the chemo," Carol told him.

"OK. I'll see you in twenty minutes," the doctor said and left.

When Dr. Denardo returned, he attempted to inject it directly into the IV tubing.

"Aren't you going to mix it with anything?" I asked.

"Like what?" he asked.

"In the Bowyer Clinic they use a cylinder with a little window and put the syringe in that instead of directly into the tubing. The saline mixes with the Cytoxan™ as it's being administered."

"Oh."

The nurse had returned. "They use a piggy back. We don't do that here."

I was about to make a fuss again but the doctor said, "I'll do it very slowly and I'll be right here with you. If you have any discomfort, I'll stop."

"OK," Carol concurred.

As long as it was all right with her, I decided to keep my mouth shut. Dick chose to wait outside. I wasn't about to leave. I had to make sure this young man knew what he was doing. He sat with Carol, injected the Cytoxan™ into the IV tube extremely slowly as he constantly asked her how she was feeling. Before long they were chatting about each other's careers. Carol seemed to be comfortable with the infusion, so I stayed in the background and kept quiet.

On Sunday morning when I arrived with my research papers, Dr. Hahn was already there. I gave her the paper about Leukeran™ and offered the rest of the loose leaf notebooks. I had three of them full of papers I had collected. Her face lit up as she thanked me.

"This is wonderful," she exclaimed, muttering her pleasure at my collection several times during the next hour or so as she skimmed through all the printed matter. "I wish every patient would take this kind of interest in their illness."

"I would have thought some doctors might feel it was an affront to their knowledge and performance," I offered. "Would you like to keep the notebooks for a while? I can get them back from you at some later date."

"That won't be necessary," she answered. "If there's anything I need to have, I can order a copy."

Drs. Saxon, Adelman and Macy had now joined us. Carol and I related the events concerning the Cytoxan™ infusion, the run-ins with the staff and the surrounding problems.

"The trouble is," Dr. Saxon said, "you often know more about what needs to be done for you then those attending you. When they realize that, they become intimidated and try to compensate.

"I spoke to Tony and he concurs with our decision to switch you to Leukeran™," he said to us. "Did you reach your contact at Mayo?" he asked Dr. Hahn.

She indicated that she had and that doctor also concurred.

"We'll start you on that in about three weeks," Dr. Saxon told Carol.

Although Carol didn't comment to the doctors, she seemed unhappy about the switch.

"Cytoxan™ is the drug of choice," she said, when all the doctors had gone. "If the best one doesn't work, what makes them think that another will?"

"The research papers were written about successes, not failures."

"Always up, aren't you, Mom," she said sarcastically.

"What choice do I have? You may be the one to prove that Leukeran™ works just as well as Cytoxan™."

"Did you check the side effects?" she asked.

"I forgot. I'll do that when I get home."

It was one of the few times I'd lied to her. I had checked and discovered that Leukeran™ had most of the same side effects as Cytoxan™. I couldn't see any reason to put ideas in her mind about things that might not happen. The power of suggestion is a great one. However, the information did not mention any problems with the bladder. That's probably why they chose that particular drug.

On Monday she was released and I took her home to my place. That was what she wanted.

When she was settled in, I decided it was time to give her the other part of her two-part gift, the emerald earrings that matched the pendant. I had planned on giving them to her when she had completed her second year of IV chemo. Since that would no longer be happening, it seemed like now was a good time. It was not only appropriate, but I hoped it would help her depression.

"Do you realize how symbolic these are, Mom?"

"What do you mean?"

"Well, there are six stones in each earring and six in the pendant. Adding them up, that represents the eighteen treatments I had."

I should have known a math major would equate the numbers.

When I first got my hands on the research paper about Leukeran™, I had looked it up in my paperback drug book. The side effects appeared to be much worse than Cytoxan™: hair loss; nausea, vomiting, and stomach upset; diarrhea; loss of appetite; infection and reduction in the body's resistance to infection; decreased blood platelets; and decreased white blood cell count from decreased neutrophils[45] and lymphocytes[46] in the blood. As with Cytoxan™, that was just the beginning. The list was also staggering. The one side effect it didn't have, however, was hemorrhagic cystitis.

While taking Leukeran™, it was imperative that Carol's blood be checked often to make sure she wasn't having any of the known problems.

The plan was to start the Leukeran™ in three weeks and continue for a year after Carol was symptom free, whatever time that entailed.

Although at this time the battle had been going on for nine years, I can't ever remember seeing Carol so depressed. I had called Dr. Haring to update him. Toward the end of the week I suggested to Carol that we try to see him. I thought he might perk her up.

I phoned Dr. Adelman to let him know we were going out to see Dr. Haring.

"If he wants any information from me, just have him call," he said.

Then I remembered that Dr. Saxon had told me he would be happy to update Dr. Haring, also.

"It makes me feel good when the doctors are so willing to cooperate with each other," I told Carol.

"What antibiotic did they give you?" Dr. Haring asked.

Carol looked at me. "I don't know, do you, Mom?"

"I think one of them was Augmentin™; I'm not sure what else."

"Dr. Adelman said he'd be in this afternoon if you want to talk to him about anything," I said as I gave him Dr. Adelman's phone number.

He left the room and returned in a short time.

"You're right. He seems like a very nice person, friendly and knowledgeable."

Carol and I nodded to each other.

"I suggested Keflex™ instead of what you're taking. We've had success with that. Dr. Adelman said he had no objection."

He wrote a prescription.

"How are you doing for pain pills?"

"Dr. Saxon gave me Percocet™."

"By the way," Dr. Haring added, "I checked with some of my oncologist friends and they tell me that Leukeran™ is probably the least toxic of the chemo drugs and has the fewest side effects."

Within twenty-four hours it was apparent that Carol was feeling better. Dr. Haring had done it again.

I was still apprehensive because of what I'd read about the Leukeran™, but continued to keep it to myself for the time being.

Carol stayed with us for most of the week. She called work every day, but made no attempt to go in. That worried me. It was so unlike her. I had to wrestle with my ambivalent feelings about that—happy that she was resting and I could take care of her—unhappy that she didn't seem anxious to get back to living.

However, when the week was up, she returned to her home and to work.

She began taking the Leukeran™ on January 9, 1988.

In March we had a repeat performance of the December infection.

Although Carol had gone to work regularly, the pain was only slightly less than it had been in December. The infection was back in full force. Actually it never went away. The only alternative was to hospitalize her again and administer an IV antibiotic.

The resident and intern assigned to her at this time arrived soon after she did, introduced themselves, and began a comedy routine that put everyone at ease and in a better mood.

It began with, "Hello, I'm Dr. Smith,* your resident, and this is Dr. Jones,* your intern. We're here to entertain you."

Carol picked right up on their routine and joined in.

With pencil poised, Dr. Smith asked, "What brings you here?"

"Mom, in the car," Carol chuckled.

Then she became serious and gave the young men her history and answered their questions.

"We'd like to examine you now. Has the Wegener's affected your hearing?"

"Huh?"

"I said, has the …"

The twinkle in Carol's eyes told them she was pulling their respective legs.

As one began to thump on her back, the other began playing a make-believe guitar and singing, "You Ain't Nothin' But a Hound Dog."

"Oh, excuse me," Dr. Smith said. "Now where were we? What do you do, Carol?"

"As little as possible," she chuckled again.

"That's not true," I chided.

She filled them in with information about her job.

"What does your father do?"

"He's a lawyer."

"We don't have to stand here and take this," Dr. Smith said.

"No, we can sit down," Dr. Jones retorted.

"I'm not interested in treating this patient. I know my rights," Dr. Smith said.

When the "performance" was complete, one young man turned the other and said, "Gee, that was fun, wasn't it? Let's find someone else and do that again."

To me Dr. Smith said, "Her doctor will be along shortly."

They left us laughing. I named them Drs. Frick and Frack and called them that during the rest of her stay.

Drs. Saxon, Adelman, and Macy paid Carol regular visits and hoped the antibiotic would do the trick, but only time would tell.

"Her frontal sinuses," Dr. Saxon explained, "have become calcified. The infection is just sitting there and can't get out."

"That's my feeling, too," I said. "What are our alternatives?"

"We might be able to stick a needle into the sinuses and drain them."

"Why isn't the Leukeran™ working?" Carol finally asked the loaded question.

"I don't know, Carol. Maybe there hasn't been enough time. I'm not ready to throw in the towel yet. How are you handling the side effects?"

"I'm handling them."

"I'm curious, Doctor. Why were we told there was one spot on Carol's lung instead of three?" I asked.

"Who told you that?"

"Dr. Black."

"I don't know. Perhaps it was a misunderstanding. There was never just one spot; there were always three. Let's give the Leukeran™ more time and I'll see you in a month," he told Carol.

Later when they had gone I said, referring to Dr. Black, "I never trusted that jerk."

After a few days Dr. Saxon released her.

"I'd like to have you see Dr. Thompson before you leave."

"He hasn't seen you in four years. Maybe he'll have some new ideas," I told Carol.

She packed her bag, dressed in her street clothes, and we went upstairs to Head and Neck.

Dr. Thompson hadn't changed much since we'd last seen him, except for a few more gray hairs.

"How are you doing, Carol?"

Wow. He called her by name.

"You tell me," she said. "I've just been released and I'm no better than when I came here four days ago."

"I'll be right back," he said and left the room.

When he returned, he had what I thought were X-rays and put them up on a light box.

As if she were reading my mind, Carol told me, "Those aren't X-rays, Mom. They're CAT scans."

"My gosh, they're a thousand times clearer than X-rays."

I was impressed. From Carol's expression, it was obviously not the first time she'd seen a scan. There were about a dozen views of Carol's skull and in many of them flesh was apparent. The area above the eyes, the frontal sinuses, were extremely cloudy. Dr. Thompson pointed those out. The right sinus was worse.

"That's where our problem is," he said.

"What should it look like?" I asked.

"Clear," he replied.

"How do we get rid of it?" Carol questioned.

"Well, antibiotics are one way," he answered.

"What's next?" she asked.

"Surgery," he answered.

"Is it possible to put a needle into the sinus cavity and draw out the infection?" I asked.

"No," he answered. "First of all there's a membrane surrounding the brain that's very strong and difficult to penetrate, and second, I don't think Carol would want someone poking a needle into her head that close to her brain who can't see where he's poking."

That was a sobering answer.

"Well, then is surgery the next step?" I asked.

"Yes."

"How?"

"We make a small incision here," he pointed to the corner of the eye near the nose, "and go up into the sinuses that way. The other choice would be to cut across the top of her head," he pointed to an area just above the hairline, "and pull the skin down to expose the forehead bone. Then we could drill through the forehead and clean the sinus cavities out."

"Cut into my head?" Carol exclaimed in horror.

"That's positively a last resort," the doctor said.

"I should hope so," I added.

"How about scars?"

"Nothing to worry about. We could even do it now and get that cleaned out for you."

"Will it work?" Carol asked.

"Sure."

"Will it last?" I asked.

"Who knows?"

"Why bother?" Carol asked.

"Relieve the pain and pressure."

"But if it's only temporary ..." Carol said.

A nurse poked her head in the open door.

"Dr. Saxon's on the phone," she said.

Without an "excuse me" or "I'll be right back," he left the room.

"What do you think?" Carol asked me.

"God, I don't know. It seems like a hell of a lot more complicated than putting a needle in your head and drawing out some pus. You're the only one who knows how much pain you're in and whether you're desperate enough to go through this kind of surgery. He hasn't changed much, has he? No beating around the bush. No long answers; just deal the hand and are you in or out?"

"I just don't know."

"Then you aren't desperate enough."

When he returned, his attitude towards the surgery seemed much less positive.

"I'm not sure we should go ahead with surgery at this time. You were just given a new antibiotic?"

"Yes."

"Why don't you give it a few weeks to see if it works?"

Good. The decision had been made.

"Thank you, Doctor. I'll let you know," Carol said.

As we were on our way out, Dr. Scott Denardo, the resident on Carol's case in December, passed us. We called to him and he recognized us.

"I've thought about you a lot," he said.

I'll bet, I thought. People always remember trouble-makers. I wondered if he'd seen any other Wegener's patients since we were here.

"How are you doing?" he asked Carol.

"Not great. I just got released after four days and they haven't done a thing."

"You're still on ..."

"Leukeran™," Carol finished his sentence, "but it's not working."

"Sometimes it takes a little longer."

"That's what I told her," I said.

"Well, good luck,"

"Thanks. That never hurts."

When we returned to Carol's room a nurse was looking for her.

"When I saw your bag I thought you weren't far away," she said. "Dr. Saxon wants to see you in his office before you leave, and your medicine is ready." She handed Carol a bottle of pills.

"Can we go up now?"

"Yes. He's waiting for you."

"I spoke to Dr. Thompson," he said.

"I know," Carol answered. "We were there."

"I think it's too soon for surgery," the doctor told us.

"Good," Carol responded.

No wonder Dr. Thompson's attitude was different after the phone call.

"Let's give the antibiotic a chance," he pleaded. "We should be seeing results from the Leukeran™ before long, also."

"I don't think it's going to work," she said. "Cytoxan™ is the drug of choice, and if that didn't work, why should a less popular one do the job?"

If this is what's been going through her mind during the last few months, no wonder she was depressed.

The phone rang and Dr. Saxon answered it.

"Remember when Aunt Bea had pneumonia last year? Penicillin is the drug of choice and she's allergic to it, so she was given a less popular drug and still got well. All those times I had bladder infections when you were little, the drug of choice is sulfa. You know I'm allergic to sulfa, so I had to take something else and I still got well. Those research papers were not written about failures, but successes. Leukeran™ does work. If by some strange happenstance it doesn't work for you, there are others that will. No one knows which one will do the job. If we did, life would be a lot simpler. They'd give you that one, all this mess would be over with, and you'd be well. But rest assured one of these drugs will work and you'll die of old age."

Dr. Saxon, having finished his phone call and listening to me, said, "I'll drink to that. I don't think surgery is necessary—at least not now. I know you're disgusted with us ..."

Carol began to protest but the doctor ignored her and continued.

"... but you're not, as we say in the business, circling the drain."

That brought a smile and chuckle to both of us.

"Far from it," he continued. "We don't know which drug will work, like your mother said, until or unless we try. All of medicine is hit and miss. It's frustrating for you and for us. But we haven't figured out a better way.

"How are you doing for pain pills?"

"Dr. Adelman gave me a prescription."

"Good. Let's give the Leukeran™ some more time. Bevra agrees with that, too. By the way, did you know that Leukeran™ is the least toxic, and has the fewest side effects, of all the chemo drugs we've discussed?"

Actually, Dr. Haring had told us the same thing.

"How are you tolerating it?"

"OK. I still have hair. Why do you suppose the Cytoxan™ didn't work?"

"We think it did—up to a point."

---

44.   Leukeran™ is the trade name for the generic drug chlorambucil.

45.   A neutrophil is a type of white blood cell that deals with defense against bacterial or fungal infections.

46.   A lymphocyte is another type of white blood cell originating from fetal stem cells.

26

Defiance

I'd been having pain in one of my shoulders and after a few tests it was apparent I would need an operation. Carol had a new kind of hospital experience—as a visitor instead of a patient.

I was amazed at how she took charge when she thought I wasn't being cared for properly. She'd certainly learned how to handle the staff and made sure I got what I wanted quickly.

Because of all we'd been through with her, I had acquired knowledge I could put to good use. When my doctor recommended surgery, I questioned his credentials, experience, and success rate. I also made sure I got a second opinion.

I was somewhat incapacitated for a while, unable to drive, and required extensive physical therapy for several months. Carol was left on her own to see after her health care. I thought she was handling it.

When I began to function reasonably normally again, I phoned Dr. Adelman to check on Carol's progress.

"So, how's she doing, Doctor?"

"I have no idea. I haven't seen her since April."

It was the middle of June. I told him about my surgery and that I'd been out of commission for a while, "But I'm back in business now. I'll tend to her."

I tried calling Carol at work but she was always too busy to talk to me and I was never able to get her at home. The answering machine hadn't been hooked up for almost a year. It began to feel like she was avoiding us again. We seldom saw her, and even the boys had little contact.

It was Ron's thirtieth birthday and we'd planned a family celebration. When it was time to leave for the restaurant there was neither sign of nor word from Carol. I could see the disappointment in Ron's face. As we pulled into the restaurant's parking lot, Dick checked the rear view mirror and discovered she was right behind us. I was furious with her for what appeared to be her lack of responsibility, and avoided saying anything more than hello for the first half of the evening for fear I'd really let her have it. I didn't even want to sit next to her—but Dick did. I noticed during the evening that he discussed my phone conversation with Dr. Adelman with Carol. He actually extracted a promise from her that she would see the doctor the following week. I wondered if she'd keep it. How could she be so callous about her check-ups? She knew the consequences. For two pins I would have gleefully wrung her neck. Had we all fought the dragon for so long to let it all go like this?

She apparently didn't keep her promise. A few weeks later I got a call from Dr. Adelman.

"Carol's pharmacy called for a refill for the Leukeran™. I cannot, in all good conscience, renew it without checking her blood. I'm not really concerned about your suing me for malpractice. I don't think we have that kind of relationship. But it's not practicing good medicine to continue refilling the drug without having her blood checked, and I have to live with myself. If you have any influence over her at all, I suggest you use it to get her in here."

Later that evening she walked in. She looked terrible. I told her about Dr. Adelman's call, but offered no admonitions of my own. It was obvious she heard and understood.

I asked the pharmacist to give her ten pills with a note to see the doctor. He complied. Months later I asked if she'd ever gone to see Dr. Adelman.

"Yup. I had to."

"Which one?"

"Both of them."

I knew she was referring to Drs. Saxon and Adelman.

Work kept her exceedingly busy and she seemed to be keeping up with it all. I'd hear from her friends Pam and Sue that sometimes she would go away with them for the weekend and spend the whole time in bed. At least she was getting the necessary rest.

She began inviting me to go shopping again. I was anxious to ask her about her health, but openings in the conversation seldom occurred. Don and Ron were not seeing much of her either, and knew as little as I did about what was going on.

Dick continued to do a lot of business traveling, and I began letting her know about all my free time. When he was gone, she and I spent many evenings at shopping malls. It didn't take long for me to realize that seeing her frequently would tell me how she was feeling just as well as asking for details she was not about to give me.

I told Ron and Don about my concerns and my decision not to ask her about her health. They concurred. It was more important to keep up a good rapport and observe than to keep pumping her with questions she didn't want to answer.

During the year, she would tell me about episodes of bloody urine. The bleeding always seemed to stop by itself within a short time. Dr. Adelman had suggested check-ups with a urologist more than once. She went so far as to make an appointment with one, but never kept it. Dr. Adelman was annoyed because he'd pulled some strings to get the appointment. But she was in pain, doped up and hesitant about driving, depressed, and disgusted. Whatever energy she had, she saved for work.

No matter how many times she was told that the Leukeran™ was working, she didn't believe it.

By the end of the year, I felt our relationship was back to normal. Once in a great while I would ask her how she was. The rest of the time I talked about everything else.

In October, 1988, she was able to take a week off and went to Florida to visit Ken. Tracey went with her. Before Carol left, I called Ken.

"See if you can find out what's going on with her health. I see her often, but she doesn't discuss anything about it with me."

When she returned, I asked Ken what she'd told him.

"About as much as she tells you," he said. "But I can tell you this—she takes her medicine religiously."

That told me she must be getting her blood checked regularly or she wouldn't have had pills to take. I liked hearing that.

Every so often Tracey would call to either give me information or ask for it. She continued to be concerned with how her friend was doing.

Once I asked her, "Do you think Carol is burning the candle at both ends?"

"Absolutely," was her answer. "She wants to make sure she isn't going to miss anything."

I had heard the same story from Don.

Six months after Carol began the Leukeran™, the spots in her lung were reduced to half the size. I know that because I saw the X-rays, side by side. She and I both felt great that day.

About a year later, during one of Carol's regular visits to Dr. Saxon, he told her, "Your lungs are clear. There are no longer any spots. The radiologist who had read them last year reported that even though he knew where to look, he could find no trace of any spots in the lung and no apparent damage from, or evidence of, their ever having been there."

The Leukeran™ did the trick.

In December, once again we had more than the holidays to think about. Cytoxan's™ after-effects were still causing problems.

After putting jury duty off twice because of the shoulder surgery, I was finally able to go. I'm one of those crazy people who loves to serve on juries whenever I am able, and had spent several days in the assembly room waiting to be called.

It seemed that everything in Pasadena was a short distance from home, the courthouse being one of them; so, coincidentally, one day I decided to go home during the lunch break and eat yesterday's leftovers. Carol always says there are no coincidences. There was a message on the answering machine with the dreaded words, "I'm hemorrhaging again."

I knew she meant from the bladder.

I called her at work and was put right through to her office.

"How long and how bad?"

"Since yesterday. It's very red and doesn't seem like it's going to stop."

"Have you called anyone?"

"Dr. Adelman, but he hasn't called me back yet."

It was a Friday—the worst day of the week to have an emergency if you need to see a doctor at the office.

"I'm in the middle of jury duty but haven't been chosen for a particular trial yet, so I can probably get excused."

"I don't even know who to see," she said. "I think I'll try Dr. Adelman again and ask him."

"Make an appointment for as late as possible today, and I'll be back home after 2:00," I said.

I called Dick's office to let him know, but had no luck catching up with him.

I returned to the assembly room and, when the lady in charge came back from lunch, I was the first one at her window.

"I'm not going to be able to stay here this afternoon. My daughter has a problem that I need to take care of immediately."

I could tell by the look on her face that she was sure I was just trying to get out of my civic duty.

I continued with my explanation.

"I went home for lunch and discovered a message from my daughter. She has been on chemotherapy, and one of the side effects of the drug is bleeding from the bladder."

The minute she heard the word "chemotherapy" her whole demeanor changed.

"Of course you can be excused ..."

"The last time this happened, she was hospitalized for a couple of days. The bladder was cauterized and they were able to stop the bleeding and release her. If it happens that way again, I should be able to return here on Monday. I brought her doctor's name and phone number and will be happy to tell him to release any information that you might require ..."

"That's not necessary. You won't have to come back on Monday. I'll just excuse you."

I thanked her and left.

When Carol still hadn't heard from the doctor, she tried again.

This time he called quickly and suggested a urologist for Carol to see. He even made an appointment for her himself. It was with a Dr. Sam Davidson.*

I picked Carol up at her apartment, and we made our way across town to the doctor together. In case she was hospitalized, we wouldn't have to worry about getting her car home.

This doctor's office was adjacent to Cedars Sinai Medical Center in the heart of Beverly Hills. The parking was expensive and the doctor's staff did not validate.

Dr. Davidson greeted us first in his office to get what information he needed and hadn't gotten from Dr. Adelman. He seemed to be pleasant enough, and had lots of pictures of him and his family skiing. Carol felt they had something in common.

The doctor informed us that he would be performing a cystoscopy here.

"May I watch?" I asked.

"Certainly, if you wish," he answered.

"Do you mind?" I asked Carol.

"No."

We were ushered into an examining room, and Carol undressed in a nearby bathroom. Then the doctor's assistant busied herself preparing Carol and the necessary instruments. I explained what problems Carol had experienced over the years. As usual, the young woman had never heard of Wegener's.

Dr. Davidson entered the room and explained to Carol what to expect from the examination.

"I'll try to be as gentle as possible," he promised. "I know it's uncomfortable."

It was obviously very painful for Carol. After he poked and prodded for a while, Carol began to groan and tears were streaming down her cheeks.

While he was poking around her bladder, he was sticking pins in my heart. When will it stop? How much more will she be put through?

While the doctor was poking, his assistant was irrigating. I was at Carol's head behind the action, holding one of her hands. As she squeezed hard I touched her shoulder with the other hand, hoping to send some positive energy through, maybe lessening the pain.

The assistant tried to be discreet with the waste pan as she emptied it. However, I strained to see what had been flushed out, and noted that it was extremely bloody even after being diluted during the irrigation.

"I'm not seeing any particular spots that are bleeding," the doctor reported.

"Then where's the blood coming from?" Carol asked.

"It's oozing from the bladder wall," he answered. "There's no one spot that I can fulgarize.[47]"

"What can we do?" I asked.

"Nothing. She's not losing enough blood to make a difference."

"That's because it's not your blood," Carol commented.

He thought Carol was teasing, but I knew she was dead serious and sarcastic.

"You'd lose more during a normal period."

I thought of Dr. Katske and what he had said four years ago when I had asked, "What happens if we don't do anything?" and he had answered, "She'll bleed to death."

I had no idea how much she was losing but, unlike a menstrual period, this was neither normal nor natural. I didn't like it.

"Get dressed," the doctor said. "I'll see you in my office."

"She's had one problem after another since all this began. She was only sixteen," I told the doctor and assistant, and gave them a brief overview of what she'd gone through.

Dr. Davidson was expensive. The fee for this visit and procedure was $637. He wanted payment then and there and would not bill Carol's insurance.

"I wonder what people do who don't have $600 lying around," I told Carol on the way home.

"They don't see a doctor in Beverly Hills," she answered.

I returned to the courthouse on Monday and completed my jury duty.

A few days later she was still seeing blood—lots of it. She called Dr. Davidson's office to report in and was told to sit tight. It might take as much as six weeks for the bleeding to stop. There was no need to concern herself.

A few weeks later it did stop. She was doing well for about a week and then it started again. When I questioned her about what she was going to do, she told me not to worry about it—as if I could actually stop.

I spoke to Dr. Adelman and got the impression that the bladder should have been checked months ago. I also got the feeling that he was annoyed that Carol wasn't taking his advice.

I offered my view of the situation.

"The last few times we've spoken, I sensed your frustration with Carol's apparent reluctance to take responsibility for her health care. I've felt that way myself for quite a while. Then the realization came to me that she *was* taking responsibility—but her own version of it. I feel as you do, that she must be checked and evaluated according to the requisite schedule. Anything less than that would seem unstable, irresponsible, and even bordering on suicidal. Through my personal research I came to an understanding of why she has chosen her present course of action—something a year ago I might have referred to as inaction.

"I must tell you, first of all, that she both likes and respects you. I've seen her interact with literally dozens of doctors since her problems began. If you were not one of her special favorites, there's no way she would have continued to consult you. But of all the doctors she's seen, she's closest to Drs. Haring and Saxon. I finally figured out why. They both accepted her way of handling her problems, even when they locked horns with her on specific methods, and both understood she had a life outside the doctor's office.

"She dealt with her health problems as her doctors saw fit for ten years. Some of what we thought would work did, some didn't. When she felt the negative advice outweighed the positive, she decided to choose her own way.

"There have been times that I felt she should have been handcuffed to the bedpost and forced to toe the line I drew. Then I realized she already felt trapped and had to find release by setting her own rules if she were to survive with her sanity intact.

"She does follow our advice and is taking care of her physical needs in her own way. But she's also tending to her emotional needs. She knows, and I had to learn, that if she doesn't have a life outside the medical center and out from under Mom's thumb, she has no reason to survive. There's no escape from the prison she's lived in for twenty-four hours of each day of the last ten years.

"You and I have a good idea of what tomorrow will bring. She has no idea what's in store for her, or even if she has a tomorrow. Just because you and I tell her she has a lot of tomorrows ahead of her doesn't make it so.

"You and I may never know the fear she lives with. She's not ignoring her problems—just putting them in their place. So far, many of her decisions have been right—for her. I do not agree with her choice not to inform her co-workers of her illness, but she's advanced at a phenomenal rate at her company. If it was known that she was battling a life-threatening disease, or on a regimen of chemo-therapy, promotions may not have occurred.

"If she didn't have friends she could be out laughing with, she might be home crying. She would never be content to view life from the sidelines as if it were a spectator sport. She has to be in the field, throwing the ball, so to speak. I wish she heeded more advice from her coaches, but she plays the game her way."

The holidays came and went, and the bleeding started again. She saw Dr. Davidson and again he did nothing that time, or any of the other several times she saw him during the next few weeks.

In the meantime I had a phone call from a lady named Donna inquiring about our support group. She told me her story and asked about Carol. When I relayed the latest bladder problems, she told me that Dr. Davidson had been her doctor, and that he was so ineffective that she eventually had to have a cystectomy.[48]

Because of that, she now had a stoma[49] and wore an ostomy[50] bag.

"Please tell Carol to find another urologist as soon as possible."

I thanked her for the information and told her about our next support group meeting. I wasn't sure what to tell Carol about Dr. Davidson. I didn't trust him but I didn't want to worry her unnecessarily. I did, however, want her to know what had happened to Donna. I was walking a fine line between protecting and informing her.

Dick, my usual source of advice, was out of town for a few days again.

The next support group meeting was one of the few that Carol didn't attend. Pondering my dilemma, I put the question to the group.

"Should I tell Carol about Donna's experience and suggest she get another doctor?"

The overwhelming consensus of the group was to give her the information and let her decide what to do with it.

She saw Dr. Davidson a few more times and said she liked him. I was wary but let her decide whether or not to continue.

Then Fate made the decision for us.

---

47.   Fulgarize is a technique in electrosurgery performed with electrical instruments in which tissue is destroyed by burning with an electric spark.

48.   A cystectomy is a surgical procedure in which all or part of the bladder is removed.

49. A stoma is an artificial opening of an organ on the surface of the body created surgically.

50. An ostomy is a surgical procedure in which an opening is made from the body to a stoma surgically created in the wall of the abdomen. Each procedure is named for the anatomic location of the ostomy, in the case of the bladder it is called a cystostomy.

27

Planned and Unplanned Trips to Denver

It was February 6, 1989, and I wondered if Carol was coming to our next support group meeting. I tried calling her at the office several times and got no answer. Finally, someone answered her phone and said she hadn't been in for two days because she had the flu.

That was strange. Carol never got the diseases other people got. I kept trying her at home and then called her pager. After the second page she finally called me back. She sounded awful.

"What's wrong?"

"I think I have the flu. I ache everywhere and I'm wiped out."

"Do you want me to take you to the doctor?"

"No. I just need to rest."

"Do you have what you need to eat or drink?"

"Yes."

"Call me if you need me."

"OK."

I wanted to know if she was still bleeding, but afraid to ask. She would tell me what she wanted me to know. Then I remembered what Dr. Saxon had said about the drugs she was taking. They were immunosuppressants and put her in the same category as someone with AIDS—prone to infections. The least little germ could lay her low. Maybe what she was feeling was the result of lowered resistance because of the Leukeran™ or Prednisone™. It never occurred to me that the loss of blood might be doing the same thing.

A couple of days later she called to say she was experiencing a lot more bleeding and asked me to get her an appointment with Dr. Davidson.

I called and was told if I could get there before five o'clock he would see her. I called her back and told her to get dressed.

"I'll be over in twenty minutes."

It was 3:30 and pouring rain. Rush hour traffic was already underway, and we had to travel through the downtown Los Angeles interchange.

"What if we don't make it before 5:00?" Carol asked.

She was reading my mind.

"Then we invoke Plan B."

"Which is …?"

"We go to Cedars-Sinai emergency room, tell them you're hemorrhaging from the bladder, did not make it to Dr. Davidson's office before it closed, and ask them to contact him or whoever is taking his calls."

We barely made it before 5:00. After a brief rundown on what was going on this time, the doctor said, "Let's scope you and see what's going on."

His assistant tried to talk me out of accompanying them into the examination room, but Carol was insistent that I remain with her.

The urine looked like grape juice again. Once again the doctor observed that there was no place to cauterize. As before, he did nothing and informed Carol that the bleeding would stop by itself. He was less than useless.

"I think you should have an IVP and let's see if the bleeding is coming from the kidneys," the doctor suggested.

"Can you do that here?" Carol asked.

"Oh yes. Let me see if we can schedule you for tomorrow."

"I'm going skiing in Colorado for a week and leaving Friday. Do you think there's any problem with that?"

"None that I can see. If you're going to bleed, you're going to bleed no matter where you are or what you're doing."

We scheduled the IVP for the next morning.

"I'll only be in during the morning," Dr. Davidson said. "I'll have my associate, Dr. Paul Hampton* call you with the results."

I was not allowed to stay with Carol during the IVP because it's done with an X-ray machine, which would expose me to radiation unnecessarily. I expected that because I had been given the same test many years ago. It was done in a short period of time. That afternoon Dr. Hampton called to say the kidneys were clear.

"She's planning on going skiing in Colorado for a couple of days. Do you see any problem with that?" I asked.

"No, but she should continue to drink a lot," the doctor answered.

"Dr. Davidson told her yesterday to cut down on her liquids as they distend the bladder and aggravate it," I reported.

"I disagree," he said. "She should be drinking as much as possible, and it's OK for her to go to Colorado. I see no problem."

On Friday morning, February 10, against my better judgment, I drove her to Burbank[51] Airport. It was obvious she wasn't feeling well, but she was still trying so hard not to let her illness cramp her style. I had offered to bring my luggage cart but she refused.

"It's just one more thing to carry," she told me, "and I have enough already."

She was right; she had more than enough. The skis and poles were in one bag; in the boot bag were the heavy ski boots; then there was her suitcase and her heavy jacket. She had checked the suitcase and the ski bag and was carrying her ski boots, jacket, and purse. As usual, the check-in counter was a long way from the boarding gate, and she had to stop a couple of times just to catch her breath. I couldn't stand watching her struggle.

"More to carry or not, this stuff is too heavy to lift," I said as I ducked into the gift shop and bought a cart. She sat down and took a much-needed breather while I arranged the things she had been carrying onto the cart and fastened them. She was able to wheel everything the rest of the way.

"I hope I can make it on the slopes," she said. "I'm having so much trouble catching my breath."

My mind was screaming: don't go. Instead, I said, "Just do what you feel like doing."

I hoped she'd get some rest.

Burbank Airport did not have raised covered walkways leading directly on to the plane. Moveable staircases were placed at the airplane's door, and passengers entered and exited that way. I watched as Carol struggled up the long stairway with her weighted pack. She waved to me and I threw her a kiss as she disappeared through the door. Although she would be at the rented condo Friday, her friends, Pam and Sue, wouldn't be in till Saturday. There was no phone at the condo. That bothered me, but there wasn't anything I could do about it.

Life seemed so easy for some people. Would it always be such a burden for her?

On Monday evening she called. I wish I could say it was unexpected.

"Mom, I can hardly walk down the street without stopping to catch my breath. By the way, I don't know if I would have made it out of the airport without the luggage cart. I couldn't have carried anything. Pam and Sue tell me I look pale."

She even sounded breathless.

"There's a hospital in Vail, isn't there?"

"Yes, a small one. That's where I had my broken wrist taken care of a few years ago."

"Get yourself in there and have them take a blood test. Then call me."

"OK, I'll do it in the morning."

She was staying in a town on the outskirts of Vail; a shuttle would be available to take her and her friends to the hospital and slopes, respectively, the next morning. They had no other transportation, and I assumed she didn't feel it was an emergency. I thought she'd had enough experience by this time to tell whether or not she was in trouble—and how deep.

It was now eleven years since Carol had been diagnosed with Wegener's granulomatosis and well over a year since her last Cytoxan™ treatment.

I didn't get much sleep that night and I'll bet she didn't either.

Tuesday morning she reported, "My blood count is way down, and I can't catch my breath. They say I'm a candidate for a transfusion."

"Where are you?" I asked.

"Vail Valley Medical Center."

"Are they going to talk to Dr. Adelman?"

"Yes. I gave them his phone number. I don't think they can take care of me here. I think they're going to transfer me to another hospital."

"Call me as soon as you know where you're going, and I'll arrange to meet you there."

Meanwhile, my friend Jean* called and asked to stop by my house for a visit. We hadn't seen each other for quite a long time. While she was there, I began to fill her in on what was going on with Carol. I'd forgotten Jean was from Colorado.

"Carol looked terrible when I took her to the airport Friday," I told her. "I bought a luggage cart. She was so weak she was struggling with the luggage; I found myself wondering how she was going to be able to ski. But I'd learned after many years of watching her battle her illness not to try to curtail her activities. She was, after all, twenty-seven and no longer had to listen to me or do what I told her."

While we were chatting, Carol called again.

"They're sending me to Denver Presbyterian Hospital. I'm supposed to see Dr. Phillips,* a rheumatologist who will be giving me a transfusion."

"How are you getting to Denver?"

"By ambulance."

Her tone was casual; the situation wasn't. Normally when you have to go to another hospital, they tell you where to go. They don't care how you get there. Ambulances are for emergencies.

I asked, "Why ambulance?"

"Because they started an IV with saline."

One can't take a bus with an IV.

"Are Pam and Sue going with you?"

"No. I took the shuttle to the hospital this morning, and Pam and Sue are skiing. I have no way to get in touch with them. I called and asked the people at the ski area if they would put a message on the board. I told them it was important."

"What board?"

"Remember there's a chalk board at the bottom of each chair lift that tells the weather conditions at the top? Well, that's where I asked them to post one."

"Will they?"

"No. They said it wasn't for personal messages."

There was no other way for Carol to make contact with her friends.

"As soon as I can get a plane out, I'll meet you at the hospital. You said Denver Presbyterian?"

"Yes."

"Keep your chin up. Don't worry. You'll be fine. I love you."

I said she'd be fine; I wasn't sure if I believed it.

As I hung up the phone, Jean, having heard my end of the conversation, said, "I have a cousin in Denver. Would you like me to call him and see if he could assist Carol in any way?"

I wasn't sure what good it would do, but I agreed. If Carol could have her hand held until I arrived, it might help.

Jean tried her cousin but got no answer.

"I'll try him later," she said.

Vail is just short of one hundred miles from Denver, an ambulance ride of close to two hours over a high mountain pass.

I phoned Dick at the office. He was in a meeting. I had never asked a secretary to interrupt him before, but there's a first time for everything. She asked me to wait on hold, and then returned to tell me he would call me back.

A few minutes later he was on the phone.

"Carol called from the hospital. She's going to need a transfusion. They're transferring her from the hospital in Vail to one in Denver, by ambulance. Can you get me on a plane out of here ASAP or should I make arrangements myself?"

I was amazed at how calm my voice sounded. My insides were churning, my heart was racing, and my mind was spinning.

"I'll take care of reservations. How did she sound?"

"Matter of fact, like she always does. But I'm sure she's petrified."

"Let me see what I can do. I'll call you back."

"OK."

I hung up the phone and turned to Jean.

"Follow me."

I went to the garage, picked out a suitcase, and then went upstairs to pack.

"I have to pick up Michael* from nursery school, so I'll be on my way," Jean said. "My cousin's name is Dr. Wilson.*"

"Is he an MD?"

"No, he's a DD."

Not knowing how serious the situation was, and not wanting to hurt Jean's feelings—after all, she meant well—I just said thank you, and immediately forgot about her cousin after she left.

A few minutes later, my parents arrived from Palm Springs. I forgot we had tickets to a show the next day.

The minute I opened the door, Mom knew there was trouble.

"Carol needs a transfusion, and they're taking her from Vail to Denver by ambulance."

I had to talk fast and keep moving or I would melt into a pile of tears. I had to keep my head. Hysterics wouldn't help anything.

I could see Mom, watching me, become visibly shaken.

The phone rang; it was Dick.

"I have reservations for both of us. We leave at 2:00 this afternoon." It was 11:30 AM. "I'll be home shortly to pack. Remember it's cold there now."

"You can get away?"

"They have no choice."

I had just finished packing enough clothes for a week when Dick arrived.

"That's too much," he said when he saw how full the suitcase was. "You'll only need enough for a few days."

I unpacked a couple of days' worth as he packed clothes for himself, and we were off.

"I have no tickets," he said, "only reservations. We'll have to buy tickets at the airport. I don't think we'll have trouble finding a place to stay in Denver." He had been there before on business but I never had.

We made the short drive to Burbank Airport, checked in, and purchased our tickets. Since neither of us had eaten, we headed for the airport restaurant. A few minutes after we sat down with our food, the loudspeaker announced Dick's name and asked that he return to the check-in area.

"Probably the office," he said and left.

He returned a few minutes later with an embarrassed grin.

"I left my American Express card with the ticket agent."

That was unusual. He never forgot things like that.

We were soon on our way. I couldn't get Donna's admonition out of my head. The closer we got to Denver, the angrier I became at Dr. Davidson. How could he have scoped and examined her and not have found bleeding spots when her urine was the color of grape juice? Could it be that he didn't know what to look for? His office is full of awards. How could someone be good enough to get all those plaques and certificates and not know what he was doing? If he did know what he was doing, why was Donna's case so botched? Did Dr. Adelman choose Dr. Davidson because he was competent, or because he knew him socially? Was it possible he was good with other urological problems and just not good with Carol's?

The view from my window seat looked like the Grand Canyon, then slowly changed to snow-covered mountains. Carol's pale face and frail body struggling with her heavy load jumped into view every time I closed my eyes, and the tears stung. She didn't ask us to come; she would have handled it. But how could we stay away?

We talked very little during our flight, but I remember asking Dick, "How can we possibly know if the blood she's getting is safe? People have contracted AIDS from blood transfusions."

"They do a lot more checking these days and, from what I've read, it seems the blood is safer today than it was in the past," he answered. "We can only hope."

The seatbelt sign lit up and the captain announced that we would be landing in Denver shortly. My impatience became stronger.

We were on the ground walking toward baggage claim when a voice boomed over the loud speaker, "Paging Richard Swart, Mr. Richard Swart. Please pick up the white courtesy phone. Paging Mr. Richard Swart. Please pick up the white courtesy phone."

I turned toward Dick.

"The office," he said, answering my unasked question. "I know I didn't leave my credit card anywhere this time."

We quickly found a courtesy phone, and as he held the receiver to his ear, he felt his breast pocket for a pen. I handed him a notepad fished from my purse. He only said two words as he wrote them down, "Reverend Wilson," and then he repeated a phone number. I could see his hand shaking as he wrote. His usually fair complexion had turned to the color of ash.

He moved to an adjacent pay phone and reached into his pants pocket for change, as I fumbled in my purse, and pulled out a handful. If I had been able to speak I would have screamed, but my voice was frozen and buried deep inside me. Panic gripped me. Who was Reverend Wilson? Was he preparing us for the worst? How bad was the worst? Was he the hospital chaplain? How did he know where to find us?

Tears spilled over onto my cheeks. A little voice in my head said: Don't let him see you cry; he can hardly control himself. His hand shook so badly as he fumbled with the coins trying to get them into the slot. He missed and dropped some. We both bent toward the floor but he beat me to the coins and retrieved them. Half of me silently screamed: make the call, while the other half mumbled: if it's bad news, I don't want to know. Voices in my head argued, *it can't be bad news*. We've only come to hold her hand. She had walked into the hospital in Vail. How serious can the situation be if she walked into the hospital?

We'd been married for thirty-three years, and I had never seen such fear in his eyes. My heart sank down into my shoes. Dick dialed the number in what seemed like slow motion. I had to know whatever it was he had to tell us. As Dick finished dialing he held out his hand and took mine. Whatever the news, we would face it together.

"Reverend Wilson, please?" I heard him ask. His voice sounded far away as if he were in a tunnel. There was a short pause and then, "Reverend Wilson? This is Dick Swart. I'm calling from the Denver airport. I was paged and ..." He let go of my hand and began writing on the notepad.

"Jean's cousin ..." I could literally see the tension draining out of him as he wrote, "... has checked on Carol ... getting blood transfusion ... doing fine."

A sob caught in my throat. Once more I felt like screaming, but this time with relief as tears streamed down my face. As Dick wiped his eyes I stopped trying to hide my terror.

"Thank you, Sir. Yes, we've made arrangements. We appreciate all you've done. I have your number. No thank you. I've rented a car. Thanks again." He hung up the receiver and turned to me.

"That scared the hell out of me," he said—as if I hadn't noticed.

I suddenly felt ten years older.

"He offered his home if we'd like to stay there. He even asked if we needed a ride to the hospital," he told me as we resumed our trek to baggage claim.

"Jean told me he was a DD."

"Why didn't you tell me?"

"Who remembered in all the commotion? Besides, Jean couldn't get him on the phone when she tried from our place, and I had no idea whether she would try again—or even remember to try."

We retrieved our luggage, picked up the rental car, and headed for the hospital.

There was snow on the ground and I remarked, "I'm glad I packed warm clothes. It looks like I'm going to need them."

As we entered Carol's room, she was sitting up with one arm attached to an IV. A bag of blood was hanging from the pole beside the bed. Once again I silently asked myself how much more?

Dick rushed to the bed and enclosed her in his arms. She looked so happy to see us.

"I was so scared," she told us.

So was I, but I wasn't going to tell her.

"I didn't need another chapter," I told her, referring to the manuscript for this book. I had partially completed it a couple of years before, but had no luck stirring up interest in it with a literary agent.

As soon as the words were out of my mouth I thought, that was a dumb thing to say.

It was one of the few times she greeted us with tears streaming down her face. She saw no tears on me; I had done my crying at the airport.

Before the day was over she had been given four units of blood.

"I left all my clothes and ski stuff at the condo near Vail. Do you think you can go get them for me?" she asked.

Just as I was wondering how to get in touch with her friends, Pam and Sue called to see how Carol was doing. We made arrangements with them to get Carol's things.

She finally fell asleep and I was able to catch my breath.

We asked at the information desk if they knew of lodging close by, and were referred to a small motel adjacent to the hospitals. There were several other hospitals on the same campus, and the motel was close enough for us to walk to and from any of them. I can't remember either before or since finding a motel as inexpensive as this one. We were given a three-room suite, complete with a kitchen. The weekly rate was something in the neighborhood of $125. They obviously catered to hospital visitors because along with the usual information, we were asked for Carol's name, which hospital she was in, and her room number. Dick gave the person at the window his American Express card. As she was making an imprint, she told us the people who usually ran the motel were away for a few days and she was helping out temporarily.

From what we could gather in our talks with the doctors who were treating Carol, it seemed that the higher altitude at Vail, and being in the pressurized airplane cabin, may have hastened the bladder hemorrhaging that precipitated this incident.

"Considering he skis himself, wouldn't you have thought Dr. Davidson would have taken the altitude into consideration?" I asked Dick.

"Obviously not," he answered.

The next morning, after visiting with Carol, we made the drive to Vail. Her friends told us what had transpired on their end.

When they arrived on Saturday, Carol was in bed resting. Both told us it was obvious that there was something drastically wrong when they took a look at her. She was as white as a sheet and looked awful.

On Tuesday morning the shuttle had dropped Carol off at the hospital and her friends at the slopes. They planned to hook up again at the end of the day at the town's covered bridge. When Carol didn't show up at their designated time, they were puzzled and wondered if she had met some guy on the slopes and gone off somewhere with him—not her usual way of doing things.

They decided to go to the ER to find out if she was still there. The hospital personnel wouldn't give them any information because they weren't family members. Coincidentally, the ambulance driver had just returned and overheard them trying to get information from the ER clerk. Carol often reminds me there are no coincidences.

"Are you looking for the little girl ..." and he proceeded with Carol's description. Although she was twenty-seven, she still looked like she was sixteen. "I took her to Denver Presbyterian," he informed them.

They then phoned Carol in the hospital while we were visiting with her.

"Did you ski at all?" I asked Carol when we returned to Denver.

"I tried the first day, but it didn't take long to realize that it was impossible. I could hardly breathe well enough to walk, let alone ski."

Carol was in the hospital for five days. She was given medicine directly into the bladder in an attempt to stop the bleeding, and it caused cramping. She was not a happy camper.

I had called Dr. Adelman to fill him in on the latest crisis in case anyone from Denver needed information. I was on the phone with him when Dr. Phillips arrived to give us an update. Dr. Adelman asked to speak to Dr. Phillips, who refused to get on the phone. He told us he was late for an appointment. I don't know why, but I didn't believe him.

As before, it was determined that she needed a cystoscopy and cauterization. The surgery was put off a couple of times and when we tried to pin down the reason, we discovered that the urologist scheduled to do the procedure was leaving on vacation. Those in charge had planned to make us wait until he returned. Once we found this out, we pushed for the surgery to be done as soon as possible with any urologist who was available.

During the week we were in Denver, Reverend Wilson visited Carol several times and told us he had been praying for her.

Carol was released on Saturday and we immediately flew home.

After we returned, I told several doctors and questioned them about the incident. Every one of them felt the altitude and the pressurized cabin in the airplane were the culprits, and that Dr. Davidson should have told Carol it was inadvisable to go skiing, especially in the higher altitudes of the Colorado resorts.

We never saw him again.

A week after we returned home, I received a phone call from the motel. They didn't accept American Express, and the temporary person in the office didn't know that. They told me they would be returning the charge slip by mail, and asked if I would mind sending them a check for the required amount.

"There are a lot of trusting people in the world," I told Dick.

---

51.   Burbank Airport, actually Burbank, Glendale, Pasadena Airport, is a small regional airport in Los Angeles County. The name was recently changed to Bob Hope Airport.

28

A Normal Disease

When Carol started working full-time after college, she began earning a substantial salary. For her second full-time job, a bank hired her in their corporate office. After six months, she received a raise and the title: Assistant Vice President. About two years later, she was promoted to Vice President, given another raise in pay, and was able to secure a nearby, subsidized parking spot in the city where parking is at a premium. Once, when she traveled for the company, she was met at the other end by a limousine waiting to take the group to the harbor for a dinner cruise. It was a good job, she enjoyed the work, and those in charge obviously liked her.

But she was becoming restless. The software consultants who contracted with the bank were earning more than she was and tried to spirit her away.

Dick and I did everything we could to dissuade her from going out on her own. We were petrified that she wouldn't be able to get health insurance, and knew she couldn't be without it. We spoke to all of her brothers and asked them to try to talk her out of it. After several attempts at that, Don put us in our respective places.

"Carol has made the best career choices of all of us. She's making much more money than the rest of us and seems to be taking care of herself nicely. I wouldn't begin to try to talk her out of it," he told us.

One consultant named Randy was working on a project that needed some more manpower, and made an offer to Carol to work for him. Both would be working as independent contractors.

In July, 1990, she made the decision to leave the bank. She worked on the project with Randy for a year until her part was completed, and then began a consulting business of her own. Phil, the man she had worked with during her college years, had formed his own company and hired her as an independent contractor for a variety of projects. During the years she worked with Phil, she doubled her income from when she was a bank vice president. She was able to buy a new car, pay it off in half the allotted time, and buy her own condominium.

She managed to extend her medical coverage from the bank as long as possible, and then applied for and got coverage with Blue Cross of California, a major medical insurer.

She took whatever time off she desired for vacations such as white water rafting in Costa Rica and sightseeing in Hawaii, Sedona, Paris, and Mazatlán. She bought a top-of-the-line mountain bike and went riding around the north rim of the Grand Canyon; other rides in Utah, Colorado, Washington, and the Canadian Rockies followed.

She replaced her old skis with longer ones commensurate with her current ability, and went on skiing trips to Lake Tahoe, Utah, Oregon, British Columbia, and even Chile. She also went on some fabulous day hikes and horseback riding trips, activities she loves.

In order to further her knowledge, she took scores of weekend and week-long seminars geared to self-improvement and self-awareness.

When she was at work, she worked hard: It was not unusual for her to put in sixty to seventy hours a week. When she played, she played hard.

She continued taking the Leukeran™ and stopped having flare-ups.

None of the chemotherapy treatments resulted in hair loss, and while on the Leukeran™ she had no stomach upsets.

She was finally beginning to live like a normal person. It was a joy to watch and about time she was able to have fun. But it wasn't to last.

In 1991, after spending more time traveling for business than he did at home, Dick decided he'd had enough and retired. He was given a fabulous retirement party. He received so many gifts we needed two cars to take them home. All the children were invited and each spoke about their father. Even my parents attended and could witness the respect and admiration that was bestowed upon him.

Although Dick would no longer be going into the office daily, there was a project in Egypt on which he agreed to consult. He made numerous trips there during the next three years.

We moved from Pasadena, rented a condo in Big Bear Lake, and awaited the completion of our new retirement home, built to our specifications. We had previously bought a lot, worked out floor plans, and hired a general contractor. We expected to live there a long time.

For our first holiday in our new mountain home, Carol invited a couple of people she worked with and their families to spend New Year's Eve with us. One of our guests' children appeared to have a rash with small red pimples or blisters. Phil, who worked with Carol, his wife Nancy, and their two young sons were among our guests. Because Nancy was a nurse, we sought her opinion on the rash. She confirmed that it looked like chicken pox. All the adults had already had the disease—except Carol. Her brothers had it before she was born. During her school years she had somehow managed not to contract it from others.

"What's the incubation time?" I asked Nancy.

"Two weeks," was her answer.

We were scheduled to go to Boston for our grand niece Bonnie's Bat Mitzvah[52] in—you guessed it—two weeks.

The disease is highly contagious and because Carol had been exposed there was nothing we could do except wait and see what transpired.

"Should we cancel our plans?" I asked Dick.

"I don't think so," he said. "The chances of her getting it are remote."

"I hope you're right," I answered.

She was still taking Leukeran™. We had no way of knowing how suppressed her immune system was.

We went ahead with our plans, arriving in Boston on a Thursday. Carol and I traveled together, and Dick met us at the airport in Boston as he returned from another trip to Egypt. The festivities took place Friday evening and most of Saturday. The evening after the ceremony and accompanying party, she came to my hotel room to show me her latest problem. She had the beginnings of what appeared to be a rash.

"I think I have chicken pox. Can that happen to someone who's 30?"

Unfortunately, we both knew the answer.

We expected to be in the hotel that was close to the celebration for three days, and then drive to Salem so that Carol could see those tourist attractions dealing with witches and witchcraft—something that had always been of interest to her and me.

There was no sense taking her to a doctor because we knew what the problem was. She spent the next couple of days in bed. Although we had no thermometer with us, a touch of her skin told us she was running a high fever. Realizing she was in no position to sightsee, we informed the hotel we would be there two more days.

"I'm sorry, you can't stay. The room is rented and there are no other rooms available," we were told at the reception desk.

"What are we going to do?" I asked Dick back in the privacy of our room.

"We're going to stay anyway. We can't move her," he answered.

"Can they kick us out?"

"By the time they get around to taking any legal action we'll be gone."

Sometimes it's great to be married to a lawyer.

"Should we tell them we're not leaving?"

"I think when we don't check out they'll figure it out."

I made calls to Drs. Saxon and Haring to find out what, if anything, we should do for Carol while we were still in Boston. Both called us first thing Monday morning and told us to discontinue the Leukeran™. By this time she had been taking it for over four years. Dr. Saxon prescribed pain medicine and a new antiviral called acyclovir. Before we went home, Dr. Haring called again to see how things were going.

The hotel had given a special rate to all those who were invited to the event. When we finally checked out, we noticed they charged us considerably more for the additional two days, but there was nothing we could do about it. After we had been at the hotel for five days, we left to go directly to the airport.

Because of Dick's extensive traveling with one airline, he had joined their club that gives frequent travelers extra perks. One of these was access to a large, separate waiting room with couches and armchairs. Carol was able to lie down there while we waited for our flight.

After we were airborne, we discovered a row of three empty seats, where Carol took advantage of the additional opportunity to lie down. I shudder to think of how many people we came in contact with that may have gotten chicken pox, but we had no choice.

Back in California we took her to her home, got a motel for ourselves nearby, and spent the evening with her. Now that we were home, we were able to take her temperature. The next morning I called Dr. Saxon and reported that it was 103° F. Carol had eaten next to nothing for several days.

"I think she needs to be hospitalized," he told us.

We drove her to the UCLA ER and she was admitted. We didn't have to ask for a private room this time; she was put on the isolation floor which had nothing but private rooms.

Because her throat was full of lesions, it hurt and she was literally unable to eat. That was a shame because the isolation section was only part of that floor; rooms in other areas were considered VIP rooms. We couldn't believe the gourmet food they were bringing in to her, such as rack of lamb and beef Wellington.

We had heard that having chicken pox as an adult is much more severe, and we were able to observe that first hand.

During the four days she was in the hospital, she was visited twice by the attending infectious disease specialist. The first visit was around 6:30 AM. She chased him out and told him to come back at a decent hour. The other time was during the late afternoon when Dick and I were in the room.

The doctor walked in with an assistant, introduced himself, and began to tell Carol about a pediatrician who was a patient down the hall and who, according to this doctor, was in much worse shape than Carol was.

"If you're telling me this, thinking it's going to make me feel better, it's not working," she snapped at him.

It's common knowledge that no matter what ails anyone else, our own illness is worse.

He snapped off his rubber gloves, tossed them into the waste basket, and stomped out of the room without saying another word.

When Dr. Saxon came to see her she told him about the incident.

"Don't worry about it," he said. "Because this is his section, he's required to check in on the patients."

During this hospitalization Carol was in pain and getting shots. When she was due for one and called for the nurse, they didn't always respond in a timely manner. I became the number one pest. I would usually give the staff a half hour to come up with the shot. If they didn't, I walked to the nurses' station, propped my crossed arms on the high counter and waited until someone looked up and recognized me.

"I'm Carol Swart's mother. She's in room (whatever). She asked for a pain shot at (whatever time). It's now (current time) and she's still waiting." I did not leave until I saw someone with a syringe going toward her room. I did that at every hospital stay she's had since then, reminiscent of Shirley MacLaine's award-winning performance in the movie "Terms of Endearment," only I didn't pace. I feel certain that each time Carol was released from a hospital, the staff was particularly glad to get rid of me.

We never saw or heard from the infectious disease doctor during the rest of Carol's hospital stay. He did, however, send a sizeable bill for services rendered.

"What should I do with this?" Carol asked.

I took the bill and wrote on it: "I don't know who this doctor is, and he performed no services for me." I asked her to sign it and then mailed it to the address on the bill. We never heard from him again.

Regarding the couple who brought their child to our home, suspecting he already had chicken pox, I asked Carol to make sure she never invited them again. We know for a fact that all the children who had been at our home that

New Year's Eve, several children who were at the Bat Mitzvah, and Peggy's husband all came down with chicken pox. It was not funny when Peggy told us her
husband, ever the jokester, had said, "Your family makes me sick."

---

52.   Bat Mitzvah is a Jewish coming-of-age ceremony for young ladies at or
      about age thirteen.

Carol and friends biking

New longer skis

Don, Carol, and friends

Carol speaking at Dad's retirement party, 1991

29

The Eyes Have It

During the years that Dick was consulting on the project in Egypt, I had the pleasure of accompanying him in 1990 and again in 1992. I was able to fulfill a life-long dream; I got to see the pyramids. While we were gone on my first Egyptian trip, Don was offered a job in San Francisco. By the time we returned home he had already moved there. I missed having him nearby, but he kept reminding us it was a great place for us to visit.

From 1991–94 Dick made so many trips to Egypt I told friends and family that the neighbors probably thought we were separated. A fax machine was purchased so that papers regarding the project could be sent to him instantaneously when he was home. We hadn't installed an extra phone line, so when faxes came in, the procedure became complicated. If I picked up a phone anywhere in the house and heard a fax tone, I had to go to the fax, pick up the receiver, press the start button, and replace the receivers on all other phones, running from one room to another. Ah, the joy of modern conveniences.

Dick had become hard of hearing but didn't wear his hearing aid to bed, so he couldn't hear the phone ring. Otherwise I would have had him running from room to room. After having been woken up and going through this procedure several times in the middle of night, because Egypt's time zone is ten hours later than California's, I decided to turn the ringer off on the bedroom phone and set the fax machine to pick up calls automatically. If anyone called before we were awake and out of bed, the answering machine picked up those calls also.

After Dick was finished with the project and the traveling, I found keeping the ringer off on the bedroom phone had another advantage—I wasn't awakened in the early morning hours so a telemarketer could ask if I wanted to change my long distance carrier. But there was also a disadvantage—a crisis call from Carol was picked up on the answering machine, and she had to fend for herself until I retrieved the messages.

On April 8, 1995, she tried to reach me early in the morning to no avail. Instead, she phoned her grandmother to tell her what was new. When I got up and checked the answering machine, there was this disturbing message from Carol:

"My eye started to swell in the middle of the night. I called Gilbert this morning to drive me to UCLA. I'll call you from there when I find out what's wrong. I also let Grandma know."

The message had been recorded at 8:30 AM. It was now 10:00. I phoned the medical center. They did not have her listed as a patient and had no knowledge of where she might be. When you go to the ER there's no record unless hospital admission is required.

When the phone rang, we both ran to get it. It was Mom. Her news was no more current than ours. All we could do was wait.

About 1:00 PM, Dr. Haring called. Dick spoke to him briefly and handed me the phone. He had spoken to Carol earlier and suggested she go to UCLA. Eyes, of course, weren't his specialty. After she got to UCLA and he checked, there was talk of a biopsy and wanted to let us know that there was a possibility of surgery.

The waiting was over.

Knowing the best way to find out anything was to be there, Dick and I packed for a possible four days away from home and headed for UCLA. We didn't even do our usual "Fort Knox" lock-up. The house was fairly isolated, and had five sliding glass doors and thirteen windows. We usually put separate locks requiring a key on all of them. Now that we sort of knew what was going on with Carol, we didn't want to waste any more time.

I made a call to Mom in case anyone was looking for us. I told her about Dr. Haring's call, and let her know we were heading "down the hill," as the locals called it, to the medical center.

Because we had entered the cellular phone era, I told Mom, "We'll have the cell phone with us in case anyone needs to reach us."

From where we now lived, it was one hundred twelve miles, a careful two-hour-plus trip down winding mountain roads. For most of the trip, Dick and I hardly spoke. I hadn't been feeling well the day before and figured it was probably a touch of the flu. All of a sudden that didn't seem important.

By this time, with the support group going strong, I had met, spoken to, or heard from Wegener's patients who had lost an eye to the disease. I was scared. The same words kept running through my mind during our long drive—please, not the eye!

When we finally arrived at the medical center it was late afternoon. Stopping at Reception, we asked if Carol had been admitted and we obtained a room number. Carol had spent seven hours in the ER.

We went straight to her room—a private room, which we learned later that she had to fight to get. She was on the phone with her back to us and we soon discovered that she was talking to Don. I put my arms around her from behind and kissed the top of her head.

"Oh my God," she exclaimed. "They're here."

She seemed pleased and relieved. "I called Dr. Haring and he said to come here. They had no idea what to do with me. I've been here since ten o'clock. I just got to this room a few minutes ago. I kept trying to find a phone to let you know where I was, but I couldn't see to dial."

"We had the cell phone with us and turned on," I told her.

Although we had entered that era, it had not yet become a habit to try the cell first.

"What's going on?" I asked.

She finished the call to Don and turned toward us. Both eyes were closed. The left was perfectly normal; her right eye stuck out from her face and looked to be about the size and shape of a small egg. The lid was discolored—a reddish purple. She looked like hell.

"When did all this happen?" I asked.

"In the middle of the night, about 2:30 this morning, I couldn't sleep, my eye was hurting really bad, and I started seeing double. When I looked in the mirror, I saw that it was swollen. I was afraid to drive."

"Did you have any warning or other symptoms?" Dick asked.

"Once or twice in the last few days I had a stabbing pain in my eye, but it didn't last."

"What did you do this morning?" I asked.

"I called Dr. Haring. He said it was really not his territory and suggested that I go to the UCLA ER. He said he would come down and take me if I couldn't get a ride with someone else. I told him I was sure I could get someone to take me, and then I called Gilbert."

"How far does he live from you?" Dick asked.

"About a mile or two."

"Did he stay?" I asked.

"He wanted to. He walked me in and waited with me until I was called to Admitting. Then, I told him it was OK to go home. I had no idea how long I'd be, and there was no sense in his waiting. He asked how I was going to get home, and I told him I would call someone."

"I'm really glad he was available. Has anyone reached Dr. Saxon?" Dick asked.

"He's out of town until Wednesday."

"What did they do in the ER?" I asked.

"They did a CT scan and took blood. They said my white count and sed rate[53] didn't indicate an infection, and I haven't had any fever."

"What do they think the swelling is from?" Dick asked.

"They don't really know."

Consultations were obtained from Rheumatology, Ophthalmology, and primary care physicians. The consensus was that it was an inflammation resulting from a flare-up of Wegener's, and a protocol of high dose steroids was administered.

A nurse came in and arranged two IV bags on a pole.

"What are those?" I inquired.

"One is a steroid, like Prednisone™ but in liquid form, to bring the swelling down, and the other is saline."

A young doctor came in, introduced himself as Dr. Morrison*, and told us he worked with Dr. Saxon.

"We called in Ophthalmology for an opinion. How does your eye feel, Carol?"

"It hurts a lot. Can I have something for the pain?"

"I've ordered some Percocet™."

"I know. I've already had it and it's not working."

"I'll order a Demerol™ injection."

"Why is your good eye closed?" I asked her.

"When I move the good eye, the other one moves along with it, making it hurt more."

Dr. Morrison left and two residents came in.

"We're from Rheumatology," one said, and introduced herself as Dr. Barry* and the doctor with her as Dr. Antonio*.

They asked a number of questions, taking notes all the while. Carol referred a lot of her history to me.

While they were there, an escort arrived with a wheelchair.

"We need a chest X-ray," he said.

We helped her out of bed and into the chair. I stayed in her room and continued giving Dr. Barry answers to her questions.

Carol was returned to us in a very short time. It must have been a slow day in X-ray. I called the family while she was gone. It was a good thing that she was getting Demerol™ shots. She began vomiting soon after she'd had the Percocet™. That's probably why it wasn't working. I got her out of her clothes and cleaned up. She hadn't eaten anything all day and had nothing solid in her stomach to bring up.

By 7:30 that evening, she had settled down. The Demerol™ had taken the edge off the pain.

About that time, Dr. Jonathan Corren came in to see her. We could tell that she knew him and liked him from her favorable reaction upon seeing him. He told her that Dr. Saxon was in Atlanta at a convention and wasn't expected back until Wednesday, but was reachable, if necessary.

Although dinner was brought in, Carol wanted nothing. She was back on the VIP floor; the menu featured steak and lobster. The food, arriving under a silver dome, was served by a very accommodating man in a tuxedo.

Dick and I found a place to stay nearby and got something to eat. Then I phoned the family again. They were all anxious to know what was going on.

Within the next twelve hours Carol showed no improvement. The Prednisone™ wasn't bringing the swelling down. Carol still couldn't open her eyes because the good one's movement continued to make the bad eye hurt more.

"I didn't sleep at all last night," she told us.

We stayed with her all day as a barrage of doctors, and those in training, visited. Talk of a biopsy continued. No one was sure who should do it, or what part of Carol should be cut.

She had surprise visitors that afternoon: Dr. and Mrs. Haring.

"I think you need a hug," the doctor told me.

I got one from both of them. I almost lost my self control, but remembered once again I had to be strong. I wish someone would tell me why.

"I had to come by and see for myself how she was doing," Dr. Haring said.

Listening to him, I got the impression that her vision could be in danger. He reminded us of his faith in Dr. Thompson's ability if the sinuses needed to be explored.

Several ophthalmologists from the Jules Stein Eye Institute, part of the medical center campus, paid her a visit and brought the CT scan. I was anxious to see it. They finally took it out of the large envelope and held it up to the light, pointing out a large gray area they kept referring to as a mass.

As the doctors hovered close, they questioned her and examined the good eye superficially using a hand-held eye chart. They seemed pleased that there was no apparent vision impairment. As they looked at the scan and spoke of the mass, Dick's eyes met mine. We said nothing, but each knew what the other was thinking. Mass meant only one thing to us: tumor. They spoke of a biopsy also. But still no one said when, or where on Carol they expected to cut.

A few hours later a young resident came in and explained that a needle biopsy on the swollen eye was going to be performed.

"Who's going to do the surgery?" Dick asked. He was sitting in a chair next to Carol's bed. The resident was standing near the bed.

"I am," she answered.

Dick asked, "How many of these have you done?"

"Me personally?" she asked.

"Yes."

"About ten."

I was behind her sitting in a chair against the wall, facing Dick. I shook my head and mouthed the word, no.

"Before we go any further," Dick went on, "I think we'd better get something clear. We're aware that this is a teaching hospital and we know those in training need the practice. We'd like you to understand this is nothing personal. We feel someone with more experience should do the biopsy."

I added, "She's had numerous crises over the years and has suffered a lot. We know there's always a chance that something might go wrong. We'd feel more comfortable with someone who's done one hundred of these procedures."

"No problem," she said. "We'll have the attending do it."

When Dr. Corren came in later, we explained what we'd been told.

"I'm going to call Andy and run this by him," he said. "Maybe I'll check with Ophthalmology first."

He returned within the hour.

"What are the statistics on this procedure?" I asked him.

The people in Ophthalmology tell me they do an average of one a day. It's similar to the procedure for removing cataracts. They have not had a problem resulting from a needle biopsy. Andy thinks it's the right thing to do."

He said the magic word: Andy. If it was OK with Dr. Saxon, it was OK with us. We trusted that he would see to it, even if remotely, that Carol would be well-taken care of.

Monday the Ophthalmology team was back with Dr. Robert Goldberg, who we learned was the Chief of Orbital and Ophthalmic Plastic Surgery.

"We've decided that a needle biopsy won't give us enough information. We're not sure what's in there and we need more than a few cells," Dr. Goldberg explained. "We have to get back there behind the eye."

Strangely enough, those were my thoughts.

"A tumor doesn't suddenly appear overnight," Dr. Goldberg explained. "Its progression is slow. An infection would produce other symptoms: fever, high white count, etc. We feel it's a reactivation of the Wegener's or possibly a fungal infection. We can't treat her until we know what we're treating. I have to find out what's causing this and remove it."

"How?" Dick asked.

The doctor explained that he would be making an incision in the eyelid below the eyebrow just under the bony socket that contains the eyeball.

"Will my eye go back in?" Carol asked.

"Yes," he answered.

"Who will be doing the surgery?" Dick asked.

"I will," Dr. Goldberg replied.

"Who will assist?" he questioned further.

"I will," Dr. Kaplan* answered.

"Dr. Kaplan is the one I gave such a hard time in the ER," Carol explained.

The doctor made no comment.

"What effect will this have on my vision?" Carol wanted to know.

"If we're lucky, none," Dr. Goldberg answered.

"I won't be seeing double anymore?"

"That's the idea."

"When are we going to do this?" I asked.

"Tomorrow morning."

"Will you be doing the surgery yourself?" I asked again. I had to make sure we weren't going to have any amateurs doing this.

"Yes, I will," he answered.

"Someone will bring the forms in for you to sign shortly and I'll see you in the morning," the doctor said. "Do you have any more questions?"

None of us did. We thanked him and he left.

Surgery was scheduled for Tuesday morning. Carol had been in the hospital since Saturday morning.

"What happened in ER?" I asked Carol when the doctors left.

"Well, they really didn't know what to do with me or who to call. After several doctors examined me, I wanted to let you know what was going on. I told them I wasn't signing anything or going anywhere until I let my parents know what's going on. Dr. Kaplan shrugged and walked out. I thought he was upset with me. If I'd known he might be operating on me, I wouldn't have given him such a hard time."

I didn't notice any animosity on Dr. Kaplan's part. I hoped he didn't hold any grudges.

The young lady resident brought in the surgical consent forms. We noted that Dr. Goldberg's name was on the form as the surgeon. Carol signed where she was told and gave it back to the doctor.

Most of the other times she'd been in the hospital, she'd hardly eaten. This time she said she was hungry. It was difficult for her to see what she was doing, so she asked me to feed her.

As she sat there with her mouth open wide awaiting each morsel she remarked, "I feel like a baby bird waiting for a worm."

The anesthetic for the surgery was to be a local. Carol wanted to make sure that she would not be conscious. The explanation didn't reassure her, so I explained how a procedure I'd had done recently was supposed to be with a local. As far as I knew, I was asleep and remembered nothing even though the doctor told me I was semi-awake and talking to him while the procedure was taking place. I assumed she would be in a similar condition.

Later that day Carol had a visit from Dr. Hahn. It appeared that she had just come by to pay her respects. The young rheumatologist residents had probably told her what was going on. It seemed that most of the doctors were convinced that the current problem was a reactivation of the WG. Dr. Hahn sat down on the bed and took Carol's hand in hers.

"How have you been, Carol?"

"Great up until this." She pointed to her eye.

"Do they think it's Wegener's?"

"They don't know. It's one of the possibilities. If it is, I'll probably have to go back on Leukeran™."

"So you've been off for a while?"

"Three years."

"How disappointing for you."

I was impressed. She didn't do any preaching or try to remind Carol of WG facts we already knew. She just let Carol know she cared. What a nice thing to do, I thought. Doctors like that probably never get sued.

"Well, I wish you luck, Carol. What does Andy think?"

"He's in Atlanta."

"Oh, yes. The allergy convention. Who's doing the surgery?"

"Dr. Goldberg."

"Not to worry, dear. You're in good hands."

We complimented her young protégés, Drs. Barry and Antonio. She agreed with us that they'll do well and left, wishing Carol good luck again.

The surgery was scheduled for 10:00 AM. Shortly before then we were told that Dr. Goldberg was behind schedule and she wasn't taken down to the eye clinic until almost noon.

About an hour later the doctors found us in the waiting room. The looks on their faces told us the news was good.

"There's no tumor, there's no sign of Wegener's and there's no fungus. She had a mucocele[54] in the frontal sinus that got infected and couldn't drain anywhere," Dr. Goldberg reported.

We'd heard the lack of drainage story before.

"The mass grew," he continued, "pressure built up, and it broke a blood vessel. When that happened it caused the swelling and pushed through the thin bone behind the eye and into the eye socket. That, in turn, pushed the eye forward.

"We removed the mass and cleaned out the orbit. Her eye went back into the socket and she tolerated the surgery well. We'll be taking the bandage off later today and she can probably go home tomorrow."

"How about her vision?" Dick asked.

"We won't know until she wakes up and tells us. I don't anticipate any change in her vision from before all this occurred."

Moments later the nurse who had brought her down to surgery came out with what appeared to be an empty gurney with an IV pole and bag attached to it.

"Aren't you coming with us?" she asked.

"Is she in there?" I asked.

"She sure is."

She certainly wasn't making much of a lump on the gurney. I walked over and looked through the bedrail. One sleepy eye looked back at me. The other was bandaged.

"Did you hear the good news?"

I saw a faint smile.

"Yes," she answered.

"Hi, sweetie," Dick called from behind me. "We got lucky."

Carol was returned to her room from recovery. When the bandage was removed later that day, she reported that she could see fine. There was no change in her vision. Her eye was back in her head where it belonged, but the incision was red and ugly. I wondered if it would fade and whether there would be a prominent scar. I hoped that if I didn't say it out loud, it wouldn't happen. It looked awful.

Carol was released on the twelfth and we took her back to her place. We weren't sure what to do with her. We wanted to take her back to Big Bear with us, but she felt it was too far from the hospital in case she needed to go back.

She came up with a plan; she got on the phone and called a few of her friends. When she told them what had happened, they decided to take turns staying with her and getting her food. She was told she would be out of commission for about a week, and would not be able to drive for two weeks. Dick and I stayed in town an extra day and then went home.

Her friends took care of her the rest of the week, and we came down from the mountains to take her to her follow-up visit. It had been a week since the surgery and the scar was practically invisible. The doctor had done a fabulous job, and more importantly, she could see just fine. We survived one more crisis.

Although Carol's vision was unaltered after the surgery to remove the mass, she was still experiencing pain and pressure behind the right eye. Scans and X-rays were taken, but there was nothing that any doctor could discern that was causing the pain.

Carol was back to taking pain medicine, and the pain was beginning to interfere with work. She took time off when she needed it and worked when the pain was manageable. She started going back to the Pain Clinic at UCLA. The doctors tried injections and various other treatments, along with the pain pills. For the most part, the relief was temporary, lasting about three days if she was lucky. Sometimes the treatments did nothing at all to relieve the pain.

By the beginning of 1997 she was unable to work regular hours. Fortunately, she had paid off her car, but, unfortunately, not her condo. With her income greatly reduced she was finding it increasingly difficult to make mortgage and utility payments. I would often call and get a disconnect message. When I couldn't reach her by phone, I panicked. I couldn't visit her because the condo was in a security building. In order to let someone in who didn't have a key, she had to answer her phone. It didn't make sense for us to drive to Pasadena with the hope of seeing her if we couldn't get into the building. One time when I hadn't spoken to Carol for what seemed like a long time, I asked Tracey to pay her a visit and report back to me. I knew Tracey had a key to her building and apartment.

When Tracey called me, she was very worried.

"Carol seemed happy to see me, but I didn't like the way she looked. She was pale and didn't seem to have any energy. The apartment was a mess. She used to keep it so nice and clean. What can we do?"

I knew she couldn't go on the way she was, but I couldn't force her to make the changes I felt were necessary.

I was besieged with other medical problems.

In 1995, less than six months after he actually retired, Dick was diagnosed with prostate cancer and later that year had to have a radical prostatectomy.[55] We were still living in Big Bear Lake, and it didn't take us long to discover that the local medical care was minimal and totally inadequate for those suffering from anything other than minor ailments. The local hospital was great for setting broken legs, after all, we lived in a ski resort town; but one couldn't even have a baby there. For most of the medical appointments, particularly where Dick was concerned, we found ourselves having to go down the hill. The closest place for the quality of care we were used to was in Palm Springs. It was about eighty-two miles and took over an hour and a half to drive there. After having spent only four years in our dream home, and realizing we were spending more time off the hill than on, we decided we had to sell it and move to the desert.

We often found ourselves asking each other, what were we thinking when we decided to retire to the mountains? As one gets older, there's no question that one needs to be where there are sufficient doctors and hospitals available.

We sold the house in 1996 and bought a new one in Palm Desert. The sale was completed in September, and the new house wouldn't be ready until February, 1997. We figured it was a great opportunity to see the country, so we started off on a road trip in October 1996.

In December we returned to a rented condo to await the completion of our *second* retirement home and moved into it in March.

Carol was already starting to feel like she couldn't function like a normal person, and the pain was getting progressively worse.

Dr. Haring suggested she see Dr. Dale Rice, a head and neck doctor at USC Medical Center who had written a book on problems such as hers. After a few appointments and a number of scans and X-rays, he suggested surgery. The plan was to cut into her head above the hairline and pull the skin down, allowing access to the frontal sinuses, and do a total obliteration.[56] It was similar to something Dr. Thompson had wanted to do a few years before. It seemed like a really drastic approach. I found out the name of the doctor's text book and looked it up online. I was able to get a print-out of the pages describing in great detail what the doctor proposed. He obviously knew what he was doing well enough to teach it to other doctors.

In the meantime, Carol asked Dr. Saxon for his opinion. His answer was, "He wrote the book. He's the one to do it."

With everyone concurring, Dick and I both felt comfortable, but Carol didn't. Although she liked and seemed to trust Dr. Rice, she was concerned because he would be drilling through her forehead into the sinuses. In addition, she was unfamiliar with the facility. She knew her way around UCLA like the back of her hand by now, but knew nothing about USC.

"Where would the surgery take place?" Dick asked, knowing that USC was responsible for running Los Angeles County Medical Center. We weren't anxious to have Carol in the hospital referred to as County General.

"My private patients go to University Hospital, right across the street," Dr. Rice told us.

That made us all feel much more comfortable, and the surgery was scheduled.

The day before the operation was to take place, Carol was notified by Dr. Rice's scheduler that the insurance information given to her was no longer valid; the policy had been cancelled due to non-payment. With all the pain and discomfort she was experiencing she neglected to make the payment in a timely manner. She had no choice but to cancel the surgery. I'm reminded that Carol always says there are no coincidences.

Carol got through the year of 1997 working when she could, but the writing was on the wall. Drs. Haring and Saxon continued to see her when it was necessary and found ways around her not having insurance.

Not too long after her insurance was cancelled, I applied for Social Security and when it was approved I became eligible for Medicare. I then had to search for an insurance policy, a Medicare supplement, for myself.

Dick kept prodding me to ask about insurance for Carol. I had previously called three agents I knew who dealt with medical insurance. They all told me she was out of luck and up the creek—uninsurable.

I called a fourth agent for information for myself and, after I arranged for my own insurance, he asked if there was anything else he could do for me.

"I also need insurance for my daughter," I told him.

After getting her name and age, he then asked, "And she's in good health?"

As Shakespeare might have said, "Aye, there's the rub."

I told him about Carol's health history and the circumstances of her cancellation.

"Is there anything you can do for her?" I asked.

I got lucky. Maybe there really are no coincidences.

"As a matter of fact there is," he answered.

I held my breath.

"There's something called the California Fair Plan that insures the uninsurable."

He explained what it was and how it worked.

"I will send you an application for normal insurance for her. Have her fill it out, write a check in the amount required, and get it back to me. I'll submit it and she will be rejected. I'll then submit a new application with a new check, along with the rejection letter, to the California Fair Plan.

"Her first check will be returned. The CFP does not insure anyone themselves but subsidizes companies to insure the uninsurable."

"It was my understanding that one couldn't approach the CFP unless there had been three rejections," I told him.

"Not so. Do what I suggested and she will be covered. There's usually a waiting list, so it may take as long as three to six months, but she will be accepted."

"Is the cost exorbitant?"

"It will probably be about the same as she has been paying," he told me.

I did exactly as he suggested, and Carol was approved by the CFP in about six weeks. The cost was slightly less than her previous insurance, and the coverage was more comprehensive. The insurer was, once again, Blue Cross of California.

By the middle of 1998, the bank foreclosed on Carol's condo. She sold what she could of her furniture, put the rest of her things in storage, and moved in with us in the desert.

53.　Sed rate is the informal term for erythrocyte sedimentation rate, the rate at which red blood cells settle out in a tube of unclotted blood, expressed in millimeters per hour.

54.　A mucocele is mucous retention cyst.

55.　Prostatectomy is the total excision of the prostate gland as performed for malignancy.

56.　Obliteration means to remove a body organ or part completely by surgery.

30

Bodies in Trouble

In December, 1998, Dick, Carol, and I made a return visit to the Mayo Clinic. Our previous visit had been so rewarding, we wondered if the doctors there had any new ideas for dealing with Carol's current problem of chronic pain.

Dr. McDonald was as wonderful as before, but he had nothing new or different to offer for her current condition—ongoing excruciating pain which she experienced twenty-four hours a day, every day. He made a point of telling us that if we were still in Rochester on Christmas Day, which was fast approaching, we were invited to dinner at his home. We had no doubt that he meant it.

Dr. DeRemee had retired, and Carol was referred to Dr. Ulrich Specks for whatever examinations she required that weren't in the domain of an ENT.

She also saw Dr. James Garrity, an ophthalmologist and a delightfully amusing man with his ongoing handshake, who gave her some ideas on getting a handle on the pain. Unfortunately none of them worked.

Consultations were arranged with orthopedics and pain management departments. According to orthopedics, they felt that her height had decreased due to bone loss, a side effect of the numerous times she was given Prednisone™. Pain management suggestions were for behavior modifications exercises.

Dr. McDonald arranged for a consultation with a plastic surgeon regarding the reconstruction of her collapsed nose. It was interesting, but nothing she wanted to pursue at that time.

We were looking for a miracle this time and, unfortunately, the Mayo Clinic was fresh out!

The general consensus among the doctors Carol saw was that there might have been some nerve damage that occurred during the surgery to remove the mass from behind her eye, or from scar tissue that formed in the aftermath. That would explain why nothing showed up on X-rays or scans.

Dr. Haring wrote a referral to the local pain clinic in the desert, and she began seeing Dr. Michael Gold, who ran the clinic, monthly. He was friendly, personable, caring, and compassionate, and tried everything there was to try including injections of various substances, cryogenics, acupressure, acupuncture, and topical analgesics.

He kept Carol on a very short leash as far as pain medicines were concerned. If the next appointment happened to fall on a day when he was in surgery—most pain management doctors are also anesthesiologists—she had to beg his associates for a new prescription.

Many of the drugs used for pain control are narcotics, which in California required a different prescription than other drugs and could not be renewed by a phone call from the doctor. Unfortunately, these drugs had also become popular with recreational drug users, which made them expensive and hard to get.

We talked about the possibility of nerve damage with Dr. Gold, and he told us there was good news and bad news. He could actually kill the nerve that served that specific place in her anatomy and it might actually kill the pain. The bad news was that if it didn't stop the pain, no doctor would have any recourse and there would be nothing left to offer her in the way of relief. Additionally, she might begin to experience phantom pain, such as an amputee might, and again there would be no way to deal with it. As if that weren't enough, Carol would have no feeling in that area near her eye. She wouldn't have the capacity to blink automatically as the rest of us do if something attacked the eye, such as wind carrying bits of leaves or dirt, or perhaps something hot coming near that area.

If that were to occur, her cornea could become scratched or damaged and her vision would suffer. Obviously, that wasn't the answer for her.

At the same time, Dick began having serious pain in his hip. He could certainly commiserate with Carol. We thought it was probably arthritis; after all, we were getting older and had to expect those old-age ailments to interfere with our lives. He was treated with the usual medicines, but nothing was working. The pain was becoming more severe, and a number of tests were taken.

In spite of his own troubles, he continued to concern himself with Carol's problems. He suggested I look into the possibility of disability payments for her. She'd certainly paid plenty of money into the system while she was working. Actually, she could have filed for disability several times in the past, but had felt that regardless of what got her down, she would be able to bounce back and make up the deficit. That definitely wasn't happening this time.

I made a call to Social Security and, after hearing the explanation of what Carol's disability was, the person on the phone looked up her work record.

"From what you're telling me, she certainly qualifies and she's already paid enough into the system to get the maximum benefits. Tell me where to send the forms," he said.

She filed for disability in February, 1999, a year that brought us great tragedy. On February 11, two months before her eighty-eighth birthday, Mom died.

I barely had time to mourn her when Dick was diagnosed with metastatic cancer of an unknown primary site. The day we got the news, I walked into the house and headed straight to the phone so I could talk to Mom and be comforted. I picked up the receiver and had half her number dialed before I remembered that she was gone—forever.

A few weeks later, Carol's claim for disability was denied, citing that she wasn't disabled or blind under Social Security rules. We were floored! How can someone who suffers from pain twenty-four/seven not be disabled? I got out the phone book and began to look for attorneys who handle this type of claim. I was amazed. There were several pages of lawyers who did nothing but Social Security appeals.

I chose one who was in the same city as we were and made an appointment. When Carol and I walked in the door, we had the correspondence that had taken place between Social Security and us, along with the forms that the doctors had submitted, as well as the complete file containing her medical history from the very beginning of her illness.

Instead of seeing the attorney, as we thought would happen, we were met by a lady who introduced herself as a paralegal.

"Tell me what Carol's disability is," she said.

Carol told her story in a nutshell.

"OK, here's the problem," the paralegal explained.

"If you're blind or visibly crippled, you will probably be approved the first time. If not, and you're under forty, you'll probably be turned down. If you're between forty and fifty, you have a 50 percent chance either way. If you're over fifty, you'll probably be approved.

"What you need to do is file an appeal."

She walked away from the desk and returned in a few moments with a form. Then she proceeded to tell us how to fill it out. In her opinion, we gave too much information and did not sufficiently explain that it wasn't the disease that prevented Carol from working; it was the resulting pain from damage that had been caused by the disease and/or the eye surgery. We might never know which.

"You have to understand that the people who are evaluating the information you sent probably do not have the education that you do. They don't understand many of the medical terms. You have to make it simple."

Carol filed a "Request for Reconsideration." There is a place on the form that states: I do not agree with the determination made on the above claim and request reconsideration. My reasons are …

Carol filled in this message:

"The return letter misstates my condition. I am *not* claiming a disability due to Wegener's Granulomatosis, a disease with which I have a twenty-year history. Rather I have suffered nerve damage and debilitating facial pain resulting from a recent surgery. It appears that I was not properly evaluated on this condition alone."

The form included a section to name a representing attorney, which she did. She submitted this new form on June 12, 1999.

On May 8, 2000, Carol's claim for disability was approved and payments began.

Meanwhile, Dick's doctors felt that the "new" cancer had nothing to do with the previous episode of prostate cancer because the pathologists were seeing a different type of cell under the microscope. The new cancer was now in the neck of the left femur.[57]

Before the year ended he had two surgeries on his upper leg. It became obvious that he would not recover and went into a deep depression. His condition required psychotherapy which lasted for several years. The few doctors who would actually give him a prognosis told him he had about two years to live.

Now I had both Dick and Carol to care for, or, if I looked at it another way, watch two people I dearly loved suffer.

Carol did her best to offer support, but she was still spending the better part of the day in bed because the pain medicine played havoc with her sleep patterns, and she often was unable to sleep at night. The doctors told her that it was not unusual for narcotics to disrupt sleep patterns; we could see that happening in spades.

Although the WG still appeared to be in remission, Carol was troubled by other ailments besides the head pain.

Several times a year she would get what looked like a pimple on one of her fingers and once or twice it appeared on her toes. It would come to a head, like an infection; she'd be given antibiotics and it would go away. These infections seemed to be coming more and more often.

During 1999–2000, she began experiencing what we used to call blood poisoning, now referred to as septicemia.[58] A finger would get infected, swell up and red streaks would begin going up her arm. Several times I had to take her to an urgent care center for antibiotic injections.

In March of 2000 she had a very swollen, infected finger, and I was able to get her in to see our family doctor. He listened to her history, took a look at the hand and arm, and felt she needed to be hospitalized. If blood poisoning gets to the heart, it could be fatal.

By the time we got home and she'd packed a few things, it was after normal admitting hours and we were sent to the ER. Those medical personnel who were in attendance kept her waiting a long time because, after all, an infection in the finger takes a back seat to the usual ER complaints.

Finally a doctor came in to see her and said, "We don't hospitalize people for an infection in their finger."

"I'm sure you don't under normal circumstances, but she's a Wegener's granulomatosis patient," I told him.

We got the usual blank stare.

"What's that?" he asked.

"An autoimmune disease that …," Carol began to answer.

Before she had a chance to finish her sentence, he left the examining room telling us, "I'll be right back."

Since AIDS had reached epidemic proportions, autoimmune had become a dirty word. When the doctor returned, he informed us that, as per Carol's doctor's orders, she would, indeed, be admitted so that antibiotics could be administered intravenously.

While she was in the hospital, a general surgeon was called in for a consultation. X-rays were taken of the offending finger and fortunately no bone damage was evident. The surgeon did excise the abscess and sent it out to be cultured. Nothing grew.

During this hospital stay she was only hooked up to an IV a few times during the day for the administration of the antibiotic; the rest of the time she was unattached and was actually able to eat.

When she was released, Carol was referred to an infectious disease specialist who saw her several times. The specialist believed that the infections stemmed from the colonization of bacteria that never left her system. An infection could be treated, but the germs were dormant between times of eruptions.

The doctor felt it would be advisable to keep Carol on a low-dose antibiotic which she was to take daily for a period of time. She was given two prescriptions, the first for the low-dose antibiotic and the second for a high potency one to use when flare-ups occurred.

They seemed to work. She took the low dose medicine for about a year, and now when eruptions occur she has been able to keep them from getting out of hand, no pun intended. She no longer takes the antibiotics on a regular basis but only when necessary.

---

57.   Femur is the leg bone that extends from the hip to the knee, also known as the thighbone.

58.   Septicemia is a systemic infection in which pathogens (microorganisms capable of producing disease) are present in the circulating blood stream, having spread from an infection in any part of the body.

31

Coast to Coast

During the summer of 2001, I had to have some minor surgery as an outpatient and should have walked out of the hospital within a few hours.

I'd had to cancel the surgery once because Carol was not in good enough shape to take me and wait to bring me home. So Don took a few days off from work and came down from San Francisco to take care of all of us, drive me to the hospital, and wait with me in recovery. That way Carol wouldn't have to worry about taking care of Dick and me when she could hardly take care of herself.

Although Dick's surgeries had healed, probably enough for him to drive, he had developed a rare form of glaucoma, one they called narrow angle. His eyesight was rapidly deteriorating.

I was told that while awakening from the anesthesia, I had what was termed a laryngeal spasm and had to be intubated.[59] I was placed in ICU overnight for observation although the tube had been removed. I was fine and came home the next day.

But the whole episode sparked questions about moving away from our home in the desert. We needed more help, but where would we go? We began to evaluate our options.

If I was out of commission for something that wasn't long lasting, such as surgery to correct something, or a broken leg, we would need someone to help with the housekeeping and take care of all of us. Live-in or daily help would be expensive and impractical, so it would have to be one of the boys.

Ron was the closest one, geographically, at two and a half hours away by car. But he traveled from time to time for his job, and had contracted diabetes himself, so living closer to him wasn't practical.

Don wanted us to move to San Francisco, but the housing costs there were way beyond our budget.

Ken had worked for the same company in Florida for several years, and was able to visit us in California at least once a year, sometimes twice. But he couldn't afford to take a leave of absence from work to care for us on the other side of the country.

So logic dictated we move to Florida. Housing costs were reasonable, and Ken would be able to help out without it creating a burden for him. There was an added advantage in that Bea and Doris had become Florida residents also.

The final hurdle was that a move might create medical insurance problems. No one in Florida wanted to insure Dick or Carol because of their health histories. I spoke to several people at our insurer, Blue Cross of California, and was able to get a written commitment that, as long as we paid the premium, it would cover us no matter where we lived.

The cost of Carol's insurance has continued to increase approximately every two years. At the time of this writing, she is paying upwards of $8,400 a year, almost 50 percent of her disability income.

Because Carol was born in California and had only been to Florida for three short trips, Dick and I thought she might like a longer visit. In August, perhaps the hottest, most humid time of year, we sent her to stay with Ken for a month.

He was moving and she could help him with packing and unpacking, returning his similar favor when she'd had to make a move.

Her original reservations showed her return date as September 13, 2001, two days after the tragedies of 9/11 took place. Obviously no airplanes were flying yet, so she stayed put.

It was an extra treat for Ken to have his sister with him longer, but Carol would shortly be running out of her pain medications. She couldn't just walk into a doctor's office or an urgent care clinic there and expect to be given narcotics.

"I had to change my reservation for eight days later," she said. "I don't know what to do about medicine. I won't have enough."

I called Dr. Gold and told him about her dilemma.

"Come in tomorrow," he offered, "and I'll give you another prescription for her."

I picked up the prescription the next day and took it to be filled. With pills in hand, packed and ready to ship, I went to the post office intending to send the medicine by express mail. There was a problem I hadn't anticipated: the airmail planes were still grounded. Now what?

I reported back to Carol, and Dick came up with a great suggestion.

"Tell her to go into the local hospital ER and explain her situation. If the doctors there need confirmation of her condition, they can call Dr. Gold in California."

It was one of those few times that the three-hour time difference would work in her favor.

I phoned Dr. Gold and apprised him of the situation, requesting that he give any physicians who called from Florida whatever information they needed in order to prescribe for Carol. He told me he would assist in any way necessary.

The next morning, before eight, Carol went to the local hospital ER. Once again, because she wasn't facing an emergency, she spent close to eight hours in the waiting area, checking every so often to see where she placed on their list.

With no knowledge of how difficult it would be to have a prescription filled, assuming the doctors there would even give her one, she begged and pleaded, hoping to get the magic piece of paper before the pharmacies closed. She had brought her prescription bottles showing what medicines had been prescribed, a Wegener's brochure for the doctors' information, and a business card of Dr. Gold's in case they wanted to phone him.

She was given prescriptions for three days' worth of pills. She actually took two different kinds of pills. One was a long-acting medicine that was to be taken every twelve hours; the other was a breakthrough pain reliever in case she was still in pain between the twelve-hour doses, which was often.

She had the prescriptions filled, and just barely had enough to tide her over before the medicine I'd sent arrived.

Because a move would affect all three of us, we needed Carol's approval.

"We'll have to find new doctors all around. How would you feel about that?" I asked Carol.

"Living here with you, I'm too far from either Dr. Haring or Dr. Saxon to see them on a regular basis. Besides, with the Wegener's in remission, my current problem is pain management, and I'm sure that specialty is practiced as much in Florida as it is here," she offered. "Besides," she added, "Dr. Gold is leaving for a job in another state," and she was unimpressed with his associates.

"You'll be leaving all your friends. How do you feel about that?" I asked.

"How often do I see any of them?"

Since she had been with us, she had hardly left the house for anything social. Regretfully, for all intents and purposes, she had no life.

We all agreed going to Florida was a logical move. With that in mind, we put the house up for sale in October.

We had been in our *second* retirement home for five years.

We found a home in Boynton Beach, and now had to find new doctors—for everybody. I began searching for pain clinics and made appointments for Carol with one after the other.

None of them seemed to be what we were looking for. The ultimate was the doctor who came into the examining room, crossed his arms and declared, "If you've come here looking for drugs, I'm not going to give you any."

We had brought copies with us, to each doctor, of Carol's medical history back to April, 1995, when the eye surgery had been performed. I don't know if any of them bothered to read any of it, or if they were intimidated with the volume of information they might have to plow through.

I could not believe that pain specialists could be so insensitive. Carol wasn't necessarily looking for pills. She was looking for anything that might help her get relief that would last longer than three days.

The only treatment that seemed to work for any length of time was one that a neurologist in California had performed just before we left there.

It was called a stellate[60] ganglion[61] nerve block[62] and gave her a significant amount of pain relief that lasted for upwards of three weeks. In Florida, two different pain specialists tried that same nerve block multiple times but with no success.

After several unsuccessful excursions to pain doctors and neurologists, a tearful Carol and I sat down with our new family doctor, Barry Schultz, looking for some guidance. What we hadn't yet known was that Dr. Schultz had been a hospice doctor before going into private practice, and was well-versed in pain management.

He requested that Carol sign an agreement that she would not seek pain medication from any other doctor, which she was happy to do. She was also required to come in for an appointment every time she needed a prescription renewal, usually monthly. He listened to what we had to say and answered the questions we asked, all while seated, with the door closed, and with his full attention. He makes it a point to ask, "What can I do for you today?" bringing our tales of woe to a conclusion. We consider ourselves lucky to have found him.

Could this be just another coincidence?

Although Carol has drug coverage with her Medicare supplement, the policy has a maximum per year. Because the narcotics are expensive, she began to reach the maximum by the beginning of fall, at which time the cost of the narcotics would jump to nearly $1200 a month. Between that and her insurance premium, the cost became prohibitive, and considerably more than her disability income. Dr. Schultz was able to find a cheaper pain medicine for her, not as effective as the expensive drug, but one that did control the pain—most of the time.

I learned that there was never a time when she was without pain. Still, she hardly complained.

In spite of his geriatric specialty designation, Dr. Schultz has been a good fit for Carol. At the time of this writing she's forty-five years old, but many of her problems are similar to those of the elderly, such as osteoporosis, menopause, and hearing loss.

After performing another bone density study, Dr. Schultz felt that Carol should be treated for the osteoporosis. He prescribed an injectable drug called Forteo to be taken daily. One of the doctor's assistants showed Carol how to inject herself. This drug added $256 a month to her co-pay, after her insurance paid its share.

One of our local support group patients told us about a head and neck surgeon, Dr. Roy R. Casiano, who practices at the University of Miami Medical Center, with an outstanding reputation for solving sinus problems.

Dr. Casiano has since performed two surgeries on Carol's frontal sinuses, creating a tiny hole in the bone and cleaning out the infectious tissue that had built up with nowhere to drain. Both times she was able to get enough relief to cut her pain medicine dosage in half for a few months. Unfortunately, the hole closes up over time, the infection returns, and we may have to repeat the surgery in the future; but at least we know where to have it done.

---

59.   When a person is intubated a breathing tube is passed into a body aperture such as the mouth or nose or into the trachea to insure a patient airway for the delivery of an anesthetic gas or oxygen.

60.   Stellate refers to a star shape or arranged in the pattern of stars.

61.   Ganglion is a knot or knot-like mass of nerve cells chiefly collected in groups outside the central nervous system.

62.   Nerve block means the injection of a local anesthetic into or near a local pain sensitive trigger point.

32

A Battle Won?

Just when we thought Carol was holding her own, toward the end of 2004 she developed a suspicious lump in her right groin. My first thought was perhaps the Cytoxan™ was still causing trouble. Anti-cancer drugs are known to cause cancer—a disconcerting paradox.

An ultrasound revealed a mass of some sort.

We took Carol to Dick's oncologist for his opinion. Both he and Dr. Schultz said it would probably have to be biopsied and removed. We were pointed in the direction of a general surgeon who performed the biopsy.

The local pathologists could not agree on what it might, or might not, be. Although it didn't appear to be cancer, the original and disturbing diagnosis was lymphoma.

After two weeks of indecision on the part of the pathologists, Dick suggested the specimen be sent to a larger facility for another opinion. The slides were sent to Johns Hopkins, and the answer came back that the lump was a neurofibroma.[63] Although it wasn't a malignant growth, it did need to be removed.

Because of the difficulty of diagnosing the lump, we had lost confidence in the local surgeon and pathologists. Carol was scheduled to see Dr. Casiano for a recheck, and we asked him if he knew of a general surgeon in Miami.

Dick and I felt that with all of Carol's history, we wanted someone at a major medical center to remove it. The mass was close to the femoral artery, and we didn't want to take any chances with less experienced surgeons. The doctor suggested we make an appointment with Dr. Alan Livingstone, the Chairman of the Department of Surgery, also at the U of M Medical Center.

"He would know the appropriate surgeon for Carol," Dr. Casiano told us.

Dr. Livingstone was friendly and personable, and we all liked him immediately. After examining Carol and reviewing her history, he told us he would be doing the surgery himself.

More tests were taken in Miami because, as usual, each doctor wants his own, and the surgery was scheduled for the end of January. That would give Carol some time to recover from the sinus surgery that Dr. Casiano would be performing at the beginning of the same month.

"I'll probably keep her overnight to make sure everything is OK," Dr. Livingstone told us.

We made appropriate plans to stay in Miami. Ken went with us as he had done before when Carol's two sinus surgeries were performed, partly as moral support for us and partly to help Dick who had become severely handicapped. However difficult it was for Dick to get around, it was more important for him to be with and support his little girl.

"The lump was very close to the surface," Dr. Livingstone reported to us, "and not a problem to remove. It lifted out easily. Although it appears to be benign, it was sent to Pathology to make sure."

When Carol was brought to Recovery, we were able to sit with her. One of the problems we have encountered when she has surgery is that she has built up a tolerance for pain medications and needs stronger drugs than the usual ones in order to relieve the post-operative pain. As with her previous two sinus surgeries here in Florida, we put the staff, and particularly the anesthesiologist, on notice that she would require stronger pain control. Those attending to patients in Recovery are unable to administer more or stronger pain medicine than the doctor orders. Each time, we had to insist that someone put in a call to whoever made the decisions, and get an order for whatever Carol needed.

We were pleasantly surprised to find Dr. Livingstone himself checking on Carol in Recovery. He proceeded to give a direct order for more pain medicine.

"She's doing so well, I'm going to send her home today," he said, and asked us to come back for a follow-up appointment in a month.

When we returned the next month, Dr. Livingstone informed us that the tumor was indeed benign, checked the incision, and told us he wouldn't need to see Carol again.

As we were on the way home, Carol said, "This is what an illness is supposed to be like. Once it's diagnosed, it should be treated and cured, not drag on indefinitely."

That would have been great but, unfortunately, all too often that's not the case.

Because of Carol's past bladder problems, we felt the need to include a urologist in her circle of consultants. Through Dr. Schultz we found Dr. Benjamin Tripp, who specializes in bladder surgery and bladder cancer. He understood the damage that cyclophosphamide can cause, recognized what Carol had been through, and knew what to look for during her periodic check-ups. We liked and felt comfortable with him right from the initial appointment. We consider ourselves lucky to have found him, also.

Because it had been a few years since Carol's last series of pain management appointments, we thought it was time to pursue an up-to-date evaluation.

After a recent appointment with Dr. Tripp, we discovered a pain doctor in the office next door to his and made an appointment.

Carol was given papers to fill out, and when she brought them back to the office she was told by the receptionist, "We can't treat you as long as you're on painkillers."

"I'm not asking for drugs. I'm looking for an alternative," Carol told her.

"Well, you have to be off drugs before we can treat you," was the response.

"If I didn't need the drugs I wouldn't need you," Carol responded.

At that point the lady handed Carol a brochure for a rehabilitation center for people with problems of drug addiction.

"Once you're off all drugs, come back and we'll make an appointment."

Carol and I couldn't believe what we were hearing and relayed the incident to Dr. Schultz at her next visit.

"It's very difficult in this day and age for doctors to spot those people who are trying to scam drugs," he told us.

"It's obvious that that pain doctor isn't the one for Carol," I added.

"We're also having trouble getting her prescriptions for the pain medications filled. The local chain pharmacies don't seem to have the drugs Carol needs in the quantity she takes.

"I called a number of independent pharmacies and finally found one who said they could fill her prescription. When I arrived and gave the prescription to a clerk, the pharmacist came out to tell me she felt her license would be in jeopardy if she filled the prescription I had brought in for the amount prescribed and refused to do so," I told the doctor.

He suggested a pharmacy that knows him, and that his other patients use with no problems. He was absolutely right; they've filled every prescription we've brought to them.

We were now more motivated than ever to find a better solution.

I started looking for Web sites that deal with chronic pain, thinking that perhaps if I could find a support group for pain sufferers, then the people attending it might give Carol some insight as to which doctors seemed to have a handle on treating someone with her problems.

Although not finding that information, I did find a Web site that pointed out how our government discriminates against those with chronic pain, and ties the hands of the doctors who treat it by limiting what they're able to prescribe. The only ones who didn't seem to have trouble getting drugs were the scammers who didn't have an actual medical need for them in the first place. War on drugs, indeed!

When Carol had the sinus surgeries, known as nasal/sinus endoscopies, she was given a pre-op evaluation by Dr. John Deo, an anesthesiologist. While discussing pain management with us, he suggested Carol consult with Dr. Dennis Patin. Dr. Deo said Dr. Patin had a lot of success in treating difficult cases.

The U of M Medical Center is over an hour away in heavy traffic, and not convenient if Carol would need to be seen weekly. But because we always had Dr. Patin in the back of our minds, I suggested it might be time to bite the bullet and make the trip.

At Carol's first appointment, Dr. Patin looked over the history and scans he asked her to bring. He seemed to be very pleasant, low key, and soft-spoken.

"Because you've been having this pain for twelve years, it may not be something I can cure," he said. "However, I'm willing to try anything, even if it's been tried before. I try to give my patients hope."

I liked his manner.

"The one treatment that seemed to work longer than three days was the stellate ganglion nerve block she received just before she left California," I told him.

"Well, we could certainly try that again. I'll set you up for one at your next appointment," he told Carol.

Then he said, "There's a new medication I'd like to try that's specifically for neuropathic pain. It's pretty expensive. I'll give you some samples. If it happens to work we can cancel the nerve block and have a social appointment next time."

Carol was to take the drug, Lyrica™, once a day for the first week and twice a day for the rest of the month until she saw the doctor again. The strength given was seventy-five milligrams.

The day after she took the first dose, she was up early in the day to tell me, "You're not going to believe this, but I'm pain free! The bad news is that I feel dizzy and kind of like I'm drunk."

I could hardly believe my ears. It was the first time in twelve years I had heard her use the words "pain" and "free" in the same sentence. It was almost too good to be true. Talk about miracles!

"Should we be kicking ourselves by not having gone to Dr. Patin a year or two ago?"

"I don't know, Mom. Maybe the time wasn't right. He did say it was a fairly new medicine."

She was correct, of course. We couldn't go backward, only forward.

During the next few weeks she began keeping track of her pain level and I was surprised and overjoyed to find that while the drunk/dizzy feeling didn't last, the drug continued to address the pain favorably. We dared not hope that this might be a solution. Nothing else had lasted very long.

At the next visit to Dr. Patin he was happy to learn the drug was working. Carol had been able to cut her pain medicine in half and, at this writing, is attempting to go lower than that, all with no visible signs of withdrawal.

"Is this drug considered a controlled substance?" I asked.

"No it's not," the doctor answered. "It can be phoned in to a pharmacy and refills are allowed. She's also taking a pretty low dose."

Although Carol is far from pain free, she's having a lot more days with little or no pain during part of the day. She seems to be more animated and energetic not to mention cheerful and hopeful.

After five months Dr. Patin had to increase the dosage slightly, but it still continues to do the job.

Only time will tell if the battle has been won, but I'm beginning to hope this might be the solution.

I also believe I'm seeing the sparkle coming back into her eyes.

---

63.   A neurofibroma is a benign, solitary encapsulated tumor.

33

Support Group Evolution

We had been having regular meetings of our local support group and had gained members.

Because of people telling people, the international group was growing, also.

Marilyn had developed a brochure telling all about Wegener's, and began writing a newsletter that she sent out six times a year to a circulation of six hundred people, using her own funds.

She charged $10 a year for membership, which included the patient and immediate family.

She listed the physicians who agreed to serve as medical consultants in the first newsletter. They were: Nabih Abdou, Arnold Chonko, and Thomas Cotton from Kansas City, MO; Thomas McDonald and Richard DeRemee from the Mayo Clinic in Rochester, MN; and Steven Weiner from Los Angeles.

In 1991, the organization had support groups in Kansas City, MO—Marilyn's group; Los Angeles—my group; and we had added groups in Minneapolis, MN; Norfolk, NE; Milwaukee, WI; Marion, IN; Cleveland, OH; Denver, CO; Dallas, TX; Ames, IA; San Francisco; and Waterford, NY.

Lists of members were available upon request, and people began writing to one another across the country.

Eventually, with the aid of an attorney friend, Marilyn incorporated the group. Bylaws were written and tax-exempt status obtained for accepting donations.

She asked me if I wanted to be a part of her organization or do my own thing. I couldn't see any advantage to re-inventing the wheel, so I told her I would be happy to join forces.

In April 1994, Marilyn arranged for the first Wegener's symposium to be held at the Airport Marriott Hotel in Kansas City, MO. At the Kansas City Airport, the electronic sign at baggage claim flashed at us: "Welcome Wegener's Granulomatosis Members."

The first symposium for WGSG could not have been better planned and organized. It was impressive. Marilyn had arranged for physician-consultants from some of the largest medical centers in the country to speak.

Dick, Carol, and I went and were astounded at the professionalism of the presentations and discussions, pre-planned break-out sessions for various body parts affected by the disease, even the arrangements for food.

There were one hundred eighty attendees from twenty-three states and two from Canada. As far as we were concerned, it was a roaring success. We now boasted of seventeen local support groups.

There was a Friday evening reception with snacks, where attendees could interact. Patients and family members were unbelievably friendly and helpful. It didn't take long for us to realize we were a part of a larger family; no one was a stranger.

At the conclusion of the symposium, Marilyn was given a standing ovation; no one deserved it more.

In 1996, Marilyn arranged another symposium, bigger and better than the last. Those we'd met at the first symposium two years before were now old friends. We could hardly wait to catch up with one another.

We began to realize that the interchanges between patients and caregivers were, for many of us, the most rewarding parts of the event.

By the second symposium, Carol had been in contact with other early Internet users. One of them, Glenn Kullman, a patient with whom Carol had been corresponding online, thought a great deal of his ENT and told her about the doctor. Carol decided she wanted to see this particular doctor, so Glenn made an appointment for her.

He came to the hotel and picked us all up, drove us to the doctor's office, discovered the doctor was at another location that day, drove us to the *other* office, and set out to wait until we finished so he could take us back to the hotel. Because the doctor would only be looking at Carol's nose, and knowing that Glenn had experienced similar symptoms, we asked him to join us in the examining room, which he did.

We marveled at how thoughtful and considerate Glenn was to do all this for someone he'd never met. As we came to know him and his family, we learned that he and his wife, Arlene, were long-time friends of Marilyn. They had helped her get the group started ten years before.

Remote as the chances were, Glenn himself was later diagnosed with WG.

At the 1996 symposium, we also had a chance to renew our acquaintance with Charles and Janet Carothers from Houston. Dick and I had met them in a chance encounter on a tour bus in Scotland.

A doctor and his wife were sitting behind us. I heard the wife say something about having a lot of bruises. Knowing that bruising is a major side effect, I asked, "Are you taking Prednisone™?"

"What do you know about Prednisone™?" the doctor asked me. I proceeded to tell him about Carol and her history with Wegener's.

Janet, sitting in front of us, overheard the discussion, turned around and asked, "Did I hear you say something about Wegener's granulomatosis?" Then, pointing to her husband, she said, "Charles has Wegener's."

During the rest of the trip, whenever and wherever time allowed, I questioned Charles extensively about his symptoms, and told him about the newly formed support group.

Collette, who by this time had gotten married and had two perfectly normal children, also came, as did Kim, a young lady we met through our local group when she moved to California; Kim's mother Karen was also in attendance. Kim and her husband later went on to head a southern California chapter.

Debra and Michael, who lived outside of Sacramento, came to a couple of our Los Angeles meetings, a trip of almost four hundred miles and close to six hours, one way. They attended this gathering.

Donna and Joe, who lived in Fresno, had also driven down to L.A. for our local meetings. Theirs was a two hundred fifty mile, four-hour trip each way. That's how anxious some people were to get information and meet other patients. They not only came to that symposium, but to every one since.

So many people from our L.A. chapter were in attendance that we got a prize for having the most participants from a single group. We have learned to be terrific cheerleaders and promoters of the symposia.

Both Carol and I were asked to be panelists, she on one that dealt with "Living With Wegener's" and I on a caregivers panel.

Caregivers sessions are restricted to non-patients and are not videotaped. That allows participants to speak freely and exchange information about how to better care for their ailing, sometimes crabby, sometimes defiant loved ones.

At this session, one of the attendees was the mother of a new patient—her sixteen-year-old daughter. The mother was beside herself and could hardly speak between the sobs. I felt so bad for her; I had walked in her shoes. As soon as the session was over and before the next one began, I walked out into the hall to offer some comfort to the lady. The first thing I could think of to do was to offer her a hug, and followed that up with my name and phone number for whenever she needed to talk.

The mother and the father have since started a support group in their area, and I am happy to report that their daughter is doing very well.

When I said to Dick and Carol, describing the encounter and its aftermath, that "I didn't do anything," they wholeheartedly disagreed; to them, it was obvious I had given the parents of the young lady what they needed—hope, and the gift of knowing that they weren't alone.

The 1996 symposium was the last that Marilyn was able to attend. She died the following year, sadly—but not, however, from Wegener's.

Shortly after Carol came to live with us, a call came in from Iva Roe, who at the time was president and executive director of the WGSG. I wasn't home so she spoke to Dick, asking him if I would consider running for the Board of Directors at the upcoming election. He told her I would.

When he updated me later, I replied: "Are you out of your mind? I've never done anything like that in my life. I wouldn't even know how to begin."

Both Dick and Carol felt that I should accept, and that I deserved to be on the board considering the work I'd done for the organization in the past. Yet I was absolutely certain that I couldn't do the job and had nothing to contribute to WGSG.

"Give it a try," Dick told me. "You are a lot more capable than you think."

At the third symposium, in 1998, I reluctantly agreed to allow my name to be placed on the ballot, and was elected. Immediately after the symposium, the new board members assembled for a short meeting to elect officers and assign duties.

"How would you like to handle the chapters and support groups?" Iva asked.

"I'd love to," I told her.

Appointed the first Chapters Chairperson, I held the post for the next six years. The board met four times a year in Kansas City. It would mean traveling by myself, something that I was apprehensive about, having only done it twice in my life.

On the Friday evening before my first board meeting, the old-timers who had known Marilyn and helped her form the organization, wanted to talk with me about my ideas for the local groups. I welcomed the opportunity to tell them what I hoped to accomplish during my tenure as a director.

Because I'd had no idea what to do when starting the Los Angeles Chapter, I felt there was a desperate need for information for those who wanted to form groups in their areas. To that end, I wrote a manual about starting and maintaining support groups.

At each symposium during my term as chapters chairperson, I conducted a meeting for group leaders at which they could tell of their accomplishments, air their grievances, and learn what worked and what didn't from other chapters. I also served as the board's Parliamentary Law consultant.

When a member offered to help form a group in his or her area, I was the earliest contact as well as the go-to person for information, assistance, and support.

In the spirit of teaching by example, I loved telling about an incident at a meeting where an elderly patient named Ruth was telling the rest of the group how her doctor didn't understand her and was reluctant to answer her questions. Carol and Collette sat down at Ruth's feet and proceeded to give her ideas on how to get her doctors to listen, insisting she write down the suggestions. They both stressed how important it was for her to understand what was going on and to report to her doctors what was or wasn't working.

At that same meeting, I had the opportunity to tell a few people in a smaller group about Carol's crisis in Colorado. When I came to the part about getting paged at the airport, I related how my friend Sandy asked me, shortly after the incident, "Did you think she had died?"

At that telling, I could no longer hold back my tears. Carol, who had been listening unseen across the room, came and held me as we cried together.

We were happy to hear later on that Ruth and her doctors were communicating much better than they had before. Problems of the elderly are often discounted or ignored because they're considered complainers, or just because of their age. I recall thinking how understanding the patients were with each other and how proud I was of the girls' compassion.

This, I explained, is what support groups are all about—patients and caregivers helping each other, knowing that none of us is alone.

I found the people involved with the board to be creative, concerned, cohesive, and exceedingly careful of how money was spent. They were the nicest, friendliest, and most competent people I'd ever worked with. Every moment I served with them was a joy.

At one of the board meetings, after having learned that Dick's health was deteriorating, a couple of people asked me if he minded my being away from home for the few days of each meeting.

It was quite the opposite: The organization had become an important part of our lives, and he thoroughly supported my participation. From time to time, he would even offer suggestions for me to present to the board. That way, WGSG could benefit from his vast experience in management and dealing with people, if only indirectly.

Glenn Kullman later did a study on the medical and socioeconomic impact of Wegener's granulomatosis on a group of seven hundred one patients, all of whom were members of the international support group. It was included in a rheumatology research paper with a number of physician-coauthors, copies of which may be obtained through the organization.

The original international support group's name, Wegener's Granulomatosis Support Group, Inc., International has been changed twice. The first change was to Wegener's Granulomatosis Association, and then in 2006 to the Vasculitis Foundation. Many of the doctors involved with the group had long been encouraging us to include other vasculitic diseases within our organizational structure.

In vasculitis, the body's immune system mistakenly attacks the body's own blood vessels, causing them to become inflamed. Inflammation can damage the blood vessels and lead to a number of serious complications.

The other diseases currently included in the umbrella organization are: Behcet's Disease, Buerger's Disease, Central Nervous System Vasculitis, Churg Strauss Syndrome, Cryoglobulinemia, Giant Cell Arteritis, Henoch-Schönlein Purpura, Hypersensitivity Vasculitis, Kawasaki Disease, Microscopic Polyangiitis, Polyarteritis Nodosa, Polymyalgia Rheumatica, Rheumatoid Vasculitis, and Takayasu's Arteritis.

Through this expansion, we hope the new Vasculitis Foundation will be in a better position to be noticed and ultimately to obtain government funding for research.

When Iva Roe retired, the board chose Joyce Kullman, Glenn's and Arlene's daughter, to be executive director and now elects its own president every two years directly after new board members are elected.

Because Joyce is not a patient, she has the health and energy to put in the hours required to keep the organization at the top of its game. And because her father, Glenn, is a WG patient, she has firsthand knowledge of what patients go through and what they need from a group such as ours to make their lives easier and the fight against their particular disease more effective.

The feedback regarding Joyce is consistent: The patients love her, the staff loves her, and the doctors she has to constantly deal with love her. I can't think of a greater recommendation.

Arlene, Joyce's mother, was Marilyn's right arm when it came to doing things for the organization, and she continues to be available for just about anything the organization needs her to do. She should be given awards for her hard work and dedication.

The office now has paid staff members who handle the business of getting information out, talking to those who call in for information, and running the registration desk at the symposia.

Each year, following a tradition started by past executive director Iva Roe, who was also a patient, Joyce and members of the VF staff attend medical conventions for physicians whose specialties are pertinent to the diseases we cover.

They set up booths, introduce themselves and the foundation, pass out literature, and encourage the physician-attendees to refer patients to us.

Support-group leaders who live in the area are notified ahead of time, and there is no trouble getting volunteers to staff the booths. The doctors are particularly interested in talking to the patient-volunteers.

We now have more than thirty physician-consultants from major medical centers all over the world who will, at no charge, advise and inform our organization of new advances in diagnostics, research, and drug treatments. They will give free advice to any physician treating a VF patient who asks for it. Many consultants also make presentations and conduct break-out sessions at our symposia.

Each newsletter contains articles written by physicians, and spotlights one or more patients with stories of their battles, written by them or their caregivers.

A list of chapters and support groups throughout the world, with names, phone numbers, and e-mail addresses of the contacts for each group, is included. Chapters' activities, submitted by leaders, are also part of each issue.

Because, unfortunately, deaths among our group occur from time to time, these are listed as well. Especially saddened to read the death of someone young, I always wonder if that person might have lived if the disease had been diagnosed sooner.

We have been getting donations that enable us to help fund research projects, determined by a committee of members and physicians; our hope is that they will lead to answers about the diseases and to ultimately find a cure.

Our domestic chapters and support groups, numbering well over one hundred, are in all fifty states and Puerto Rico; our international groups number in the thirties, encompassing twenty-one countries.

In 2007, the first European symposium took place in Cambridge, England.

The biggest problem groups have had is finding places to meet. Libraries don't want us; hospitals don't want us; churches and restaurants don't want us, all citing liability in case an attendee gets hurt on the premises. Members often have had to resort to meeting in each other's homes.

We meet where we can and hope that wherever we gather we can bring each other comfort, support, and education.

Many of our members have participated in local health fairs, usually put on by hospitals, to acquaint people with who we are and what we do. That gives us the opportunity to introduce our organization to the public by passing out brochures, newsletters, shirts, pens, notepads, etc. We never know whose life may be saved because they got the information just in time to be properly diagnosed and treated.

Creative people are constantly coming up with ways to raise money. There have been chapters that have walked for VF, eaten for VF, biked for VF, golfed for VF, bowled for VF, etc. Local businesses have been generous in their support, many donating food, bottled water, and so on for the activities. There have even been a few Vasculitis Foundation-sponsored cruises.

All such activities have to be approved by the Foundation. Money collected, minus costs, if any, is sent directly to our headquarters in Kansas City.

We sell T-shirts, sweatshirts, water bottles, tote bags, even a member-generated cookbook; and each year, we add new items, hoping to promote awareness of the Vasculitis Foundation.

The organization continues to have an international symposium every other year, and the one in 2006 was the first to include diseases besides Wegener's granulomatosis.

For those unable to attend symposia, videotapes and DVDs are available for purchase. It's not as good as being there, but for those who can't, it's the next best thing.

At the 2006 symposium, Sheri Lyn Schwar, a Takayasu patient, presented a book she had written about her battle with that disease called, *Vasculitis—Sick and Tired of Being Sick and Tired*. I urge anyone who purchased this book to buy Sheri's book also. She writes with great passion, and has so much to teach us about her condition and her courage.

The diseases now under the VF umbrella have been addressed on every scripted, prime-time medical show on television. Also, we are now named on hospital check-sheets with our own diagnosis number.

Dr. Saxon pointed out the WG diagnosis code on UCLA's check-sheet a few years ago and remarked, "Your group is directly responsible for this."

The southeast Florida support group leader, because of health problems of her own, stepped down in 2006, and I took over the leadership in her place.

Carol and I both continue to help the organization in any way we can and whenever we're asked.

34

Carol Finds the Reason

In late 1995, Carol was fascinated with the Internet and made a point of searching for information on Wegener's from time to time. She came across a Web site created by a physician from somewhere in Florida.

Upon reading his description, she found some errors. E-mailing him a response, she offered corrections, telling him she'd been a patient for seventeen years. Fortunately, he was a doctor without an ego problem, and e-mailed her back thanking her for the information. He was very gracious and grateful for her input. He corrected his Web site and, with her permission, used what she had told him.

That gave her an idea. She began to discuss with her co-workers the possibility of creating a Web site that would serve the organization, which was now formally called: Wegener's Granulomatosis Support Group, Inc., International.

Phil, the man who had given Carol a job years ago while she was on chemo, owned the consulting business where she was working and knew all about her health problems. Over a six month period, with the technical input she gleaned from him and his employees, along with information that she knew personally about Wegener's, Marilyn, and the organization, she created the layout and wording for a Web site. She asked me to edit it for grammar and content. Then she sent a copy of what she proposed to Marilyn for her opinion and approval.

Marilyn loved the idea, and Carol got the Web site up and running in January, 1996. WGSG, Inc. was online.

Phil then offered to host it. It wasn't until years later that I learned that one had to pay an Internet Service Provider approximately $200 a month to host a Web site. He never asked Carol or the organization to compensate him during the time she was in charge of maintaining it. Nor did he or his employees ever get compensated for their time spent in designing and developing the software. It was a labor of love.

The following is the text from the March/April Newsletter of the same year, as Carol wrote it and Marilyn printed it, telling the international group about the new Web site.

Connected
By Carol Swart, WG patient

Welcome to Connected! This is a brand new column dedicated to the world of cyberspace and to help each other stay connected and tuned in using e-mail and the Internet. The goals of this column are as follows:

To update you with information on the progress of our very own WGSG Home Page and related information;

To help find new WG patients and link them up in an electronic support system;

To provide patients, physicians, family members, and friends with the most up-to-date information on WG and WGSG by showing you how to access that information electronically.

I believe that within cyberspace lies huge potential for exposure of WG to patients, physicians, and the general public. And exposure is the name of the game. If more patients were informed of and understood critical information such as medications, side effects, coping strategies, and signs of relapse, they might be more apt to take a more active role in their recovery process. If more physicians knew about the characteristics of this disease, they might be more apt to think of it when a patient comes to them with similar symptoms. Faster diagnosis means better recovery rates. And finally, if more lay people have heard of the disease and how it affects the lives of patients and their families, they might be more apt to support us by diverting some of their yearly charitable donations to our group or towards WG research. Exposure is the key.

As a brief history of this project, I am a consulting software engineer in the Los Angeles area, and a WG patient of seventeen years. My associates here at the office were working on an Internet-based product, so I overheard lots of related discussions. One day I got the idea to put WGSG on the net and asked my office mates if they would help me do it. They agreed. So we registered our acronym of WGSG. Then I got to work organizing and typing in as much information as I could get my hands on. And the rest, as they say, is history.

There are primarily three groups of people that we hope to attract through our presence on the Internet:

1. *First, there will be patients who have just been diagnosed with WG who are interested in obtaining information about the disease. Chances are their physicians do not know much about it. And even if they do, they probably have little or no "user-friendly" descriptions, just medical jargon. In the past, they might have gone to the local library to do some research; today they will log into the Internet and search by keyword. Once they enter the words, "Wegener's Granulomatosis" and click the "search" button, a link to our home page will appear and they will be connected!*

2. *Secondly, there will be physicians who do not work near a major medical center who acquire one or more patients with WG. They will use the Internet to do a similar keyword search to find us and we can subsequently put them in touch with consulting physicians.*

3. *Thirdly, there will be people who will find us linked up to various organizations such as NORD, AARDA, groups with non-profit status, and so forth. These people may be interested in contacting us perhaps because they're doing their own research, compiling lists of support groups, or classifying diseases and conditions. Once people know who we are and why we exist, the sky's the limit!*

Since this Web site is a new endeavor for all of us, we all are learning together. With my jumping-off point and your comments and suggestions, we can work together to create an informative and appealing presentation of our organization to the world. For some people, it will be all they ever see of us. For others it will be the very thing that started them on the road to recovery and good health. For those people, and everyone in-between, let's not take this endeavor lightly.
WGSG Home Page: http://www.wgsg.org[64]

When people searching the web began to find us via our new homepage, the Web site began averaging fifty hits a week, and requests for new patient information began coming in faster than Marilyn could send the packets out. She called to tell me that she was thrilled and overwhelmed with the response, and that she was going to have to corral more people to help her put information packets together.

In the e-mails that Carol received, some had already lost a loved one to WG, and wished that the Web site existed for them to access when they had needed it. When Carol brought the early e-mails to me, I sat down to read them and found tears streaming down my cheeks as other patients and family members told their stories—particularly those about the ones who didn't make it.

In the May/June Newsletter, 1996, the one following the announcement of the new Web site, Marilyn inserted the following note:

HATS OFF to the Internet Home Page!

Hats off to Carol Swart, WG patient, and to those who helped her set up our Internet Home Page and related articles. It is very impressive and superbly done. We owe a debt of gratitude to them, as this service is hard to come by, not only monetarily but done so professionally.

To give you an example, the first month the WGSG was on the Internet, we gained ninety new members from all over the country, as well as the world; Peru, Italy, England, Canada and Australia are some of the countries. It looks like we will be close to that number in April.

Thank you from all of us, especially from the new patients whom we were able to reach because of you, Carol.

When I read that note in the Newsletter I asked Marilyn how many members we had previously been adding each year. I was astounded when she told me we were lucky to find thirty.

Phil showed Carol how to set up his laptop computer and allowed her to bring it to the 1996 symposium—an unusually generous and trusting favor. Most of the time that wasn't taken up by meetings and break-out sessions was spent gathered around the computer so that Carol, and others who were technically savvy, could show the rest of the people what was on the Web site and how to access it.

After the Web site had been in existence for a year, the membership tripled, going from about six hundred members to about eighteen hundred. There was no question that Carol had made her mark, and those who run the organization consistently offer her recognition and gratitude.

For all those who had said from time to time, including Carol herself, there must have been a reason why she was stricken with Wegener's, we realized she had found it. Through her creation, other patients, caregivers, family members, and friends of patients would find comfort, support, and valuable information. They would be able to electronically visit and interact with each other all over the world.

At the symposium in 1998, Carol was recognized for her contribution to the organization and to patients from every corner of the globe, by her creation of the Web site, with a certificate and a beautiful crystal clock. It represented the gift of time that patients might acquire because of access to knowledge that was previously unavailable or hard to find. It also represented the appreciation of her time

No one feels silly saying, "I love you."

I've learned not to let insignificant occurrences upset me, as they might have done in the past. I've become more tolerant about who spends what holidays with us. If any of the children have plans that take them away on holidays, or my birthday, I don't get my feelings hurt. I know they love me three hundred sixty-five days a year. Missing a particular day won't change that. I often let them know how much they all mean to me, and how much joy they have given me.

But getting to this place was an arduous trip.

There were so many times that I felt guilty. Did Carol see enough doctors? Did I do enough, early enough? Could any of her suffering have been prevented?

Who knows? We all did the best that we could with the knowledge and information we had at the time. That's all anyone can be expected to do. We were lucky it worked.

Since I couldn't find any books about coping with Wegener's, I began to read about how others coped with different illnesses. I found it didn't matter what the illness was; those of us providing care have many of the same problems. Two books were particularly helpful: *Once My Child, Now My Friend*, by Elinor Lenz, offered suggestions for harmonizing relationships with grown offspring; and *Living With Chronic Illness*, by Cheri Register, gave me insight on how a patient feels about parents and friends hovering and talking constantly about being sick.

When I told Carol I had begun to read about other people's illnesses she said, "That must be depressing."

"Actually, it's not," I told her. "Most of the people I read about recovered. The ones who didn't were teachers, showing us the way to face the inevitable."

I'm not really sure how close Carol has come to death's door. She may know, but I don't think I want to, never having been prepared to lose her. The statistics seemed to be in her favor. There was always the possibility that she might be in the tiny percentage of those who lose the battle, but I couldn't let myself think about that. If I lost hope, who would hold the rest of the family up by the armpits?

Sometimes, when Carol didn't seem to be showing progress, I would get depressed and wonder if she would ever get better or just go through life with all her problems—or worse. Then I would talk to her and hear the laughter in her voice. She's having a good day, I'd think. She's really better. She's going to get well.

With each crisis, I experienced monumental fear—until she emerged victorious.

Often, I didn't know what to do or say to make things better. Then I realized I didn't have to say anything beyond, "I love you and I'm here for you." We have shared some beautiful silences.

I also felt guilty if I indulged in something fun when Carol was ailing. When I told her this, she let me know how upsetting that was to her. She didn't want me to stop living because she was sick. She made it clear that when I did things that were fun, or took interesting trips, it made me more interesting to her.

The emotional pain that Dick and I suffered is every bit as ongoing as Carol's physical pain. People have remarked, "I don't know how you handle it."

What other choice is there? If we had a choice, of course, Carol would never have been stricken with WG. But we have to play the hand we're dealt, and that means handling what comes, from one day to the next.

When an acquaintance learned that I refused to cry in front of Carol or Dick, she commented that it seemed like my whole family was suffering from years of denial—acceptance being the first step toward emotional recovery.

Whatever helps one to cope is neither wrong nor right; it's just his or her way. We all have to learn what works for us. Some cry in public, some in private, and some only in their hearts. For me, a good cry turned out to be a great tension reliever.

We've all heard people say that you shouldn't feel sorry for yourself. We catch ourselves feeling bad, and that makes us feel guilty. There's nothing wrong, however, with feeling sorry or angry because this happened to us. It's only wrong if it impedes our recovery.

One's emotional state has a great deal to do with one's health. A lot has been written about that by experts. While anyone who walks around with a perpetual smile on his or her face looks like an idiot, it's a good idea to try to look at the bright side of any situation.

Pushing bad thoughts to the back of my mind has become my favorite exercise.

I have less patience now with people's petty grievances. Still, I had to learn that it's not fair to minimize the problems of other family members. They need compassion and hugs, too.

It's amazing how much physical and emotional good can come from a hug. I can give them out by the bushel and do, at every opportunity. I wish I could squeeze some of my good health into Carol's body.

I wonder—will her life ever be the same again? The answer is unequivocally *no*. How could it be? She's lived through a nightmare and survived it. The way she's coped makes me so proud. She could have spent time moaning about the terrible thing that happened to her, so the whole family could pity her, and would probably have gotten anything she wanted. But she has chosen not to use her illness for anything except to make her stronger.

Because she's been fighting back at the disease, Carol has also become more assertive—not just in medical situations, but in her daily life and career as well.

Having fun also has been good for Carol's health, and her doctors concur with this. If she'd spent her life sitting in a corner feeling sorry for herself, instead of out skiing, hiking, horseback riding, whitewater rafting, bicycle riding, etc. she'd be lousy company and wouldn't have any friends. She also wouldn't have had anything to take her mind off her physical problems. Acting like an invalid can lead to becoming one.

I used to be concerned about her participation in sports, thinking she's doing too much; she should be resting more. Then I learned the benefits of exercise, and heard from her friends that if she didn't feel up to it, she didn't partake. But she was with people who cared about her, and that made her happy.

Because of Carol's cheerful disposition, we tend to forget at times the seriousness of her condition. Friends or relatives will ask me how she is, but if she's having a bad siege do they really want to know? They tend to change the subject or relate a story about someone else who's sick. But most people will get over their illnesses in a short time. Carol will never be over this.

Sometimes I wonder if those of us who love Carol will spend the rest of our lives trying to make it up to her because she's been sick. We probably will. Will it help her? Probably not. But that won't stop us.

I used to wish for things money could buy. My fondest wish now would be for Carol to be rid of this disease forever.

I used to dream of the day when I could hold a child of hers in my arms for the first time. Now I dream of the day when I can say of my child: "The disease is cured and her pain is gone."

There are no guarantees for any of us, and we often must make our own luck. This is the only body we have, and we have to put up a fight for control when the body starts calling the shots instead of the brain.

Carol wants to be well for all the obvious reasons, but she also wants to be well for those of us who love her. How long the wellness will last is anybody's guess. Wegener's is unpredictable and can return at any time with no warning. Without a crystal ball, none of us knows what tomorrow will bring. We're all under the pressure of wondering what course the disease will take next.

If we don't have answers to all of the questions, it doesn't mean there aren't any; it just means we haven't found them yet. It's important to keep searching.

There will be times we won't like the answers we find. Coping with those is part of life.

I'm not sure at this point whether or not I believe in God, fate, or destiny. I do, however, believe in Carol and her will to survive. I also believe in her doctors.

Looking back over the years since she's been diagnosed and treated, we realize that those doctors we've come to know and love are the ones who weren't afraid to listen and learn. The ones who helped her the most are the ones who let her participate in her care. And she knows in her heart that they truly care whether she lives or dies. They always maintained hope and so did she.

One of the most important things we've learned is that a doctor should recognize his or her own limitations, to be aware of what he or she doesn't know.

If Dr. Mysko had kept treating Carol for upper respiratory infections for months and months, instead of suggesting we see a specialist, things might have been a lot worse. Whenever it was suggested to Dr. Haring that another opinion might be in order, he offered his assistance in every way possible, never once discouraging us. If a doctor doesn't want a second opinion, I don't want that doctor.

Information we have found and passed along about Wegener's has never intimidated the doctors treating Carol. They have, in fact, searched our minds in their attempt to learn all they could about this unique disease. They've been very interested in Carol's actions, reactions, symptoms, and suggestions. Recovery takes teamwork.

Good doctors want to know that what they're doing is the right thing for their patients. Other opinions may confirm that, and show us that what is being done in the way of treatment is what should be done. If they differ, we may need to seek additional advice; there may be more than one way to deal with medical issues. It's important for us to get all the facts in order to make informed decisions.

Illness can be educational, and the years have taught us a lot.

We've all learned to take better care of ourselves. Carol encourages me to read labels of foods and medicines. We make every attempt to educate ourselves as to what will make us well when we get sick; or better still, how to live a healthy life and try to avoid getting sick in the first place.

Waiting too long before seeing the doctor for an ailment could add to suffering, and might even cost lives. If something isn't getting better within a reasonable period, we know it's time to see the doctor.

Communication between doctor and patient, and also between the doctor and the patient's family, is a very important part of treatment. If doctors won't say what's going on and why, I have learned to grab hold of their sleeves and hold them down for questioning. They owe us that.

When Carol has been hospitalized, except for the first time when we didn't know any better, we've learned to speak up for her when necessary. It's enough to be afraid of the disease; one needn't be afraid of the system.

Not every doctor has a great bedside manner. They're human beings with different personalities and they, like the rest of us, have fears, insecurities, problems at home, sometimes lack of knowledge, etc. These things are bound to interfere with their practice from time to time. If we take the time to let them know what we're thinking or feeling, they'll be better equipped to work with us as patients or family members.

It's important not to be timid or embarrassed to tell the doctor what ails us. Many are good and great and wonderful, but very few are mind readers.

I remember asking Mom when she complained about an ailment, or that a medicine didn't work, "Did you tell the doctor?"

Invariably the answer was, "No."

She had to be reminded that doctors can't help us if we don't let them know what is or isn't working.

We know to take a list of medicines and supplements to every doctor's appointment, and keep a copy in wallet or purse in case of an accident or emergency.

At doctors' visits, it's also important to take a list of complaints, along with an advocate—someone who knows what's going on in your life and cares. Whether a patient or a caregiver, we're only human and bound to forget things. The person with us may be listening well enough to catch something the doctor said when we weren't.

Once we have a better understanding of the situation at hand, we're better equipped to cope with the advice, or perhaps even to question it. A little detective work can turn up a particular substance that could be a trouble-maker.

The doctors always told us the truth and gave us hope. Drs. Haring and Saxon respected her wishes and never fought her on issues or decisions. Working as a team, they never fought with each other, either. The depth of their commitment to pulling her out of her illness must be counted as a major part of her victory.

It's my sincere hope that Carol's story will help someone else get diagnosed early enough to save a life. Maybe a parent, spouse, sibling, or child will seek help for their loved one with similar symptoms sooner. A loved one might find it easier to cope after reading about us.

We've discovered that many WG patients weren't diagnosed for years, and in some instances the disease caused a lot of destruction that didn't have to happen. In spite of it all, they have continued going to school or work, and leading active lives. They are all heroes and I salute them.

We know we can't change what's happened to Carol or the destruction it has caused. Even if it's possible to give her a new nose, whether a prosthesis or through plastic surgery, we won't be able to give her back what's missing inside.

What we can do, however, is join the fight, to research ways to cure this disease. Sales of this book will benefit the Vasculitis Foundation, to further its efforts toward awareness, education, and research, along with offering comfort and support.

There are many people from the Vasculitis Foundation who have enriched our lives by our having known them, whether they're patients or caregivers. They have given us support and comfort along with an education.

Carol's not used to losing. As a young child, her artwork won awards at contests. She won an essay contest in the sixth grade. I've recounted already her awards from high school and public speaking. In this battle against Wegener's, the biggest contest of her life, I'm certain she will be victorious again.

At this time there are few jobs, if any, that will allow someone to work at odd hours with no promise of continuity, number of hours, or days. She talks about being able to go back to work someday. If the new drug, Lyrica™ continues to work, perhaps that day isn't too far away.

There have been times when I've looked at other families' smooth paths and been jealous. Their children got married, landed good jobs, got promoted, and had babies. I console myself with the realization that my child has made a difference in the world that will live long after we're both gone. She has created something that will give people comfort and support. And we're often reminded by the people running the Foundation that Carol has no idea how many people she has helped, or how many lives she has saved, by her creation of the Web site.

Carol and I truly believe we were put on Earth for a reason. If her mission was to create a vehicle for reaching a worldwide audience with a message of education and support, and mine to tell the story, then perhaps we've fulfilled our missions. In any case, we have not stopped, and will not stop, working at it.

I promise that anyone who asks me for help in starting a group will always get what's necessary in a timely manner, with as much speed as is humanly possible. After trying to get information from other support groups and finding them lacking, I, as a Board member, composed the booklet about how to start support groups. No one will have to ask for my help twice.

I promise those patients seeking comfort and support to provide what I can as long as I'm on this Earth.

I promise those patients or caregivers with whom I've had contact that I will never forget who they are and will make every effort to stay in touch.

It does my heart good when I speak to a new patient or caregiver who expresses astonishment at our speedy contact. They found out about the Vasculitis Foundation in the morning and by afternoon they have had phone calls or e-mails from at least two people addressing their needs.

If Carol hadn't gotten sick, there would be no reason for this book. I wish there had never been a story to tell. But as long as it happened, and if there's a chance that it might help someone else who has fought, or is fighting, a similar battle, then it must be told.

My feeling about having written this book is expressed in these lines from the Emily Dickinson poem quoted at the beginning:

> "If I can ease one life the aching,
> … I shall not live in vain."

Epilogue:
By
Carol D. Swart

Long before the story you just read was fashioned into book form, Mom and I were always cognizant that this was *her* story about my life, not mine. For completeness, she wanted to make sure I had a forum to clarify, rebut, or add my own insights to anything she wrote.

However, with respect to the details of my fight with Wegener's, the question of what happened is covered with amazing grace and accuracy. There is little for me to add, except to say I never believed my life was in danger, despite early medical crises or predictive literature.

Instead, I would like to describe my early recollections about my health, how I kept my sanity throughout the ordeal, and what I have learned from the experience.

Ultimately, I have come to believe—as Mom has written—that there are no coincidences in life, and that everything happens for a reason. Determining what those reasons are is the hard part, especially since they unfold over time.

I can't remember a time in my life when I wasn't sick. It seems I was always encumbered with some kind of illness or physical limitation that separated me from the other kids or got in the way of my life.

As a young child, I remember my parents closing the heat vent in and removing all the stuffed animals from my bedroom, trying to keep the dust levels to a minimum.

I also remember Mom taking me to a health food store to buy "special chocolate" (i.e., carob) and wheat-free spaghetti in accordance with my pediatrician's recommendation. He thought that these common allergens of dust and food might be contributing to my asthma.

I don't believe those changes made much of a difference.

In grade school, physical exertion was not my friend. I remember having bouts of asthma that would keep me either indoors or on the sidelines. As a tomboy and good athlete, this was very disappointing. I felt different, limited, and perhaps even defective in some small way.

It also caused me to grow up fast in this regard: I had to be cognizant of my breathing, aware of my environment. For example, freshly cut grass on the school grounds or ball field might hasten an asthma attack; and when Los Angeles County issued smog alerts indicating worse-than-normal air quality, I was not allowed to go outside, even for recess.

Any time my breathing became strained, I had to be mature enough to say when, to bow out of the game or activity before an asthma attack could take hold; or in the extreme case, to notify an adult if I started wheezing badly.

Fast-forward to high school—and a day that would haunt me for decades.

With my asthma outgrown and well behind me, I decided to take advantage of a beautiful spring day and ride my bike to school. That afternoon, while working on a chemistry assignment in the science lab, I picked up a small glass vial containing a clear liquid. Trying to identify the contents, I unscrewed the cap and breathed in the fumes.

An organic smell virtually bowled me over, making me nauseous and disoriented for quite some time. Still feeling the effects hours later as I set out for home, I rode passed a large construction site engulfed in dust, making the air heavy and my breathing difficult.

Looking back, I believe these assaults on my respiratory system may have been a factor in or initiator of the WG disease process.

Six months later came one of those quintessential teenage moments: looking at photos of my friends and myself, clowning around, having fun, all I could see was my nose. How disproportionate it looked; how I longed for a smaller, cuter one!

I have since learned the meaning of the phrase, "be careful what you wish for."

The appearance of my nose would soon become the least of my worries: My world was about to come crashing down around me.

Not long after I was diagnosed with Wegener's, but before any treatments were administered, Dr. Haring did something quite heroic that would completely change the course of my life: he sent me to a psychologist. Highly perceptive and way ahead of his time in this regard, Dr. Haring was somehow able to see past the patient with complicated medical issues, and into the heart and soul of a scared but analytical sixteen-year-old with an uncertain future, who would need help expressing fears and gaining perspective.

Through the years, Dr. Haring would continue to ask me about my mental and emotional health: How was I handling the stress? Do I have supportive friends in the picture? What am I doing for fun? Had I ever thought about suicide?

He understood that my attitudes and emotions would always play a part in my disease and recovery process, and wanted to make sure my thoughts were not spinning out of control. This, on top of all the other things he did with respect to my health care, has landed him at the top of my list of heroes.

The psychologist he recommended was a woman who specialized in patients with chronic medical problems. In the short time we worked together, she showed me that there are things I can do, steps I can take, to help myself live a healthier life.

First and foremost, she taught me self-hypnosis, guided imagery, and meditation. During these sessions, she would hook me up to a temperature probe. If my body temperature rose, then I was successfully *in the zone*. Before this, I had heard of the mind-body connection but was unaware of how applicable it was to my situation.

She also taught me progressive relaxation techniques to help calm my mind and relax my body. We practiced using guided imagery, a mental exercise that helped me visualize such things as pain reduction, a properly working immune system, and me as a healthy and happy individual.

She helped me realize that my thoughts and words carry energy and therefore have power; that I should choose what I think and say carefully.

All of these new ideas ignited my curiosity and gave me a glimpse into the world of personal empowerment. My actions, attitudes, and levels of excitement, as well as my thoughts and perceptions—good or bad—all are in my hands!

At the end of our time together, I felt transformed into a different person, somehow better and more equipped to handle whatever life might throw at me.

So, instead of sitting around whining about my rotten health, taking on the role of victim and asking "Why me?" to no one in particular, I could choose a different attitude, and take actions that would make a positive difference in my life.

This concept resonated heavily with me because basically I am a doer, an achiever. Like most of my fellow Wegener's patients, I can't just sit back, do nothing, and wait for something to happen.

The problem was I didn't know exactly what I could or should be doing to further my cause. Since I had always been a good student, I decided to take on the subjects of health, wellness, and personal empowerment as if they were part of my school curriculum. I began reading popular books as well as those less mainstream or more esoteric, spending countless hours in libraries and bookstores.

Early into my junior year of college, I started my first set of chemo treatments. I was living in an apartment near campus and enjoying having my very own kitchen. This was the first time I remember putting into practice all those health and wellness concepts I had spent so much time reading about. With each new healthy-eating book I reviewed, I modified my diet accordingly. I tried removing dairy, wheat, and citrus foods from my diet; went through my vegetarian phases, with and without eggs; did the macrobiotic and juicing diets; and worked with dozens of others.

My grocery shopping trips took hours because I had to check every label, verify each food source. It took years for me to find a happy medium where I could accept invitations to homes and restaurants without feeling guilty about breaking my current diet.

Healthy eating was one way for me to feel I was gaining control over my health. When I was preparing a nutritious meal, I was automatically in a better mood, spending precious time in a state of personal empowerment over my sick body. What a wonderful feeling that was!

It was not long before I found other steps to take that might also make a difference in my health, life, or attitude. Any subject was fair game because I would have done anything to get well. I started taking vitamins, and learned about herbs, supplements, and nutritional guidelines.

I stopped watching daily news shows to shield myself from negative thoughts and images. I went to see chiropractors, hands-on healers, and chakra-balancing experts. I had my astrological chart prepared. I worked with art, automatic writing, and non-dominant hand writing therapists. Countless hours were spent in standard talk therapy and personal-growth workshops. I even worked with an equestrian therapist.

I surrounded my living space with quartz crystals, mirrors, and plants according to feng shui principles; and slept on a mattress and pillow filled with magnets. Oh, and don't forget exercise! I walked and jogged, hiked and biked, skied and skated, played racquetball, did jazzercise, and took the stairs as much as I possibly could.

Although this quest for knowledge went on for years, the motivation was always the same: if I don't know what made me sick, how will I know what makes me well? So, I just tried every life-affirming idea that came my way, one by one. Plus, as long as I kept busy, I wasn't thinking about my next treatment, the pain in my sinuses, or the time I was missing from school.

Many of the wellness concepts I focused on resulted in major health benefits: I went into remission and have been off all WG-related drugs ever since. A few items did work, but not necessarily as expected. For example, my income tripled over a period of three jobs and four years.

Most, however, did more for my emotional health and awareness, which, I have come to realize, is just as important. Even if a particular benefit was temporary, it may have lasted long enough for me to enjoy more time on the slopes, an extended evening with friends, or a good night's sleep.

Living with Wegener's was not all bleak. I had plenty of fun in my life as well, in spite of my diagnosis and crummy health. Depending on the type of vacation or activity, I learned to either take things slowly and rest often, or push myself to not get left behind. More often that not I relied on pain medicine to help me through the day.

At times, I even secretly agreed with Mom that I probably shouldn't have gone out, but I was not about to give in or back down. These getaways and activities helped me switch focus from my disease and treatment difficulties to the joy of friends and the peacefulness of nature.

Besides simply having fun, I had two other motivating factors that kept me in the game.

First, I feared that if I stopped accepting invitations to all these crazy outings, my friends would stop inviting me.

Second, how many more times in my life will I be able to ski, ride or hike? This disease has not hit my kidneys, and only briefly touched my lungs and joints, but who knows what the future holds? My bladder still hemorrhages from time to time, with angry red spots that don't seem to heal. I have an advanced case of osteoporosis. People who have been through chemo are more likely to get cancer later on in life. And, statistically speaking, I'm more likely than not to have a relapse.

In addition to these known complications, there are plenty of unknowns that the experts avoid talking about even when pressed. For example, will I experience delayed side effects from any of the dozens of medicines I have taken? Will my life span be shortened due to all I've been through?

Regardless of what logic or genetics tells us, no one really knows what will affect me in the future. How could they? I'm pretty much leading the pack in this regard. No one else I'm aware of has lived with Wegener's as long as I have. So, I wasn't about to let anything fun or interesting pass me by if I could help it.

The old fears rarely seep into my consciousness anymore. But when they do, Mom is terrific about rebutting my arguments and eventually assuaging them. Although any of the above complications *could* happen, chances are extremely low that they will after fifteen years of remission. In fact, regardless of what the medical literature says, I believe I am as close to the "C" word—cured—as one could be, given my circumstances.

Although I still struggle with certain medical issues, mostly due to the damage caused by past disease or treatment history, my overall health is actually quite good. One of my continuing goals is to learn to read the cosmic message board without having to upset my physical body in the process.

More good things than bad have happened to me as a result of my having had WG. I have been challenged in so many ways, and found strength I may never have known. I have met some amazing, brave, and generous people who have given me comfort, faith, and encouragement along the way. While working on the WGSG Web site, I have felt useful and appreciated on a worldwide scale.

Through the years I have gathered a great deal of information about health and wellness and the mind-body connection that I would not have learned otherwise. Perhaps in sharing my knowledge with others, I can help them on their path to becoming healthy and strong.

Somewhere along the way, I learned that I can't heal my body without looking after the health of my mind, emotions, and spirit as well. All components work together in harmony and can't be separated from one another.

I learned that one of the things I fought the hardest—having someone come to my appointments with me—is one of the most important things I can do for my sanity and peace of mind. That's why I still, at forty-five years old, bring Mom or one of my brothers to consultation appointments, or anywhere else they want to tag along. I don't have to solve all my problems by myself.

Finally, I learned that I can be calm even when surrounded by turmoil. Every day that I feel good is a gift; every person who has helped me along my obstacle course of life, an angel. And every time I see opportunity or coincidence, I am inspired because I know *There Must Be a Reason.*

I wish all fellow patients as much comfort, support, knowledge, and success, in your quest for health and wellness as I have had. I hope my story inspires you on your road to recovery.

A special note of thanks goes to my brothers, Ken, Ron, and Don for encouraging me throughout the bad times, and enhancing my social life when I wasn't well enough to spend time with friends. Thanks for helping me through the aftermath of treatments, for making innumerable hospital visits bringing silly gifts to cheer me up, and for helping to shield me from nagging parents. You always knew how to make me laugh, even when I felt like crying.

Thanks to Tracey for never giving up on a friend; for reminding me that other people have feelings too; for applying your unique sense of humor to my most difficult situations; and for letting me know that the world is still out there waiting, whenever I'm ready to rejoin the living.

Thanks to John for listening to all the gory details of my illness and then prodding me for more; for always being willing to make the four-hour drive to Mammoth (Mom, read: five-hour drive); and for making it safe for me to express my thoughts, feelings, hopes, and fears, even if I didn't quite know what they were.

Thanks to Dad, my original and lasting hero, for being with me at all my surgeries, important appointments, and crisis situations. You always knew the direction in which to lead us towards solutions, and how to deal with the truly difficult people. Your presence in my hospital rooms gave me strength, inspiration, and the will to recover, and the little stuffed animals didn't hurt either.

Thanks to Mom for accompanying me on almost all my appointments, whether I wanted you there or not; for getting the support group going so I wouldn't be alone in my battle; and for putting up with all the crabbiness I conveniently forgot about, but found documented herein for the whole world to remember. Thanks also for keeping in touch with my friends, returning their calls when I didn't feel like picking up the phone; and for exemplifying all things good and kind and selfless in this world.

You all are my heroes, and I couldn't have survived without you.

Carol with current nose, 1993

Afterword:
By
Andrew Saxon, MD

Being Marcus Welby, MD or any of the other TV doctors must have been fun. Generally you got to cure patients, solve their social, economic, and personal problems, and even if the patient died, it was generally a happy ending with all the loose ends tied up. And he never made mistakes.

Unfortunately, treating patients in the real world is not like that. Many of the difficulties physicians have are exemplified in the diagnosis and management with diseases such as Wegener's granulomatosis. The first thing that you lose sleep over is have you made the right diagnosis? Rare diseases are rare and some are damned rare.

Thus, when a patient comes in with non-specific symptoms such as stuffy nose, back pain, and headache, your mind does not immediately jump to unusual illnesses. The medical proverb is, "When you hear hoofbeats, think horses, not zebras."

On the other hand, always in the back of your mind is the fact that even the simplest, most ordinary symptoms may be the harbinger of some rare and potentially fatal disease. And it is your job not to miss it. Thus you have to balance your desire not to overlook a disease with your commitment to the patient's well-being by not doing unnecessary, expensive, and potentially harmful examinations and tests.

And then, when you think about a diagnosis and try to prove it, the answers may simply not be there at that one point in time. Thus in the early stages of Wegener's granulomatosis, before the kidneys and lungs are affected and only the upper airway is involved, the diagnosis may be difficult or impossible to make with assurance. You have a young patient with a potentially treatable and potentially fatal disease, and you can't prove it in spite of the best efforts you and medical science have to offer. You lose lots of sleep over this.

The quandary is particularly relevant in patients with diseases similar to Wegener's granulomatosis because the treatment for one of these diseases is completely different than the treatment for another disease that may mimic it—Lethal Midline Granuloma. Treatment for each of the diseases is ineffective in the other and both involve chemotherapy, immunosuppression, and/or radiation therapy, which themselves can lead to life-threatening complications. You lose more sleep over this.

And then you finally either make a diagnosis or at least commit the patient and yourself to a therapy. You are going to take a young, relatively healthy-appearing individual and make them sick or potentially make them sick in order to make them better. This is the dilemma that is faced, I am sure, by my colleagues in oncology continually, but knowing that they have done it many times before does not make me feel any better.

What I take strength in is the knowledge that I am doing the right thing and, by giving the patient therapies which are unpleasant and make her feel worse, in the end I am going to make her better. But I sure feel better and sleep better once the patient starts to improve.

And then is she better? While it is easy to prove that some patients are getting better by following various tests, in patients like Carol it can be extraordinarily difficult to document that the patient is getting better and not worse. Blood tests, as in her case, may not give the answer and simply examining the nose is a very sensitive and painful way to try to determine whether improvement is occurring.

And then while on an alternative therapy—because of complications from initial standard therapy—new lesions appear in the lung and clearly the battle is being lost. What do you do? Do you go back on the initial therapy that caused severe bladder problems and likely will cause them again? Do you try a newer therapy with intravenous treatment which works but may or may not work quite as well? You call around to everybody you know who is an "expert" like yourself and get them to hold your hand, even though they know that you don't know the answer either and that you will have to make the decision. You try to diffuse your anxiety by being sure you are not missing something, though you know you are not to begin with.

And then you finally get the patient into remission and you have to decide when to stop therapy. But there is no absolute way of deciding when the remission began, and you will have to make a decision as to when to stop. If you keep treating longer than necessary, you expose the patient to continued side effects and potential long-term negative effects of the chemotherapy. But if you stop too soon the whole problem may come back. And you lose more sleep.

Amidst all of this, the patient is trying to lead a normal life. Sometimes it is hard for us as physicians to remember that the patients have things to do in their lives other than see the doctor and take medicines because we, as physicians, only see the patients in this setting.

It is easy to forget that they are college students, wives, husbands, and somebody's daughter, and that all their personal interrelationships and activities need to be factored into the patient's life—not just trips to the doctor, taking medicines, taking tests. Because we sometimes forget this as physicians, we occasionally get frustrated and angry that the patients aren't as compliant as we would like in that they don't follow our instructions perfectly.

Sometimes because of our own perspective, we think of ourselves as being the most important figure in these individuals' lives, forgetting that the patient has a very complex social network that is the true fabric of the person's life. Their illness and their physicians are just a part of this fabric.

Indeed, in the end, the physicians who take care of the patient and not just the illness become more than just a part of the patients' illness and become woven into the fabric of the patient's life in general. And in this is the reward that makes all that loss of sleep worthwhile.

Abbreviations

AARDA: American Autoimmune Related Diseases Association

AIDS: Autoimmune Deficiency Syndrome

AMA: American Medical Association

CAT: Computerized Axial Tomography

CBC: Complete Blood Count

CDC: Centers for Disease Control

DAR: Daughters of the American Revolution

DMPG: Department of Medicine Professional Group

ER: Emergency Room

ENT: Ear, Nose and Throat doctor

HBO: Home Box Office

ICU: Intensive Care Unit

IRA: Individual Retirement Arrangement

IRS: Internal Revenue Service

IVP: Intravenous Pyelography

LAX: Los Angeles International Airport

MRI: Magnetic Resonance Imaging

NASTAR: National Standard Race

NIH: National Institutes of Health

NORD: National Organization of Rare Disorders

PDR: Physician's Desk Reference

UCLA: University of California at Los Angeles

UCR: University of California at Riverside

USC: University of Southern California

VIP: Very Important Person

VF: Vasculitis Foundation

WGSG: Wegener's Granulomatosis Support Group

Bibliography

Abdou, Nabih I.; Kullman, Glenn J.; Hoffman, Gary S.; Sharp, Gordon C.; Specks, Ulrich; McDonald, Thomas; Garrity, James; Goeken, James A.; and Allen, Nancy B. 2002. Wegener's Granulomatosis: Survey of 701 Patients in North America. Changes in Outcome in the 1990s. *Journal of Rheumatology* 29:2: 309–16.

Beers, Mark H. and Berkow, Robert. *The Merck Manual*. Boston, MA: Merck Publishers, Fourteenth Edition, 1982.

Bruning, Nancy. *Coping with Chemotherapy*. New York, NY: Avery Publishers, 2002.

Cousins, Norman. *Anatomy of an Illness As Perceived by the Patient*. New York, NY: W.W. Norton & Co., Inc., 1979.

Dickens, Charles. *A Tale of Two Cities*. London, England: Penguin Classics, 1840–41.

Dickinson, Emily. *Favorite Poems of Emily Dickinson*. New York, NY: Avenel Books, 1890.

Keane, Bil. *I Need a Hug*. Robbinsdale, MN: Fawcett Gold Medal Books, 1985.

Lenz, Elinor. *Once My Child, Now My Friend*. Clayton, Victoria, Australia: Warner Books, 1985.

Breu, Giovanna. 1986. Disfigured by Disease. *People Magazine* December 8:

Register, Cheri. *Living with Chronic Illness*. New York, NY: Bantam Books, 1987.

Schwar, Sheri Lyn. *Vasculitis—Sick and Tired of Being Sick and Tired*. Lincoln, NE: iUniverse, Inc., 2006.

Thomson Healthcare Staff, Editors. *Physicians' Desk Reference*. Montvale, NJ: Thomson Healthcare, 2008.

Resources

AARDA: American Autoimmune Related Diseases Association

National Office: 22100 Gratiot Avenue, East Detroit, MI 48021
Phone: 568-776-3900
Fax: 568-776-3903
Web site: www.aarda.org
Email: aarda@aarda.org

Washington Office: 750 17th Street, N.W., Suite 1100, Washington, DC 20006
Phone: 202-466-8511

Literature Requests
Phone: 800-598-4668

AIN: Autoimmune Information Network

P.O. Box 4121, Brick, NJ 08723
Toll Free: 877-AIN-4900
Phone: 732-262-0450
Fax: 732-262-0452
Web site: www.aininc.org
Email: autoimmunehelp@aol.com

NFCA: National Family Caregivers Association

10400 Connecticut Avenue, Suite 500, Kensington, MD 20895-3944
Toll Free: 800-896-3650
Phone: 301-942-6430
Fax: 301-942-2302
Web site: www.thefamilycaregiver.org
Email: info@thefamilycaregiver.org

NORD: National Organization for Rare Disorders

55 Kenosia Avenue, P.O. Box 1968, Danbury, CT 06813-1968
Toll Free: 800-999-6673 (voice mail)
Phone: 203-744-0100
Fax: 203-798-2291
TDD: 203-797-9590
Web site: www.rarediseases.org
Email: orphan@rarediseases.org

VF: Vasculitis Foundation

Joyce A. Kullman, Executive Director
P. O. Box 28660, Kansas City, MO 64188-8660
Toll Free: 800-277-9474
Phone/Fax: 816-436-8211
Web site: www.vasculitisfoundation.org
Email: vf@vasculitisfoundation.org

Shannon Morgan, Patient Support Coordinator, Florida Office
6289 Aspen Glen Lane, #203, Boynton Beach, FL 33437
Phone: 561-732-6744
Email: vfpatientsupport@aol.com

Products

Web sites for products mentioned in the preceding story are offered below for information purposes only. Their use or purchase are not suggested or endorsed by the author or publisher, and they receive no compensation from the manufacturer or distributor of these products.

The Alkalol Company

This company makes an all-natural nasal rinse solution by the same name, along with the nasal wash cup known as the "pink pig".
P.O. Box 273, Boston, MA 02133-9998
Toll Free: 800-967-4904
Phone: 617-248-8822
Web site: www.alkalolcompany.com
Email: info@alkalolcompany.com

Hydro Med Inc.

This site contains information on the Grossan Nasal Irrigator system with pulsating action similar to a Water-Pik™.
10200 Sepulveda Blvd., Suite 150, Mission Hills, CA 91345
Toll Free: 800-560-9007
Fax: 818-893-6208
Web site: www.hydromedonline.com
Email: sales@hydromedonline.com

Medical Specialties of California

Information regarding the disposable cold cap discussed in this story was unavailable. However, a reusable product known as Penguin Cold Cap Therapy can be found at the following address:
Tara House, 274 Hither Green Lane, London, SE13 6TT, United Kingdom

Phone-USA: 714-630-9010
Phone-Int'l: +44 (0) 208-695-0111
Fax-Int'l: +44 (0) 208-697-7111
Web site: www.msc-worldwide.com
Email: sales@msc-worldwide.com

About The Artist

Brought together via the Internet and two artists on opposite coasts, Sigi Oberlaender and his wife and Myrna and Carol were coincidentally booked on the same cruise! Myrna and Carol had chosen that particular cruise through the sponsorship of the Vasculitis Foundation. Meetings on the Lido deck cemented their alliance as it became apparent that Sigi had been chosen by fate to create the portraits that became the covers for this book.

Sigi Oberlaender was born in Poland to German parents. He was raised and educated in Germany where he attended college and became a chemical process engineer. While serving in the German Air Force, he began taking classes in color composition.

Although Sigi's work as an engineer took him to various parts of the world, he has always painted. After taking a watercolor workshop, he became a serious watercolorist and has since shown his work in various exhibitions too numerous to list here.

In the United States, in just the last decade alone, Sigi has had solo exhibitions in Florida at the Museum of Art and Science, the Henegar Center for the Arts, and the International Airport in Melbourne; the General Consulate of Germany and the Kennedy Gallery in Miami; Jazz Fest, the Brevard Watercolor Society, and the Public Library in Cocoa Beach; and the Kennedy Space Center in Cape Canaveral. Additional solo exhibits have been held in Georgia, Alabama, and North and South Carolina.

On the international front, Sigi has also shown his work solo in Germany and Colombia.

He is the recipient of numerous awards and a member of various art societies.

He likes to experiment, and has created various types of 3D paintings. In a striking community effort, Sigi, along with students of Brevard County schools, created a mural entitled "Landing of Ponce de Leon." Measuring eight by fourteen feet and consisting of 380 enameled copper tiles, this project is installed at Ponce de Leon Park in Melbourne Beach, Florida.

Sigi painted a violin for a fundraiser for the Brevard Symphony, and has created the artwork for the covers of several other books now in print.

One of his specialties is painting portraits in any kind of media.

His work can be found in corporate and private collections in the United States, Europe, and South America.

He currently teaches art and architecture, devoting the rest of his time to painting in various mediums.

Sigi resides in central Florida with his wife Rosi.

About The Author

Throughout the pages of this book, you have come to know Myrna Swart as a mother, a caregiver, and a take-charge advocate who would do anything to make her daughter's life easier. You read how she drove all over southern California, hovered over the nurses' stations at hospitals, and started a local support group that has now reached international proportions. But there are a number of things you don't know about Myrna.

She began her working career as a legal secretary, continued as an award-winning real estate salesperson, and ended as a loan processor. As a volunteer, she has served on various civic committees, and organized self-run programs at schools her children attended.

Although this is her first published work, Myrna's writings are numerous and varied including short stories, poetry, song lyrics, and travelogues describing her experiences in Europe, Asia, North Africa, Canada, and much of the United States.

Her manual entitled "How to Start and Maintain a VF Chapter," is currently in use by the Vasculitis Foundation.

An award-winning public speaker, Myrna, along with her daughter, created and performed workshops on speech construction. More recently, they have written and begun presenting workshops offering information about living with chronic illness, which she hopes to turn into her next book.

Before learning how to read and write, Myrna, as a young child, was taught how to knit, a craft she shared with her mother; between the two of them, her children enjoyed wearing great looking sweaters.

A needlecraft lover, Myrna has created beautiful works of art in embroidery, latch-hooked rugs, and needlepoint canvases, including scenes such as the Eiffel Tower, Mont Saint Michel, the Pyramids of Giza, and the Parthenon, along with famous paintings such as Rembrandt's "Night Watch."

A music lover, Myrna began impressing her friends and family during episodes of the TV show, "Name That Tune." She possesses an uncanny knowledge of old movies, and if there were a "Name That Movie" game where a few frames at a time are shown, she would excel in that as well.

Myrna loves to ballroom dance and in her younger years she was known to clear the floor when she and her partner shifted into high gear, inspiring the other dancers to move to the sidelines to watch. She enjoys ballet as well as musical theater and fulfilled one of her dreams attending live performances of the Kirov and Bolshoi ballets.

Known for her parties since her teenage years, Myrna is a gracious hostess, a gourmet cook, and enjoys entertaining.

Finally, Myrna loves to explore the history of words and sayings. She is an avid reader, and does crossword puzzles in ink.

After more than forty years in southern California, Myrna is now back home in south Florida where she lived as a child. The mother of four, Myrna is retired and, with all her projects, wonders how she ever found time to work.

978-0-595-47001-3
0-595-47001-7

Made in the USA
Monee, IL
02 August 2020

37473136R00249